Contents

List of Maps

Preface

Each year UK residents take 70 million overseas trips to destinations throughout the globe. This accounts for eight percent of all international travel from the more than 200 other countries in the world. This staggering figure translates to millions of enjoyable holidays, productive business trips, eye-opening gap year experiences, and reunions with family and friends. However, it also translates into illness and injury abroad, and cases of infectious disease imported to the UK. It can be expected that up to 60 percent of travellers to low-income regions of the world will develop an episode of travellers' diarrhoea that interrupts planned activities at least a quarter of the time. More seriously, there are about 1,500 cases of malaria in returned travellers and several deaths. Nearly all of these cases of malaria are preventable if both the traveller and health professional are aware of the risk, the correct medication is prescribed, and the traveller takes precautions against mosquito bites and takes all of their malaria tablets.

It is here that the key issues of travel medicine are brought sharply into focus. The travelling public needs to be well informed not only about their destination and all of its cultural richness, but also aware of the potential risks during their journey. Equally, there needs to be a cadre of GPs, practices nurses, and other health professionals who are knowledgeable about the risks on a country by country basis, and who are confident in advising their patients about each of the measures necessary to keep them healthy while travelling. Health professionals and travellers need to be aware of specific diseases as diverse as malaria, typhoid, and yellow fever, as well as the geographic risk of each. Health professionals need to know how to prevent these diseases, (e.g. by practising vector avoidance measures, taking malaria prevention tablets, or receiving a vaccine), and they should also be able to balance the benefits of the measures recommended against their potential drawbacks. This is the essence of making a risk assessment for the individual traveller and managing that risk.

NaTHNaC and other national and international resources such as Health Protection Scotland, the World Health Organization and the US Centers for Disease Control and Prevention provide travellers and health professionals with the latest information and advice about travel health. NaTHNaC was formed at the end of 2002 as an initiative of the English Department of Health, and one of its first actions was to provide a national telephone advice line for health practitioners who have particularly complex queries. It receives it's funding today from the Health Protection Agency and has gone from strength to strength since its inception. The advice line currently takes nearly 10,000 calls annually and in 2004 NaTHNaC instituted a programme of registration, training, standards and audit for the 3,500 Yellow Fever Vaccination Centres in England, Wales and Northern Ireland. This has brought oversight and consistency of practice to these centres and has become a global model for the management of yellow fever centres. At the end of 2007, NaTHNaC added country-specific advice about vaccine-preventable disease and other health risks to its website. This is linked to a listing of global health events that may be a threat to British travellers that is updated daily. The collation of these outbreak events by country, date or disease is globally unique and has helped attract nearly 75,000 visitors to the NaTHNaC website each month.

Preface

The Yellow Book now completes a package of resources for travel health professionals that elevates NaTHNaC to being a world leader in travel medicine. The Yellow Book is the background and support to NaTHNaC's dynamic information on the website. It guides the clinician through the consultation process, provides them with the rationale and support to handle complex travel or travellers, and gives detailed information on the major diseases that a traveller may encounter. It also answers the common questions about how to handle the ill returned traveller.

We are confident that this will be an invaluable resource for the busy practitioner, supporting them in the challenges of their day to day practice.

We welcome your comments.

Justin McCracken
Chief Executive
Health Protection Agency
London, June 2010.

Section 1

Introduction to UK Travel Health

Section 1 – contents

1.1 Provision of Travel Health Services in the UK

Over the past two decades, the specialty of travel health has grown dramatically in the UK. As more people travel internationally, often with complicated itineraries and challenging health needs, the demand for travel health advice is increasing.

Travel health advice in the UK is provided by health professionals working in primary care (general practice), occupational health, specialist travel clinics (NHS and private sector), the armed forces and in schools/universities. Most are 'nurse-led' services, supervised by a nominated doctor. Recently, interest in the specialty has extended to pharmacists.

Although travel health services can be accessed in the UK, the range of services available at clinics varies. Some offer basic health and immunisation advice, others provide comprehensive assessment, specialist advice and a tailored service. There is currently little guidance for UK travellers on the range of services they can expect from healthcare providers.

There are two authoritative sources of travel health advice in the UK:
The National Travel Health Network and Centre (NaTHNaC) was founded in 2002 by the Department of Health (England), in partnership with the Health Protection Agency, the London School of Hygiene and Tropical Medicine, the Hospital for Tropical Diseases and the Liverpool School of Tropical Medicine. NaTHNaC provides national guidance on travel health for England. The Travel Health section of Health Protection Scotland (HPS) founded TRAVAX in 1984 and FitforTravel in 1988. TRAVAX provides national guidance on travel health for Scotland. Wales and Northern Ireland are able to follow either source. NaTHNaC and TRAVAX/FitforTravel both provide country-specific information for health professionals and travellers on their websites. See Resource Guide: C – Sources of Specialist Advice.

NaTHNaC is freely available to all users. TRAVAX is available free to the NHS within Scotland and by subscription outside of Scotland.

In recent years in the UK, there has been movement towards developing and maintaining improved standards of travel health advice. To date, competencies have been formulated by the Royal College of Nursing (RCN). See Resource Guide: A31 – Key Resources.

In 2005, the Faculty of Travel Medicine was established within the Royal College of Physicians and Surgeons of Glasgow (RCPSG). In 2006, the RCPSG was the first medical Royal College to admit non-medical professionals, including nurses and pharmacists. The Faculty is committed to promoting standards in travel health and supporting their multi-disciplinary membership. See Resource Guide: C – Sources of Specialist Advice.

Specific travel health training is available in the UK. See Resource Guide: 1.1.1. Currently the only existing mandatory programme of registration, training, standards and audit is for yellow fever vaccination. This is required by all designated UK Yellow Fever Vaccination Centres, who must adhere to a strict code of practice. In England, Wales and Northern Ireland this programme is administered by NaTHNaC. In Scotland, it is administered by Health Protection Scotland. See Resource Guide: C – Sources of Specialist Advice.

1 Introduction to UK Travel Health

1.1 Provision of Travel Health Services in the UK

Appropriate training, professional support and evidence-based travel health resources are now widely available in the UK. Health professionals who advise travellers should ensure that they have adequate levels of knowledge, experience and resources, as well as sufficient time to deliver a high standard of care.

The British Travel Health Association (BTHA), a membership organisation, was established in 1999 and aims to provide information, education and stimulate research for all disciplines involved in the field of travel health. See Resource Guide: A3 – Key Resources.

1.2 The UK Travel and Tourism Industry

The UK travel and tourism industry is a substantial and vibrant industry sector, and a major employer and supplier of travel services. Travel has moved from being a 'luxury' to a regular activity for many. During challenging economic times, the travel sector shows tremendous resilience, with the underlying trend in the UK and globally, remaining one of growth.

In recent years, travel and the travel industry has changed in many ways, most notably due to the emergence of 'low-cost carriers' or budget airlines, and the various new forms of online booking.

The majority of leisure air travellers book through the traditional channels of travel agents and tour operators, where established mechanisms for disseminating health and other advice operate. In total, more than 58 million visits overseas were made by UK residents in 2001.By 2006, this had increased to more than 69 million overseas visits by UK residents, an average of more than one visit per person. The average masks a widening range of individuals, from those who do not travel to those who travel regularly, and includes a diverse range of activities. There are some 8 million business travellers and 10 million visits to friends and relatives (VFRs). The land and sea routes to and through France remain extremely important, but the sector that has seen the greatest growth and change in structure, and which may represent the greatest challenge for travel medicine, is the air travel sector. See Resource Guide: 1.2.1.

In 2008, some 46 million leisure trips were made by air. Significantly, only 23.6 million of those trips were protected by the Civil Aviation Authority Air Travel Organisers' Licence (CAA ATOL) financial protection scheme for organised travel arrangements. See Resource Guide: 1.2.2. Within that number, only 17 million customers travelled on traditional 'package' holidays provided by major travel groups on charter flights. Travellers whose arrangements fall outside the organised sector are much less likely to receive appropriate travel and health advice through the booking process.

The distribution of travel products has also changed dramatically in this time. There has been a consistent move away from the high street to a mix of call centre, home-worker and online activity. These channels of distribution are not exclusive and one common scenario is the use of traditional brochures and advice sourced in the travel agency, followed by internet research, supported by enquiries on specific issues with a call centre, and the completion of the transaction by telephone or online.

So What Does This Mean for Travel Medicine?

1. Destinations
While Spain and France remain the most popular destinations by volume, Egypt and Turkey have received increasing numbers of UK visitors in recent years. Travellers can hop onto a charter or scheduled flight, booking as late as they like, and travel to ever more exotic destinations. Affordable travel extends worldwide, for the student backpacker, young explorer, family traveller or business tourist. Charter flights to Brazil, China and Cape Verde are recent innovations in the market.

2. Perception of Risk
The perception of 'risk' has been reduced and a new generation thinks nothing of wandering the world in a largely unplanned way – a great freedom, but one that makes the provision of planning appropriate, complete, healthcare advice an ever greater challenge.

1.2 The UK Travel and Tourism Industry

3. Types of Tourism
Within the mainstream market, the cruise industry continues to expand, bringing new and ever larger ships into service. Luxury travel has experienced steady growth and has demonstrated resilience through the economic crisis. There has also been an emergence of the Responsible Tourism movement into the mainstream, including 'voluntourism' and the development of an increasing range of authentic and accessible products. Catering for the needs of these complex travellers can be challenging. See Special Risk Travel Section 3.

4. Travel Insurance
There is a trend towards a greater willingness to travel uninsured, with serious consequences for treatment and in particular repatriation, even within the European Union (EU). In addition to road traffic accidents, mental health issues, personal security, sexual assault, alcohol and substance abuse issues are now the daily workload of Foreign Office Consular officers and travel company teams around the world. See Resource Guide: 1.2.3.

5. Travel Industry Regulations of the Provision of Travel Health Advice
The 1992 UK Package Travel Regulations (implementing the 1990 EU Package Travel Directive), which only apply to packages and not to flight or accommodation only bookings, require that general information be provided about 'health formalities' required for the journey and stay. A failure to provide this information in brochures can lead to a criminal conviction and a fine. See Resource Guide: 1.2.4 and 1.2.5.

Similarly, the Association of British Travel Agents Code of Conduct provides that brochures 'must contain adequate information pertaining to both recommended and compulsory health requirements of countries featured. Clients should be advised to check with their own doctor before their departure as to which inoculations are available and necessary for specific areas'. See Resource Guide: 1.2.6.

The travel industry has stated that it will continue to work towards ensuring that appropriate information and advice is available to the traveller before, during and after their holiday. It is recognised that partnerships of industry, health professionals, educators and government are required to achieve this. An example of a successful partnership of this kind is the Foreign and Commonwealth Office 'Know Before You Go' campaign. See Resource Guide: A15 – Key Resources.

1.3 Travel Medicine and Disease Surveillance

Travel medicine involves assessing an individual's health risks when travelling to a particular destination/s and providing advice to help reduce that risk. Disease surveillance (monitoring) helps to provide the evidence for pre-travel health recommendations. It consists of two main activities:

1. Surveillance of global disease patterns – this gives a general indication of which diseases occur where and can alert practitioners to outbreaks, new diseases, or old diseases occurring in new places.

2. Surveillance of illness in returned travellers – identifies particular risks for UK travellers to specific destinations and particular risks for specific groups of travellers such as those who had visited friends and relatives (VFRs); see Special Risk Travel: 3.2.11.

Surveillance of global disease patterns

Travel medicine is dynamic. It is important that healthcare professionals are aware of recent outbreaks and changes in disease epidemiology. Reports of global outbreaks are readily available online. Local, national and international media organisations often initially describe outbreaks. Official sources, such as national governments and the World Health Organization (WHO) may take longer to verify outbreaks, but provide an essential source of reliable information.

How to find information on global disease outbreaks
Various online sources publish outbreak information in easily accessible formats. NaTHNaC's Outbreak Surveillance Database (available at: www.nathnac.org/countrysearch.aspx) provides information on infectious disease outbreaks worldwide that may be of importance to UK travellers. Information held in this database can be searched by disease, country and date. It is open-access and updated daily.

Data is gathered from a wide range of sources including:

- WHO Disease Outbreak News (www.who.int/csr/don/en/index.html): Detailed, usually verified information on selected disease outbreaks.
- ProMED-Mail (www.promedmail.org): Information on disease outbreaks in humans, animals and plants; often unverified.
- ReliefWeb (www.reliefweb.org): Collates reports on humanitarian issues from state authorities, non-governmental organisations and the media.
- Media reports: Scanned from a variety of news aggregation services.

Outbreaks resulting in changes in travel health recommendations or practice are described in more detail in NaTHNaC's Clinical Updates[1] (available at: http://www.nathnac.org/pro/clinical_updates/index.htm). These include in-depth outbreak descriptions and targeted travel health advice. The NaTHNaC[1] website also links directly to the Foreign and Commonwealth Office's country-specific safety and security advice.

Using disease outbreak information in the pre-travel risk assessment
Reports of changes in disease incidence are key elements of pre-travel risk assessment. Health professionals must be aware of major disease outbreaks at the traveller's destination so that they can effectively convey risks to the traveller; see Table 1-1.

1   Alternatively see Travax http://www.travax.nhs.uk/ or Fit for Travel http://www.fitfortravel.nhs.uk/

1 Introduction to UK Travel Health

1.3 Travel Medicine and Disease Surveillance

Table 1-1. Factors to consider when interpreting disease outbreak information

Information Source	• Is the information from a reliable source? E.g. national or international health authority (e.g. World Health Organisation).
	• If the information is from an informal source, is it plausible? Has it been widely reported? Are official sources quoted? Be aware of the possibility of errors, for example misreporting or under-reporting of case numbers.
	• Lack of reporting does not necessarily mean absence of disease. Levels of both official and unofficial reporting differ between countries and within regions. Outbreaks may go unreported. Bias will occur if English language reports are the only sources reviewed.
	• Have cases been laboratory confirmed? If not, are there other possible causes?
Disease	• Is the risk still current? When was the outbreak reported? Has there been an increase or decline in case numbers?
	• What is the severity and likelihood of transmission of the disease? See Disease Guide Section 5.
Traveller	• Are they travelling to, or near the area affected by the outbreak? Using an atlas, compare the area affected by disease and the traveller's destination.
	• What is the likelihood of the traveller being exposed? E.g. outbreaks in schools may be less likely to affect travellers than those in hotels. Some travellers can be at higher risk due to their planned activities.
	• What are the implications of exposure for this particular traveller and what preventive measures are available? What is the traveller's past medical history? What activities are they undertaking? What is the impact of not taking preventive measures?

1.3 Travel Medicine and Disease Surveillance

Surveillance of illness in returned travellers

Illness in returned travellers can also act as a sentinel, alerting public health authorities to disease risks in a particular country. This is important for destinations where public health systems are less robust and outbreaks of disease may not be readily detected or routinely reported.

How to find information on UK surveillance of travel-associated illness

In the UK, national data on travel-associated illness are collated and analysed by the Health Protection Agency (HPA) Centre for Infections (CfI) for England, Wales and Northern Ireland and Health Protection Scotland (HPS) for Scotland.

In the UK, the main sources of data on travel-associated illness include:

- Routine laboratory reporting from NHS laboratories and weekly returns from Scottish NHS laboratories.
- HPA and HPS reference laboratory reports.
- Enhanced surveillance schemes.
- Direct reports from local health protection staff in regional units/boards.

Surveillance reports on travel-associated illnesses are regularly produced and summarise the data available; see Table 1-2.

Table 1-2. UK surveillance information

Information available	Location
National surveillance information for England, Wales and Northern Ireland and UK travel trends	Travel page of HPA website http://www.hpa.org.uk/
Quarterly imported infections reports England and Wales	Health Protection Report http://www.hpa.org.uk/hpr/infections/travel.htm
Imported infections reports for Scotland	Health Protection Scotland travel health page http://www.hps.scot.nhs.uk/travel/

How valid is surveillance data on travel-associated illness?

The reports of illness that are captured by surveillance often represent the more severe end of the clinical spectrum. Mild infections may not be reported as the traveller self-treats or the practitioner does not submit diagnostic samples. In addition, data obtained through routine laboratory reports frequently lack reliable travel history information, meaning travel-associated infections may be under-reported or incomplete.

What can be done to improve data on travel-associated infections?

The gold standard for improving data on travel-associated infections is enhanced surveillance of individual infections. Detailed travel and clinical histories, including dates of travel and onset, and reason for travel are then collected. Enhanced studies are resource intensive and are not realistic for most diseases. **Improvement of routine reporting is essential.**

1 Introduction to UK Travel Health

1.3 Travel Medicine and Disease Surveillance

Laboratory reports indicating confirmed infections are preferable for surveillance, rather than statutory Notifications of Infectious Diseases (NOIDS). These notifications are reported on clinical suspicion for public health purposes only and are not always laboratory confirmed. Information on laboratory reports is only as reliable as the investigation request form completed by the practitioner. **To ensure accurate laboratory diagnosis and improve surveillance, complete clinical and travel history must be included at this stage.**

When requesting laboratory investigations, the information in Box 1-1 should always be included.

Providing this information:

- Assists laboratories with clinical diagnosis. This means results are more rapidly available, making patient treatment more effective.
- Contributes to improved understanding of travel-associated illness and evidence-based pre-travel advice.

Box 1-1. Travel history for laboratory requests

1. Has the patient travelled in the last year? It is just as important to state that there has been no recent travel abroad as it is to state that the patient has travelled. Include new entrants/visitors to the country.
2. Country of travel (give town/region if known).
3. Dates of travel.
4. Reason for travel (e.g. holiday, business, or visiting friends and relatives etc).
5. Recent risk activities (e.g. contact with animals, caving, unprotected sexual exposure, healthcare work, medical/dental treatment abroad etc.).
6. Onset date of symptoms.
7. Relevant clinical symptoms.

Section 2

The Pre-Travel Consultation

EUROPEAN HEALTH INSURANCE CARD

3 Name

4 Given names

6 Person

5 Date of birth

7 Identification

8 Identification number of the card

Section 2 – contents

2.1 Introduction

The risk of illness and injury for those travelling overseas is well recognised. Approximately 8% of travellers require medical care during travel. Many more will experience illness such as travellers' diarrhoea. The primary aim of the pre-travel health consultation is to identify and reduce these risks by offering advice and informing travellers whilst promoting effective preventive measures. Advice which is accurate, achievable and tailored to the individual's travel plans and specific health needs, will increase compliance.

The pre-travel health consultation is a two step process:

- **Risk Assessment** (2.2) – identifies potential health risks and individuals who are at increased risk who may need special consideration.
- **Risk Management** (2.3) – provides advice and preventive strategies to reduce health risks, including tailored advice for those with special needs. See Special Risks Section 3.

Both steps are discussed in detail in this book. Some risks, however, are dynamic and change rapidly, for example disease outbreaks at specific destinations. In addition to this book, therefore, health professionals must also access up-to-date references and online resources during their travel health consultations to ensure the care and advice they offer is current and complete. Internet access is essential. See Resource Guide: C – Sources of Specialist Advice.

A guide to using this book in a travel health consultation is given in Chart 2-1.

Communication
Effective communication skills are necessary when conducting a pre-travel consultation. The aim is a two-way interactive dialogue which actively involves the traveller and encourages informed decision-making. Travel health consultations can be lengthy and adequate time is essential. Most travellers need a minimum of 20 minutes. Those with special risks usually require more detailed information and so will need longer.

There is a limit to the amount of knowledge travellers will retain, so written advice should be provided and the traveller should be directed to reliable online sources. See Resource Guide: B – Resources for Travellers.

Documentation
The travel health professional is responsible for careful documentation of all aspects of the pre-travel consultation, including vaccine records. See Resource Guide: A31 – Key Resources. These must be kept for a minimum of 10 years for an adult and 25 years for a child (or 8 years following a child's death). Each traveller should also be provided with a written record of any vaccinations given and, if applicable, a note of when future doses are due. See Chart 2-3 in Risk Management Checklist.

2.1 Introduction

2 The Pre-Travel Consultation

2.1 Introduction

Competence and Training
Travel health, like any specialty, requires a basic level of knowledge for safe and effective practice. Clear guidance is available from the Royal College of Nursing; see Resource Guide: A31 – Key Resources. Specific travel health training, including certificate, diploma and masters level courses, is available in the UK; see Resource Guide: 1.1.1. NaTHNaC and Health Protection Scotland provide training specifically about yellow fever. Travel health professionals should also be aware of their limitations and know when and how to seek specialist advice. See Resource Guide: C – Sources of Specialist Advice.

Chart 2-1. Using this book in a travel health consultation

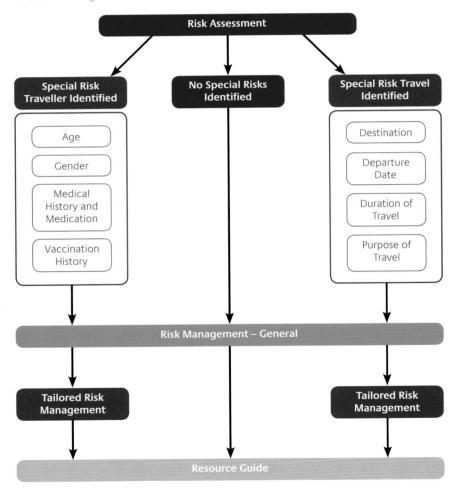

2.2 Risk Assessment

Risk assessment is fundamental to pre-travel health consultation. It is a two-step process of gathering information firstly about the traveller and secondly about their trip. Accurate risk assessment can be used to guide risk management advice and strategies. All travellers should be given the advice included in the Risk Management Section 2.3 of this book. Risk assessment should also identify travellers with special risks; see Box 2-1. These travellers need additional, tailored, risk management advice; see Special Risks Section 3.

In order to emphasise the most important risks for the individual traveller, health professionals must prioritise advice on risk management and address the priorities in the time available.

Information needed for effective risk evaluation can be gathered by asking travellers to complete a risk assessment form prior to their appointment and by verifying the information with the traveller during the consultation. See Chart 2-2. Risk Assessment Form.

Careful documentation of the pre-travel health consultation is essential.

Box 2-1. Special Risk Identifiers

Special Risk Traveller (3.1)

- Age
    - Child (See 3.1.2)
    - Older age (See 3.1.11)

- Gender
    - Women (See 3.1.17)
    - Pre-conception, pregnancy and breastfeeding (See 3.1.12)

- Medical history and medication
    - Allergies (for vaccine allergies see 2.4)
    - Cardiovascular and cerebrovascular disease (See 3.1.1)
    - Diabetes (See 3.1.3)
    - Disability (See 3.1.4)
    - Gastrointestinal conditions (See 3.1.5)
    - Haematological conditions (See 3.1.6)
    - Hepatic conditions (See 3.1.7)
    - HIV/AIDS (See 3.1.8)
    - Immunocompromised (See 3.1.9)
    - Neurological conditions, e.g. epilepsy (See 3.1.10)
    - Psychological conditions, e.g. depression (See 3.1.13)
    - Renal conditions (See 3.1.14)
    - Respiratory conditions (See 3.1.15)
    - Rheumatological conditions (See 3.1.16)

- Vaccination history
    - Principles of vaccinations (See 2.4)

Special Risk Travel (3.2)

- Destination
    - Destination-specific advice and disease outbreak information should be found online, e.g. NaTHNaC Country Information Pages[1] www.nathnac.org
    - Altitude (See 3.2.2)

- Departure date
    - Last minute travel (See 3.2.6)

- Duration of stay
    - Long-term (See 3.2.7) including backpacker/expatriate/volunteer/work

- Purpose of visit
    - Adventure (See 3.2.1)
    - Cruise (See 3.2.3)
    - Diving (See 3.2.4)
    - Healthcare worker (See 3.2.5)
    - Medical tourism (See 3.2.8)
    - Natural disasters (See 3.2.9)
    - Pilgrimage (See 3.2.10)
    - Visiting friends and relatives (See 3.2.11)

2.2 Risk Assessment

2 The Pre-Travel Consultation

2.2 Risk Assessment

Chart 2-2. Risk Assessment Form

Note for Health Professionals: Special Risk Identifiers highlighted in **BLACK and BOLD** below. See Special Risks Section 3.

For completion by the traveller:	All information is treated as confidential.

Name:	Date of birth:	
Address:	Telephone:	Email:

Travel Details (Check atlas and country-specific online resources, e.g. www.nathnac.org[1])

Date of travel:	Total length of travel:	
Country	Region	Length of stay
1.		
2.		
3.		
4.		
5.		
6.		

Do you have travel health insurance? Yes ☐ No ☐

Purpose of trip (circle all that apply) Tourism Business (< 1 month)
Adventure | Cruise | Diving | Healthcare worker | Long-term (backpacker/expatriate/volunteer/work)
Medical tourism | Natural disasters | Pilgrimage | Visiting friends & relatives (VFRs)

Medical History
Are you well today? Yes ☐ No ☐
Do you take any medicines/pills? (Prescribed/self-treatment/over-the-counter, including contraception). Yes ☐ No ☐
Please list all medication:
Do any of the following apply to you:

	Yes	No	Details
Allergies (including food, latex, medication etc.)			
Anaemia			
Bleeding/clotting disorders (including deep vein thrombosis)			
Heart disease (e.g. angina, high blood pressure)			
Diabetes			
Disability			
Epilepsy/seizures			
Gastrointestinal (stomach) complaints			
Liver problems			
HIV/AIDS			
Immune system condition			
Mental health issues (including anxiety, depression)			
Neurological (nervous system) illness			
Kidney problems			
Respiratory (lung) disease			
Rheumatology (joint) conditions			
Spleen problems			
Any other conditions			

Women only: Date of last period?
Are you pregnant, breastfeeding or planning pregnancy whilst travelling? Yes ☐ No ☐

1   Alternatively see Travax http://www.travax.nhs.uk/ or Fit for Travel http://www.fitfortravel.nhs.uk/

2.3 Risk Management

Chart 2-3. Risk Management Checklist

		For Health Professional Use	
		Discussed (✓)	Comments
✚	1. Medical Preparation		
✈	2. Journey Risks		
	3. Safety Risks		
☼	4. Environmental Risks		
	5. Food and Water-borne Risks		
	6. Vector-borne Risks		
	7. Air-borne Risks		
♂ ◊	8. Sexual Health and Blood-borne Viral Risks		
	9. Skin Health		
	10. Psychological Health		

Travel vaccine/s	Date(s) received	Vaccine discussed / recommended	Administration details: date, immunisation site, manufacturer, batch number and administrator (e.g. initials)
BCG Mantoux			
Cholera			
Diphtheria/ Tetanus/ Polio			
Hepatitis A			
Hepatitis B			
Hepatitis A/B			
Hepatitis A/ typhoid			
Japanese encephalitis			
Influenza			
Meningitis ACWY			
MMR			
Rabies			
TBE			
Typhoid			
Yellow fever			
Other			

Antimalarials	√	Comments
Atovaquone/proguanil		
Chloroquine		
Doxycycline		
Mefloquine		
Proguanil		
Bite avoidance only		
Emergency standby		
Other Advice		

2.3 Risk Management

2 The Pre-Travel Consultation

2.3 Risk Management

Guide to Icons

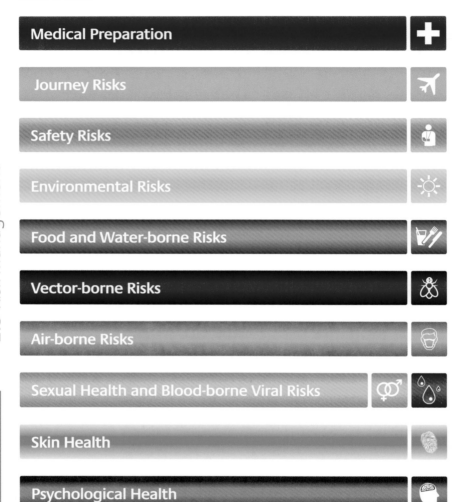

Medical Preparation

Journey Risks

Safety Risks

Environmental Risks

Food and Water-borne Risks

Vector-borne Risks

Air-borne Risks

Sexual Health and Blood-borne Viral Risks

Skin Health

Psychological Health

2.3.1 Medical Preparation

- Destination-specific risk management advice can be found on the NaTHNaC Country Information Pages[1] www.nathnac.org.
- All travellers should allow adequate time to plan and prepare for their trip in consultation with a travel health professional. Ideally this should begin around 4 to 6 weeks before the trip; however, it is never too late to seek travel health advice. Refer travellers to Resource Guide: B – Resources for Travellers.
- A dental check-up is recommended prior to travel, particularly for long-term or remote travel. Access to reliable dental services may be limited during travel.
- See Resource Guide: 2.3.1.

Travel Medical Kit

- Travellers should consider carrying a personal travel medical kit tailored to their needs and appropriate for their itinerary. See Box 2-2.
- If they purchase a commercial kit, the traveller should review the contents to be sure that they meet their needs. The traveller should know when and how to use each item in the kit. Written instructions are recommended.
- A doctor's letter (on headed paper) explaining that the contents of the kit are for personal medical purposes is recommended to aid passage through customs. Certificates for this purpose are often included in commercially bought kits.
- A list of items included in the kit and their function is recommended so that they can be replaced after use. Names of medications and the correct dosage regimes should be included. As trade/brand names of drugs can differ around the world, generic names are most useful. Manufacturer's instructions on the insert leaflet should be followed and expiry dates and storage recommendations checked.
- Travellers should be discouraged from purchasing medical supplies overseas where quality may not be assured.
- Sharps, such as needles, lancets and scissors, should be packed in hold luggage.
- It is recommended a travel medical kit is carried in a rip-resistant waterproof nylon bag to prevent spoiling.
- Introductory first aid courses, such as those provided by St John's Ambulance, are widely available and should be considered by travellers, especially those travelling long term, to remote areas, or with children. See Resource Guide: 2.3.1a.
- A first aid manual could be carried. See Resource Guide: 2.3.1b.

Travelling with a Medical Condition

- Travellers with a pre-existing medical condition may need specific pre-travel risk management advice tailored to their condition.
- An assessment of fitness to travel by a GP and/or specialist is recommended for all travellers with any pre-existing medical condition, ideally prior to booking a trip.
- Travellers should be fit to fly if travelling by aircraft. An IATA approved Medical Information Form (MEDIF) may be required by airlines. See Risk Management: 2.3.2 Journey Risks – Fitness to Fly.
- A letter detailing the medical condition and a list of prescribed medications should be carried by the traveller, in case of the need to seek medical assistance.
- If appropriate, identification aids such as MedicAlert® bracelets should be worn. See Resource Guide: A23 – Key Resources.

---

1 Alternatively see Travax http://www.travax.nhs.uk/ or Fit for Travel http://www.fitfortravel.nhs.uk/

2.3 Risk Management

2 The Pre-Travel Consultation

2.3.1 Medical Preparation

- The traveller should comply with regular and travel-specific medication.
- When prescribing medication for the purpose of travel, potential contraindications and drug interactions must be checked by the prescriber. Adjustments to regular medication, and plans for monitoring overseas, should ideally be made in advance of travel.

Travelling with Medication

- A copy of all prescriptions, including generic names for medications, should be carried.
- Adequate supplies of personal medication should be taken. Obtaining re-supplies of reliable quality may not be possible; counterfeit drugs are an increasing risk worldwide.
- Medication (and medical equipment) should be kept in their original labelled packaging and split between hand and hold luggage in case of loss during transit.
- Storage requirements for medication must be checked in advance. Arrangements for control of temperature during transit with certain medications may be needed.
- Transportation of certain medication across borders, such as controlled drugs (e.g. narcotics) and drugs which act on the central nervous system (e.g. psychotropics), may be forbidden or require special permission. This includes substances which may be found in small amounts in some over-the-counter medication, as well as prescribed medication. Travellers should review medication regulations for the countries to which they are travelling with the relevant authorities including the Home Office and embassies of the destination country/countries. See Resource Guide: 2.3.1c.
- A letter from the prescribing physician written on letterhead stationery should be carried for controlled substances and injection medications.
- A Health Information Sheet, *Medicines – transportation by travellers*, is available to download from NaTHNaC[1]. See Resource Guide: A26 – Key Resources.
- Travellers should be advised not to take medication for the first time during the journey, in case of allergic reaction/anaphylaxis.

Travel Insurance

- Obtaining travel insurance, covering all intended destinations and activities, and including emergency medical care and repatriation, is essential. A full declaration of pre-existing medical conditions must be made; an incomplete declaration may invalidate cover.
- A European Health Insurance Card (EHIC) should be carried in countries in the European Economic Area and Switzerland, where these are accepted. It is valid for up to 5 years. In an emergency overseas, UK residents can access state-provided necessary treatment equivalent to care available to citizens in the country being visited. A financial contribution may still be required. Travellers should be aware of their eligibility and limitations of this scheme. EHIC is not a substitute for travel insurance. See Resource Guide: A9 – Key Resources.
- Travellers should be aware of driving licence and insurance requirements when hiring vehicles overseas. Regular eye tests are advised for all drivers.

---

1   Alternatively see Travax http://www.travax.nhs.uk/ or Fit for Travel http://www.fitfortravel.nhs.uk/

2.3.1 Medical Preparation

Self-Treatment During Travel

- Travellers should consider carrying medication for self-treatment of minor illness. Travellers must be advised, and receive written instructions, of appropriate use of such medication and know when and where to seek further medical advice.
- Travellers should be informed of the signs and symptoms of Travellers' Diarrhoea (TD) and the appropriate use of self-treatment measures, including rehydration and/or medication. See Box 2-7. The need to seek prompt medical attention for fever, bloody diarrhoea, jaundice or persistent symptoms must be emphasised.
- Travellers should be informed of the signs and symptoms of malaria and of the need to seek urgent medical attention. Appropriate use of emergency standby treatment should be discussed and written guidance given. See Table 5-3 in Disease Guide Section 5.

Accessing Medical Care During Travel

- Travellers should obtain as much information as possible about medical facilities at their destination. Healthcare may be limited and, in some areas, non-existent. Emergency plans should be discussed in advance.
- See Resource Guide for sources of information about medical services overseas:
  - International Association for Medical Assistance to Travellers (IAMAT) (2.3.1d)
  - Joint Commisssion International (2.3.1e)
  - The International Society of Travel Medicine (ISTM) (2.3.1f)
  - British Embassy/High Commission/Consulate (2.3.1g)
  - Commercial databases (2.3.1h)

Box 2-2. Travel medical kit (including medications for travel)

Travel medical kit

Where appropriate, the following items should be considered for inclusion in a travel medical kit:

- Alcohol hand sanitiser
- Antiseptic cleansing wipe/cream
- Assorted dressings – bandages/plasters/gauze/swabs
- Condoms
- Cotton wool
- Feminine hygiene products
- First aid quick reference card
- Insect repellent/insecticides
- Measuring spoon/syringe
- Plastic/neoprene gloves
- Roll of tape/safety pins
- Scissors
- Sterile saline solution for washing eyes or wounds
- Spare contact lenses/prescription glasses

2.3 Risk Management

2 The Pre-Travel Consultation

(continued)

2.3.1 Medical Preparation

Box 2-2. Travel medical kit (including medications for travel) (continued)

- Sun cream
- Thermometer
- Tweezers/tick removers
- Water purification tablets/solution
- Wound closure strip

Medications for travel

Before recommending or prescribing any medication, health professionals must check a traveller's medical history, current health status, medications and allergies, to identify any drug contraindications.

Check British National Formulary (BNF); see Resource Guide: A2 – Key Resources.

According to individual requirements, the following medications should be considered for inclusion in a travel medical kit:

- Analgesia/antipyrexia medication
- Antihistamines (oral & topical)
- Antimalarials (where appropriate)
- Antimotility agent
- Antacid agent
- Antibiotics (where appropriate)
- Antiseptic agent
- Topical antifungal agent
- Calamine lotion
- Decongestant (note: pseudoephedrine is illegal in some countries)
- Eye/ear drops
- Steroid cream, e.g. hydrocortisone 1% cream
- Motion sickness tablets
- Oral rehydration sachets

2.3.2 Journey Risks

- Destination-specific advice can be found on NaTHNaC's Country Information Pages[1] www.nathnac.org.
- Refer travellers to Resource Guide: B – Resources for Travellers.
- See Resource Guide: 2.3.2.

The journey itself poses potential risks to a traveller.

Travellers should be advised not to take medication for the first time during the journey, in case of allergic reaction/anaphylaxis.

Fitness to Fly

- Cabin air pressure is the equivalent of an altitude of 1,800m to 2,400m. This air pressure is tolerated well by healthy individuals; however, it can exacerbate some underlying medical conditions.
- All travellers with pre-existing medical conditions should be reviewed by a medical professional and assessed as fit to fly, ideally prior to booking a trip.
- Travellers should check individual airline regulations and consult with their medical departments as appropriate. A Medical Information Form (MEDIF) may need to be completed by the traveller and their doctor, valid for the dates of travel. A more permanent record of medical information, the Frequent Travellers' Medical Card (FREMEC), may be acceptable to some airlines. Forms can be obtained from the airline's medical department.
- Guidelines for medical professionals on assessing fitness to fly are given by the UK Civil Aviation Authority. Table 2-1 summarises the contraindications and considerations for flying listed in these guidelines. See Resource Guide: A6 – Key Resources.
- A guide for healthcare professionals about the impact of flying on passenger health is available from the British Medical Association. See Resource Guide: 2.3.2a.
- See Special Risks Section 3.

2.3 Risk Management

2 The Pre-Travel Consultation

1   Alternatively see Travax http://www.travax.nhs.uk/ or Fit for Travel http://www.fitfortravel.nhs.uk/

2.3.2 Journey Risks

Table 2-1. Contraindications and considerations for flying

Category	Contraindications	Considerations
Cardiovascular disorders	• Uncomplicated myocardial infarction (MI) within 7 days. • Complicated MI within 4 to 6 weeks. • Unstable angina. • Decompensated congestive heart failure. • Uncontrolled cardiac arrhythmia. • Uncontrolled hypertension. • Coronary artery bypass graft (CABG) within 10 to 14 days. • Angioplasty/stent placement within 5 days. • Severe symptomatic valvular heart disease.	Medical clearance required up to 21 days post MI/CABG.
Ear, nose and throat disorders	• Otitis media and sinusitis. • Middle ear surgery within 10 days. • Tonsillectomy within 7 days.	Medical/nursing escort with wire cutters needed for travellers with wired jaw.
Eye disorders	• Retinal detachment repair within 2 to 6 weeks, depending on gas used during surgery. • Intraocular procedure or penetrating eye injury within a week.	Absorption of gas used during procedure may take up to 6 weeks. Specialist advice must be sought.
Gastrointestinal disorders	• Abdominal surgery within 10 days. • GI tract bleed within 24 hours. • Laparoscopic surgery within 24 hours.	Medical clearance required up to 10 days post laparoscopic surgery.
Haematological disorders	• Sickle cell crisis within 10 days.	Haemoglobin below 10 g/dl requires assessment and possibly oxygen. If in-flight oxygen is necessary, this should be arranged with the airline well in advance of travel.
Neurological disorders	• Cerebrovascular accident (CVA) or sub-arachnoid haemorrhage within 3 days. • Generalised seizures within 24 hours. • Brain surgery within 10 days.	Medical clearance required up to 10 days post CVA or subarachnoid haemorrhage. Cranium must be free from air following brain surgery.

(continued)

2.3 Risk Management

2 The Pre-Travel Consultation

2.3.2 Journey Risks

Table 2-1. Contraindications and considerations for flying (continued)

Category	Contraindications	Considerations
Orthopaedic	• Application of plaster cast within 24 hours for flights under 2 hours, 48 hours for longer flights. • If there is an urgent need for travel, a bi-valved cast can be applied.	Travellers with full length or above the knee plaster casts or who require leg elevation must reserve appropriate seats to ensure necessary leg room.
Pregnancy	• Not recommended after 36 weeks gestation in an uncomplicated single pregnancy. • Not recommended beyond 32 weeks in an uncomplicated multiple pregnancy. • If there are risk factors for premature labour, flying is not recommended after 33 weeks gestation.	Many airlines will not allow women to fly after 36 weeks gestation. Most airlines require a medical letter after 28 weeks gestation, stating that the pregnancy is progressing normally, there are no anticipated complications and confirming the expected date of delivery. The date of the return journey should be considered.
Uncontrolled psychotic conditions	• Individuals with unpredictable, violent or disruptive behaviour. • Displaying symptoms which are likely to compromise flight and passenger safety. • The flight environment may potentially exacerbate the condition.	Close liaison with the supervising specialist and the airline are essential when assessing fitness to fly. Compliance with medication, previously history and, ideally, a period of stability prior to travel are important indicators of fitness. However, psychiatric conditions, by their very nature are unpredictable; patients with well-managed illness usually still require an escort.

(continued)

2.3 Risk Management

2 The Pre-Travel Consultation

2.3.2 Journey Risks

Table 2-1. Contraindications and considerations for flying (continued)

Category	Contraindications	Considerations
Respiratory disorders	• Active or infectious respiratory disease. • Pneumothorax – until at least 2 weeks post-drainage and evidence of complete resolution on chest radiograph. • Commercial flights are contraindicated for those with a current closed pneumothorax. • Major chest surgery within 10 days.	The ability to walk 50 metres without severe dyspnoea is a basic indication that the aircraft environment can be tolerated. Medical clearance may be required if travelling within 21 days of pulmonary surgery. If in-flight oxygen is necessary, this should be arranged with the airline well in advance of travel. Severe asthma, COPD, cystic fibrosis or severe restrictive diseases require a pre-flight medical assessment.
Scuba diving	Within 24 hours.	Specialist advice must be sought in regards to flying after decompression sickness (DCS). Travel should be delayed for at least 48 hours (and at least 72 hours for arterial gas embolism) following completion of treatment and full resolution of symptoms.

Deep Vein Thrombosis (DVT) and Venous Thromboembolism (VTE)

- The World Health Organization's Research into Global Hazards of Travel (WRIGHT) indicated that the risk of venous thromboembolism (VTE) approximately doubles following flights of 4 hours or more. However, the overall risk, if seated and immobile for 4 hours or more remains relatively low, at 1 case per 6,000 healthy individuals. See Resource Guide: 2.3.2b.

- See Box 2-3 and Box 2-4.

- A Health Information Sheet, *Travel-related DVT*, is available to download from NaTHNaC[1]. See Resource Guide: A26 – Key Resources.

---

1   Alternatively see Travax http://www.travax.nhs.uk/ or Fit for Travel http://www.fitfortravel.nhs.uk/

2.3.2 Journey Risks

■ Anticoagulant therapy, such as low molecular weight heparin may be necessary for travellers with an increased risk of DVT/VTE; specialist advice should be sought when necessary.

Box 2-3. DVT risk factors

Moderate risk:
- Past history of DVT/VTE, unless taking anticoagulant therapy.
- Haematological disorders such as thrombocythaemia.
- Pregnancy and up to 6 weeks postpartum.
- Congestive cardiac failure/recent myocardial infarction.
- Surgery lasting more than 30 minutes, performed 4 weeks to 2 months ago.
- Oestrogen therapy, such as the combined oral contraceptive pill.
- Obesity.
- Lower limb fracture in plaster.
- Dehydration.

High risk:
- Malignancy.
- Surgery lasting more than 30 minutes, within the last 4 weeks.
- Haematological disorders such as Factor V Leiden mutation or antithrombin deficiency.
- Polycythaemia.

Box 2-4. DVT prevention measures

- Avoid dehydration.
- Avoid excessive consumption of alcohol.
- Mobilise as much as possible at regular intervals during travel.
- Regularly flex and extend the ankles encouraging blood flow from the lower legs.
- Take regular deep breaths.
- Avoid stowing hand luggage by feet as it may restrict movement.
- Wear properly fitting flight socks. See Resource Guide: A2 – Key Resources.
- The use of aspirin is NOT recommended.

- Those with DVT high-risk factors should also be considered for:
- Anticoagulant therapy such as low molecular weight heparin, prior to the journey, unless currently anticoagulated with warfarin.
- Referral to a haematologist is appropriate.

Motion Sickness

■ 'Motion sickness' describes the symptoms caused by exposure to movement during a journey on any form of transport, notably boats, aircraft and cars. Symptoms include abdominal discomfort, malaise, nausea and vomiting, flushing, sweating and light-headedness.

2.3 Risk Management

2 The Pre-Travel Consultation

2.3.2 Journey Risks

- When at sea, most travellers adapt within 2 to 3 days, although approximately 5% remain symptomatic.
- Rates of motion sickness peak between the ages of 3 and 12 years; children under 2 years of age are rarely affected. Women are more commonly affected. Pregnancy is an added risk factor.
- Motion sickness can be reduced by:
  - Sitting in the middle seats of boats/aircraft/cars.
  - Fixing vision on the horizon or other stable object.
  - Use of distraction, e.g. listening to music or playing games; reading should be avoided.
  - Large meals should be avoided.
  - Antiemetic medication should be started in advance of the journey.
  - See Table 2-2.

Table 2-2. Drugs used to prevent/reduce motion sickness (in alphabetical order)*

Drug	Minimum age	Presentation/Dose	Adverse events
Cinnarizine	5 to 12 years	15mg (oral) 2 hours prior to travel, then 7.5mg every 8 hours, if necessary.	Drowsiness, gastrointestinal disturbance. Also rarely: lichen planus, lupus-like skin reactions, sweating and weight gain.
	Adults/children over 12 years	30mg (oral) 2 hours prior to travel, then 15mg every 8 hours, if necessary.	
Cyclizine	6 to 12 years	25mg oral.	Drowsiness, headache, rash, dry mouth.
	Adults/children over 12 years	50mg oral up to 3 times daily.	
Hyoscine Hydrobromide (Scopolomine Hydrobromide)	3 to 4 years	75µg oral 30 minutes prior to start of journey, then every 6 hours if required.	Constipation, bradycardia, dilation of pupil with loss of accommodation, dry mouth, dry and flushed skin, reduced bronchial secretions and urinary urgency and retention.
	4 to 10 years	75 to 150µg oral 30 minutes prior to start of journey, then every 6 hours if required.	Rarely: confusion, giddiness, nausea and vomiting.
	Adults/children over 10 years	50 to 300µg oral 30 minutes prior to start of journey, then every 6 hours if required.	Very rare: angle-closure glaucoma.
	Patch not suitable for children under 10 years.	1mg self adhesive skin patch (Scopoderm TTS®), every 72 hours.	

(continued)

2.3.2 Journey Risks

Table 2-2. Drugs used to prevent/reduce motion sickness (in alphabetical order)*
(continued)

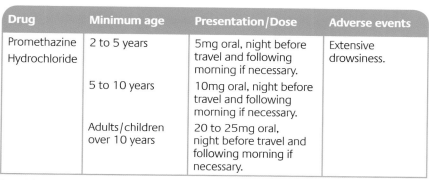

Drug	Minimum age	Presentation/Dose	Adverse events
Promethazine Hydrochloride	2 to 5 years	5mg oral, night before travel and following morning if necessary.	Extensive drowsiness.
	5 to 10 years	10mg oral, night before travel and following morning if necessary.	
	Adults/children over 10 years	20 to 25mg oral, night before travel and following morning if necessary.	

*Drug information should be checked in the British National Formulary (BNF);
See Resource Guide: A2 – Key Resources.

Jet Lag

- 'Jet lag' describes the symptoms caused by disruption to the body's circadian rhythms as a result of crossing multiple time zones. Symptoms include appetite loss, headache, malaise and sleeping difficulties such as night time insomnia and/or day time drowsiness.
- Adaptation to a new time zone may take several days; eastward travel usually requires more time to adapt than westward travel.
- The effects of jet lag can be reduced by breaking the journey with a stopover, eating light meals, limiting alcohol and caffeine consumption, gentle exercise and exposure to sunlight during daylight hours on arrival.
- Melatonin is sometimes used for the prevention of jet lag by travellers. It is however not licensed or available for this purpose in the UK.

Fear of Flying

- See Risk Management: 2.3.10 Psychological Health.

2.3 Risk Management

2 The Pre-Travel Consultation

2.3.3 Safety Risks

- Destination-specific advice can be found on NaTHNaC's Country Information Pages[1] www.nathnac.org.
- See the Foreign and Commonwealth Office website www.fco.gov.uk. Travellers should be encouraged to register their contact details and travel plans online at FCO LOCATE. See Resource Guide: A14 – Key Resources.
- Refer travellers to Resource Guide: B – Resources for Travellers.
- See Risk Management: 2.3.1 Medical Preparation – Travel Insurance.
- See Resource Guide: 2.3.3.

Whilst some aspects of safety are out of an individual's control, the importance of maintaining a heightened sense of awareness, especially in unfamiliar environments, should be discussed, along with the risk reduction measures detailed below.

Transport Safety

According to the WHO *Global status report on road safety* 2009, over 1.2 million people die on the world's roads every year, and an estimated 50 million are injured. Over 90% of deaths occur in low- and middle-income countries. See Resource Guide: 2.3.3a. Road traffic accidents account for significantly more morbidity and mortality in travellers than infectious diseases.

- Travellers should familiarise themselves with the rules of the road at their destinations.
- Care should be taken when crossing roads. Some countries have different standards of driving, for example, vehicles may not stop at zebra crossings and jaywalking can be illegal.
- Travel at night should be avoided whenever possible, especially if road conditions and lighting are poor.
- Drivers should familiarise themselves with their vehicle and route prior to a journey. Seat / safety belts should be worn, when available, and vehicle doors should be locked at all times.
- Child restraint seats may be unavailable and ideally should be brought from the UK.
- Cyclists / motorcyclists should always wear a protective helmet, even if it is not a legal requirement.
- Travellers should ensure that their insurance covers them for driving or travelling as a passenger on a motorcycle.
- Travellers must be reminded not to drive after drinking alcohol or taking drugs, to avoid excessive speed and not to drive when tired.
- Local advice regarding the use of taxis should be followed.
- Buses, trains, boats and ferries may be old, poorly maintained and subject to overcrowding.
- Travellers should not hitchhike.
- Recognisable airlines and scheduled flights should be used whenever practical. The Department of Transport and the European Commission publish regularly updated lists of airlines banned from operating in the UK and the European Union. See Resource Guide: 2.3.3b and 2.3.3c.

1   Alternatively see Travax http://www.travax.nhs.uk/ or Fit for Travel http://www.fitfortravel.nhs.uk/

2.3.3 Safety Risks

Water Safety

The most serious, but largely preventable risk associated with water is drowning. Worldwide, approximately 450,000 people drown annually. Alcohol is a major risk factor. See Resource Guide: 2.3.3d.

- Travellers should be aware of local warnings regarding tides and weather conditions and only swim from designated safe beaches.
- Suction outlets, filters and grilles can be dangerous or inadequately maintained in swimming pools and water parks.
- Drugs and alcohol should be avoided before swimming or participating in water sports.
- Water sports such as water skiing, windsurfing and canoeing carry a risk of injury and should only be undertaken if qualified. Safety standards in low-income regions may not be rigorous.
- Beginners should ensure they receive tuition from qualified, experienced instructors and that equipment is properly maintained.
- Lifejackets should be worn whilst participating in water sports and travelling by boat. Depth of water should always be checked before diving.
- Children must be supervised at all times in or near water. This includes on balconies, at the beach and around swimming pools.

Accommodation Safety

- Travellers should familiarise themselves with fire exits and inspect accommodation for potential health hazards, including electrical and structural hazards.
- Travellers should be alert to the risk of carbon monoxide poisoning. Regulations regarding service and maintenance of gas facilities may not be thorough or enforced.
- Campsites can have security issues and can be located in areas prone to flooding.

Personal Safety

- The FCO website provides general and destination-specific safety and security advice. Travellers should research their destination before departure (ideally prior to booking a trip) and follow advice, including the travel warnings. See Resource Guide: A12 – Key Resources.
- Travellers should register their contact details and trip plans on FCO LOCATE, so that the local British Embassy and/or crisis staff can provide better assistance in an emergency such as a tsunami or terrorist attack. See Resource Guide: A14 – Key Resources.
- Travellers should ensure family and friends are regularly kept informed of plans, record emergency contact details in their passport and carry emergency numbers, including those of next of kin, insurers, and the British embassy at their destinations.
- Photocopies of all travel documents, including passports, should be taken and kept separate from the originals and/or stored online using a secure data storage site. Travelling alone, particularly at night, should be avoided.
- Travellers should familiarise themselves with cultural sensitivities and dress and behave appropriately.
- Avoid wearing jewellery or any obvious displays of wealth and remain vigilant at all times with valuables including money.

2.3.3 Safety Risks

- Local people should not be photographed without permission and photographing airports and military buildings must be avoided.
- Crimes, including theft or muggings, should be reported to local police.
- A Health Information Sheet, *Personal safety during travel*, is available to download from NaTHNaC[1]. See Resource Guide: A26 – Key Resources.

Sport and Recreational Risks

- Injuries from contact sports increase risk of blood-borne viral illnesses (BBVs) in risk regions.
- Helmets should be worn by travellers riding a horse, bicycle or motorbike.
- Skiers should follow weather/avalanche warnings carefully, wear appropriate clothing and use sun protection, including goggles.
- Walkers and hikers should obey local safety and weather advice.
- Trekking in remote areas without an experienced guide is not recommended.
- Involvement with drugs increases the risk of becoming a victim of crime. Penalties for drug use, possession and dealing are likely to be more severe than in the UK, and can include the death penalty. Travellers should never carry parcels/packages for others.
- Nightclubs and bars may disregard fire hazards and can become significantly overcrowded.

2.3 Risk Management

2 The Pre-Travel Consultation

2.3.4 Environmental Risks

Travellers from the UK may arrive overseas unprepared physically or mentally for the hazards of more extreme environmental conditions. Environmental risks include those relating to altitude, sun exposure, temperature, humidity, air and water pollution, aquatic risks, and risks associated with the flora and fauna. Such risks are not to be underestimated; appropriate research and preparation should be encouraged.

Some individuals will intentionally travel to destinations with extreme environmental conditions such as high altitude, intense heat or extreme cold. Travellers to extreme climates should be physically fit, equipped, and competent in skills required to survive. Preparation is vital.

Travellers with pre-existing medical conditions should be medically assessed and understand the potential consequences of exposure to environmental risks on their health; specialist advice should be sought where necessary.

- Environmental conditions may be changed by natural disasters. See Special Risk Travel: 3.2.9 Natural Disasters.
- A Health Information Sheet, *Natural Disasters – advice for travellers to affected areas*, is available to download from NaTHNaC[1]. See Resource Guide: A26 – Key Resources.
- Refer travellers to Resource Guide: B – Resources for Travellers.
- See Resource Guide: 2.3.4.
- Worldwide location and seasonal weather forecasts are available from the Met Office. See Resource Guide: 2.3.4a.

Altitude

- See Special Risk Travel: 3.2.2 Altitude.
- A Health Information Sheet, *Altitude illness*, is available to download from NaTHNaC[1]. See Resource Guide: A26 – Key Resources.

Sun

Travellers can be exposed to stronger sunlight; unless protected, there is an increased risk of skin damage from exposure to the sun's ultraviolet rays (UVA and UVB rays). Surfaces such as snow, sand and water reflect UV rays and can result in increased sun exposure. UVA rays are associated with skin ageing, and increasingly have been linked to malignant melanoma; UVB rays are associated with sunburn, skin ageing and cancer. See Resource Guide: 2.3.4b.

- **Sunburn**
  Sunburn is the visible appearance of damage to skin cells. Sunburnt skin should be covered and further sun exposure avoided. Skin moisturisers, a cool compress, analgesia and anti-inflammatory medication can help alleviate the discomfort of sunburn; a medical opinion should be sought in severe cases. In the tropics, severe sunburn can develop in under an hour.

- **Prickly heat**
  Prickly heat (miliaria) is an itchy, red rash that occurs in hot and humid weather. It is a result of blockage of the sweat glands and typically affects the hands, chest and feet. The rash lasts for 2 to 3 days and usually resolves spontaneously. Prickly heat can be avoided by keeping cool and limiting sun exposure. Antihistamines can be used to relieve itching.

2.3 Risk Management

2 The Pre-Travel Consultation

---

1   Alternatively see Travax http://www.travax.nhs.uk/ or Fit for Travel http://www.fitfortravel.nhs.uk/

2.3.4 Environmental Risks

■ **Skin cancer**
Benign and malignant transformation of skin cells can result from UV radiation damage. A history of childhood, and/or intense intermittent, sun exposure are risk factors for skin cancer. Those with fair or freckled skin are at increased risk. Individuals with a history of skin cancer must be advised to reduce future sun exposure as much as possible.

Travellers should be informed of skin damage reduction measures, see Box 2-5. Travellers should be directed to the information on Sunsense: Protecting Yourself from Ultraviolet Radiation. See Resource Guide: 2.3.4c. A Health Information Sheet, *Sun Protection*, is available to download from NaTHNaC[1]. See Resource Guide: A26 – Key Resources.

Box 2-5. Skin damage reduction measures

1. Sun exposure should be limited during the hours between 10am and 3pm when the sun is usually at its strongest.
2. Skin should be covered as much as possible with appropriate clothing. A wide brimmed hat should be worn to protect the head and face. Loose, breathable clothing in natural fabrics will offer cooler cover.
3. Sunscreen should be liberally applied before exposure to sun, and reapplied regularly, particularly after swimming. The Sun Protection Factor (SPF) is a measure of protection afforded by sunscreen. Sunscreen with an SPF of 15 means that it takes 15 times as long to get sunburnt with sunscreen applied compared to no sunscreen. Sunscreen with an SPF of at least 15 is strongly recommended. Children, and those with fair or sun-sensitive skin, require a higher SPF.
4. Travellers should be informed of signs of skin damage and be encouraged to check moles or freckles regularly for change; a prompt medical opinion should be sought if changes, including discolouration, increasing size or bleeding, occur.

Heat and Humidity

- Most travellers will adapt to persistently high temperatures in approximately 10 days.
- Humidity reduces the rate of evaporation of sweat and can make it more difficult to control core body temperature.
- Rapid dehydration can occur in hot conditions.
- Until acclimatised, and to avoid the risk of heat-related effects, travellers should limit physical exertion and maintain an adequate fluid intake. Small (but not excessive) amounts of salt can be added to food, provided adequate fluid levels are maintained, dehydration is not present and there are no medical contraindications.
- Salt tablets are not recommended as they can cause gastric irritation.
- The combination of persistent heat, inadequate acclimatisation, loss of fluids/electrolytes and over-exertion, can lead to heat exhaustion.

---

1   Alternatively see Travax http://www.travax.nhs.uk/ or Fit for Travel http://www.fitfortravel.nhs.uk/

2.3.4 Environmental Risks

- Feeling cold in hot conditions can be a sign of heatstroke. Sweating can also cease, although this is not a universal sign. Rest in a cool environment, with adequate hydration is recommended. A medical opinion should be sought, particularly if irritability and/or confusion develop. Rapid evacuation from the hot environment may be required.

- Oral rehydration solutions can help to maintain electrolyte balance. They are primarily used to replace fluid and electrolytes following episodes of diarrhoea. Instructions for their use should be followed carefully.

- The young and the elderly are particularly susceptible to heat-related illnesses and can take longer to adapt.

- Caucasians living in hot climates have a risk of developing renal stones when a fluid/electrolyte balance is not maintained.

- See Resource Guide: 2.3.4d.

Cold

- Appropriate clothing should be worn in cold conditions. It should consist of several layers of breathable fabric (wool, down or fleece) with tough windproof and waterproof exterior 'shell' garment. Particular care must be taken to ensure that extremities (fingers, toes, and nose) are well protected. Spare clothing should be carried.

- There can be a risk of injury from slipping and falling on snow or ice. Footwear should have good grip and ideally provide upper as well as sole insulation.

- Wind and/or rain/snow soaked clothes can lead to hypothermia.

- Hypothermia, with a core body temperature below 34.5°C, can cause individuals to become confused, irrational and uncoordinated. It can lead to unconsciousness and death. Shelter, warm drinks, food and dry clothing should be provided urgently; a medical opinion should be sought. Rapid evacuation from the cold environment may be necessary.

- Frostbite is rare in a healthy person in temperatures above -20°C; the risk increases as the temperature drops. In very cold climates metal jewellery can chill and cause local frostbite; jewellery should be removed. Skin should be checked regularly for signs of frostbite; these include a waxy appearance of the skin and loss of sensation. When suspected, shelter should be found and the affected part re-warmed slowly as soon as possible; a medical opinion should be sought.

- Ultraviolet rays reflecting off snow and ice can cause snow-blindness, which is sunburn of the front of the eye. A painful gritty sensation in the eye with swelling of the eyelids results and requires several days away from sunlight for recovery. Sunglasses or goggles should be worn to protect the eyes from glare in snowy conditions.

- Sunscreen with an SPF of at least 30 must be applied to exposed areas such as the face.

- Adequate provisions including food, fluids, spare clothing and a travel medical kit should be carried.

- See Resource Guide: 2.3.4d.

2.3.4 Environmental Risks

Air Pollution

- The WHO global update 2005 stated that air pollution is a major environmental risk to health and is estimated to cause approximately 2 million premature deaths worldwide per year.

- Significant air pollutants include particulate matter from the burning of fossil fuels, ozone, nitrogen dioxide and sulphur dioxide mostly from industrial emissions. Higher pollution levels have been shown to increase morbidity and mortality in the local population.

- Avoiding exposure can be difficult for travellers. The effects of pollution can be reduced by avoiding strenuous exercise and remaining indoors during peak emission times, if these are known. Smoking should be discouraged.

- Travellers with pre-existing respiratory conditions are at risk of exacerbations. See Special Risk Traveller: 3.1.15 Respiratory Conditions.

- Travellers involved in work with the potential for exposure to pollutants such as dust, silica, asbestos, or chemicals, should be advised that prevention and control measures that are applied and regulated in the UK, may not exist or be enforced overseas.

- Ideally, any exposure to hazardous substances / processes should be avoided. If this is not possible, exposure should be limited and appropriate personal protective equipment used. The Health and Safety Executive provide guidance on personal protective equipment. See Resource Guide: 2.3.4e.

- The WHO provides air quality guidelines for particulate matter, ozone, nitrogen dioxide and sulphur dioxide. See Resource Guide: 2.3.4f.

Water Risks

- Travellers should be aware of:
  - Safety risks associated with water. See Risk Management: 2.3.3 Safety Risks.
  - Water-borne disease risks. See Risk Management: 2.3.5 Food- and Water-borne Risks.
  - Water-associated disease risks, e.g. leptospirosis, marine toxins and schistosomiasis. See Disease Guide Section 5.

- Travellers should avoid freshwater swimming / wading / paddling in areas known or suspected to be at risk for schistosomiasis.

- Travellers intending to swim or dive in the salt water should be aware of local hazards of marine life such as jellyfish, sea urchins, coral and fish.

- Appropriate protective clothing, including footwear, should be worn.

- If stung, jellyfish tentacles should be removed using gloves and urgent medical attention sought. Application of vinegar inactivates the nemacysts of most jellyfish species, with the exception of Portuguese Man o' War.

- Sea urchin spines should be removed as soon as possible. Initial first aid treatment of sea urchin stings is immersion in hot water, taking care not to burn the affected area.

- Rivers and lakes can become contaminated with organic or inorganic chemical compounds. In some regions this may cause contamination of the water supply.

- Lead in water can result from industrial sources. Lead exposure is primarily through food and water, although exposure from air, dust, soil and paint contribute to overall exposure.

2.3.4 Environmental Risks

Flora and Fauna

- Travellers should be aware of the potential hazards associated with an environment's flora and fauna. Plants can have sharp thorns, contain saps that are corrosive or capable of causing skin photosensitivity reactions.
- Travellers should be advised to avoid direct skin contact with local flora.
- Travellers should be advised to avoid algal blooms. See Resource Guide: 2.3.4g.
- Medical attention should be sought should skin irritation not be adequately treated by simple cooling measures and antihistamine use. See Resource Guide: 3.2.1 Adventure.
- Traveller should be aware of the venomous snakes, scorpions and spiders that are native to the area in which they are travelling. See Disease Guide Section 5.
- It is not appropriate to carry snake or scorpion anti-venom. Local specialist advice should be sought. Urgent medical attention must be sought following possible envenomation. Knowledge of first aid measures is essential. See Resource Guide: 2.3.1a and 2.3.1b.
- See Risk Management: 2.3.6 Vector-borne Risks.

2.3 Risk Management –

2 The Pre-Travel Consultation

2.3.5 Food- and Water-borne Risks

Travellers' diarrhoea (TD) is the most common cause of illness in travellers, with 20% to 60% of travellers affected. Eating contaminated food and, to a lesser degree, drinking contaminated liquids are the predominant way of acquiring TD. TD is caused by a wide variety of infectious agents worldwide, the most common being bacterial agents enterotoxigenic *Escherichia coli* (ETEC), other *E. coli* strains, Campylobacter, Salmonella, Shigella, as well as viruses including norovirus and rotavirus, and protozoa such as *Giardia* and *Cryptosporidium*. Cholera is rare in travellers. Less common, but still important are poisonings that occur after ingestion of toxic marine foods. A change in bowel habit can also be caused by stress, a change in diet, increased alcohol consumption, and hot weather.

Pre-Travel Preparation

- Travellers should be informed of diseases transmitted by food and water. See Table 2-3 and Disease Guide Section 5.
- Refer travellers to Resource Guide: B – Resources for Travellers.
- Destination-specific advice can be found on NaTHNaC's website Country Information Pages[1] www.nathnac.org.
- Travellers should practise food, water and personal hygiene measures. Water purification should be discussed, as local drinking water may not be potable in many locations. See Box 2-6.
- Vaccines are available for the prevention of cholera, hepatitis A, poliomyelitis and typhoid. See Resource Guide: Appendix 1 – Vaccine Compendium.
- A travel medical kit containing oral rehydration sachets and a water disinfectant agent, where appropriate, should be carried from the UK.
- Travellers should be informed of the signs and symptoms of TD and the appropriate use of self-treatment measures, including rehydration and/or medication. See Box 2-7. The need to seek prompt medical attention for fever, bloody diarrhoea, jaundice or persistent symptoms must be emphasised. See Resource Guide: 2.3.5a and 2.3.5b.
- Travellers should be informed that gastrointestinal illnesses can result in reduced effectiveness of regular medication, including oral contraception. Additional precautions may be required.
- Antibiotic or other (e.g. bismuth subsalicylate) prophylaxis is not recommended for most travellers. See Resource Guide: 2.3.5c. The impact that an episode of TD will have on the traveller and their planned activities, as well as any medical conditions, should be considered prior to prescribing chemoprophylaxis. When prescribed, drug interactions should be avoided.
- See Resource Guide: 2.3.5.

---

1   Alternatively see Travax http://www.travax.nhs.uk/ or Fit for Travel http://www.fitfortravel.nhs.uk/

2.3.5 Food- and Water-borne Risks

Table 2-3. Diseases transmitted by food and water

Category	Disease	Usual modes of transmission	Prevention
Bacterial	Brucella	Unpasteurised dairy products	Avoidance
	Campylobacter	Food or water	Avoidance
	Cholera	Usually water, occasionally food	Avoidance & vaccine
	E. coli	Food	Avoidance
	Salmonella	Food	Avoidance
	Shigella	Food and water	Avoidance
	Typhoid / paratyphoid	Food and water	Avoidance & vaccine
Helminths	Roundworms	Soil-contaminated food	Avoidance
	Whipworms	Soil-contaminated food	Avoidance
Protozoa	Amoeba	Food and water	Avoidance
	Cyclospora	Food and water	Avoidance
	Cryptosporidium	Food, water and human-to-human	Avoidance
	Giardia	Water, human-to-human	Avoidance
Toxic marine poisoning	Scromboid	Mahi-mahi, tuna, mackerel, bonito, herring, sardine, anchovy	Avoidance
	Ciguatera	Barracuda, snapper, grouper, sea bass, moray eel	Avoidance
	Pufferfish	Pufferfish	Avoidance
	Shellfish	Bivalve shellfish or mussels	Avoidance
Viral	Hepatitis A	Food and water	Avoidance & vaccine
	Hepatitis E	Usually water, occasionally food	Avoidance
	Norovirus	Food and water	Avoidance
	Poliomyelitis	Food and water	Avoidance & vaccine
	Rotavirus	Food and water	Avoidance

2.3 Risk Management

2 The Pre-Travel Consultation

2.3.5 Food- and Water-borne Risks

Avoidance of Food- and Water-borne Diseases During Travel

Travellers should avoid the following food items:

- Salads.
- Uncooked fruits and vegetables, unless they have been cleaned and peeled by the traveller.
- Unpasteurised dairy products, e.g. milk, cheese and ice cream.
- Raw or undercooked seafood or meat.
- Food from street traders.
- Cooked food that has been allowed to stand at room temperature, or is likely to have been exposed to flies such as food in buffets.
- Raw vegetables fertilised with human or animal waste (night soil).

Ideally only food that has been freshly prepared, thoroughly cooked and is served piping hot should be consumed; most enteropathogens are inactivated at temperatures above 60°C. The phrase **'Boil it, cook it, peel it or forget it!'** is often used to summarise common sense advice for travellers.

Travellers should be advised regarding water and drinks that:

- Untreated water from taps, bore holes or wells in regions without effective water treatment provisions should not be used to drink or to clean teeth. Ice should also be avoided.
- Only bottled water provided in sealed, tamper-proof containers and bottled by known manufacturers, and that has been certified according to national and international water quality standards, should be drunk. Where bottled water is not available, a suitable effective method of water purification should be used. See Box 2-6. See Resource Guide: 2.3.5d and 2.3.5e.
- Carbonated bottled beverages, pasteurised or canned juice, sports beverages, and pasteurised, boiled or sterilised milk (without ice) are normally safe. Care should be taken to ensure bottled or canned drinks have intact seals and that the outside of the container is clean. Consumption of homemade or non-commercial, unpasteurised juices should be avoided.
- Drinks made with boiling water, including tea and coffee are generally safe.
- Swallowing water whilst swimming should be avoided.
- Seawater should be avoided when posted warnings suggest conditions conducive to fish poisonings, such as the presence of excessive amounts of dinoflagellates in breeding areas, known as 'red tides'.

A Health Information Sheet, *Food and water hygiene*, is available to download from NaTHNaC[1]. See Resource Guide: A26 – Key Resources.

Travellers should be advised regarding personal hygiene that:

- Human-to-human transmission occurs in conditions of poor faecal-oral hygiene.
- Hands should be washed after visiting the toilet, and always before preparing or eating food.
- Only swim in chlorinated water or that which is unlikely to be contaminated with sewage and do not swim in pools whilst experiencing diarrhoea.

1   Alternatively see Travax http://www.travax.nhs.uk/ or Fit for Travel http://www.fitfortravel.nhs.uk/

2.3.5 Food- and Water-borne Risks

Box 2-6. Water purification methods

Water can be purified by four methods: boiling, filtration, chemical disinfection and ultraviolet (UV) light. Filtration and chemical disinfection, and filtration and UV light, are usually used in combination. The most appropriate method for an individual traveller should be discussed. The necessary equipment should be purchased in the UK.

1. Boiling

Water can be purified by bringing it to a boil. This will kill all disease causing pathogens, however, it may not always be convenient.

If water is not boiled, filtration followed by chemical disinfection is recommended.

2. Filtration

A water filter must be designed and certified for small volume water purification.

Ceramic, membrane and carbon block filters are the most common types.

Filters will remove protozoa and some bacteria but viruses are too small to be captured in the filter. Some filters decrease viral contamination through a combination of filtration and electrostatic attraction, but are not able to rid water of viral contamination completely.

The filter pore size should be < 1 μm to ensure removal of *Cryptosporidium* in clear water.

Reverse osmosis (very fine pore filtration that holds back dissolved salts in the water) and ultrafiltration (fine pore filtration that passes dissolved salts but holds back viruses and other microbes) devices can theoretically remove all pathogens.

3. Chemical disinfection

If it is not possible to boil water, chemical disinfection of clear, non-turbid water is effective for killing bacteria and viruses. It is not as reliable in killing protozoan parasites. For example, *Giardia* is generally killed by properly performed chemical disinfection, but *Cryptosporidium* and *Cyclospora* are more difficult to kill.

Chlorine and iodine are the chemicals most commonly used.

A recent European Union (EU) directive has announced that iodine will no longer be sold or supplied for use in disinfecting drinking water after October 25, 2009. If sourced outside of the EU, travellers should be informed that iodine use over a long period of time is not recommended for pregnant women, those with a history of thyroid disease, and those with known hypersensitivity to iodine, as excess iodine can interfere with the functioning of the thyroid gland.

If turbid water (i.e. not clear, or with suspended solid matter) is to be disinfected with chemicals, it should be cleared beforehand by, for example, letting the impurities settle, or by filtering.

A product that combines chlorine disinfection with coagulation/flocculation (i.e., chemical precipitation) should be used, when available, as these products remove significant numbers of protozoa, in addition to killing bacteria and viruses.

(continued)

2.3.5 Food- and Water-borne Risks

Box 2-6. Water purification methods (continued)

Often, after chemical treatment, a carbon filter is used to improve taste and, in the case of iodine treatment, to remove excess iodine.

Silver, contrary to widespread perception, is not an effective disinfectant and is not recommended for water disinfection.

4. Ultraviolet (UV) light water purification

Portable, battery-operated devices utilising UV light can be used to purify water. Water must be free of particulate material before treating.

Box 2-7. Self-treatment guide: Travellers' diarrhoea

- During any diarrhoeal illness travellers should maintain adequate hydration.

- Specific oral rehydration solutions can be drunk by young children, the elderly and those with chronic medical conditions. Instructions must be followed.

- Mild, uncomplicated diarrhoea without fever is typically self-limiting; rest and hydration are usually all that are required.

- Fluid intake should be maintained with boiled, bottled or purified water. Breast and/or bottle feeding should continue for babies.

- Antimotility drugs, such as loperamide, can be taken to control watery diarrhoea in the short term. They are contraindicated in bloody diarrhoea, fever and in children less than 4 years, and should be used cautiously in children under 12 years.

- Diarrhoea with blood in the stool, fever or dehydration needs medical attention if self-treatment measures are not effective within 24 hours.

- Babies, young children, the elderly and those with pre-existing medical conditions are more susceptible to complications, particularly dehydration and should seek early medical advice.

- Single dose antibiotic therapy can be used; if symptoms are unresponsive, treatment can continue for 3 days. Fluoroquinolones, such as ciprofloxacin, are the drugs of choice outside Asia. Azithromycin should be used in South and South East Asia, where fluoroquinolone-resistant *Campylobacter* is a more common cause of TD.

- Rifaximin can be used as an alternative treatment for TD, but is unlicensed in the UK.

2.3.6 Vector-borne Risks (including animals)

Pre-Travel Preparation

- Significant and/or potentially life-threatening illnesses are transmitted by vectors (including animals). See Table 2-4 and Disease Guide Section 5. Travellers should be informed of the risk of vector-borne disease, according to the distribution, seasonality and biting habits, and risks associated with animals, at their destination.

- Destination-specific advice can be found on NaTHNaC's Country Information Pages[1] www.nathnac.org.

- Vector-borne illnesses are best prevented by personal protection measures. See Box 2-8. See Resource Guide: 2.3.6a.

- A Health Information Sheet, *Insect bite avoidance*, is available to download from NaTHNaC[1]. See Resource Guide: A26 – Key Resources.

- Refer travellers to Resource Guide: B – Resources for Travellers.

- The traveller should carry with them all measures that they intend to use during travel to reduce exposure to vector-borne diseases.

- Appropriate medication for self-treatment of bites should be carried. See Risk Management: 2.3.1 Travel medical kit.

- Vaccines are available for the prevention of Japanese encephalitis, rabies, tick-borne encephalitis and yellow fever. See Disease Guide Section 5 and Resource Guide: Appendix 1 – Vaccine Compendium.

- Antimalarial medication is available for the prevention of malaria. See Malaria below.

- Travellers should be advised of signs and symptoms of vector-borne diseases and be encouraged to seek prompt medical attention.

- See Resource Guide: 2.3.6.

Table 2-4. Vector-borne diseases

Vector-borne diseases	Activity	Diseases
Animals (and bats); animal products	Bite, scratch, lick, bodily fluid.	Rabies; Brucellosis, Q fever, Anthrax
Fleas	Live on or bite a variety of mammals, including humans.	Rickettsia, plague
Flies		
Sand fly (*Phlebotomus and Lutzomyia* spp.)	Bite during hours of darkness. Found in forests, stone/mud walls & animal burrows.	Leishmaniasis
Black fly (*Simulium* spp)	Bite during daylight hours and live near fast-flowing streams.	Onchocerciasis
Tsetse fly (*Glossina spp.*)	Active in day. Live in woods in savannah and dense foliage by streams.	African trypanosomiasis
Lice	Live on mammals, including humans. Transferred by direct contact.	Rickettsia

(continued)

1 Alternatively see Travax http://www.travax.nhs.uk/ or Fit for Travel http://www.fitfortravel.nhs.uk/

2.3 Risk Management

2 The Pre-Travel Consultation

2.3.6 Vector-borne Risks (including animals)

Table 2-4. Vector-borne diseases (continued)

Vector-borne diseases	Activity	Diseases
Mites	Live in or on soil, plants, animals and mould, depending on species.	Rickettsia
Mosquitoes *Aedes* spp.	Day biting	Chikungunya fever, dengue fever, filariasis, yellow fever
Anopheles spp.	Most active between dusk and dawn	Malaria, filariasis
Culex spp.	Most active between dusk and dawn	Japanese encephalitis, West Nile Virus, filariasis
Haemogogus spp.	Mainly active in day	Yellow fever
Rodents	Contact with or aerosolisation of urine	Hantavirus, leptospirosis, lassa fever, plague
Reduviid bug (Triatomine)	Feeds at night. Lives in dry forested areas such as burrows, nests and mud houses.	American trypanosomiasis (Chagas disease)
Ticks (several species)	Found in undergrowth, forest fringes, grasslands, during spring, summer or early autumn. Brush off onto clothing or skin.	Tick-borne encephalitis, rickettsia, Lyme disease, erlichiosis, babesiosis, CCHF

Malaria

- See Disease Guide Section 5. Travellers should be informed of the ABCD of malaria prevention.
- Antimalarial medication is available for the prevention of malaria. The Health Protection Agency (HPA) Guidelines for Malaria Prevention in Travellers from the United Kingdom should be followed. See Resource Guide: A5 – Key Resources.
- Destination-specific malaria advice can be found on NaTHNaC's Country Information Pages[1] www.nathnac.org.
- Travellers should be advised of signs and symptoms of malaria and be encouraged to seek prompt medical attention.
- Rapid Diagnostic Tests (RDTs) are not recommended for use by travellers for self-diagnosis of malaria.
- Emergency standby treatment for malaria should be recommended for those taking antimalarials AND visiting remote areas where they are unlikely to be within 24 hours of medical attention. See Table 5-3 in Disease Guide Section 5.

---
1   Alternatively see Travax http://www.travax.nhs.uk/ or Fit for Travel http://www.fitfortravel.nhs.uk/

2.3.6 Vector-borne Risks (including animals)

Box 2-8. Personal protective measures during travel

1. Outdoors

Minimise outdoor exposure. When it is not possible:

- Repellents: apply to all exposed non-sensitive areas of skin.

  - DEET (N, N-diethyl-m-toluamide) is the preferred insect repellent. It is suitable for all individuals over 2 months. There is no evidence that any groups, including pregnant women, are at increased risk of adverse events from DEET.

    Increasing concentrations of DEET correlate with extended duration of protection (see table below). There is no additional benefit to concentrations greater than 50%. Intervals between applications depend on concentration used, activity, and humidity, as sweating reduces duration of protection.

Duration of protection –DEET based repellents	
20% DEET	1 to 3 hours
30% DEET	Up to 6 hours
50% DEET	Up to 12 hours

  Combination products of DEET/sunscreen are not recommended. If both products are needed, sunscreen should be applied first, ideally 20 minutes before DEET. There is rare skin sensitivity to DEET.

  - Picaridin – (Bayrepel®, KBR 3023, Autan®) (1 piperidecarboxylic acid, 2- (2-hydroxyethyl)-1-methyl-propylester) is reported as having repellent properties comparable to DEET. In the UK, a 20% strength product is recommended.
  - Oil of lemon eucalyptus (p-menthane-3, 8-diol) gives approximately the same protection as 15% DEET. Lemon eucalyptus essential oil is a different product and is not recommended as an insect repellent.
  - Citronella oil-based repellents should not be used due to their short duration of action.

- Insecticides – Synthetic pesticides, called pyrethroids (e.g. permethrin), can be used in sprays to kill mosquitoes. They should not be applied directly to skin, but can be used on clothes and mosquito net. Smouldering pyrethroid coils can be used to deter flying insects outside. It is recommended that insecticides be used in addition to, and not in place of, DEET.

- Clothing – Light-coloured, long-sleeved shirts, trousers, socks and covered shoes should be worn to cover as much skin as possible. Outer clothing can be treated with permethrin.

- Tick checks should be carried out regularly following potential exposure. Ticks should be extracted as soon as possible, using tweezers/tick removers placed as close as possible to the skin. The tick should be pulled slowly, with care not to squeeze stomach contents into the bite site. See Figure 2-1.

2.3 Risk Management

2 The Pre-Travel Consultation

(continued)

2.3.6 Vector-borne Risks (including animals)

Box 2-8. Personal protective measures during travel (continued)

- Direct contact with animals/animal products should be avoided. This includes petting or feeding animals, especially dogs, or adopting them as pets. Children must be closely supervised, and all bites reported.

2. Indoors

- Sleeping in an air-conditioned room is ideal. All open windows and doors should have intact insect screens.
- If sleeping in an area where insects can enter, travellers should sleep under an intact, strong, insecticide impregnated bed net with a mesh size no larger than 1.5mm. Mosquito nets should be hung according to instructions, tucked under the mattress/hammock and kept in a good state of repair. Cot nets are available for infants. Babies should sleep under nets during daytime naps.
- An aerosol insecticide room spray and vapouriser device should be used.

There are several measures that are less/**NOT** effective and NOT recommended:

- Bath oil.
- Citronella oil-based repellents – very short durations of action.
- Citrosa plant (geranium houseplant).
- Eating garlic or a yeast extract spread such as Marmite.
- Electronic (ultrasonic) or electrocuting devices.
- Odour-baited mosquito traps.
- Orally administered vitamin B1.
- Skin moisturisers that do not contain an approved active repellent.
- Tea tree oil.

Figure 2-1. Technique for removal of a tick

A. Grab the tick at the mouth parts as close as possible to the skin.

B. Pull straight out.

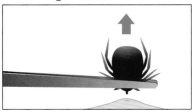

Acknowledgement: Adapted from Centers for Disease Control and Prevention

2.3 Risk Management

2 The Pre-Travel Consultation

2.3.7 Air-borne Risks

See Risk Management: 2.3.4 Environmental Risks – Air Pollution.

Pre-Travel Preparation

- Travellers should be informed of air-borne disease risks at their destination/s. See Disease Guide Section 5. Refer travellers to Resource Guide: B – Resources for Travellers.
- Destination-specific advice can be found on NaTHNaC's Country Information Pages[1] www.nathnac.org.
- Air-borne diseases are best prevented by personal protection measures. See below.
- Vaccines are available for the prevention of influenza, pneumococcal pneumonia and tuberculosis (TB). See Disease Guide Section 5 and Resource Guide: Appendix 1 – Vaccine Compendium. Vaccinations should be administered according to UK schedule and NaTHNaC[1] destination-specific travel advice.
- Travellers should be advised of signs and symptoms of respiratory diseases, how to use over-the-counter medication for treatment of mild, self-limiting respiratory conditions, and where and when to seek medical care. In most cases, travellers should not take with them the neuraminidase inhibitor, oseltamivir (Tamiflu®) for either prevention or self-treatment of influenza.
- Those who are symptomatic with a respiratory illness should delay their travel, and seek medical advice.
- A recent diagnosis of pulmonary TB is a contraindication to travel. Infected individuals must postpone travel until they are confirmed as non-infectious by their supervising physician.
- See Resource Guide: 2.3.7.

Personal Protective Measures During Travel

- The risk of disease transmission on aircraft is low.
- Transmission can occur from an infectious traveller to others seated in close proximity (usually within 2 rows) over lengthy periods of time.
- There is the most information about transmission of TB during air travel. In this case, sitting within 2 rows of an infectious traveller during a flight of 8 hours or longer presents the highest risk. See Resource Guide: 2.3.7a.
- Travellers should be advised to:
  - Avoid crowds and mass gatherings where possible.
  - Cover your nose and mouth with a tissue when you cough or sneeze and dispose of the tissue promptly.
  - Practise good personal hygiene including washing hands with soap and water, using waterless alcohol-based hand gels and avoidance of hand to nose/mouth/eyes contact.
  - Follow public health guidance at the destination.
- Individuals travelling to areas with recently reported cases of avian influenza should be advised to:
  - Avoid visiting live animal markets and poultry farms.
  - Avoid contact with surfaces contaminated with animal faeces.
  - Do not eat or handle undercooked or raw poultry or egg dishes.

2.3 Risk Management

2 The Pre-Travel Consultation

---

1   Alternatively see Travax http://www.travax.nhs.uk/ or Fit for Travel http://www.fitfortravel.nhs.uk/

2.3.7 Air-borne Risks

- Do not attempt to bring any live poultry back to the UK.
- Do not pick up or touch dead or dying birds.
- There is little evidence of the effectiveness of wearing masks in public gatherings, however, properly fitted, special grade masks can be worn in situations such as healthcare settings.

After Travel

- See The Post-Travel Consultation Section 4.
- Travellers with exposure to a respiratory illness should monitor their health. They should contact their GP, and inform them of their travel history if they become ill.
- Following exposure to influenza, they may develop a febrile illness with cough, sore throat, runny nose, headache or muscle aches, which develop within 7 days of their return. The onset of symptomatic TB may be several weeks following return.

2.3 Risk Management

2 The Pre-Travel Consultation

2.3.8 Sexual Health and Blood-borne Viral Risks

Travellers may engage in risk-taking behaviours, such as unprotected sex and recreational drug use during travel; studies have found this to be particularly true in adolescents/young adults, expatriates, military personnel, and those visiting friends and relatives (VFRs). Factors during travel which facilitate risk-taking behaviours include a sense of freedom from usual restraints, increased alcohol consumption and drug use on holiday, loneliness, peer pressure and opportunity.

Pre-Travel Preparation

- Travellers should be informed of sexual health and blood-borne viral risks (BBVs) at their destination/s. See Disease Guide Section 5. See Resource Guide: 2.3.8a and 2.3.8b. Refer travellers to Resource Guide: B – Resources for Travellers.
- Destination-specific advice on hepatitis B can be found on NaTHNaC's website Country Information Pages[1] www.nathnac.org.
- Vaccination against hepatitis B is available. See Disease Guide Section 5 and Resource Guide: Appendix 1 – Vaccine Compendium.
- Transmission of sexually transmitted infections (STIs) and BBVs is best prevented by avoidance and/or use of personal protective measures. See below.
- Travellers should be informed that contraception, including post-coital contraception, pregnancy, abortion and post-exposure screening services may not be easily accessible during travel. Contraception should be carried from the UK. See Resource Guide 2.3.8c and 2.3.8d.
- Travellers should carry a travel medical kit containing sterile needles and syringes for use in a medical/dental emergency, where the safety of local supplies cannot be guaranteed. See Risk Management: 2.3.1 Medical Preparation – Travel medical kit.
- Vaccinations should be administered according to UK schedule and NaTHNaC[1] destination-specific travel advice.
- Travellers should be advised of signs and symptoms of STIs and BBVs, and know where and when to seek medical care. See Disease Guide Section 5. See Risk Management: 2.3.1 Medical Preparation – Access to Medical Care Overseas.
- Cultural and legal acceptance of risk-taking behaviours varies worldwide; travellers should research their destination/s carefully and abide by local customs and law. See Resource Guide: A15 – Key Resources.
- For potential occupational exposure to BBV risks. See Special Risk Traveller: 3.2.5 Healthcare Workers.

Personal Protection Measures during Travel

1. Protection measures to reduce sexual risks should be discussed with travellers. These include:
   - Abstinence.
   - Condoms should always be used to avoid STIs.
   - Contraception should be used to avoid unplanned pregnancy.
   - High-risk sexual practices should be avoided.
   - The number of partners should be limited.
   - Sex with commercial sex workers is known to increase risk of exposure to STIs.

2.3 Risk Management

2 The Pre-Travel Consultation

---

1   Alternatively see Travax http://www.travax.nhs.uk/ or Fit for Travel http://www.fitfortravel.nhs.uk/

2.3.8 Sexual Health and Blood-borne Viral Risks

- Prompt medical advice must be sought for any symptoms/signs of STIs (pain, dysuria, discharge, swelling or ulcers); travellers should refrain from any sexual activity until the condition is diagnosed and treatment is complete.

- STIs and BBVs can be asymptomatic. Travellers concerned about potential exposure should be advised to seek post-exposure testing and/or prophylaxis at a reliable centre at the earliest opportunity. See Algorithm 4-7 in The Post-Travel Consultation Section 4.

2. Preventive measures to reduce blood and bodily fluid transmission of infections should be discussed with travellers. These include:

- Avoiding contact with non-sterile needles including those which may be used in body piercing and tattoos, acupuncture and injecting-drug use.

- If exposure to needles is to occur, needles should be verifiably sterile and single use only. Sharing should always be avoided.

- Medical and dental treatment overseas should be avoided where possible.

- For those travelling for the purpose of receiving medical and/or dental treatment. See Special Risk Travel: 3.2.8 Medical Tourism.

- Blood transfusions should be avoided, and substitutes used, where possible prior to evacuation, unless the safety of the blood supply is up to UK standard.

- Membership with The Blood Care Foundation (fee for service) entitles the member to the worldwide delivery of clean blood and plasma in an emergency. See Resource Guide: 2.3.8e.

Travel can increase the likelihood of becoming a victim of crime, including sexual assault; vigilance is important. See Resource Guide: 2.3.8f.

2.3.9 Skin Health

A traveller's skin may be at risk from environmental factors (sun, cold etc.), bites/ stings, infections, injury, and side effects from drugs. The skin can also reflect a systemic illness acquired overseas, typically with a rash. Consultations for skin rash in returned travellers are common. Conditions most frequently seen are diffuse macular rash, bacterial infections, eczema, pruritus, scabies, urticaria, insect bite reactions, dermatophytosis, cutaneous larva migrans (CLM), leishmaniasis, schistosomiasis, and drug eruptions.

Individuals with pre-existing skin conditions should be medically assessed prior to travel and receive specific advice on how to avoid exacerbations as detailed below.

- Refer travellers to Resource Guide: B – Resources for Travellers.
- See Resource Guide: 2.3.9.
- See Algorithm 4-3 in The Post-Travel Consultation Section 4.

Environmental Risks

- See Risk Management: 2.3.4 Environmental Risks – Sun, Cold, Water, Flora.

Bites/Stings

- See Risk Management: 2.3.6 Vector-borne Risks – Bite Avoidance.

Skin Infections

1. Bacterial Infections

    - See Disease Guide Section 5 – Anthrax, Diphtheria, and Lyme Disease.
    - Travellers should be advised to avoid direct contact with animals or animal products.
    - Any skin wound can become secondarily infected with *Staphylococci* and *Streptococci* if not kept clean and dry. Travellers should carry a topical antibacterial agent to self-treat mild infections; a medical opinion should be sought if the infection persists/worsens.

2. Fungal Infections

    - See Disease Guide Section 5 – Fungal Skin Infections.
    - Fungal infections, including tinea pedis (athlete's foot), tinea corporis (ringworm) and vaginal candidiasis (thrush) are more common in humid environments.
    - Skin should be kept as clean and dry as possible.
    - Occlusive footwear should be avoided and use of antifungal powder considered.
    - Unnecessary antibiotic use should be avoided to reduce the risk of candidiasis.
    - Wet items of clothes and footwear should be allowed to dry thoroughly before re-wearing. Socks should be changed regularly.
    - Travellers should carry with them a topical antifungal cream to self-treat mild fungal infections.

3. Parasitic Infections

    - See Disease Guide Section 5 – Cutaneous Larva Migrans, Helminth Infection, Myiasis, Leishmaniasis, Onchocerciasis, Schistosomiasis and Tungiasis.
    - Travellers should wear protective footwear.
    - A towel should be used when lying down on the ground to avoid direct contact with potentially contaminated soil or sand.

2.3 Risk Management

2 The Pre-Travel Consultation

2.3.9 Skin Health

- Insect bite avoidance measures are essential.
- Drying clothes indoors and ensuring they are carefully ironed (ironing eliminates eggs laid in clothes) helps reduce risk of myiasis.
- Ectoparasites (e.g. scabies (mites) and pediculosis (lice)), cause skin manifestations such as itch and rash, and are spread through contact with infected people. Over-the-counter self-treatment should be sought.

4. Viral Infections

- See Disease Guide Section 5.
- Viral rashes (exanthems) can be a key symptom of many viral illnesses, including chikungunya, dengue, measles, rubella, parvovirus (slapped cheek syndrome) and varicella (chickenpox).
- A rash, often accompanied by arthralgia, fever, lethargy, lymphadenopathy, sore throat and diarrhoea, can also be a feature of HIV seroconversion.

Skin Wounds

- All travellers should carry a travel medical kit including an antiseptic agent, plasters and dressings.
- Wounds should be cleaned, ideally with an antiseptic solution (e.g. iodine, alcohol), dried thoroughly and covered on 3 sides with a clean dry dressing. Dressings must be replaced regularly and immediately if they become wet.
- Skin wounds can take longer to heal in hot, humid conditions; exposure to altitude also delays wound healing.
- Travellers should be informed of signs of wound infection and advised to seek early medical assistance should these occur. Medical assistance should always be sought for large and/or penetrating injuries and following any animal bite.

Drug Reactions

- Skin flushing and/or urticarial rash can be a feature of an anaphylactic drug reaction. Other symptoms include: bronchospasm, facial/laryngeal oedema, hypotension and dizziness leading to collapse, nausea and vomiting. This is a medical emergency – prompt recognition and appropriate treatment are vital.
- Cell-mediated hypersensitivity reactions to topical medicines can cause contact dermatitis.
- Urticaria and maculopapular skin rashes are characteristic of serum sickness or immune complex reactions to injection of serums (e.g. anti-tetanus serum) or administration of antibiotics and some anti-thyroid drugs.
- Certain medications which may be prescribed for use during travel, including tetracycline antibiotics (e.g. doxycycline) and acetazolamide (Diamox®) can rarely cause phototoxicity resulting in a reaction resembling sunburn on exposed areas of skin. When prescribed, sun protection measures should be emphasised. These medications should be avoided if possible in travellers with photosensitive skin.

Travellers with Pre-existing Skin Conditions: Eczema and Psoriasis

- See Resource Guide: 2.3.9b.
- Eczema can improve with exposure to mild sun and after swimming in seawater; potential irritants include sand, heat and wind.
- Exposure to sun often benefits travellers with psoriasis; exposure to cold can cause exacerbation.

2.3.9 Skin Health

- Thickened areas of skin can reduce the ability to sweat, resulting in skin irritation. Light cotton clothing helps to keep skin dry and cool.
- Adequate supplies of all skin treatments should be carried from the UK.
- Emollients should be applied to the skin 30 minutes before applying sun cream and before swimming. Emollients should be applied more regularly in cold weather to avoid drying of the skin.
- Insect repellents should not be applied to areas of broken skin.
- Chloroquine can exacerbate psoriasis and should be avoided in travellers with this condition.

2.3.10 Psychological Health

Psychological stress can result from the journey itself, exposure to different cultures, economies, languages, laws and societies, as well as isolation from friends, family and familiar surroundings. Discussing these issues during the pre-travel consultation can help prepare a traveller.

Pre-Travel Preparation

- Travellers may have psychological barriers about aspects of their pre-travel preparation. Their ideas, concerns, and expectations should be openly discussed, and risk management strategies tailored accordingly.
- Anxiety about vaccine safety, fear of needles or pain associated with injections can prevent travellers seeking appropriate travel advice and immunisations. Concern about potential side effects has also been linked to decisions to decline antimalarials.
- Travellers should be counselled against risk-taking behaviours such as excessive alcohol intake, illegal drug use, extreme sports, and sexual experimentation, in response to psychological stress.
- Refer travellers to Resource Guide: B – Resources for Travellers.
- See Resource Guide: 2.3.10.

Fear of Flying

- Fear of flying, concern about terrorism and claustrophobia can cause significant anxiety. Delays, airport security procedures and lost luggage can further exacerbate anxiety.
- Use of alcohol and/or recreational drugs as a coping mechanism should be discouraged.
- Prescription of a short-acting benzodiazepine can be considered for some travellers.
- Psychological therapy is regarded as the most effective treatment for a phobia of flying; some airlines run courses to help travellers overcome their anxieties.
- See Resource Guide: 2.3.10a.

Culture Shock

- Culture shock is a phenomenon describing the difficulties experienced when travelling or living in an unfamiliar culture and can present as anxiety, depression and/or hostility to the new culture.
- Factors such as age, expectations, preparation, previous travel experiences, pre-existing psychological health issues and willingness to integrate, all influence a traveller's ability to cope.
- Travellers from high-income countries visiting low-income countries often find the economic disparity they observe psychologically challenging. Feelings of guilt or anger may make cultural adaptation difficult.
- Gradual adjustment to a new culture is usual. Decompensation is usually a gradual mental deterioration and has been associated with stress of travel, illegal drugs and lengthy separation from home. Symptoms include reduced decision-making abilities, difficulty carrying out routine activities, short-/long-term memory loss, social withdrawal, anxiety and depression. Travellers should be informed of the potential for culture shock and decompensation and adjustment strategies discussed; travellers should know when and how to seek help.

2.3 Risk Management

2 The Pre-Travel Consultation

2.3.10 Psychological Health

- See Risk Management: 2.3.1 Medical Preparation – Accessing Medical Care During Travel.
- Children can also experience psychological issues particularly if going to live overseas. Psychological distress may be displayed as behavioural change, developmental delay (particularly language delay) and/or developmental regression such as a return to thumb sucking or bed-wetting. Early specialist advice should be sought. See Special Risk Traveller: 3.1.2 Children.
- See Resource Guide: 2.3.10b.

Other Concerns

- Unexpected events compromising personal safety such as accidents, crime, illness, or natural disasters can impact psychological health.
- Those travelling within groups may experience issues with group dynamics; equally, travelling alone can cause significant isolation and homesickness.
- Unresolved family, relationship or work issues, coupled with the pressures of travel, can precipitate psychological stress, even in previously resilient individuals.

Returning Home

- Returning home after prolonged periods travelling/living overseas can result in psychological stress whilst readjustment occurs. This 'reverse culture shock' can be as, or more, stressful than culture shock and is most often seen in long-term travellers returning from low-income countries. Support from family, friends and colleagues can assist readjustment; psychological referral may be necessary for some. See Resource Guide: 2.3.10c.

2.3 Risk Management

2 The Pre-Travel Consultation

2.4 Principles of Vaccination

Vaccination is a key intervention in travel medicine. Travellers often believe that vaccine-preventable diseases are common during travel, and vaccination is often the reason that travellers initially seek pre-travel advice.

In reality, such diseases are uncommon in travellers, usually occurring less than 1 case per 1,000 overseas visits. Nevertheless, vaccination is one of the most important public health interventions for global infectious disease control and offers protection for travellers at risk of exposure.

Importantly, if health professionals are clear about the indications and contraindications for each vaccine, and can confidently convey this to travellers, they will have time to focus on the prevention of other more common travel-associated health risks.

There are several important points to consider when administering travel vaccines:

- Is the traveller up to date with routine UK vaccines?
- Do the itinerary and planned activities increase the risk for specific diseases?
- Does the traveller have time to complete a vaccine series before departure?
- What are the considerations and contraindications to vaccines, including allergy?
- How can the risks, including potential vaccine adverse events and benefits of vaccination be conveyed to the traveller?
- What are the cost considerations for travel vaccinations?
- How is informed consent from the traveller obtained and recorded?
- Which preventive strategies need to be conveyed in addition to vaccination?
- What are Patient Group Directions (PGDs) and Patient Specific Directions (PSDs) and when should they be used?
- What are the guidelines regarding vaccine storage and transportation?
- How should a vaccine be correctly administered?
- How should vaccine administration be recorded?
- Where can up to date information/advice about vaccination be found?

Is the traveller up to date with routine UK vaccines?

A pre-travel consultation is an ideal opportunity to assess the traveller's status for vaccines which are routinely administered in the UK. Offering/updating childhood vaccines is an important preventive measure, and also reduces risk of importation of disease into the UK. Ideally, past vaccination records should be reviewed. Travellers can be exposed to diseases overseas, such as measles, for which they may not have been immunised in childhood. See Resource Guide: A32 – Key Resources, 'The Green Book'.

Immunisation schedules in other countries may differ to those in the UK. For those born/raised overseas, health professionals should check the immunisation programmes listed on the World Health Organization country profile pages. See Resource Guide: 2.4.1.

2.4 Principles of Vaccination

Do the itinerary and planned activities increase the risk for vaccine-preventable diseases?

Risk Assessment (see 2.2) and Risk Management (see 2.3) are key factors in making informed travel health decisions, including vaccination. The itinerary, season, duration and purpose of travel must be considered as well as any pre-existing health conditions. These factors are then matched against destination-specific risks of vaccine-preventable diseases; see NaTHNaC Country Information Pages[1] www.nathnac.org. The risk assessment should identify those with special risks; risk management advice should then be appropriately tailored. See Special Risks Section 3.

Does the traveller have time to complete a vaccine series before departure?

Vaccine courses often consist of several doses administered at specified intervals. These schedules have been developed following clinical trials demonstrating efficacy or immune response and have been used to support the application for vaccine licensing. Ideally, travellers should contact their GP or travel clinic 4 to 6 weeks prior to departure to discuss what may be recommended for travel. This allows time to complete a series of multiple-dose vaccines, if necessary. At times, some courses may be accelerated. See Table 3-7 in Special Risk Travel: 3.2.6 Last Minute Travel.

The issue of whether it is acceptable to administer fewer than the number of recommended doses is not resolved and needs to be individualised to the patient and vaccine. While it is theoretically possible that a single dose of a course may provide partial protection, the traveller must be informed that this cannot be guaranteed. Specialist advice can be sought for travellers who do not have time to complete a vaccine course before departure. See Resource Guide: C – Sources of Specialist Advice.

What are the considerations and contraindications to vaccines, including allergy?

First, the traveller's age and pre-existing medical conditions need to be considered. See Special Risks Section 3. Then it is necessary to understand different vaccine types and routes of administration before giving a vaccine.

Vaccines are composed of:

- Inactivated whole cells of viruses or bacteria.

- Inactivated components of viruses or bacteria.

OR

- Live bacteria or viruses that have been attenuated (weakened).

Most vaccines are given by intramuscular or subcutaneous injection. The exceptions are:

- BCG (tuberculosis vaccine) which is injected intradermally. Intradermal vaccination is a specialist technique requiring additional training.

- Cholera and live typhoid vaccines are given orally.

Details of the composition and routes of administration of individual vaccines can be found in the vaccine section of each disease chapter. See Disease Guide Section 5.

2.4 Principles of Vaccination

2 The Pre-Travel Consultation

2.4 Principles of Vaccination

An active immune response to vaccines begins within a few days of administration and peaks in approximately 10 to 14 days. For single dose vaccines, most individuals respond and will be protected 1 month after administration. Some primary vaccine courses need 2 or 3 doses to complete the series. Each subsequent dose enhances earlier doses or stimulates an immune response in those who have not responded to the initial dose. Booster doses following completion of a primary course may be needed. If recommended, they are given after a specified interval for each vaccine. Check up to date chapters of the 'Green Book' (Resource Guide: A32 – Key Resources, 'The Green Book') and vaccine Summary of Product Characteristics (SPC) (Resource Guide: A8 – Key Resources). Also see Resource Guide: Appendix 1 – Vaccine Compendium.

Individuals with normal immune systems can receive any of the vaccines with no more than the usual risks of associated adverse events. Very young children under the age of 2 years, have difficulty developing an immune response to polysaccharide only vaccines. Therefore, when polysaccharide vaccines are given to this group, they are usually conjugated (attached to a carrier protein such as diphtheria) so that a more robust immune response develops. When polysaccharide vaccines are conjugated, not only are antibodies produced, but also memory T cells. This facilitates a longer duration of protection and boosts an immune response when exposure to the antigen occurs, either via natural exposure or subsequent vaccination. See Special Risk Traveller: 3.1.2 Children.

Immunocompromised individuals usually cannot receive live, attenuated vaccines. Information on the specific vaccine, medical condition and advice from the relevant specialists must be obtained before vaccination. Although inactivated vaccines are usually safe in immunocompromised persons, their immune response may be inadequate. Therefore, a measure of immunity, such as blood antibody testing, may be necessary following vaccination, or additional protection measures may be needed. See Special Risk Traveller: 3.1.9 Immunocompromised Travellers.

Pregnant women present another special risk group. If the risk of disease exposure is considered high during travel, most vaccines can be offered. Caution should be used when considering live vaccines. See Special Risk Traveller: 3.1.12 Pre-conception, Pregnancy and Breastfeeding.

Occasionally, immunoglobulins are given in order to provide immediate protection prior to, or, more commonly, after exposure to a disease. This is called passive immunity. Immunoglobulins are not vaccines, they are proteins derived from purified human or animal plasma, and contain antibodies against a specific disease. Rabies immunoglobulin (RIG) is the most common immunoglobulin used in travellers. It may be administered after a potential rabies exposure for those who have not previously received rabies vaccine. It gives immediate protection by inactivating the virus at the site of exposure, as well as protecting against virus circulating systemically. Following the introduction of inactivated hepatitis A vaccines in the 1990s, hepatitis A immunoglobulin is no longer available for travel-associated risk.

A history of a **vaccine allergy** can be difficult to interpret. In general, a vaccine is absolutely **contraindicated** if a person has a confirmed anaphylactic reaction to a previous dose of the vaccine or a product contained in the vaccine (including residual egg protein, if the vaccine is cultured in egg, e.g. influenza and yellow fever vaccines). Egg allergy is most common. Specialist advice may be needed before administering vaccines to these persons. All centres administering vaccines must be

2.4 Principles of Vaccination

adequately prepared to deal with anaphylaxis. A hospital allergy testing clinic may offer such a service.

How can the risks, including potential vaccine adverse events, and benefits of vaccination be conveyed to the traveller?

Making a decision in travel medicine involves balancing the potential risk and consequences of acquiring a disease with the potential risk of adverse events following vaccination. For most vaccines, the adverse events are mild (local soreness at the injection site with occasional fever and aches), self-limited and of short duration over a few days. Thus, if the health professional has determined that there is a sufficient risk of disease during travel, the vaccine is generally offered.

However, other vaccines, such as yellow fever, can be associated with severe, albeit rare, adverse events. In these situations, it is necessary that the health professional has a good understanding of these events and their frequency, so that they can understand and explain them clearly. This enables the traveller to make an informed choice about whether or not to receive the vaccine. It is this interaction, the open discussion of the benefits of vaccination in preventing disease, the risk of the disease and the safety profile of the vaccine that distinguishes excellence in the pre-travel consultation. Some clinics may wish to use specific health information sheets that summarise key concepts for the traveller. See Resource Guide: B – Resources for Travellers.

What are the cost considerations for travel vaccinations?

As part of the General Medical Services contract, GP practices receive 2% of their global sum payments for providing vaccinations and immunisations (V&I), including certain travel vaccinations, to their patients. If a practice chooses not to provide this service then it loses the 2%. Practices providing V&I services must make hepatitis A, typhoid, cholera, and polio vaccinations available to patients intending to travel to certain countries and under certain circumstance as set out in 'The Red Book' (see Resource Guide: 2.4.2) without charge as part of public health measures to reduce the risk of imported disease. For all other travel vaccinations, a private charge can be levied provided the GP does not then seek remuneration from their Primary Care Trust for providing the service.

Some travellers will consider cost when making a decision about whether or not to receive a vaccine. When this is an issue, the health professional should help prioritise the vaccines by considering which the most likely risks to the traveller are during their journey.

How is informed consent from the traveller obtained and recorded?

Prior to providing any medical intervention, patient consent must be obtained. Clear guidance about consent is given by the Department of Health in 'The Green Book'; see Resource Guide: A32 – Key Resources, 'The Green Book'. Individuals must be informed about the process, benefits and risks of vaccination, and be given the opportunity to discuss any concerns. Information can be conveyed verbally, in writing via leaflets, fact sheets or posters, or through video presentations.

All adults aged 18 and older are assumed to have the capacity to consent to immunisation. Teenagers between 16 and 17 years are also presumed in law to be competent to consent. Those under 16 years, who fully understand what is involved in the proposed procedure, are referred to as 'Gillick competent' and can also give

2.4 Principles of Vaccination

consent, although ideally their parents/guardians will be involved. Consent can be given in writing, verbally or implied by co-operation. The key issue for valid consent is that the process of giving information and answering questions has been followed, and accurately recorded. A signature indicates that a discussion has occurred and a decision made. However, it is not a legal requirement. See Resource Guide: 2.4.3.

Which preventive strategies need to be conveyed in addition to vaccination?

Risk management includes behavioural measures to decrease exposure or the risk of acquiring an infectious disease; in many cases, the addition of vaccination is appropriate. This is the challenge of the risk assessment and risk management decision. Whether or not a vaccine is given, all travellers should practise additional prevention measures, as vaccines may not give full protection. Taking these precautions can help to avoid other, non-vaccine preventable diseases. See The Pre-Travel Health Consultation: 2.3 Risk Management.

What are Patient Group Directions (PGDs) and Patient Specific Directions (PSDs) and should they be used?

The legal framework for the use of PGDs in the UK has been in place since 2000, following an Amendment in the Medicines Act 1968. All travel related vaccines administered by a non-prescriber should be given either using a PGD or PSD as authorisation.

- A PGD is a written instruction for the supply or administration of a prescription only medicine by non-prescribing registered health professionals to groups of patients who have not been identified before presentation for treatment.

- A PSD is a written instruction from an independent prescriber, e.g. GP to another healthcare professional, e.g. nurse. PSDs can be written by a doctor or nurse prescriber, for named patients who have presented for a specific medicine. This can take the form of a prescription for the individual, a signed direction for a stock medicine to be administered, or a signed list of named individuals to whom the prescriber has authorised that a named prescription only medicine can be administered.

Current interpretation of the Medicines Act 1968 dictates that the use of PGDs in the public and private sectors is different.

1. For those working in the private sector in England, Wales and Northern Ireland (and registered with the Care Quality Commission (CQC); see Resource Guide: 2.4.4), a PGD can be used for all travel vaccines. For those working in the private sector in Scotland, legislative arrangements governing the regulation of private services are not yet in place. See Resource Guide: 2.4.5.

2. For those working in the public sector a PGD can be used to administer vaccines given according on the NHS to the GMS contract, e.g. hepatitis A, typhoid and polio. A PGD cannot be used for travel related vaccines that are not available on the NHS according to the GMS contract (e.g. yellow fever, tick-borne encephalitis, meningococcal meningitis ACWY, and rabies pre-exposure (for travel)). A PSD should be written for any vaccines provided for travel that are not available on the NHS.

2.4 Principles of Vaccination

What are the guidelines regarding vaccine storage and transportation?

Clinics should designate an individual, as well as a deputy, who is responsible for the safe storage of vaccines. For each vaccine, the manufacturer's recommendations for storage should be followed; most will be stored at + 2°C to + 8°C. All vaccines must be stored in a designated vaccine refrigerator. Domestic refrigerators must not be used; nothing other than vaccines or pharmaceutical products should be placed in the fridge. Blood and body fluid specimens must never be stored in vaccine fridges and blood / specimen fridges must not be used for vaccine storage.

Refrigerators should be:

- Capable of measuring minimum and maximum temperatures.
- Fitted with an external digital minimum and maximum memory display.
- Capable of automatic defrosting.
- Connected to an electricity supply that cannot be interrupted.

Temperature should be recorded at least once each working day, with temperature logs created. An independent thermometer in the body of the fridge could also be considered. See Resource Guide: A32 – Key Resources, 'The Green Book'.

How should a vaccine be correctly administered?

All healthcare professionals advising on immunisation or administering vaccines must have received specific training in immunisation, including the recognition and treatment of anaphylaxis. They should maintain and update their professional knowledge and skills and follow guidance given in the Health Protection Agency's *National minimum standards for immunisation training 2005*. See Resource Guide: 2.4.6.

Vaccine preparation, injection technique, choice of needle length and gauge (diameter), and injection site are all important considerations, since these factors can affect both the immunogenicity of the vaccine and the risk of local reactions at the injection site. See Resource Guide: A32 – Key Resources, 'The Green Book'.

How should vaccine administration be recorded?

When a traveller is a registered patient of a clinic, a record of vaccination must be made in their medical notes. If they are not a registered patient, then a separate record should be developed. Vaccination should be recorded with the following information:

- Date of vaccination.
- Vaccine name, product, batch number and expiry date.
- Dose.
- Site of administration.
- Name, signature and designation of vaccinator.

Developing a standard form, either a paper or electronic copy, will lead to consistent vaccine recording for all travellers. Electronic records allow rapid retrieval of information. This can be particularly helpful in the event of an adverse event or product recall. A record should also always be given to the traveller.

2.4 Principles of Vaccination

Where can up to date information/advice about vaccination be found?

- See Disease Guide Section 5.
- See Resource Guide: A32 – Key Resources, 'The Green Book'.
- See Resource Guide: A8 – Key Resources, Summary of Product Characteristics.
- See Resource Guide: Appendix 1 – Vaccination Compendium.
- See Resource Guide: C – Sources of Specialist Advice.

Note: Where the information in the Summary of Product Characteristics (SPC) differs from that given in the 'Green Book', the 'Green Book' should be followed.

2.4 Principles of Vaccination

2 The Pre-Travel Consultation

Section 3

Special Risks –
Traveller and Travel

Section 3 – contents

Section 3.1

Special Risk – Traveller

3.1.1 Cardiovascular and Cerebrovascular Disease

Cardiovascular disease is the leading cause of death in adult travellers. The stress and physical challenges of travel can precipitate either a new cardiovascular or cerebrovascular event or exacerbate an existing condition. Travellers should be advised to read the holiday and travel top tips from the British Heart Foundation. See Resource Guide: 3.1.1a.

- Risk management advice should follow that of the general traveller and be tailored as described below.
- Destination-specific risk management advice can be found on the NaTHNaC Country Information Pages[1] www.nathnac.org.
- See Resource Guide: 3.1.1.

Medical Preparation

- Comprehensive travel insurance is essential for all travellers. A full declaration of medical conditions should be made to the insurers. All equipment and planned activities should be covered.
- Travellers with a history of cardiovascular or cerebrovascular disease should discuss the suitability of the proposed trip with their GP and/or specialist.
- Travellers should be advised, and receive written instructions, on the use of medication for self-treatment of minor illness, and know when and how to seek medical assistance.
- Potential drug interactions should be carefully checked prior to prescribing any medication; specialist advice should be sought when necessary.

Vaccination

Influenza/pneumococcal disease

- Individuals with congenital heart disease, hypertension with cardiac complications, chronic heart failure and individuals requiring regular medication or follow up for ischaemic heart disease should be vaccinated according to the UK schedule against influenza and pneumococcal disease.

Malaria

- Some antimalarials are contraindicated for use in individuals with cardiac conditions. Potential drug interactions should be considered carefully and avoided where possible. See Table 3-1.
- For those taking anticoagulants, careful monitoring of the International Normalised Ratio (INR) is strongly recommended when commencing additional medication and until stable control is established.
- Travellers should start taking their antimalarials at least 1 week (and ideally 2 to 3 weeks in the case of mefloquine) prior to their departure to allow time for adjustments to be made if necessary. A baseline INR should be checked before, and 1 week after, starting the antimalarials. The dose of warfarin should be adjusted accordingly and the INR rechecked if there is a demonstrated effect.

3.1.1 Cardiovascular and Cerebrovascular Disease

- For trips exceeding 2 to 3 weeks, the INR should be checked at regular intervals at their destination/s. Travellers should be aware that the sensitivity of thromboplastin reagent used to measure INR may vary between laboratories and countries, and make interpretation and comparison of results difficult. Medical advice should be sought when necessary.
- Once the antimalarials have been discontinued, depending on INR results, the traveller can resume their normal maintenance dose of warfarin.
- See Resource Guide: 3.1.1b and 3.1.1c.

Journey Risks

- Recent myocardial infarction, congestive cardiac failure, history of deep vein thrombosis (DVT) and peripheral vascular disease are risk factors for flight-associated DVT. See Risk Management: 2.3.2 Journey Risks – DVT.

Fitness to Fly

- Travellers with a history of cardiovascular or cerebrovascular disease should have a medical evaluation prior to flying and be assessed as fit to fly according to the guidelines stated by their airline.
- Contraindications to flying with a history of cardiovascular or cerebrovascular disease are given by the Civil Aviation Authority (CAA), and summarised in Table 2-1 in The Pre-Travel Health Consultation Section 2. See Resource Guide: A6 – Key Resources.
- Hypertension is not a contraindication to flying providing it is controlled and stable.
- Supplemental oxygen may be required for those with heart failure or cerebrovascular disease; airlines must be consulted in advance and appropriate provision made. There may be a charge for in-flight oxygen.
- Proper functioning of implanted cardiac devices (defibrillators/pacemakers) should be ensured before departure. These devices are unlikely to be affected by airport security systems and are not a contraindication to flying when the cardiac condition is stable. Carrying a card from their physician or device manufacturer is advised in order to alert security personnel using hand-held magnetic security devices.

Environmental Risks

Altitude

- Travellers with vascular disease should discuss their plans with their GP and/or specialist, ideally prior to booking their trip. They should limit their activities during the first days and allow extra time to acclimatise.
- Those with good exercise tolerance at sea level usually tolerate travel to altitude although there is always an increased risk of exacerbation of pre-existing cardiovascular or cerebrovascular disease due to hypoxia.
- Recent myocardial infarction or poorly controlled heart failure are contraindications to ascent to high altitude. Those with cardiac failure can experience deterioration in cardiac function at altitudes above 3,000m.

3.1.1 Cardiovascular and Cerebrovascular Disease

- Following an uncomplicated myocardial infarction, a 3 month programme of cardiac rehabilitation is recommended, including control of risk factors and progressive exercise training, prior to assessment by a specialist of the suitability of travel to altitude.

- Persons with mild stable angina or those who have had successful bypass surgery can usually travel to altitude without ill effects.

- Those with existing pulmonary hypertension can experience an increase in pulmonary artery pressure, even at moderate altitudes; travel to altitude is not recommended. If unavoidable, supplemental oxygen is recommended at altitudes of 2,000m or above.

- There is little evidence of adverse events associated with well controlled hypertension at altitude. A rise of 5 to 10mmHg systolic and diastolic blood pressure is recognised to occur, however it is transient and rarely requires intervention. There is no indication for increased dosages of anti-hypertensive medication.

- Acetazolamide (Diamox®), when used for prevention of altitude illness, has a minimal antihypertensive effect. It can be taken with other diuretics used for high blood pressure.

- Health professionals should ensure that the travellers who routinely use diuretics, have normal blood electrolytes prior to starting acetazolamide (Diamox®) and advise good hydration in order to avoid complications associated with the use of 2 drugs causing diuresis. Test doses prior to travel are advised.

- The combination of acetazalomide (Diamox®) and aspirin should be avoided due to the potential for enhanced metabolic acidosis.

Food- and Water-borne Risks

- Alcohol and some foods may interact with the metabolism of warfarin and alter INR. Specialist advice should be sought before travel.

- Dehydration in travellers taking diuretics and/or ACE inhibitors can result in a rapid fall in blood pressure, and should be avoided.

- Travellers should be advised, and receive written instructions, on the use of medication for self-treatment of travellers' diarrhoea, and know when and how to seek medical assistance. See Box 2-7 in The Pre-Travel Health Consultation Section 2. Prompt treatment of gastrointestinal infections is essential.

Skin Health

- Wound management advice should be emphasised in consultation with travellers with peripheral vascular disease.

3.1 Special Risk Traveller

3 Special Risks

3.1.1 Cardiovascular and Cerebrovascular Disease

Table 3-1. Contraindications to antimalarials for those with cardiac conditions (in alphabetical order)*

Antimalarial	Potential drug interaction	Nature of interaction
Atovaquone/ Proguanil	Warfarin	Isolated reports that proguanil increases the anticoagulant effect of warfarin. It is unknown if there is an interaction with atovaquone/ proguanil.
Chloroquine	Amiodarone	Increased risk of ventricular arrhythmias.
	Digoxin	Possible increase in plasma concentration of digoxin.
Doxycycline	ACE inhibitor: Quinapril	Absorption of tetracyclines reduced by quinapril.
	Warfarin	Possible increased anticoagulant effect of warfarin.
Mefloquine	Amiodarone Quinidine	Increased risk of ventricular arrhythmias.
	Beta-blockers Calcium channel blockers Cardiac glycosides	Increased risk of bradycardias. Use with caution.
Proguanil	Warfarin	Isolated reports that proguanil increases the anticoagulant effect of warfarin.

*Drug information should be checked in the British National Formulary (BNF); see Resource Guide: A2 – Key Resources.

3.1 Special Risk Traveller

3 Special Risks

3.1.2 Children

Children and young people of all ages travel for holidays, education, 'gap years', to visit friends and relatives, and to live long term. Children and young people have specific travel health issues that differ from those of adults.

Parents/guardians should be informed of the risks and benefits of preventive and therapeutic interventions available for the child, including vaccination. Advice should be given with the best interests of the child in mind; careful discussion and due consideration of parental ideas, concerns and expectations are also required. Clear documentation of the consultation as well as the decisions taken by the parents or guardians on behalf of the child is essential, especially where interventions such as vaccinations are declined.

Teenagers between 16 and 17 years are presumed in law to be competent to consent. Those under 16 years, who fully understand what is involved in the proposed procedure, are referred to as 'Gillick competent' and can also give consent, although ideally their parents/guardians will be involved. See The Pre-Travel Consultation: 2.4 Principles of Vaccination. See Resource Guide: 2.4.3.

- Risk management advice should follow that of the general traveller and be tailored as described below.
- Destination-specific risk management advice can be found on the NaTHNaC Country Information Pages[1] www.nathnac.org.

Medical Preparation

- Comprehensive travel insurance is essential for all travellers. A full declaration of medical conditions should be made to the insurers. All equipment and planned activities should be covered.
- Preparing children for overseas travel requires knowledge of childhood disease and vaccination practices in the countries to be visited. Childhood diseases no longer seen in the UK still occur in many countries. Details of the childhood vaccination programmes in other countries are available from the World Health Organization (WHO). See Resource Guide: 3.1.2a
- A travel medical kit that is appropriate for the child should be carried. Parents/guardians should be advised, and receive written instructions, on the use of medication for self-treatment of minor illness, and know when and how to seek medical assistance.
- Parents/guardians planning to take children to live abroad should be encouraged to take a basic first aid course.
- Some medication is available in syrup form. Some tablets can be crushed and mixed with jam, fruit purée or sweetened condensed milk in order to reduce the bitter taste and therefore aid compliance. See Resource Guide: 3.1.2b British National Formulary for Children.
- All medication must be stored out of reach of children.
- Information regarding medical facilities at destination should be obtained prior to departure as suitable paediatric facilities, including intensive care, can be limited or non-existent.
- Comprehensive travel health insurance is essential for each child.

3.1 Special Risk Traveller

3 Special Risks

3.1.2 Children

Vaccination
- Check up-to-date chapters of the 'Green Book'; see Resource Guide: A32 – Key Resources.
- Check vaccine Summary of Product Characteristics; see Resource Guide: A8 – Key Resources.
- See Resource Guide: Appendix 1 – Vaccine Compendium.
- See Table 3-2. Children's Vaccines.
- Children in the UK receive vaccines as part of the national childhood immunisation programme. If travel plans mean that children intend to travel before the optimal age of administration, parents/guardians must be informed that the child may be susceptible to disease.
- Adjusting schedules by shortening intervals between doses, starting vaccines at an earlier age, or offering 1 or 2 doses of a vaccine series, should be avoided. Nevertheless, there are accepted guidelines for altering vaccination schedules if required.
- Maternal antibodies can interfere with the infant's ability to develop their own antibodies, particularly to live, viral vaccine. This is reflected in the age limitations for use of some vaccines, including MMR.
- Premature infants should be vaccinated at the same chronological age as full-term babies, except for hepatitis B vaccine that should be administered beginning at 1 month of age for babies at risk due to travel.
- Very premature infants (born ≤ 28 weeks of gestation) who are in hospital should have respiratory monitoring for 48 to 72 hrs when given their first immunisation, particularly those with a previous history of respiratory immaturity. If the child has apnoea, bradycardia or desaturations after the first immunisation, the second immunisation should also be given in hospital, with respiratory monitoring for 48 to 72 hrs.
- Polysaccharide antigens, used in Vi typhoid are T-cell independent and poorly immunogenic in children below 2 to 3 years.
- The conjugate ACWY should be used 'off label' in infants and children under five years. Children over five years and adults can receive either the conjugate vaccine or polysaccharide but should be informed that the conjugate vaccine is likely to provide longer lasting protection. See Table 3-2.
- When possible, children remaining overseas long term should have vaccine doses during visits back to the UK, or travel to a reliable medical centre where the quality and storage of vaccines, and the sterility of syringes and needles, can be assured.
- Children less than 1 year of age should be vaccinated in the anterolateral thigh and older children, in the deltoid of the upper arm. A 25mm (1 inch) needle length should be used. See Resource Guide: A34 – Key Resources.

Rabies
- Children are at a higher risk of rabies than adults as they can have increased contact with animals, be bitten on the head/neck/upper limb, and may not report bites, scratches or licks.

3.1 Special Risk Traveller

3 Special Risks

3.1.2 Children

- Animal avoidance, reporting potential exposures, immediate first aid measures, and the need to seek prompt medical attention should be emphasised in discussion with parents or guardians and children. Unfamiliar animals in the street or 'tame' animals living in the wild should not be touched. See Resource Guide: 3.1.2c.
- There is no contraindication to post-exposure vaccine.

Meningococcal meningitis

- The immune response to the quadrivalent (ACWY) polysaccharide meningococcal meningitis vaccine is poor below the age of 3 months, and gradually increases from 3 months to 5 years of age. Children, who were under 5 years when they were first vaccinated, should be given a booster dose after 2 to 3 years if they remain at continued risk. Children over 5 years should be given a booster dose every 5 years if they remain at continued risk.
- Vaccination for children travelling to Hajj or Umrah is a visa requirement from the age of 2 years.

Malaria

- Children should travel to malarial endemic areas only when the trip is essential, as infection can be life-threatening. All preventive measures should be employed to protect the child.
- Antimalarials must be adjusted for the child's weight. See Table 5-1 in Disease Guide Section 5.
- There are insufficient quantities of prophylactic medication in breast milk to protect breastfeeding infants; separate administration of weight-adjusted antimalarials is necessary.
- Specialist advice should be sought before prescribing mefloquine to children with a past medical history of Attention Deficit Hyperactivity Disorder (ADHD).
- All medication must be stored out of reach. Chloroquine can be fatal in overdose.
- Emergency Standby Treatment (EST), including atovaquone/proguanil and arthemether/lumefantrine, can be given to children according to their weight, from 5kg. Doxycycline is contraindicated for children younger than 12 years. Specialist advice should be sought before prescribing EST for children.

Journey Risks

Fitness to Fly

- A child's fitness to fly should be carefully assessed by the travel health professional and paediatrician if necessary, particularly for children with a recent or current history of illness.
- Healthy babies can usually travel by air from 48 hours after birth, but it is preferable to wait 7 days. Air travel is discouraged for premature babies until they have been medically evaluated and the alveoli have fully expanded. Emergency transport in an incubator, with medical supervision, can be arranged from 48 hours after birth if necessary.

3.1 Special Risk Traveller

3 Special Risks

3.1.2 Children

- Approximately 15% of children experience ear pain when flying, especially during descent and landing. Equalisation of middle ear pressure can be achieved by encouraging sucking, chewing or swallowing. Swallowed air can cause pain in the abdomen. Decongestants are not recommended.
- Ideally flights should be avoided during current or recent ear and respiratory infections.

Motion Sickness

- Motion sickness can occur at any age, but is more common in children between 3 and 12 years. Promethazine hydrochloride can be given to children of 2 years and older. Drowsiness and, rarely, paradoxical stimulation, are potential side effects.

Jet Lag

- Medication to aid sleep is not recommended for children.

Safety Risks

- Children are at increased risk of injuries, including traffic injuries, falls, drowning, poisoning, burns and dog bites. Careful supervision is essential.

Personal Safety

- Children should carry emergency contact details. Parents should carry photos of their children.
- A notarised permission letter should be carried if a child is not travelling with both parents / guardians.
- Risk-taking behaviour is common in teenagers. Security issues should be discussed and they should be discouraged from visiting urban areas alone, especially at night.

Transport Safety

- Road traffic accidents are the leading cause of death in children overseas. Children should be educated about road safety prior to travel. Appropriate child restraint systems should be used in vehicles. These may not be available locally and should be brought from home.

Water Safety

- Drowning is the second leading cause of death in children overseas. Parents should closely supervise children at all times when in or near water. Children should be taught to swim; buoyancy aids should be worn when necessary.

Accommodation

- Accommodation should be carefully inspected for hazards and child-proofed, where possible. Children should be supervised near balconies.
- Children should be observed whilst playing. They should not play with animals, and should be kept out of contact with dangerous objects and products such as medication, repellents and pesticides.

3.1.2 Children

Environmental Risks

Altitude

- See Special Risk Travel: 3.2.2 Altitude.
- Travel to high altitude with children should be undertaken with caution.
- The incidence of altitude illness in children is the same as for adults. However, interpreting a child's symptoms of irritability, difficult sleeping, reduced appetite and pallor, can be difficult, particularly at a very young age. Symptoms typically last for 24 to 48 hrs and then resolve with acclimatisation.
- High-altitude pulmonary oedema (HAPE) has not been reported in children <2 years of age who reside in low-altitude areas and ascend to high altitude. Due to a physiologic difference, HAPE has been observed in children <2 years who were natives of high-altitude areas, upon their return from a trip to low altitude. High-altitude cerebral oedema (HACE) has not been reported in children <9 years.
- As in adults, time at intermediate altitude, slow ascent, and adequate acclimatisation, should be encouraged to prevent altitude illness. This is preferable to prophylaxis, and reduces the need for treatment.
- Symptomatic medication for the treatment of headache can be used, e.g. paracetamol.
- Specialist advice should be sought before prescribing acetazolamide (Diamox®) for children. It is effective at a dose of 3 to 5 mg/kg/day in divided doses. It has been used in newborns to stimulate ventilation and appears to be safe in children of all ages. Cutting of tablets is required to adjust the dose for children; an approximate, rather than an exact dose, will suffice.
- Dexamethasone is effective for treatment of altitude illness in children. Supplemental oxygen over 24 hrs is also effective, although in most circumstances, descent should be undertaken.
- Children with pre-existing medical conditions can develop complications when travelling to altitude. Specialist advice about the suitability of travelling to altitude should be sought.
- Children are at higher risk of cold exposure and sunburn at high altitudes. Suitable cold weather clothing should be worn and high factor UVA/B sunscreen (SPF 30 or higher) used.

Food- and Water-borne Risks

- Gastrointestinal illness can be more severe in children resulting in dehydration.
- Breastfeeding reduces the risk of diarrhoea in infants and should be continued if an infant has diarrhoea. Formula milk should be ready-made and pre-packed or bottle feeds prepared using boiled and cooled, or bottled mineral water. If bottled water is used, sodium levels must be below 200mg per litre.
- Dairy products must be pasteurised.
- Good hygiene should be practised, including sterilisation of bottles and dummies, cleaning toys and using bottled or purified water for brushing teeth.

3.1.2 Children

- Children should be taught to wash their hands with soap and warm water, particularly after using the toilet.
- Accidental ingestion of contaminated recreational water is a common route of entry for gastrointestinal pathogens.
- Dehydration can be life-threatening in children, particularly under 2 years. Parents/ guardians should be able to recognise early signs of dehydration, know how/when to use oral rehydration solutions and know when to seek medical help. See Box 3-1.
- Urgent medical attention is necessary for children with bloody diarrhoea, dehydration, drowsiness, fever, persistent vomiting or severe abdominal pain.
- Following medical advice, azithromycin (10mg/kg/day for 3 days) can be used to treat travellers' diarrhoea in children over 6 months. Parents/ guardians will need to cut a tablet if the intended dose is less than 250mg, to an approximate amount. Splitting the dose into twice a day schedule can reduce side effects.
- The use of fluoroquinolones (i.e. ciprofloxacin) in children should be restricted to situations where there is not an alternative for treatment of bacterial diarrhoea.
- Antimotility medications are usually not necessary, and are not recommended for children under 4 years. They should be used only after consultation with a health professional.

Vector-borne Risks

- A plan for bite avoidance for children should be followed.
- Up to 50% DEET can be used safely on children from 2 months of age. Eyes, mouth and hands should be avoided and repellent stored out of reach.
- Depending on their age, children may not report bites from insects or animals. Parents must remain vigilant and regularly inspect a child's skin for bite marks or insects such as ticks.

Sexual Health and Blood-borne Viral Risks (BBVs)

- Risk-taking behaviour, including sexual behaviour and the use of drugs and alcohol overseas, and their potential physical and psychological impact, should be discussed with teenagers.

Skin Health

- Children should be discouraged from walking barefoot in order to reduce risk of injury and infection.
- Children are at increased risk of short- and long-term damage to the skin from solar radiation. Good sun protection is essential.
- Head lice (pediculosis) and/or scabies can be transmitted through close human-to-human contact whilst at play. Treatment should be administered with topical permethrin.

3.1.2 Children

Psychological Health

- Pre-existing psychological condition can be exacerbated by travel; autistic children may find the stresses of travel difficult.
- Children can experience adaptation difficulties, particularly those living overseas long term. Information to prepare children, and parents, for travelling is available. See Resource Guide: 2.3.10b.
- Parents should identify and report problems early; signs of anxiety in a child include psychological symptoms, such as sleeplessness and mood swings, and physical symptoms including headaches, stomach aches and enuresis (bed-wetting), particularly if these are prolonged and without apparent cause.

Box 3-1. Signs of dehydration in children

- Increased thirst.
- Decreased urination.
- Feeling weak or light-headed.

Signs of dehydration in young children might also include:

- Dry mouth or tongue.
- Few or no tears when crying.
- No wet nappies for 3 hours or more.
- Drowsiness.
- Sunken eyes, cheeks, abdomen, or fontanelle (soft spot on top of the head).
- Irritability or listlessness (low energy).
- Decreased skin turgor (skin that flattens very slowly when pinched and released).

Contact a doctor if diarrhoea is accompanied by:

- Signs of dehydration.
- Blood in the stools or black stools.
- Frequent vomiting so fluids cannot be replaced by mouth.
- Severe abdominal pain.
- High fever.
- Drowsiness.
- No improvement after 24 hours or persistent diarrhoea lasting longer than 3 to 4 days.

Severe dehydration may require treatment with intravenous fluids. Do not depend on taking liquids by mouth to treat severe dehydration.

3.1 Special Risk Traveller

3 Special Risks

3.1.2 Children

Table 3-2. Children's vaccines*

Routine Vaccines	Routine age to start vaccine course	Early administration	Primary course	Additional doses	Comments
Diphtheria	2 months	Seek specialist advice.	3 doses (DTaP/IPV/Hib) at 4 week intervals.	4th dose (DTaP/IPV or dTaP/IPV) pre-school. 5th dose (Td/IPV) school leaving.	Wherever possible primary immunisation schedule should be completed before travel.
Haemo-philus influenzae type b (Hib)	2 months	Not Applicable (N/A)	3 doses (DTaP/IPV/Hib) at 4 week intervals.	4th dose (Hib/MenC) at 12 months of age.	Wherever possible primary immunisation schedule should be completed before travel.
Human Papilloma virus (HPV)	12 to 13 years for girls	N/A	3 doses, month 0, 1 to 2, and 6.	N/A	
Measles, mumps, rubella (MMR)	13 months	6 months	2 doses, 2nd dose pre-school.	N/A	If first dose is given under 12 months of age, 2 further doses should be given as in routine schedule.
Meningitis C	3 months	2 months	Age under 1 year: 2 doses at 4 week interval. Aged 1 year and older: single dose.	Children who received 2 doses should have a 3rd dose (Hib/MenC) at 12 months of age.	
Pertussis	2 months	Seek specialist advice.	3 doses (DTaP/IPV/Hib) at 4 week intervals.	4th dose (DTaP/IPV or dTaP/IPV) pre-school.	Wherever possible primary immunisation schedule should be completed before travel.

(continued)

3.1.2 Children

Table 3-2. Children's vaccines* (continued)

Routine Vaccines	Routine age to start vaccine course	Early administration	Primary course	Additional doses	Comments
Pneumo-coccal Conjugate Vaccine (PCV)	2 months	N/A	Age under 1 year: 2 doses at 2 month interval. Age 1 year to under 2 years: single dose (PCV).	Children who received 2 doses should have a 3rd dose at 13 months of age.	
Poliomyelitis	2 months	Seek specialist advice.	3 doses (DTaP/IPV/Hib) at 4 week intervals.	4th dose (DTaP/IPV or dTaP/IPV) pre-school 5th dose (Td/IPV) school leaving.	Wherever possible primary immunisation schedule should be completed before travel.
Tetanus	2 months	Seek specialist advice.	3 doses (DTaP/IPV/Hib) at 4 week intervals.	4th dose (DTaP/IPV or dTaP/IPV) pre-school 5th dose (Td/IPV) school leaving.	Wherever possible primary immunisation schedule should be completed before travel.

Vaccines for at risk groups	Age to start vaccine course	Early administration	Primary course	Additional doses	Comments
Pneumo-coccal Polysac charide Vaccine (PPV)	2 years	N/A	1 dose after the 2nd birthday and at least 2 months after the final dose of PCV.	N/A	Check up to date chapters of the 'Green Book'. See Resource Guide: Appendix 1 – Vaccine Compendium.

3.1 Special Risk Traveller

3 Special Risks

(continued)

3.1.2 Children

Table 3-2. Children's vaccines* (continued)

Vaccines for at risk groups	Age to start vaccine course	Early administration	Primary course	Additional doses	Comments
Seasonal influenza	6 months	N/A	Age 6 months to 12 years: 2 doses at 4 to 6 week interval if receiving vaccine for first time. Age 13 years and older: single dose.	Annually	Check up to date chapters of the 'Green Book'. See Resource Guide: Appendix 1 – Vaccine Compendium.
Tuberculosis	Birth	N/A	Single dose.	N/A	Check up to date chapters of the 'Green Book'. See Resource Guide: Appendix 1 – Vaccine Compendium. 0.05 ml for children under 12 months of age. Mantoux test required prior to administration in children aged 6 years or older.
Varicella	12 months	N/A	Age 12 months to under 13 years: single dose. Age 13 years and older: 2 doses at 4 to 8 week interval.	N/A	

(continued)

3.1 Special Risk Traveller

3 Special Risks

3.1.2 Children

Table 3-2. Children's vaccines* (continued)

Travel Vaccines	Age to start vaccine course	Early administration	Primary course	Additional doses	Comments
Cholera	2 years	N/A	Age 2 to 6 years: 3 doses at 1 to 6 week intervals. Age 6 years and older: 2 doses at 1 to 6 week interval.	For adults and children over 6 years, a single booster dose is recommended for those at continued risk. For children aged 2 to 6 years, a single booster after 6 months is recommended for those at continued risk.	No clinical data are available on the protective efficacy of booster doses. If more than 2 years have elapsed since the last vaccination, the primary course should be repeated.
Hepatitis A	12 months	N/A	2 doses at 0 and 6 to 12 months.	20 years if at continued risk.	Hepatitis A can be a less serious illness in children under 6 years, however, vaccine is recommended in children at risk from 12 months as they can still transmit the illness to others.
Hepatitis B	Birth	N/A	3 doses at 0, 1 and 6 months; or 3 doses at monthly intervals with 4th dose at 12 months.	Single reinforcing dose at 5 years.	

(continued)

3.1 Special Risk Traveller

3 Special Risks

3.1.2 Children

Table 3-2. Children's vaccines* (continued)

Travel Vaccines	Age to start vaccine course	Early administration	Primary course	Additional doses	Comments
Hepatitis A and B	12 months	N/A	Ambirix®: 2 doses at 0 and 6 to 12 months. Twinrix®: 3 doses at 0, 1 and 6 months.	Hepatitis A: single dose at 20 years. Hepatitis B: single dose at 5 years.	
Japanese encephalitis – 'Green Cross®' vaccine	12 months to 17 years	N/A	3 doses at days 0, 7 and 28.	Single booster at 12 months, and then every 3 years if at continued risk.	Half dose (0.5ml recommended for children aged 1 to 3 years).
Japanese encephalitis – Ixiaro® vaccine	18 years and over	N/A	2 doses at days 0 and 28.	Revaccination every 3 years.	Ixiaro® is currently unlicensed in children under 18 years of age however in older teenagers prescribers may wish to consider 'off label' use.
Meningococcal ACWY – conjugate vaccine	2 months and older	N/A	Infants under 1 year: 2 doses 1 month apart. If first dose is given at 2 months then this dose and the second dose should replace the MenC vaccine. If given after a dose of MenC vaccine leave one month before administering MenACWY. Individuals from one year and older: single dose.	Boosting for children and adults not yet known. Check up to date chapters of the 'Green Book'. See Resource Guide: Appendix 1 – Vaccine Compendium.	Recommended for infants and children up to 10 years 'off label'.

(continued)

3.1.2 Children

Table 3-2. Children's vaccines* (continued)

Travel Vaccines	Age to start vaccine course	Early administration	Primary course	Additional doses	Comments
Meningo-coccal ACWY – poly-saccharide vaccine	5 years	N/A	Age 5 years and older: single dose (note: conjugate is likely to provide longer lasting protection).	Every 5 years to those at continued risk.	Meningococcal ACWY conjugate vaccine is preferred for children under 5 years.
Rabies	Birth	N/A	3 doses on days 0, 7 and 21 or 28.	Every 3 to 5 years if at continued risk.	No minimum age: pre-exposure vaccine recommend-ed according to risk of exposure taking into consideration the age at which child begins to walk or crawl.
Tick-borne encephalitis	12 months	N/A	3 doses: day 0, 1 to 3 months later, and 5 to 12 months after 2nd dose.	3 years if at continued risk.	TicoVac® 0.25ml Junior for children age 1 year to under 16 years.
Tuberculosis (BCG)	Birth	N/A	Single dose.	N/A	Recommend-ed for children under 16 years who are travelling for more than 3 months in a country with an annual incidence of TB of ≥ 40 cases/ 100,000. Mantoux test required prior to administration in children aged 6 years or older.

3.1 Special Risk Traveller

3 Special Risks

3.1.2 Children

Table 3-2. Children's vaccines* (continued)

Travel Vaccines	Age to start vaccine course	Early administration	Primary course	Additional doses	Comments
Typhoid (Vi antigen)	2 years	Can be considered from 12 months of age if risk of typhoid high.	Single dose.	3 years if at continued risk.	Vaccine may be less effective in children under 2 years of age.
Yellow fever	9 months	6 months, only if risk considered exceptional. Specialist advice must be sought. See Resource Guide: C – Sources of Specialist Advice.	Single dose.	10 years if at continued risk.	Vaccine should never be administered to children under 6 months of age due to risk of encephalitis.

*Vaccine information should be checked in the 'Green Book' and Summary of Product Characteristics; see Resource Guide: Appendix 1 – Vaccine Compendium.

3.1.3 Diabetes

- Risk management advice should follow that of the general traveller and be tailored as described below.
- Destination-specific risk management advice can be found on the NaTHNaC Country Information Pages[1] www.nathnac.org.
- Travellers with diabetes should read information from Diabetes UK. See Resource Guide: 3.1.3.

Medical Preparation

- Comprehensive travel insurance is essential for all travellers. A full declaration of medical conditions should be made to the insurers. All equipment and planned activities should be covered. Diabetes UK offers specialist policies.
- Methods of glucose monitoring, insulin storage and delivery, and a safe means of disposal of sharps, should be discussed.
- Additional quantities of insulin should be supplied.
- Obtaining insulin overseas is discouraged; names, brands, strengths and qualities of insulin vary considerably worldwide. An altered dose may be required; a conversion table is available from Diabetes UK. See Resource Guide: 3.1.3a.
- Illness in a traveller with diabetes can lead to hypo- or hyper-glycaemia. Travellers should be advised, and receive written instructions, on the use of medication for self-treatment of minor illness, and know when and how to seek medical assistance.
- Travellers with diabetes should wear identification, such as that available from the MedicAlert® Foundation, and inform travel companions and tour company of their condition. See Resource Guide: A23 – Key Resources.

Journey Risks

- Insulin should be carried in hand luggage; insulin stored in the aircraft hold may freeze and efficacy would then be affected.
- Diabetic travellers may need to adjust insulin doses when crossing 6 or more time zones. Methods by which this can be achieved should be discussed with a diabetic specialist. See Resource Guide: 3.1.3b.
- Changes in activity levels, stress and jet lag can affect blood glucose levels.
- Frequent monitoring of blood glucose levels is essential.
- 'Diabetic' meals on aircraft may contain very little carbohydrate and are considered unnecessary. It is advisable to carry snacks in case of delays and on long-haul flights.

Environmental Risks

- Insulin should be stored away from direct sunlight and protected from temperature variations by use of a thermal insulated bag/flask.

3.1 Special Risk Traveller

3 Special Risks

3.1.3 Diabetes

- Insulin remains stable for up to 1 month when stored at room temperature (20°C). It will deteriorate more rapidly in warmer climates.
- Insulin is absorbed more quickly in warm temperatures and more slowly in cold temperatures. Blood glucose levels should be monitored frequently and insulin dosing adjusted as needed.
- The performance of glucometers, test strips and insulin delivery devices can be affected by temperature, humidity and altitude. Urine dipstick tests may provide a more reliable method of basic monitoring whilst at altitude. Specialist advice should be received prior to travel to these environments.
- Dehydration can affect blood glucose levels and adequate hydration should be maintained.

Food- and Water-borne Risks

- Availability of suitable food and drink (including unsweetened drinks) varies.
- Simple carbohydrate sources, such as glucose tablets and sweets, should be carried to relieve symptoms of hypoglycaemia; complex carbohydrate sources, such as cereal bars and biscuits, should also be carried to supplement/replace a meal.
- Gastrointestinal illness can quickly affect blood glucose. Blood glucose levels should be monitored frequently during illness. Travellers should know how to adjust their medication, use self-treatment measures, and know when and how to seek medical assistance. See Box 2-7 in The Pre-Travel Health Consultation Section 2.

Sexual Health and Blood-borne Viral Risks (BBVs)

- Female travellers with diabetes are at increased risk of urinary tract infections.
- The risk of vaginal candidiasis is also increased, particularly if taking an antibiotic such as doxycycline for malaria prevention.
- Travellers should be advised of self-treatment options and know when to seek medical advice.

Skin Health

- Travellers with diabetes, especially those with peripheral neuropathy, should avoid injury to their feet. They should wear comfortable, well-fitting shoes and avoid walking barefoot.
- Feet should be checked regularly for injury, and kept clean, dry and moisturised.
- Toenails should be well-trimmed and broken skin covered with a sterile dressing.
- Insect bite avoidance is important; bites should be kept clean and not scratched. An antihistamine can reduce itching.

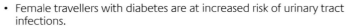

3.1.4 Disability

- Risk management advice should follow that of the general traveller and be tailored as described below.
- Destination-specific risk management advice can be found on the NaTHNaC Country Information Pages[1] www.nathnac.org.
- The ABTA checklist, Accessible Travel, for disabled and less mobile persons should be used by travellers with disabilities and by travel agents, to ensure an appropriate booking is made. Disabled Persons Transport Advisory Committee offers practical guidance in 'Door to Door: a travel guide for disabled people'. See Resource Guide: 3.1.4a.

Medical Preparation
- Comprehensive travel insurance is essential for all travellers. A full declaration of medical conditions and disabilities should be made to the insurers. All equipment and planned activities should be covered.

Journey Risks
- See Resource Guide: 3.1.4b.
- Transport modes should be chosen carefully to best suit the traveller's needs.
- Arrangements should be made for the transportation of equipment on flights, i.e. wheelchair, portable batteries, respirators or oxygen. Restrictions with regard to security and luggage allowance still apply.
- Assistance may be required to access information, transit transport hubs, and use toilet facilities. Transport staff (including aircrew) will not be able to assist with toileting, lifting or other personal needs; an escort may need to be arranged in advance.
- Enquiries should be made regarding the availability of lifts or moving walkways if stairs are difficult to manage.
- Repair kits or spare equipment should be carried for emergency use.
- The Pet Travel Scheme provides information for those travelling with assistance dogs. See Resource Guide: 3.1.4c.

Deep Vein Thrombosis (DVT)
- Travellers with restricted mobility can be at increased risk of a DVT. Preventive measures should be emphasised and arrangements made to enable mobilisation. See Risk Management: 2.3.2 Journey Risks – DVT.

Safety Risks
- See Resource Guide: 3.1.4d.
- See Resource Guide: 3.1.4e.

Transport Safety
- For those intending to hire a car, the Blue Badge Scheme now operates throughout the EU; adapted cars may be available for hire and should be pre-booked. See Resource Guide: 3.1.4f.

3.1 Special Risk Traveller

3 Special Risks

---
1 Alternatively see Travax http://www.travax.nhs.uk/ or Fit for Travel http://www.fitfortravel.nhs.uk/

3.1.4 Disability

Accommodation

- Accommodation should be chosen carefully to best suit the traveller's needs.
- The travel company and accommodation owner should be advised of the nature of the disability in order to provide assistance in the event of emergency evacuation.
- An effective communication method should be agreed for those with sight or hearing impairment.

Environmental Risks

- Travellers with peripheral neuropathy can be at increased risk of heat or cold injuries. Appropriate clothing should be worn.

Food- and Water-borne Risks

- Gastrointestinal illness can be difficult for those with restricted mobility. Travellers should be advised, and receive written instructions, on the use of medication for self-treatment of travellers' diarrhoea, and know when and how to seek medical assistance. See Box 2-7 in The Pre-Travel Health Consultation Section 2.

Skin Health

- Travellers who use mobility aids such as walking sticks, crutches or wheelchairs can be at increased risk of skin breakdown in high or low temperatures.
- Protective measures such as relieving pressure regularly and keeping skin clean and dry should be discussed.

Psychological Health

- The acceptance of disability in other cultures can differ; disability often draws attention from inquisitive but well meaning observers. Travellers should firmly but politely decline assistance if it is not required.

3.1.5 Gastrointestinal Conditions

Travellers with pre-existing gastrointestinal (GI) conditions such as gastro-oesophageal reflux, inflammatory bowel disease (Crohn's disease and ulcerative colitis), irritable bowel syndrome, malabsorption (coeliac disease and intestinal resection), colostomy or ileostomy, and malignant disease, may be at increased risk of ill health during travel. These travellers should be encouraged to read information from their respective patient associations. See Resource Guide: 3.1.5.

- Risk management advice should follow that of the general traveller and be tailored as described below.
- Destination-specific risk management advice can be found on the NaTHNaC Country Information Pages[1] www.nathnac.org.
- See Resource Guide: 3.1.5.

Medical Preparation

- Comprehensive travel insurance is essential for all travellers. A full declaration of medical conditions should be made to the insurers. All equipment and planned activities should be covered.
- Travellers with a history of a GI condition should discuss the suitability of the proposed trip with their GP and/or specialist.
- Travellers with a stoma should ensure they carry adequate supplies of appliances. Stoma bags may need to be changed more frequently in hot climates and replacement equipment may not be readily available.

Journey Risks

- Specific dietary requirements should be arranged in advance with airlines and at accommodation. Specific dietary products and supplements may not be available overseas.
- Intestinal gas increases by around 30% at a cabin altitude of 2,438m (8,000ft).

Fitness to Fly

- Flying should be avoided for 24 hours following surgical procedures during which gas has been introduced into the colon or abdominal cavity.
- Flying should be avoided for 10 days after abdominal surgery due to the risk of tearing of sutures, bleeding or perforation following intestinal gas expansion during flight.
- During the days before travel travellers with a stoma should avoid food and drink that increase intestinal gas. Over inflation of stoma bags can be reduced by adding an extra flatus filter to the bag.

Environmental Risks

- Travellers with a stoma can be at increased risk of fluid and electrolyte loss as a result of increased stoma output, particularly in hot, humid climates or during physical activity. Adequate hydration is essential.

3.1 Special Risk Traveller

3 Special Risks

---

1   Alternatively see Travax http://www.travax.nhs.uk/ or Fit for Travel http://www.fitfortravel.nhs.uk/

3.1.5 Gastrointestinal Conditions

Food- and Water-borne Risks

- GI infection acquired during travel can result in exacerbation of a pre-existing GI condition. Travellers should adhere to strict food, water and personal hygiene precautions.
- Food and drink known to aggravate any pre-existing GI condition should be avoided.
- Travellers taking proton pump inhibitors (PPIs) may be at increased risk of gastrointestinal infection as a result of decreased gastric acid production.
- Travellers should be advised, and receive written instructions, on the use of preventive treatment and/or carriage of self-treatment for travellers' diarrhoea. See Box 2-7 in The Pre-Travel Health Consultation Section 2.
- These travellers should be encouraged to seek early medical care in event of illness or exacerbation.

Vector-borne Risks

- Absorption of antimalarials can be compromised in those who have undergone resection of the gastrointestinal tract. Specialist advice should be sought.

Air-borne Risks

- Coeliac disease can be associated with hyposplenia and/or diabetes and as a result these travellers can be at increased risk of bacterial sepsis. If there is evidence for hyposplenism, pneumococcal and influenza vaccination should be given according to the UK schedule.

3.1.6 Haematological Conditions

Coagulation Disorders (including anticoagulant medication)
Bleeding disorders (e.g. haemorrhagic telangiectasia, and autoimmune disorders such as idiopathic thrombocytopaenia (ITP)) and clotting disorders (e.g. haemophilia, Christmas disease, and Von Willebrand disease) result in reduced or ineffective coagulation either as a result of abnormalities in the blood vessels or platelet function. Such conditions are inherited or acquired. Acquired disorders can occur as a result of an underlying disease, e.g. autoimmune disorders, malignancy, splenic dysfunction and infection, or as a result of extrinsic factors such as blood transfusion and medications, e.g. warfarin and heparin.

Haemoglobinopathies – Sickle Cell Syndromes and Thalassaemias
Sickle cell syndromes (sickle cell trait (heterozygous carriers), sickle cell disease (homozygous carriers)) and the thalassaemias (thalassaemia trait, β thalassaemia, α thalassaemias) are inherited disorders of haemoglobin that are found most frequently in people of African, Asian, Middle Eastern and Mediterranean descent. The most frequent complications of sickle cell disease are painful crises, acute anaemia and infections; these can be life-threatening. Long-term sequelae of sickle cell disease and thalassaemias include chronic haemolytic anaemia, liver, renal and splenic dysfunction.

Hyposplenia and Asplenia
The most common cause of asplenia is surgical splenectomy either as a result of trauma, or as treatment for an underlying condition. Hyposplenia or asplenia can result in poor antibody responses and poor killing of bacteria as well as the inability to eliminate red blood cells that have been infected by blood parasites.

Porphyria
Porphyria is a rare deficiency in the enzymes required to convert porphyrins into haem for use in red blood cells; a toxic build up of porphyrins results. There are at least 7 types of porphyria classified as acute or non-acute. Acute porphyria presents with abdominal pain, nausea and vomiting. In severe cases tachycardia, hypertension, anxiety, confusion and seizures occur. Drugs that interfere with porphyrin metabolism, alcohol, reduced calorie intake and infection can trigger an acute attack. Non-acute cutaneous porphyria primarily results in fragile and sensitive skin that can blister or ulcerate after trauma or exposure to sunlight. Management involves avoiding trigger factors and for some, venesection (removal of units of blood) can help.

- Risk management advice should follow that of the general traveller and be tailored as described below.
- Destination-specific risk management advice can be found on the NaTHNaC Country Information Pages[1] www.nathnac.org.
- See Resource Guide: 3.1.6.

Medical Preparation
General Recommendations
- Comprehensive travel insurance is essential for all travellers. A full declaration of medical conditions should be made to the insurers. All equipment and planned activities should be covered.
- Travellers with haematological conditions must discuss their travel plans with their specialist in advance of their trip.

1 Alternatively see Travax http://www.travax.nhs.uk/ or Fit for Travel http://www.fitfortravel.nhs.uk/

3.1 Special Risk Traveller

3 Special Risks

3.1.6 Haematological Conditions

- Travellers should be advised, and receive written instructions, on the use of medication for self-treatment of minor illness, and know when and how to seek medical assistance.
- Potential drug interactions should be carefully checked prior to prescribing any medication; specialist advice should be sought if necessary.
- These travellers should be encouraged to read information from their respective patient associations. See Resource Guide: 3.1.6 Patient Associations.

- Travellers with haematological conditions may be more likely to need invasive medical interventions overseas and therefore, be at increased risk of exposure to blood-borne viruses; Hepatitis B vaccination should be considered.

Coagulation Disorders

- It is particularly important that this group know their blood group and carry documentation in case of the need for an emergency blood transfusion.
- For those taking anticoagulants, careful monitoring of INR is strongly recommended when commencing additional medication and until stable control is established. See Malaria below. See Resource Guide: 3.1.6a.
- For trips exceeding 2 to 3 weeks, the INR should be checked at regular intervals at their destination/s. Travellers should be aware that the sensitivity of thromboplastin reagent used to measure INR may vary between laboratories and countries, and make interpretation and comparison of results difficult. Medical advice should be sought when necessary.
- Illness can lead to bleeding or abnormal clotting. Careful monitoring of INR during illness is recommended.
- There is a risk of haematoma after vaccination of some individuals with coagulation disorders. Vaccines normally given by the intramuscular route should be given by deep subcutaneous injection to reduce the risk of bleeding. A fine needle (<23 gauge) should be used and firm pressure applied to the site, without rubbing, and for >2 minutes.
- Travellers should start taking their antimalarials at least 1 week (and ideally 2 to 3 weeks in the case of mefloquine) prior to their departure to allow time for adjustments. A baseline INR should be checked before, and 1 week after, starting the antimalarials. The dose of warfarin should be adjusted accordingly and the INR rechecked if there is a demonstrated effect.
- Once the antimalarials have been discontinued, the traveller can resume their normal maintenance dose of warfarin.

Haemoglobinopathies – Sickle Cell Syndromes and Thalassemias

- Sickle cell **trait** provides some protection against severe *Plasmodium falciparum* malaria by preventing the full development of the parasite in the human host. Nevertheless, antimalarials should still be taken.

3.1.6 Haematological Conditions

- Individuals with sickle cell **disease** are at high risk of severe malaria. Travel to malaria endemic areas should be discouraged. Where travel plans cannot be changed, the importance of personal protection measures against mosquito bites and compliance with prescribed antimalarials should be stressed.
- Renal and liver function should be taken into consideration before prescribing antimalarials.

Hyposplenia/Asplenia

- Lifelong antibiotic cover (usually oral penicillin or erythromycin) is recommended by the British Committee for Standards in Haematology. See Resource Guide: 3.1.6b.
- Hyposplenic or asplenic individuals should be considered to be at lifelong risk of invasive infection from *Haemophilus Influenzae* type b, *Streptococcus pneumonia* and *Neisseria meningitides*.

- In addition to routine vaccinations, hyposplenic/asplenic travellers should receive Hib, pneumococcal and Meningococcal C conjugate vaccines. Meningococcal ACWY should be given if travelling to endemic areas, even if conjugate C vaccine has been given previously. Influenza vaccines are also recommended.
- Hyposplenic/asplenic individuals can be at risk of severe parasitaemia following infection with malaria parasites *(Plasmodium spp.)* or from tick-borne babesiosis *(Babesia)*. See Disease Guide Section 5.
- Travel to malaria- and babesia-endemic areas should be considered carefully. Where travel plans cannot be changed, the importance of personal protection measures against mosquito and tick bites, and compliance with prescribed antimalarials, should be emphasised.
- Parasitaemia is likely to develop more rapidly and be more severe. Travellers should be advised to seek medical advice urgently should symptoms suggestive of malaria or babesia occur.
- Malaria parasites may not be adequately cleared from the bloodstream during treatment. A follow up malaria parasite screen should be considered for returned travellers with a history of malaria, or treatment for possible malaria, during travel.

Porphyria

- Diagnosis and management of acute attacks of porphyria can be difficult. The British Porphyria Association can provide details of specialists overseas. See Resource Guide: 3.1.6c.
- Venesection may not be available or advisable. Specialist advice should be sought.
- A copy of the safe drugs list available from Welsh Medicines Information Centre should also be taken. See Resource Guide: 3.1.6d.
- Persons travelling to malaria risk areas should have been free from acute porphyria attacks for at least 2 years.
- Specialist advice regarding antimalarials should be sought for all travellers with porphyria. Those with acute intermittent porphyria or cutaneous porphyria may be advised not to take doxycycline.

3.1.6 Haematological Conditions

Journey Risks

General Recommendations
- Travellers with haematological conditions should discuss their travel plans with a specialist.
- Severe anaemia should be corrected before embarking on air travel. If haemoglobin is < 7.5 g/dl a medical assessment of fitness to fly should be made.

Coagulation Disorders
- Thrombocythaemia (increased platelet count) increases the risk of DVT. Additional precautions such as the use of compression stockings and anticoagulant medication (e.g. subcutaneous heparin) should be discussed with a specialist.
- See Risk Management: 2.3.2 Journey Risks – DVT.

Haemoglobinopathies – Sickle Cell Syndromes
- Supplemental oxygen is recommended for all those with sickle cell disease. Arrangements must be made with the airline before travel.
- Individuals with sickle cell disease can develop problems related to hypoxia during unpressurised aircraft flights; these should be avoided. There is no risk in those with sickle cell trait.
- Airline travel should be deferred for 10 days following a sickle crisis.

Porphyria
- Some porphyria suffers have reported acute attacks following long haul flights. Travellers should have been free of attacks for some time before contemplating long haul travel. Specialist advice should be sought.
- Disturbance of sleep due to travel and jet lag can increase the risk of an acute attack.

Environmental Risks

Coagulation Disorders
- Travellers with some clotting disorders can be at increased risk of clotting when dehydrated. Specialist advice should be sought.

Porphyria
- Dehydration can trigger an acute attack of porphyria; care should be taken to maintain adequate hydration.

Porphyria
- Adequate sun protection is essential for those with cutaneous porphyria. A sun block of at least SPF 60 is recommended. A specialist reflective sunscreen available on prescription may be obtained as needed. Protective clothing is essential.

Haemoglobinopathies – Sickle Cell Syndromes and Thalassaemias
- There is an increased risk of sickle crisis at altitudes over 2,000m for those with sickle cell disease. Travel to altitude should be discouraged.

3.1 Special Risk Traveller

3 Special Risks

3.1.6 Haematological Conditions

- Travellers with sickle cell trait and other haemoglobinopathies, such as beta-thalassaemia, can also be at risk of a sickle crisis at low-oxygen tensions found at high altitudes.
- Specialist advice should be sought.

Food- and Water-borne Risks

- Principles of food, water and personal hygiene should be emphasised. Travellers should be advised, and receive written instructions, on the use of medication for self-treatment of travellers' diarrhoea, and know when and how to seek medical assistance. See Box 2-7 in The Pre-Travel Health Consultation Section 2. Prompt treatment of gastrointestinal infections is essential.

Coagulation Disorders

- Changes in diet, alcohol consumption, and gastrointestinal illness can affect anticoagulant control. Travellers who take anticoagulants should know how to monitor their control and alter their medication.
- Ciprofloxacin and doxycycline can enhance the anticoagulant effect and should be avoided.

Hyposplenia/Asplenia

- *Listeria, Escherichia coli, Klebsiella, Salmonella enteritidis* and *Streptococcus suis* have each been associated with overwhelming infection in hyposplenic or asplenic individuals. Strict food, water and personal hygiene should be practised. Antibiotics should be carried.
- See Resource Guide: 3.1.6e and 3.1.6f.

Porphyria

- Acute attacks of porphyria can be triggered by consumption of alcohol, dehydration and long periods without eating.
- Nausea and vomiting can occur due to porphyria. Antiemetics should be carried.

Vector-borne Risks

Hyposplenia/Asplenia

- The bacteria *Capnocytophaga canimorsus* may cause serious infection following a dog or cat bite. Prophylactic antibiotics following bites should be given to hyposplenic and asplenic individuals.

Skin Health

Coagulation Disorders; Hyposplenia/Asplenia; Porphyria

- Avoidance of injury, and careful skin hygiene to prevent skin breakdown and bruising/bleeding, are essential for travellers with certain haematological conditions, such as those with coagulation disorders.
- Travellers with hyposplenia/asplenia and cutaneous porphyria are at increased risk of skin infection caused by *Staphylococcus aureus* and *Streptococcus pyogenes* (Group A streptococci). Prophylactic antibiotics should be considered following skin wounds.

3.1 Special Risk Traveller

3 Special Risks

3.1.6 Haematological Conditions

Psychological Health
Porphyria

- Emotional and physical stress can trigger an acute porphyria attack. Stress avoidance and management strategies should be discussed.

3.1 Special Risk Traveller

3 Special Risks

3.1.7 Hepatic Conditions (Liver)

Worldwide, chronic infections with hepatitis B or C are the most common causes of chronic liver disease. Chronic and excessive alcohol ingestion is also a major cause of liver disease. Less common causes are primary biliary cirrhosis, primary sclerosing cholangitis and autoimmune chronic active hepatitis. Destruction of the liver parenchyma in chronic liver disease can lead to liver cirrhosis and portal hypertension. Clinical signs, related to liver failure and portal hypertension, include ascites, oesophageal varices and encephalopathy. Cirrhosis is irreversible. Liver disease is not a contraindication to travel, however, a careful risk benefit analysis must be undertaken.

- Risk management advice should follow that of the general traveller and be tailored as described below.
- Destination-specific risk management advice can be found on the NaTHNaC Country Information Pages[1] www.nathnac.org.
- See Resource Guide: 3.1.7.

Medical Preparation

- Comprehensive travel insurance is essential for all travellers. A full declaration of medical conditions should be made to the insurers. All equipment and planned activities should be covered.
- Travellers with liver disease should discuss the suitability of the proposed trip with their GP and/or specialist, ideally prior to booking.
- The liver is important in the metabolism of many drugs, and liver disease is known to be a common cause of altered drug pharmacokinetics. Drug metabolism and drug interactions must be considered carefully prior to the prescription of medication taken during travel. There is a risk of drug accumulation in severe liver impairment. See Resource Guide: 3.1.7a.
- It is important to establish the degree of liver impairment in order to make an accurate risk assessment.
- No obvious marker exists for characterising hepatic function with respect to prediction of drug elimination capacity, in contrast to renal impairment. Therefore, dose recommendations may not be as accurate for hepatic impairment as they are for renal impairment.
- The Child-Pugh classification can be used to grade hepatic dysfunction as either 'Mild', 'Moderate' or 'Severe'. See Resource Guide: 3.1.7a.
- Those with advanced liver failure, ascites, active oesophageal varices or a newly diagnosed hepatic condition are usually advised not to travel. Those with mild or chronic conditions should be advised that access to appropriate medical care may be limited. Even in areas with adequate medical provision, specialist liver facilities may not be readily available.
- These travellers should be encouraged to read information from their respective patient associations. See Resource Guide: 3.1.7.

3.1 Special Risk Traveller

3 Special Risks

3.1.7 Hepatic Conditions (Liver)

 Vaccination

Hepatitis A

- Individuals with chronic liver disease are at substantially higher risk of developing serious complications if they become infected with hepatitis A.
- Immunisation against hepatitis A is recommended for all patients with severe liver disease, regardless of cause. Vaccination should also be offered to those with milder liver disease.

Hepatitis B

- Individuals with chronic liver disease are at substantially higher risk of developing serious complications if they become infected with hepatitis B.
- Immunisation against hepatitis B is recommended for all travellers with severe liver disease, regardless of cause. Vaccination should also be offered to those with milder liver disease.
- Hepatitis B vaccination may be less immunogenic in those with alcoholic liver disease, particularly if cirrhosis is present. Post-vaccination serology should be obtained.
- A higher dose (40 micrograms) may be recommended for immunocompromised travellers, and for transplantation candidates. Specialist advice should be sought.

Influenza / pneumococcal disease

- The incidence of pneumococcal disease is higher in those with chronic liver disease.
- The mortality rate from pneumococcal disease is higher in alcoholics with chronic liver disease.
- Influenza in individuals with chronic liver disease can cause complications.
- Travellers with chronic liver disease should be up to date with pneumococcal and annual influenza vaccines.

Malaria

The choice of antimalarials for a person with a liver condition is guided by their Child-Pugh score and should usually be made by a specialist. Most antimalarials are metabolised or excreted by the liver. There is a risk of drug accumulation in severe liver impairment. See Table 3-3.

- Individuals with severe liver disease should be strongly advised not to travel.
- The importance of compliance with malaria prevention advice and early medical intervention for symptoms must be emphasised. Malaria in a traveller with a liver condition can result in severe complications.

3.1.7 Hepatic Conditions (Liver)

Table 3-3. Antimalarial use in those with liver impairment*

Degree of liver impairment	Child-Pugh score	Antimalarial (in alphabetical order)
Mild	5 to 6	Atovaquone/proguanil: can be used. Chloroquine: can be used. Doxycycline: caution. Mefloquine: can be used. Proguanil: can be used.
Moderate	7 to 9	Atovaquone/proguanil: can be used. Chloroquine: avoid. Doxycycline: avoid. Mefloquine: can be used. Proguanil: can be used.
Severe	10 to 15	Atovaquone/proguanil: seek specialist advice. Chloroquine: avoid. Doxycycline: avoid. Mefloquine: avoid. Proguanil: avoid.

*Drug information should be checked in the British National Formulary (BNF); see Resource Guide: A2 – Key Resources.

Food- and Water-borne Risks

- Individuals with certain liver conditions may be advised to consume a restricted diet, such as high protein, low salt, reduced fat or sugar free. These diets may be difficult to follow during travel.
- Travellers should be advised, and receive written instructions, on the use of medication for self-treatment of travellers' diarrhoea, and know when and how to seek medical assistance. See Box 2-7 in The Pre-Travel Health Consultation Section 2. Prompt treatment of gastrointestinal infections is essential.
- Drug metabolism and drug interactions must be considered carefully prior to the prescription of medication for self-treatment of gastrointestinal illness. Tetracyclines should be avoided or used with caution; ciprofloxacin has rarely been associated with drug-induced acute liver injury. Specialist advice should be sought if necessary.

3.1 Special Risk Traveller

3 Special Risks

3.1.7 Hepatic Conditions (Liver)

Skin Health
- Itching (pruritus) is a common feature of liver conditions and may be accentuated in hot/humid climates.

Psychological Health
- Liver disease can cause confusion and disorientation (hepatic encephalopathy), leading to altered consciousness. This condition can have rapid onset. Specialist medical care may not be available in some areas.
- Travellers with alcohol-related liver conditions may find it difficult to abstain from alcohol during travel. Appropriate pre-travel counselling should be received.

3.1 Special Risk Traveller

3 Special Risks

3.1.8 HIV/AIDS

HIV infection causes progressive loss of immunity. The advent of highly active antiretroviral therapy (HAART) has transformed HIV infection from a frequently fatal disease into a chronic manageable condition. Many HIV-positive individuals are travelling extensively; careful planning and preparation is required. These travellers should be encouraged to read information provided by HIV patient associations. See Resource Guide: 3.1.8.

- Risk management advice should follow that of the general traveller and be tailored as described below.
- Destination-specific risk management advice can be found on the NaTHNaC Country Information Pages[1] www.nathnac.org.

Medical Preparation

- Comprehensive travel insurance is essential for all travellers. A full declaration of medical conditions should be made to the insurers. All equipment and planned activities should be covered.
- Standard travel insurance policies may decline those with HIV/AIDS; the Terrence Higgins Trust provides information on available specialist policies. See Resource Guide: 3.1.8 Patient Associations.
- Travel plans should be discussed with an HIV specialist and travel health professional.
- HIV-positive travellers must check each country's entry restrictions (including the transport of medicines) and allow time to complete regulatory procedures. See Resource Guide: 3.1.8a.
- It is recommended that a current CD4 cell count (within 4 weeks), along with clinical judgement, should be used to determine immune competence of HIV-positive persons. As a guide, asymptomatic HIV-positive persons with CD4 counts:
  - >400 cells/µl are considered immune competent.
  - 200 to 400 cells/µl are considered to have limited immune deficiency.
  - <200 cells/µl are considered to have severe immune deficiency.
- Individuals with HIV/AIDS with a CD4 count <200/µl are susceptible to certain infections that can have severe consequences.
- A newly commenced antiretroviral regimen should be known to be effective and well tolerated for at least 3 months prior to travel.
- Adequate supplies of all medications must be carried; antiretroviral drugs may not be available in some areas.
- Interruptions to HAART should be avoided.
- Travellers with HIV/AIDS should know how to seek medical advice for HIV/AIDS-related illness occurring during or after travel. Expertise in HIV/AIDS medicine may not be available during travel. Advice from specialists in the UK may be received if arranged in advance.
- See Resource Guide: 3.1.8b.

3.1 Special Risk Traveller

3 Special Risks

---

1 Alternatively see Travax http://www.travax.nhs.uk/ or Fit for Travel http://www.fitfortravel.nhs.uk/

3.1.8 HIV/AIDS

Vaccination

- The British HIV Association (BHIVA) guidelines for immunization of HIV-infected adults should be checked. See Resource Guide: 3.1.8c.
- The advice of an HIV specialist and travel health specialist should be sought. See Resource Guide: C – Sources of Specialist Advice.
- The CD4 cell count, along with clinical judgement, should be used to determine suitability for vaccination.
- Response to vaccination, particularly in those with immune deficiency, is often sub-optimal; post-vaccination serology can help guide booster frequency. Consideration can be given to delaying immunisation until the CD4 cell count has recovered with HAART; this may not always be possible or practical.
- Vaccination can result in a transient rise in HIV viral load and a drop in CD4 count. These changes are not considered clinically significant and should not prevent appropriate vaccination.
- Inactivated and polysaccharide vaccines are safe to administer. Travellers should be up to date with the UK schedule.
- Live vaccines should be avoided where possible. When travel is unavoidable, some live vaccines can be administered to asymptomatic HIV-positive travellers with a stable (at least 3 months) CD4 count >200 cells/μl.
- Box 3-2 and Box 3-3 summarise vaccination guidelines from the British HIV Association (BHIVA).
- Individuals with symptomatic HIV/AIDS infection and/or CD4 counts < 200 cells/μl must NOT be given live vaccines.

Hepatitis A

- Vaccination is indicated for those at increased risk of exposure, including travellers to endemic areas and all MSM (men who have sex with men) travellers.
- Routine pre-vaccination serology is not usually recommended, but can be considered in travellers with possible prior exposure.

Hepatitis B

- All HIV/AIDS individuals seronegative for HBV should be vaccinated as soon as possible following HIV/AIDS diagnosis.
- Immune response should be tested 4 to 8 weeks after the last vaccine dose.
- Persistent non-responders should be vaccinated with higher doses of antigen, as recommended for those with other forms of immune suppression.

Influenza

- Increased rates of complications from influenza, including mortality can occur in individuals with HIV/AIDS.
- Annual vaccination is recommended.
- Live, intranasal influenza vaccine is contraindicated.

3.1 Special Risk Traveller

3 Special Risks

3.1.8 HIV/AIDS

Measles

- Measles can be more severe in persons with HIV/AIDS.
- MMR vaccine can be given to asymptomatic individuals with a CD4 count >200 cells/µl who have not previously been immunised against measles, following discussion with an HIV/AIDS specialist. BHIVA recommend serological confirmation of protection status prior to travel to endemic areas unless 2 vaccinations are clearly documented. Individuals born before 1970 are likely to have had natural measles infection and are not susceptible.
- If seroconversion following measles vaccine is in doubt, following a potential exposure to measles, immunoglobulin treatment can be considered with specialist advice.

Pneumococcal

- HIV/AIDS increases susceptibility to pneumococcal disease. If not already received, pneumococcal vaccine should be considered.

Polio

- HIV/AIDS travellers should be up to date according to the UK schedule. Consideration should also be given to immunising close contacts.
- Live oral polio vaccine (no longer available in the UK) is contraindicated in individuals with HIV/AIDS (regardless of CD4 cell count) and their close contacts.

Rabies

- Reduced response to pre-exposure vaccination can occur in persons with lower CD4 counts; documentation of seroconversion 4 weeks after vaccination is recommended.
- Urgent post-exposure treatment in the event of rabies exposure should be emphasised, regardless of prior vaccination status.

Tuberculosis (TB)

- HIV/AIDS increases risk of acquisition of TB. Globally TB is the most prevalent HIV-associated opportunistic infection.
- HIV-infected individuals should avoid high-risk environments such as hospitals, prisons or homeless shelters whenever possible.
- BCG vaccination is contraindicated.
- Isoniazid prophylaxis can be considered for those intending to stay in a country endemic for TB (annual incidence of ≥40 cases/100,000) for ≥3 months or longer, and for those with close contact with local populations, e.g. HIV-positive healthcare workers. Specialist advice must be sought.
- Specialist referral should be made for post-exposure screening.

Typhoid

- Typhoid immunisation with an inactivated vaccine should be considered for travellers with HIV/AIDS going to endemic areas.
- Live oral typhoid vaccine is contraindicated in HIV/AIDS infection, regardless of CD4 count.

3.1 Special Risk Traveller

3 Special Risks

3.1.8 HIV/AIDS

Yellow fever (YF)

- Travel to areas at risk of YF should be considered carefully.
- YF vaccine can be considered, following specialist advice, in those who are clinically well, with a suppressed viral load, and a CD4 count >200 cells/µl, if risk of YF exposure is high and unavoidable.
- If there is a substantial risk of exposure, patients unable to receive YF vaccine should not travel.
- A medical exemption letter can be issued when travel must be undertaken to a risk area with a requirement for vaccination and YF vaccine cannot be administered.
- Reduced response to vaccine can occur; documentation of seroconversion 2 to 3 weeks after vaccination is recommended if possible.

Malaria

- Travellers with HIV/AIDS can have a higher risk of severe malaria. Travel to malaria endemic areas should be considered carefully.
- Strict bite avoidance measures and compliance with antimalarials are necessary.
- Potential drug interactions should be determined when prescribing antimalarials. Antimalarials are effective in this group. Drug information should be checked in the British National Formulary (BNF); See Resource Guide: A2 – Key Resources. See Resource Guide: 3.1.8d and 3.1.8e.
- Use of artemether/lumefantrine as emergency standby treatment for malaria is contraindicated in those taking protease inhibitors. Atovaquone/proguanil is recommended.
- Treatment of malaria in travellers with HIV/AIDS should be carried out in a specialist setting.

Food- and Water-borne Risks

- Travellers with HIV/AIDS are at increased risk of some gastrointestinal infections, such as salmonellosis, *Campylobacter, Isospora belli, Cryptosporidium sp.*, and their complications such as chronic infection, bacteraemia and relapse.
- Principles of food, water and personal hygiene should be emphasised. Travellers should be advised, and receive written instructions, on the use of medication for self-treatment of travellers' diarrhoea, and know when and how to seek medical assistance. See Box 2-7 in The Pre-Travel Health Consultation Section 2. Prompt treatment of gastrointestinal infections is essential.
- Travellers with advanced HIV/AIDS can consider prophylactic use of ciprofloxacin or azithromycin following specialist discussion.
- Potential drug interactions should be carefully checked prior to prescribing any medication; specialist advice should be sought if necessary.

3.1.8 HIV/AIDS

Vector-borne Risks

Leishmaniasis

- HIV/AIDS travellers with a CD4 count < 200 cells/μl have a higher risk of visceral leishmaniasis.
- Strict use of personal protective measures must be emphasised to avoid sand fly bites.

Air-borne Risks

Fungal infections

- Respiratory fungal infections (mycoses) are uncommon in travellers, but can cause life-threatening opportunistic infections in HIV/AIDS travellers, often several years after exposure.
- Exposure to dust, soil, bird and bat droppings should be avoided. Care should be taken during eco/adventure/cave trips or during excavation/ construction/agricultural work. Masks and gloves can help reduce exposure to fungal spores when working with plants, hay or peat moss.

Sexual Health and Blood-borne Viral Risks (BBVs)

- Travellers with HIV should practise safe sex and avoid body piercing/ tattoos. This will reduce risk of onward HIV transmission, and protects against acquisition of a different HIV strain and other sexually transmitted infections (STIs) and BBVs. See Disease Guide Section 5.
- HIV-positive injecting-drug users (IDU) must be made aware of potential legal and health consequences, especially overseas. Drug paraphernalia should not be shared.

Psychological Health

- HIV/AIDS carries a stigma in some areas of the world and discrimination may be encountered.

3.1 Special Risk Traveller

3 Special Risks

3.1.8 HIV/AIDS

Box 3-2. Inactivated vaccines in HIV-infected persons

The following vaccines can be given safely to HIV-infected persons:

Cholera WC/rBS (oral)
Hepatitis A
Hepatitis B
Haemophilus influenzae type b (Hib)
Influenza (inactivated)
Japanese encephalitis
Meningitis C
Meningitis ACWY (polysaccharide and conjugate)
Pneumococcal
Rabies
Polio (inactivated)
Tick-borne encephalitis
Typhoid (Vi polysaccharide)

Box 3-3. Live vaccines in HIV-infected persons

The following vaccines can be considered for HIV-infected persons if CD4 count is above 200 cells/μl (Specialist advice should be sought):

Measles, Mumps Rubella (MMR)
Varicella
Yellow fever

The following vaccines are **contraindicated** in all HIV-infected adults regardless of CD4 cell count:

- BCG (tuberculosis)
- Influenza intranasal – also contraindicated in close contacts; this vaccine is not currently used in the UK.
- Polio oral – also contraindicated in close contacts; this vaccine is not currently used in the UK.
- Smallpox – in the absence of recognised risk of infection, risks of vaccine outweigh disease risk.
- Typhoid – Ty21a oral

3.1.9 Immunocompromised Travellers (excluding HIV/AIDS)

Immunocompromising disease and/or drugs can result in an inability to contain some infectious diseases. Steroids can suppress clinical signs of infection and allow diseases to reach an advanced stage before being recognised. Response to vaccines may be reduced and live vaccines are often contraindicated due to a risk of vaccine-associated generalised infection. Specialist advice should be sought, as necessary.

Conditions that may be cause immunocompromise are:

- HIV/AIDS. See Special Risk Traveller: 3.1.8.
- Hyposplenia/asplenia. See Special Risk Traveller 3.1.6.
- Primary immunodeficiency syndromes, e.g. severe combined immunodeficiency syndrome, Wiskott-Aldrich syndrome.
- Active generalised malignancy.
- Chronic inflammatory and autoimmune disease, e.g.:
  - Myasthenia gravis. See Special Risk Traveller: 3.1.10.
  - Rheumatic disease, e.g. Rheumatoid arthritis, myasthenia gravis. See Special Risk Traveller: 3.1.16.
  - Gastrointestinal disease, e.g. ulcerative colitis.
  - Systemic lupus erythematosus (SLE).
- Transplant recipients (solid organ and bone marrow transplant) who are taking immunosuppressive medication to prevent rejection of the transplant.
- Generalised radiotherapy.
- Immunosuppressive drugs, e.g.:
  - Antiproliferative drugs (e.g. azathioprine).
  - Anti-TNF drugs (e.g. etanercept, infliximab).
  - Corticosteroids and other inhibitors (e.g. prednisolone, ciclosporin).
  - Cytotoxic drugs including antimetabolites (e.g. methotrexate) and other antineoplastic drugs (e.g. taxanes).
  - Chemotherapy.
  - Disease-modifying antirheumatic drugs (e.g. azathioprine, cyclophosphamide, leflunomide).

Immunosuppression does **NOT** usually result from:

- 'Low dose' steroid therapy of a dose and/or duration of less than that stated in appendix below (including alternate day use of short acting steroids).
- Non-systemic corticosteroids, such as aerosol, topical or intra-articular (joint) use.
- Hormone antagonists such as those used in the treatment of breast and prostate cancers.
- Replacement therapy with physiological doses of corticosteroids (e.g. hydrocortisone and fludrocortisone) in those with conditions such as adrenal deficiency states.

When in doubt, specialist advice should be sought.

There is the potential for an altered immune response in pregnant women, children and older travellers. See Special Risk Traveller: 3.1.12, 3.1.2, and 3.1.11.

3.1 Special Risk Traveller

3 Special Risks

3.1.9 Immunocompromised Travellers (excluding HIV/AIDS)

- Risk management advice should follow that of the general traveller and be tailored as described below.
- The suitability of an itinerary should be discussed in detail, ideally before a trip is booked.
- Destination-specific risk management advice can be found on the NaTHNaC Country Information Pages[1] www.nathnac.org.
- See Resource Guide: 3.1.9.

Medical Preparation

- Comprehensive travel insurance is essential for all travellers. A full declaration of medical conditions should be made to the insurers. All equipment and planned activities should be covered.

Vaccination

- Immunocompromised individuals should be vaccinated according to the UK schedule. Check up to date chapters of the 'Green Book'; See Resource Guide: A32 – Key Resources.
- See British Society for Rheumatology, Vaccinations in the immunocompromised person; Resource Guide: 3.1.9b.
- See The Royal College of Paediatrics and Child Health, Immunisation of the immunocompromised child Resource Guide: 3.1.9c.
- Inactivated vaccines can be administered safely to immunocompromised individuals, although they may have a lower immune response than immunocompetent individuals.
- Inactivated vaccines should be administered at least 2 weeks before commencement of immunosuppressive treatments when possible. If not, vaccination can be carried out at any time and re-immunisation considered after treatment is finished and immune recovery has occurred. Where available, serologic (blood) testing can act as a guide.
- Live vaccines can cause severe or fatal infections in immunocompromised individuals due to unchecked replication of the vaccine strain. For this reason, live vaccines should not be given to individuals with impaired immune response, whether caused by disease or treatment, without specialist advice.
- Live vaccines should be administered at least 2 weeks and preferably 4 weeks or more, in advance of commencement of immunosuppressive treatments. Specialist advice should be sought.
- Live vaccines should be postponed for the duration of treatment, **and** until:
  - at least 3 months after stopping high dose systemic steroids; See Box 3-4.
  - at least 6 months after stopping other immunosuppressive drugs or generalised radiotherapy.
  - at least 12 months after discontinuing immunosuppressive drugs following bone marrow transplantation, or longer where the patient has developed graft-versus-host disease.

1   Alternatively see Travax http://www.travax.nhs.uk/ or Fit for Travel http://www.fitfortravel.nhs.uk/

3.1.9 Immunocompromised Travellers (excluding HIV/AIDS)

- Individuals who have received a bone marrow or a stem cell transplant may need to repeat primary immunisations. See Recommendations of the Infectious Disease Working Party of the European Bone Marrow Transplant (EBMT) Resource Guide: 3.1.9d.
- Prophylaxis with antibiotics or antiviral drugs may be indicated for certain immuncompromised travellers; specialist advice should be sought.

Hepatitis B

- Hepatitis B vaccination should be given. Titres should be checked 4 to 6 weeks after completion of the primary course.

Influenza/pneumococcal disease/*Haemophilus influenzae* b/meningococcus

- Influenza and pneumococcal vaccines are recommended for all those with immunosuppression. In addition, *Haemophilus influenzae* type b and meningococcal C vaccines are recommended for those with hyposplenia/asplenia.

Rabies

- Monitoring of the immune response after rabies vaccination, via a serologic (blood) test for rabies virus neutralising antibodies, is recommended. Failure to seroconvert with an acceptable antibody response should be discussed with a specialist.
- Post-exposure prophylaxis should be administered using all 5 doses of vaccine, with awareness that the immune response may still be inadequate. Rabies virus neutralising antibody testing is recommended after completing the series.

Yellow fever (YF)

- If YF risk is unavoidable, specialist advice should be sought. Those unable to receive YF vaccine should be advised against travel to areas at risk of YF. A letter of medical exemption can be given when travel is unavoidable.

Malaria

- Drug interactions should be considered carefully; specialist advice should be sought.

Journey Risks

Deep Vein Thrombosis (DVT)

- Malignancy is a risk factor for DVT. Travellers should discuss their travel plans with their oncologist. Anticoagulant therapy (e.g. heparin) or other preventive measures may be advised.
- See Risk Management: 2.3.2 Journey Risks – DVT.

Environmental Risks

Sun

- Chemotherapy and radiotherapy can make skin more sensitive to the sun. Measures to protect the skin from sun should be taken.

3.1.9 Immunocompromised Travellers (excluding HIV/AIDS)

Food- and Water-borne Risks

- Immunocompromised travellers can be at increased risk of complications from diarrhoeal illnesses. Self-treatment medications should be carried and used where appropriate.
- Prophylactic antibiotics can be considered in special circumstances; this should be discussed with a specialist.

Air-borne Risks

- Unless already immune, patients should avoid close contact with people who have measles, chickenpox or shingles. Use of human normal immunoglobulin (HNIG) should be considered after exposure to measles. Use of varicella zoster immunoglobulin (VZIG) should be considered after exposure to chickenpox in persons who are not immune. Prompt administration of prophylactic acyclovir may also be beneficial.
- Immunocompromised individuals are at increased of tuberculosis and invasive fungal disease. Where possible, travellers should avoid exposure and seek medical advice post-exposure; BCG is contraindicated.

Box 3-4. Corticosteroids and immunosuppression

Travellers who take corticosteroids (and other immunosuppressive drugs) should carry with them a steroid treatment card and declare their medical history and medication when receiving treatment for any illness or injury overseas. See British National Formulary (BNF) Steroid Treatment Card; Resource Guide: 3.1.9a.

Dose of steroid (including oral, parenteral, rectal administrations), which should be considered immunosuppressive:

Prednisolone (or equivalent ≡):

Adult: Equal to, or more than, 40mg/day for 1 week or more.

Child: Equal to, or more than, 2mg/kg/day for 1 week or more,
OR
Equal to, or more than, 1mg/kg/day for 1 month or more

Equivalent Steroid Doses
Prednisolone 5mg
≡ Betamethasone 750micrograms
≡ Cortisone acetate 25mg
≡ Deflazacort 6mg
≡ Dexamethasone 750 micrograms
≡ Hydrocortisone 20mg
≡ Methylprednisolone 4mg
≡ Triamcinolone 4mg

Occasionally those on lower dose steroids may also be immunosuppressed. Specialist advice should be sought.

3.1.10 Neurological Conditions

Individuals with a neurological condition include those with epilepsy, multiple sclerosis (MS) and other demyelinating diseases, Guillain-Barré syndrome (GBS), myasthenia gravis (MG), and cerebrovascular accidents (CVAs)/strokes and other brain injuries. These travellers should be encouraged to read information from their respective patient associations. See Resource Guide: 3.1.10 Patient Associations.

- Risk management advice should follow that of the general traveller and be tailored as described below.
- Destination-specific risk management advice can be found on the NaTHNaC Country Information Pages[1] www.nathnac.org.
- See Resource Guide: 3.1.10.

Medical Preparation
- Comprehensive travel insurance is essential for all travellers. A full declaration of medical conditions should be made to the insurers. All equipment and planned activities should be covered.
- Travellers should discuss their travel plans with their specialist.

Vaccination
- Individuals with neurological disease may be immunocompromised due to either their medical condition or drug treatment.
- Live vaccines are contraindicated in immunocompromised travellers. If there is doubt about the level of immune compromise, specialist advice should be sought.
- Inactivated vaccines are safe to administer in immunocompromised travellers, however the immune response can be sub-optimal. Serological testing can be considered post-vaccination.
- Yellow fever vaccination is contraindicated in those who are immunocompromised and those with abnormalities of the thymus gland such as travellers with MG.
- There is no association between hepatitis B, tetanus, varicella and BCG vaccines and relapses of MS. There is insufficient evidence of an association for all other vaccines. See Resource Guide: 3.1.10a.
- The risk of relapse following vaccination in those travellers with a history of GBS is rare. See Resource Guide: 3.1.10b.
- Febrile convulsion is not a contraindication to vaccination, providing the febrile episode has resolved.
- Epilepsy or a family history of epilepsy is not a contraindication to vaccination.

Journey Risks
- Mobility can be compromised in those with a neurological condition. Necessary arrangements at each stage of the journey will need to be considered in advance.
- Seizures can be triggered by stress or environmental changes. Travel companions should be familiar with managing a seizure.
- Medication should be taken as usual. Careful adjustment of the timing of a

1   Alternatively see Travax http://www.travax.nhs.uk/ or Fit for Travel http://www.fitfortravel.nhs.uk/

3.1 Special Risk Traveller

3 Special Risks

3.1.10 Neurological Conditions

dose may be necessary when crossing time zones. Specialist advice should be sought.

Fitness to Fly

- Health professionals should follow guidelines issued by the UK Civil Aviation Authority (CAA). See Resource Guide: A6 – Key Resources.
- The interval between a neurological event and fitness to fly depends on the stability of the condition, as assessed by a specialist, and the requirements of individual airlines and insurers. Specialist advice should be sought.

Safety Risks

Water Safety

- Those with an unstable neurological condition should avoid activities, including swimming and diving, where loss of consciousness or awareness would result in danger to themselves or others. See Special Risk Travel: 3.2.4 Diving.
- Supervision is recommended for those with a stable neurological condition in order to maximise personal safety.

Environmental Risks

Altitude

- High-altitude travel is not contraindicated for those with a stable neurological condition. However, exacerbation of the condition, including seizures, may be life-threatening in a remote setting.

Heat / Cold

- Extremes of heat and cold should be avoided as they can trigger seizures in some individuals. Suitable clothing should be worn and adequate hydration maintained.

Food- and Water-borne Risks

- Fluoroquinolones can rarely induce convulsions and should be used with caution in travellers with neurological conditions. An alternative drug for the self-treatment of gastrointestinal illness should be prescribed.

Vector-borne Risks

- Prophylactic and treatment doses of certain antimalarials can exacerbate the symptoms of MG. Chloroquine and doxycycline should be avoided or used with caution. Specialist advice should be sought. See Resource Guide: 3.1.10c.
- Doxycycline has been rarely associated with raised intracranial pressure. An alternative antimalarial should be prescribed in those with pre-existing raised intracranial pressure.
- Mefloquine rarely can cause sensory and motor neuropathies. It is prudent to use an alternative antimalarial in those with pre-existing neuropathies.
- Mefloquine and chloroquine are contraindicated in travellers with epilepsy, as they can lower the seizure threshold. The drug interaction between doxycycline and carbamazepine is not thought to be clinically significant and there is no need to adjust the dose of doxycycline.

3.1.11 Older Travellers

For older travellers, factors such as pre-existing medical conditions and reduced ability to adapt to different environments can increase risk of morbidity and mortality. Careful pre-trip preparation can reduce risks. These travellers should be encouraged to read information from patient associations. See Resource Guide: 3.1.11 Patient Associations.

- Risk assessment and management: guidance for older individuals travelling overseas should follow that of the general traveller, with awareness that travel associated health risks can increase with age.
- Suitability of itineraries should be discussed in detail, ideally before a trip is booked.
- Destination-specific risk management advice can be found on the NaTHNaC Country Information Pages[1] www.nathnac.org.
- See Resource Guide: 3.1.11.

Medical Preparation

- Comprehensive travel insurance is essential for all travellers. A full declaration of medical conditions should be made to the insurers. All equipment and planned activities should be covered.
- Insurance options for older travellers, particularly those with pre-existing medical conditions, may be limited and are likely to be expensive. Age Concern/Help the Aged offer advice on tailored policies. See Resource Guide: 3.1.11 Patient Associations.
- A pre-travel medical assessment of cardiopulmonary function for those with pre-existing cardiac or respiratory disease is strongly recommended. See Special Risk Traveller: 3.1.15 Respiratory Conditions.
- Pre-existing medical conditions and drugs taken to treat these conditions should be considered prior to prescribing medications for travel.
- Supplies of routine medications should be carried in hand luggage. A medical letter detailing conditions and treatment should be carried.
- Older travellers may require medical/dental care overseas.
- The availability and quality of healthcare and possible need for emergency medical evacuation should be discussed.

Vaccination

- Older age is an important consideration in the assessment of yellow fever vaccination. See Yellow Fever below.
- Older travellers may not have received routinely administered vaccines according to the UK schedule. The travel health consultation is an opportunity to administer/update them.
- Standard adult doses and schedules should be used.
- See Resource Guide: 3.1.11a.

Influenza/pneumococcal disease

- Travellers of 65 years and over should be up to date with routine immunisations according to the UK schedule for their age, including influenza and pneumococcal vaccination.

3.1 Special Risk Traveller

3 Special Risks

3.1.11 Older Travellers

Yellow fever (YF)

- Travellers aged 60 years and over, who receive YF vaccine for the first time, are at increased risk of rare, serious vaccine-associated adverse events (neurologic and viscerotropic). In this age group, the rate is approximately 25 cases per million doses, compared to an estimated 3 to 5 cases per million doses in younger individuals.
- YF vaccine should be given to older travellers following a comprehensive assessment that balances the risk of acquiring YF disease at the destination with the risk of a serious adverse event following vaccination. Specialist advice should be sought as necessary.
- All cases of serious neurologic and viscerotropic adverse events have occurred in primary vaccinees; revaccination does not have this association.
- See Resource Guide: 3.1.11b, 3.1.11c and 3.1.11d.

Malaria

- A change in the dose of antimalarials is not required on the basis of age in adults. Specialist advice should be sought when necessary.
- Consider potential drug interactions when prescribing antimalarials.
- Older travellers are more likely to develop severe malaria and/or complications, especially if they have pre-existing medical conditions.

 ## Journey Risks

- The method of transport and travel itinerary should be discussed in detail.
- This is especially important if mobility is compromised or an increased level of activity is required.

Fitness to Fly

- Older travellers can have contraindications to air travel. Health professionals should follow guidelines issued by the UK Civil Aviation Authority (CAA). See Resource Guide: A6 – Key Resources.
- Travellers must inform their airline, at least 48 hours in advance, of specific requirements such as the need for assistance or oxygen.
- Forgetting to take medication on long journeys can lead to complications. For example, failure to take diuretics can lead to pulmonary and peripheral oedema.
- The physical demands of travel should not be underestimated.
- Long distances are often necessary to transit transport hubs, whilst carrying heavy luggage, negotiating crowds and coping with delays/cancellations. Older travellers should be reminded of these stresses and be encouraged to allow additional time for their journeys.

Deep Vein Thrombosis (DVT)

- Older travellers may have pre-existing risk factors for deep vein thrombosis (DVT). Periods of immobility during the journey can further exacerbate these conditions and increase the risk of DVT and pulmonary embolus.
- Advice on DVT prevention/risk reduction should be provided. See Risk Management: 2.3.2 Journey Risks – DVT.

3.1.11 Older Travellers

Motion Sickness

- Older travellers may experience less air and sea sickness due to reduced vestibular function with age.

Safety Risks

Transport Safety

- Older drivers can have more difficulty adapting to a different driving culture overseas. Additional time should be allowed to become familiar with the vehicle and roads.
- Age restrictions on vehicle hire may apply in some countries.

Accommodation

- Older travellers with mobility issues may have special accommodation requirements such as ease of access, additional handrails and need for emergency assistance. These should be confirmed at the time of booking.

Personal Safety

- Reduced mobility, balance and reaction times, combined with unfamiliar surroundings can increase risk of injury.
- Heightened awareness, additional care and protective footwear should be encouraged.
- Vigilance, especially at night, should be emphasised, in order to avoid being a victim of crime.
- Local advice in regard to safety and areas to avoid should be followed.

Environmental Risks

Altitude

- Older people with normal cardiopulmonary function are less susceptible to acute mountain sickness (AMS) than younger persons. See Resource Guide: 3.1.11e.
- Some older travellers have a lower tolerance of reduced oxygen pressures at altitude.
- A pre-travel medical assessment is strongly recommended, particularly for those with existing cardiovascular or respiratory disease.
- Exacerbations of angina and breathlessness can occur.

Heat / Cold

- Susceptibility to heat-related illnesses can be increased. This can be due to reduced thirst reflex, and reduced perspiration and dilatation of peripheral blood vessels.
- Hot climates can increase the risk of postural hypotension in those taking antihypertensives or antiparkinsonism drugs.
- Diuretic dosages may need to be adjusted to allow for extra fluid lost through sweating.
- Older travellers should maintain hydration, especially in hot and humid climates and allow time for temperature acclimatisation.

3.1.11 Older Travellers

- Age increases susceptibility to hypothermia due to a reduced capacity for heat-generating mechanisms such as shivering.
- The importance of appropriate clothing should be emphasised.

Food- and Water-borne Risks

- Older travellers can be vulnerable to the complications of gastrointestinal illness such as fluid loss, dehydration and associated electrolyte imbalance, particularly in the heat. Adequate hydration is essential.
- Older travellers should be advised, and receive written instructions, on the use of medication for self-treatment of travellers' diarrhoea, and be instructed to seek medical attention early. See Box 2-7 in The Pre-Travel Health Consultation Section 2.

Air-borne Risks

- Older travellers may be more susceptible to respiratory infections and their complications.

Sexual Health and Blood-borne Viral Risks (BBVs)

- The need for medical/dental intervention can increase the risk of exposure to BBVs.
- Older volunteers/healthcare workers face the same hazards as their younger colleagues and should be advised accordingly. Hepatitis B vaccination should be given. See Disease Guide Section 5 and Resource Guide: Appendix 1 – Vaccine Compendium.
- Measures to prevent sexually transmitted infections (STIs) should be discussed. See Disease Guide Section 5.

Skin Health

- Older travellers are at increased risk of sun damage and its consequences.
- Careful hygiene, including measures to prevent skin breakdown, are essential.

Psychological Health

- Adaptation to social, cultural and language differences may be more difficult due to reduced visual, auditory and/or memory functions.
- Assistance with planning a sensible itinerary and awareness of the psychological demands of travel should be emphasised.

3.1.12 Pre-conception, Pregnancy and Breastfeeding

Pregnancy during travel carries important risks that should be considered carefully prior to booking the trip. Pregnant women with a significant obstetric history, an inadequately controlled or newly diagnosed medical condition, or who are planning travel to malarial areas, or areas without access to medical care, should be advised against non-essential travel. If travel is essential, the advice below should be discussed. See also Special Risk Traveller: 3.1.17 Women.

These travellers should be encouraged to read information on pregnancy and travel. See Resource Guide: 3.1.12 Websites.

• Risk management advice should follow that of the general traveller and be tailored as described below.

• Destination-specific risk management advice can be found on the NaTHNaC Country Information Pages[1] www.nathnac.org.

• See Resource Guide: 3.1.12.

 Medical Preparation

• Comprehensive travel insurance is essential for all travellers. A full declaration of medical conditions, including pregnancy, should be made to the insurers. All equipment and planned activities should be covered.

Pre-conception

• Women should be advised to delay conception for 28 days after receiving live vaccines. There is a theoretical risk of virus transmission to the foetus.

• Vaccinating prior to conception is preferable to vaccination during pregnancy.

• The recommended interval between finishing antimalarials and trying to conceive is:

  • 1 week following doxycycline use, 2 weeks following atovaquone/proguanil use and 3 months following mefloquine use.

  • Women planning conception in countries with a high risk of chloroquine-resistant *P. falciparum* malaria should seek specialist advice.

Pregnancy

• The early pregnancy scan (usually performed between 10 to 13 weeks gestation) should ideally be performed prior to travel to ensure the viability of the pregnancy and confirm the gestation.

• Pre-natal records and next of kin details should be carried when travelling.

• Appropriate gynaecological, obstetric and neonatal care may be limited or non-existent in some areas. Emergency plans should be made in advance of travel.

• Travel with a pre-existing obstetric condition is not recommended. Those who are determined to travel should seek advice from their obstetrician.

• Women must declare their pregnancy and medical history to insurers. Failure to do so is likely to invalidate insurance.

3.1 Special Risk Traveller

3 Special Risks

3.1.12 Pre-conception, Pregnancy and Breastfeeding

- Women should check that their insurance provides comprehensive cover for pregnancy related complications, including premature delivery and neonatal intensive care.

Vaccination

- Inactivated vaccines can usually be safely given during pregnancy. Antibodies pass transplacentally to the foetus and this can provide a degree of protection for several months after birth.
- Live vaccines are generally contraindicated in pregnancy due to theoretical risks to the foetus. Termination of pregnancy is not advised after inadvertent administration of a live vaccine.
- Pregnant women should be advised against travel to yellow fever (YF) endemic areas. If travel is essential, YF vaccine can be considered, even in the first trimester, if the risk of disease outweighs the risks associated with vaccine. Specialist advice should be sought.
- MMR or any rubella-containing vaccine, BCG and varicella vaccines are contraindicated in pregnancy.

Malaria

- Women must be informed that malarial destinations are not suitable in pregnancy.
- Malaria in pregnancy increases the risk of maternal death, miscarriage, stillbirth and low birth weight, with associated risk of neonatal death.
- Pregnant women are more at risk of being bitten by mosquitoes, increasing their vulnerability to malaria. If travel is essential, the importance of effective bite avoidance, compliance with appropriate antimalarials and early medical intervention for symptoms must be emphasised.
- Contraindications, side effects and drug interactions must be considered carefully prior to prescription of antimalarials in pregnancy.
- Chloroquine and proguanil are safe in all trimesters. These drugs offer poor protection against malaria in many areas due to widespread *P. falciparum* drug resistance. Pregnant women who take proguanil should also take 5mg of folic acid daily.
- Doxycycline is contraindicated.
- Mefloquine can be safely prescribed in the second and third trimesters provided there are no contraindications.
- Safety of mefloquine in the first trimester has not been established and caution is advised. Use is justified if travel to a malarial area is essential and the chloroquine-resistant *P. falciparum* malaria risk is high. Specialist advice should be sought.
- Safety of atovaquone/proguanil has not been established in pregnancy and caution is advised. Use may be considered if travel to a malarial area is essential, the chloroquine-resistant *P. falciparum* malaria risk is high, and mefloquine is contraindicated. Specialist advice should be sought.

3.1.12 Pre-conception, Pregnancy and Breastfeeding

Breastfeeding

- See Resource Guide: 3.1.12a.
- Lactation should be well established prior to travel.

Vaccination

- Breastfeeding is not a contraindication for any vaccines.
- There is a theoretical risk that YF virus could be transmitted to the breastfed baby. Ideally, YF vaccine should be avoided whilst breastfeeding; however, as in pregnancy, if the disease risks outweigh the theoretical risk of vaccination, YF vaccine can be given.
- Vaccination of a mother will not protect the breastfed baby.

Malaria

- Atovaquone/proguanil is not generally recommended due to lack of safety data. It can be considered if travel to a malarial area is essential and mefloquine contraindicated. Specialist advice should be sought.
- Chloroquine and proguanil are safe.
- Doxycycline is contraindicated.
- Mefloquine is safe.
- Any amount of medication that passes into breast milk does not protect an infant from malaria; infants require their own appropriate antimalarials.

Journey Risks

Fitness to Fly

- Commercial air travel is considered safe in uncomplicated pregnancy up to 36 weeks and up to 32 weeks for a multiple pregnancy. Pregnant women should check the airline's requirements when booking flights. The second trimester is regarded as the safest time to fly.
- After 28 weeks most airlines require a medical certificate confirming the estimated date of delivery and that there are no complications.
- The date of the return journey should also be considered.
- Women with high-risk pregnancies, including placental abnormalities or risk of premature labour, should avoid flying.
- See Resource Guide: 3.1.12b.

Deep Vein Thrombosis (DVT)

- Pregnancy increases the risk of DVT; this is especially a concern when flying, as legroom may be restricted. On long haul flights pregnant women should wear properly fitted elastic compression stockings, exercise as much as possible and avoid dehydration.
- See Risk Management: 2.3.2 Journey Risks – DVT.

Motion Sickness

- Motion sickness can exacerbate pregnancy-induced nausea.

3.1.12 Pre-conception, Pregancy and Breastfeeding

Environmental Risks

Altitude

- Foetal oxygen supply can be compromised at altitude. Data is reassuring for altitudes up to 2,500m; however at higher altitudes potential complications include bleeding, low foetal heart rate and premature labour. Specialist advice should be sought.
- Pregnant women should be advised against travel to altitudes >3,500m. Altitudes >2,500m should be avoided in late or high-risk pregnancy.
- Pregnant women travelling to altitude should avoid exercising until they become acclimatised. Acetazolamide (Diamox®) is not recommended in pregnancy and whilst breastfeeding.
- See Special Risk Travel: 3.2.2 Altitude.

Food- and Water-borne Risks

- Unpasteurised dairy products, under-cooked meat and soft cheeses must be avoided.
- The affect of gastrointestinal illness in pregnancy can be significant for both mother and foetus. Careful food, water and personal hygiene should be emphasised.
- Medications licensed for use in pregnancy and breastfeeding should be prescribed to treat gastrointestinal illness; it may be appropriate to prescribe azithromycin off licence in some cases. Specialist advice should be sought.

Vector-borne Risks

- Pregnant women are more susceptible to mosquito bites. Mosquito bite avoidance measures should be emphasised.
- Insect repellents containing up to 50% DEET can be used; there is no evidence of harm in pregnancy when applied appropriately.

Psychological Health

- Anxiety during pregnancy, bonding and breastfeeding difficulties, and post-natal depression can be exacerbated by travel. These issues should be discussed prior to travel and/or specialist advice sought when necessary.

3.1.13 Psychological Conditions

Travel can be stressful. Individuals with a predisposition for psychological ill health can experience this for the first time during travel. Those with pre-existing psychological conditions, including phobia, anxiety, depression, mania, schizophrenia, eating disorder and substance misuse, may experience an exacerbation. Psychological health issues are significant causes of ill health among long-term travellers.

Enquiry regarding a traveller's mental health should be a standard part of the pre-travel consultation. With appropriate advice, most people with stable psychological conditions can travel successfully.

- Many causes of stress during travel cannot be predicted or prevented; some causes of stress can be reduced through careful preparation. Risk management advice should follow that of the general traveller and be tailored as described below.
- Suitability of itineraries should be discussed in detail, ideally before a trip is booked.
- Destination-specific risk management advice can be found on the NaTHNaC Country Information Pages[1] www.nathnac.org.
- See Resource Guide: 3.1.13a.

Medical Preparation

- Comprehensive travel insurance is essential for all travellers. A full declaration of medical conditions should be made to the insurers. All equipment and planned activities should be covered.
- All travellers should research their journey and destination before departure, in order that to anticipate psychological challenges, reduce their impact and increase their ability to cope on arrival.
- Travel to areas with a contrasting culture and unfamiliar language, away from normal support networks, can result in psychological distress. Irregular food and fluid intake, insomnia and substance misuse can compound this stress.
- Stable psychological conditions, and past history of psychological disorder, are not contraindications to travel. Advanced planning is essential and should involve discussion with all relevant health professionals (e.g. GP, psychologist and psychiatrist).
- It may be necessary to advise against travel if the psychological condition is new or unstable. Travel within 6 months of an exacerbation or change of treatment is generally not recommended.
- Individuals with unstable conditions, who cannot defer travel, should be encouraged not to travel alone. Ideally, they should travel with a supportive companion. Particular attention should be paid to the risk of violence or suicide.
- Avoidance of risk-taking behaviours, including use of excessive alcohol and recreational drugs that can exacerbate psychological conditions and interact with medication, should be discussed.
- A careful check should be made for potential drug interactions between routine medications used to treat psychological/psychiatric conditions and medication to be prescribed (or obtained over-the-counter) in association with travel.

3.1 Special Risk Traveller

3 Special Risks

---

1 Alternatively see Travax http://www.travax.nhs.uk/ or Fit for Travel http://www.fitfortravel.nhs.uk/

3.1.13 Psychological Conditions

Travelling with Medication

- Supplies of medications should be carried in hand luggage. It is essential to take sufficient quantities as supplies may not be available overseas. Medication should be continued for the entire duration of the trip.
- In certain countries, it is a criminal offence to carry psychotropic medication (for example, benzodiazepines) without proof of prescription. A medical letter detailing conditions, treatment and certifying the need for medicine, preferably in a language that is understood in the country of travel, should be carried at all times.
- Certain medications used to treat psychological conditions may be forbidden, or require special permission, for use in some countries. Travellers must check with relevant embassies prior to travel.
- Individuals with alcohol and/or drug addiction disorder should have successfully completed a comprehensive treatment programme before considering travel. The large variation among countries in the legal status of drug misuse should be emphasised.

Access to Medical Care

- Access to appropriate mental health services, including facilities for monitoring of drug levels, may be limited. Culturally and linguistically appropriate healthcare professionals as well as interpreters may also be rare or non-existent. Emergency medical evacuation plans should be discussed.
- Travel to remote areas with limited medical care requires careful additional consideration and planning in event of an exacerbation.

Vaccination

- There are no known contraindications to vaccines for those with psychological conditions.

Malaria

- Consider potential drug interactions and side effects when prescribing malaria antimalarials.
- Mefloquine is contraindicated in any individual with a personal or first-degree family history of neuropsychiatric disorder, including psychosis, depression, seizures or generalised anxiety disorder.
- Drugs such as phenytoin, carbamazepine and barbiturates reduce the half life of doxycycline. However, a dose adjustment of either doxycycline or the antiepileptic is not recommended.
- Cerebral malaria should always be considered as a differential diagnosis in a traveller with fever and psychological disturbance during/after travel to a malarial endemic area.

3.1.13 Psychological Conditions

Journey Risks
- The psychological challenge of any journey should not be underestimated. Length of trip, delays, crowds, jet lag and security checks can increase stress and exacerbate pre-existing conditions.
- Abnormal or nervous behaviour whilst transiting immigration may be regarded suspiciously and could result in arrest or detention.

Fitness to Fly
- Any travel, including flying, is not advised during episodes of acute psychosis, mania or significant depression.
- Travellers with fear of flying can be helped by developing coping mechanisms. Cognitive behavioural self-help books or therapy with a psychotherapist, and/or exposure-based psychological treatment offered by some airlines, can be of use.
- Use of anxiolytic medication should be discussed with a physician.

Jet Lag
- Use of sleeping tablets should be discussed with a physician.
- Excessvie tiredness can worsen some psychological conditions.

Environmental Risks
Altitude
- Acetazolamide (Diamox®) should be used cautiously in those taking lithium, as it can decrease lithium levels. Gradual acclimatisation is preferable and should be strongly encouraged in order to negate the need for acetazolamide (Diamox®) use in such individuals.

Food- and Water-borne Risks
- Absorption and efficacy of drugs can be reduced by gastrointestinal illness. Lithium levels can be elevated by dehydration. Prompt medical advice should be encouraged.

Sexual Health and Blood-borne Viral Risks (BBVs)
- Travellers with bipolar disorder may be more prone to risk-taking behaviour, especially during manic episodes. Risk management advice should be emphasised.

Skin Health
- Some medications used to treat psychiatric conditions, including amitriptyline, citalopram, chlorpromazine, fluoxetine, can cause photosensitivity. Care should be taken to avoid concurrent prescribing of other photosensitising drugs such as doxycycline.
- Appropriate recommendations regarding sun avoidance should be emphasised.

3.1 Special Risk Traveller

3 Special Risks

3.1 Special Risk Traveller

3 Special Risks

3.1.14 Renal Conditions

Travellers with a renal condition may have mild to severe renal dysfunction secondary to a wide spectrum of disorders. They may also be post-renal transplantation or on dialysis.

- Risk management advice should follow that of the general traveller and be tailored as described below.
- Destination-specific risk management advice can be found on the NaTHNaC Country Information Pages[1] www.nathnac.org.

Medical Preparation

- Comprehensive travel insurance is essential for all travellers. A full declaration of medical conditions should be made to the insurers. All equipment and planned activities should be covered.

- Travellers with a history of a renal condition should discuss the suitability of the proposed trip with their GP and/or specialist, ideally prior to booking.

- Arrangements to receive dialysis during travel require careful advanced planning. Ideally, a UK specialist should advise on appropriate treatment during travel. Details of international clinics are provided by several organisations such as the Global Dialysis Directory. See Resource Guide: 3.1.14a.

- Travellers should know about the blood or peritoneal dialysis units at their destination, in particular with regard to potential blood-borne virus transmission.

- All documentation required by the overseas clinic should be completed prior to travel by a specialist and include documentation of hepatitis B, C, HIV and MRSA status. Travellers should be aware of the policies of their UK dialysis clinic with regard to dialysis and screening on return.

- Peritonitis is a risk for those undergoing peritoneal dialysis. A 'standby' course of antibiotics can be carried, with instructions for use. Urgent medical care must still be sought.

- There may be a charge for dialysis and associated services in countries outside the UK; these charges will not be covered by the NHS. Appropriate insurance is essential for these travellers.

Vaccination

Hepatitis B

- Travellers with chronic renal failure requiring dialysis or those anticipated requiring haemodialysis or renal transplantation in the near future, should have received hepatitis B vaccine; there is a vaccine (Fendrix®) specifically formulated for use in renal patients.

Influenza/pneumococcal disease

- Travellers with chronic renal conditions, including nephrotic syndrome, chronic renal failure and renal transplantation, should be up to date with pneumococcal and annual influenza vaccination according to the UK schedule.

---

1   Alternatively see Travax http://www.travax.nhs.uk/ or Fit for Travel http://www.fitfortravel.nhs.uk/

3.1.14 Renal Conditions

Malaria
- Health professionals should consider the severity of renal impairment prior to prescribing antimalarials for those travelling to malarial endemic areas. See Table 3-4. See Resource Guide: 3.1.14b.

Table 3-4. Antimalarials in patients with renal disease (in alphabetical order)*

Drug	Glomerular filtration rate (GFR) 20 to 50 mL/min	GFR 10 to 19 mL/min	GFR <10mL/min	Continuous ambulatory peritoneal dialysis	Haemodialysis	Continuous arterio-/veno-venous haemodiafiltration
Atovaquone/ Proguanil	Contraindicated if GFR <30mL/min. 1 adult tablet if GFR 30 to 60mL/min	Contraindicated	Contraindicated	½ adult tablet	½ adult tablet	Unknown dialysability. Contraindicated
Chloroquine	Normal dose	Normal dose	50% normal dose	50% normal dose	50% normal dose	Normal dose
Doxycycline	Normal dose	Normal dose	Normal dose	Normal dose	Normal dose	Normal dose
Mefloquine	Normal dose	Normal dose	Use with caution	Use with caution	Use with caution	Normal dose
Proguanil	100mg/day (GFR 20 to 59mL/min)	50mg/48 hours	50mg/week	50mg/week	50mg/week	Unknown dialysability. Dose 50mg/48hours

*Drug information should be checked in the British National Formulary (BNF); see Resource Guide: A2 – Key Resources.

3.1.14 Renal Conditions

Food- and Water-borne Risks

- Travellers with a renal condition should be encouraged to keep well hydrated particularly in warmer climates as dehydration can worsen conditions such as chronic renal failure. Dehydration can also promote the development of kidney stones in susceptible travellers.
- Oral rehydration solutions should be carefully checked for their sodium and potassium content to avoid conflict with any special dietary requirements.
- Principles of food, water and personal hygiene should be emphasised. Travellers should be advised, and receive written instructions, on the use of medication for self-treatment of travellers' diarrhoea, and know when and how to seek medical assistance. See Box 2-7 in The Pre-Travel Health Consultation Section 2. Prompt treatment of gastrointestinal infections is essential.
- Potential drug interactions should be carefully checked prior to prescribing any medication; specialist advice should be sought if necessary.

3.1.15 Respiratory Conditions

- Risk management advice should follow that of the general traveller and be tailored as described below.
- Destination-specific risk management advice can be found on the NaTHNaC Country Information Pages[1] www.nathnac.org.
- Travellers with a respiratory condition should be encouraged to read information from the British Lung Foundation including their guide: 'Going on holiday with a lung condition'. See Resource Guide: 3.1.15a.

Medical Preparation

- Comprehensive travel insurance is essential for all travellers. A full declaration of medical conditions should be made to the insurers. All equipment and planned activities should be covered.
- Travellers with a history of a respiratory condition should discuss the suitability of the proposed trip with their GP and/or specialist, ideally prior to booking.
- A course of antibiotics and/or corticosteroids can be carried, with instructions for use in event of an acute exacerbation of a respiratory condition, whilst seeking medical assistance.
- Those requiring home oxygen should consult their oxygen supplier for details of the availability of oxygen at their destination.

Vaccination

- Travellers with chronic respiratory conditions, including COPD, cystic fibrosis, chronic bronchitis and emphysema, should be up to date with pneumococcal and annual influenza vaccination, according to the UK schedule.

Journey Risks

Fitness to Fly

Before flight

- Commercial aircraft are pressurised to cabin altitudes up to 2,438m (8,000ft). At this altitude the partial pressure of oxygen falls to the equivalent of breathing 15.1% oxygen at sea level and a healthy passenger's SpO_2 will fall to 85% from 91%.
- Altitude exposure may therefore exacerbate hypoxaemia in patients with lung disease, including chronic obstructive pulmonary disease (COPD) and cystic fibrosis, particularly in those who are hypoxaemic at sea level.
- Travellers with a respiratory condition should have a medical evaluation, ideally including measurement of pulse oximetry and spirometry, prior to flying. See Box 3-5 for those travellers with a history of respiratory conditions who should be considered for evaluation.
- If these are unavailable, the '50-metre walk' test has traditionally been used. The ability to walk 50 metres without distress is a crude indicator of an individual's ability to tolerate the relative hypoxia experienced during air travel.

3.1 Special Risk Traveller

3 Special Risks

3.1.15 Respiratory Conditions

- In those who are screened who have resting sea level oximetry between 92% and 95% and who have additional risk factors, a hypoxic challenge test is recommended. Additional risk factors include hypercapnia; FEV1 <50% predicted; lung cancer; restrictive lung disease involving the parenchyma (e.g. pulmonary fibrosis), chest wall (kyphoscoliosis) or respiratory muscles; ventilator support; cerebrovascular or cardiac disease; within 6 weeks of discharge for an exacerbation of chronic lung or cardiac disease.

- The British Thoracic Society Standards of Care Committee recommendations 'Managing passengers with respiratory disease planning air travel' should be followed. See Resource Guide: 3.1.15b.

- See Table 3-5 for a guide to the main respiratory conditions which contraindicate flying.

- Travellers should also check they are fit to fly according to the guidelines stated by their airline and ensure required documentation is complete.

- Patients with infectious tuberculosis (TB) must not travel by public air transportation until confirmed non-infectious. HIV-negative patients in whom drug resistant TB is not suspected and who have completed 2 weeks of effective anti-tuberculous treatment are usually considered non-infectious. For HIV-positive patients 3 smear negative sputum examinations on separate days, or a single negative sputum culture result, are required while on effective anti-tuberculous treatment.

- Travellers with TB and influenza-like illness should postpone their flight until fully recovered. See Resource Guide: 3.1.15c.

- Lung cancer *per se* is not a contraindication to flying. However, associated respiratory disease should be considered in its own right.

3.1.15 Respiratory Conditions

Box 3-5. Travellers with respiratory conditions recommended for pre-flight evaluation

- Asthma.
- Chronic Obstructive Pulmonary Disease (COPD).
- Restrictive disease.
- Cystic fibrosis.
- Air travel intolerance with respiratory symptoms (dyspnoea, chest pain, confusion or syncope).
- Co-morbidity with other conditions worsened by hypoxaemia (cardiovascular or cerebrovascular disease).
- Pulmonary tuberculosis.
- Passengers from an area with recent local transmission of Severe Acute Respiratory Syndrome (SARS).
- Within 6 weeks of hospital discharge for acute respiratory illness.
- Recent pneumothorax.
- Risk of or previous venous thromboembolism.
- Pre-existing requirement for oxygen or ventilator support.

Table 3-5. Contraindications to flying

Respiratory condition	Contraindication	Comments
Active or infectious respiratory disease	Flying is contraindicated until non-infectious.	Most persons with TB will be non-infectious after 2 weeks of active treatment. Patients with drug resistant TB require 2 negative consecutive sputum-cultures.
Pneumothorax	Flying is contraindicated until at least 2 weeks after lung re-expansion.	
Major chest surgery	Flying is contraindicated until 2 weeks after procedure.	Medical clearance may be required if travelling within 3 weeks of surgery.

During flight

- Supplementary in-flight oxygen, usually prescribed at a rate of 2L/min and administered by nasal cannula, is recommended for travellers whose SpO_2 is below 92% at sea level.
- Travellers requiring oxygen during flight should arrange this directly with the airline well in advance of travel. Some airlines do not permit use of supplemental oxygen during take off or landing. Travellers requiring oxygen should therefore always discuss this first with the airline.

3.1 Special Risk Traveller

3 Special Risks

3.1.15 Respiratory Conditions

- Individuals with cystic fibrosis or tracheotomies may find the low humidity of the aircraft cabin uncomfortable. Hydration during the flight is encouraged.
- Those requiring battery-powered continuous positive airways pressure (CPAP) machines for sleep apnoea on long haul flights should inform the airline. CPAP machines must be switched off prior to landing.
- Those requiring portable nebulisers need to have these approved by the airline. The use of a spacing device used in conjunction with a metered dose inhaler has been found to be as effective as nebulisers in treating asthma.
- Ventilator-dependent travellers should inform the airline of their requirements at the time of reservation. A doctor's letter is required outlining diagnosis, necessary equipment, recent blood gas results and ventilator settings. A medical escort is required as the ventilator may have to be switched off for take off and landing and the traveller manually ventilated. Arrangements must be made for proceeding through air terminals before and after the flight.
- Excess alcohol should be avoided before and during the flight, particularly in those with obstructive sleep apnoea and who are at risk of thromboembolism.

Environmental Risks

- Many cities suffer from high levels of air pollution that can exacerbate respiratory conditions.

Heat / Cold

- Cold air can cause bronchospasm in those with asthma; adequate supplies of prescribed inhalers should be carried.
- Salt loss in those with cystic fibrosis is considerable. When travelling to hot climates these individuals should take sodium chloride tablets under the careful guidance of their specialist.

Altitude

- Travellers with a respiratory condition should discuss their plans with their GP and / or specialist, ideally prior to booking a trip to altitude. They should also be advised to limit their activities during the first days of acclimatisation and to allow extra time to acclimatise.
- Some travellers with asthma report that their symptoms improve with altitude. However, they should be advised to continue their usual medication even if their symptoms improve. There is no evidence to suggest that asthma increases the risk of altitude illness.
- Individuals with COPD or cystic fibrosis who experience dyspnoea and / or hypoxia during mild exercise at sea level are likely to experience worsening symptoms at high altitude; such travellers should avoid high-altitude destinations.
- Travellers requiring CPAP for sleep apnoea should use their machine whilst sleeping at altitude.
- Travellers with pulmonary hypertensive disorders should not travel to altitude. If such travel cannot be avoided, supplemental oxygen should considered for altitudes above 2,000m. See Resource Guide: 3.1.15d.

3.1.16 Rheumatological Conditions

There are a wide range of rheumatological and autoimmune connective tissue conditions (e.g. Rheumatoid arthritis (RA) and Systemic lupus erythematosus (SLE)). Travellers with such conditions may be immunosuppressed as a result of the medical condition and/or the medication used in its management.

- Risk management advice should follow that of the general traveller and be tailored as described below.
- Destination-specific risk management advice can be found on the NaTHNaC Country Information Pages[1] www.nathnac.org.
- See Resource Guide: 3.1.16.

Medical Preparation

- Comprehensive travel insurance is essential for all travellers. A full declaration of medical conditions should be made to the insurers. All equipment and planned activities should be covered.
- Disease activity, abnormalities of immune function and immunosuppressive medications can make this group of travellers more susceptible to infection and less responsive to vaccination. Risk management advice should be emphasised.
- These travellers should be advised to seek medical advice urgently if infection is suspected. Risks of complications from illness, as well as from their treatment overseas, may be higher in this group.

Vaccination

- See British Society of Rheumatology guidelines Resource Guide: 3.1.16a and 3.1.16b.
- Live virus vaccines are contraindicated in those immunocompromised by an underlying medical condition or drug treatment. If there is doubt about the level of immunocompromise, specialist advice should be sought.
- Inactivated vaccines can be given, however the immune response may be sub-optimal. Serological testing can be considered post-vaccination.
- Reports of SLE induction or exacerbation following immunisation are rare. See Resource Guide: 3.1.16c.

Influenza/pneumococcal disease

- Travellers with rheumatological conditions should be up to date with routine vaccinations according to the UK schedule, including pneumococcal and influenza vaccines where indicated.

Malaria

- Doxycycline can cause photosensitivity and should be avoided in travellers with dermatological manifestations of SLE.
- When chloroquine (with or without proguanil) is to be recommended for antimalarials, individuals who are taking daily treatment doses of hydroxychloroquine can remain on this, and do not need to take additional chloroquine.

---

1   Alternatively see Travax http://www.travax.nhs.uk/ or Fit for Travel http://www.fitfortravel.nhs.uk/

3.1.16 Rheumatological Conditions

- Potential drug interactions should be carefully checked. Specialist advice should be sought. Plasma ciclosporin levels may be increased by concomitant use of chloroquine or doxycycline; these combinations should be avoided. Doxycycline is known to increase the risk of methotrexate toxicity; this combination should be avoided.

Environmental Risks

Sun

- Photosensitivity is common in SLE. In addition, sun exposure can exacerbate the condition. Travellers with SLE should avoid exposure to sunlight without the use of sun protection.

Cold

- Peripheral neuropathy can be present. Those affected may be prone to cold damage, particularly of the extremities. Suitable clothing should be worn.

Altitude

- Those with SLE can be sensitive to sulphonamide type drugs such as acetazolamide (Diamox®). Specialist advice should be sought.

Food- and Water-borne Risks

- Due to an increased susceptibility to gastrointestinal infection, self-treatment antibiotics may be appropriate for some individuals. Specialist advice should be sought.

Skin Health

- Peripheral neuropathy can be present. Skin can be fragile when steroid treatment has been used. The importance of good foot care should be emphasised.

3.1 Special Risk Traveller

3 Special Risks

3.1.17 Women

Women have specific travel health issues that differ from those of men and which should be discussed.

- Risk management advice should follow that of the general traveller and be tailored as described below.
- Destination-specific risk management advice can be found on the NaTHNaC Country Information Pages[1] www.nathnac.org.
- See Resource Guide: 3.1.17.

Medical Preparation

- Comprehensive travel insurance is essential for all travellers. A full declaration of medical conditions should be made to the insurers. All equipment and planned activities should be covered.
- Women should keep up to date with routine cancer screening according to UK schedules, such as cervical smears and mammograms.
- Care must be taken to ensure long-term female travellers are not inadvertently excluded from such programmes. Specific arrangements may be necessary.
- Follow-up and/or treatment should ideally be completed prior to travel.
- Menstrual irregularities can occur during travel; jet lag, exercise, cold, and high-altitude ascent, are likely modifying factors.
- Sanitary protection can be difficult to obtain overseas. Adequate supplies should be carried from the UK.
- Hormonal medication, including contraceptives, hormone replacement therapy and emergency contraception, as well as certain contraceptive devices may not be available during travel. Adequate supplies should be carried and taken from the UK.
- Drug interactions should be checked prior to prescription of medication recommended for travel.
- Access to specialist gynaecological or infertility treatment can be limited or non-existent in some areas. Where such services are available, they may not meet UK standards of care.

Malaria

- Doxycycline may reduce the effectiveness of combined oral contraceptives. Additional barrier methods of contraception should be used during the first 3 weeks of doxycycline use. After 3 weeks, additional contraception is no longer required.
- If the pill or patch-free week coincides with the first 3 weeks of doxycycline use, the contraceptive-free week should be missed.
- Doxycycline does not reduce the effectiveness of the progesterone only pill.
- Pregnancy must be avoided whilst using doxycycline as use may affect foetal bone growth.

---

1   Alternatively see Travax http://www.travax.nhs.uk/ or Fit for Travel http://www.fitfortravel.nhs.uk/

3.1.17 Women

Journey Risks

- The gradual adjustment of the time at which contraceptive pills are taken whilst crossing time zones should be discussed.

Fitness to Fly

- Women taking oral (or transdermal) combined hormonal contraceptives are at an increased risk of deep vein thrombosis (DVT) during travel involving periods of immobility over 5 hours. The risk can be reduced by lower extremity exercise during the journey and by wearing properly fitted, graduated compression flight socks.
See Risk Management: 2.3.2 Journey Risks – DVT.

Safety Risks

Personal Safety

- Women travellers can be targeted by criminals. Women should be encouraged to read advice from the Foreign and Commonwealth Office. See Resource Guide: 3.1.17b.

Environmental Risks

Altitude

- See Special Risk Travel: 3.2.2 Altitude.
- See Medical Commission UIAA recommendations for women going to altitude Resource Guide: 3.1.17a.
- Iron deficiency can impede acclimatisation at high altitudes. Iron supplementation is advised for women with low levels.

Food- and Water-borne Risks

- Vomiting and persistent diarrhoea can interfere with the absorption of oral contraceptives. If vomiting occurs within 2 hours of taking the pill, another pill should be taken as soon as possible.
- In cases of persistent vomiting or diarrhoea lasting more than 24 hours, additional contraceptive precautions should be used during the illness and for 7 days after recovery. If the vomiting and diarrhoea occurs during the last 7 tablets, the next pill-free interval should be omitted.

Sexual Health and Blood-borne Viral Risks (BBVs)

- As with all travellers, women should be advised to avoid unsafe sexual practices and BBV risks including unprotected sex, injecting-drug use, body piercing and tattoos.
- Post-exposure sexually transmitted infection (STI) and BBV screening or treatment (such as HIV PEP) may not be available. Travel to a distant medical centre, or back to the UK may be necessary. See Disease Guide Section 5 and see Algorithm 4-7 in The Post-Travel Consultation Section 4.
- Abortion is illegal in some countries. Travel to a distant medical centre, or back to the UK may be necessary.

3.1.17 Women

Psychological Health

- The expected behaviour and role of women in other countries can differ to that in the UK. Cultural adaptation may be necessary. See Resource Guide: 3.1.17b.
- The inherent pressures of travel can result in the emergence or reoccurrence of a psychological condition.

3.1 Special Risk Traveller

3 Special Risks

Special Risk – Travel

3.2.1 Adventure

Adventure tourism is expanding rapidly, with travel to challenging environments and participation in demanding activities, often with an associated increased risk to health. Travellers often underestimate the level of fitness and preparation that can be necessary for this type of travel. Significant preparation should be undertaken. These travellers should be encouraged to read information from expeditions, mountain and wilderness societies. See Resource Guide: 3.2.1 Websites.

Adventure tour operators vary in their organisation and adherence to safety standards; extensive research on the part of the traveller is strongly recommended.

- Risk management advice should follow that of the general traveller and be tailored as described below.
- Destination-specific risk management advice can be found on the NaTHNaC Country Information Pages[1] www.nathnac.org.
- See Resource Guide: 3.2.1a, 3.2.1b and 3.2.1c.

Medical Preparation

- Comprehensive travel insurance is essential for all travellers. A full declaration of medical conditions should be made to the insurers. All equipment and planned activities should be covered.
- Travellers should know how to access medical facilities and what to do in event of a medical emergency.
- A travel medical kit should be carried. See Risk Management: 2.3.1 Medical Preparation – Travel medical kit. First aid training should be considered. See Resource Guide: 2.3.1.
- Travellers should be advised, and receive written instructions, on the use of medication for self-treatment of minor illness, and know when and how to seek medical assistance.
- A dental assessment is recommended prior to remote travel.
- Adequate physical fitness is necessary, and travellers should prepare themselves appropriately.

Vaccination

Hepatitis B

- There can be an increased risk of injury during adventurous travel resulting in medical care. A personal sterile travel medical kit should be carried and hepatitis B vaccination considered.

Rabies

- Pre-exposure rabies vaccination should be considered for those undertaking activities such as caving and cycling, which can increase the risk of exposure to rabies. It should also be considered for long-term travel, travel to remote areas, and to areas where access to timely post-exposure immunoglobulin and vaccine is limited.
- Urgent medical attention should be sought if bitten. Travel to a distant specialist centre may be required to access reliable post-exposure care. Insurance, including repatriation for such an eventuality, is essential.

1   Alternatively see Travax http://www.travax.nhs.uk/ or Fit for Travel http://www.fitfortravel.nhs.uk/

3.2 Special Risk Travel

3 Special Risks

3.2.1 Adventure

Malaria

- There is an increased risk of morbidity and mortality from malaria in areas remote to medical assistance. Compliance with all malaria prevention measures should be emphasised.
- Emergency standby treatment for malaria should be recommended for those taking antimalarials and visiting remote areas where they are unlikely to be within 24 hours of medical attention.
- Rapid Diagnostic Tests for malaria are not recommended for use by travellers; they can be carried by health professionals accompanying an expedition to remote malarious areas, provided care is taken to transport and store them correctly in order to prevent deterioration in their performance in the field.

Safety Risks

- Risks associated with activities can be minimised by ensuring that equipment and personal protective clothing are appropriate.
- Those travelling as part of a group should be aware that their decisions and behaviour can impact the safety and efficient working of the group.

Environmental Risks

- Adventure travellers can be at risk of injury and illness when exposed to unaccustomed environmental conditions. Risk management advice should be tailored to the itinerary and planned activities (e.g. altitude, heat, cold).
- Local advice should be taken, particularly in regards to terrain and weather, and reputable/registered guides employed where necessary.
- Diseases transmitted through exposure to water (e.g. leptospirosis, schistosomiasis) should be discussed as appropriate. See Disease Guide Section 5.
- Leeches can be a problem in wet environments. They can be avoided by wearing boots and minimising exposed skin. DEET should be used on exposed skin.

Food- and Water-borne Risks

- Access to safe food and water may be limited.
- Advice on water purification methods should be given. Potable bottled water may be limited, and boiling may not be practical. Combining chemical disinfection with filtration of water is often the most appropriate.
- Ability to maintain personal hygiene can be limited. Discuss methods to maintain hand hygiene, e.g. use of alcohol-based hand sanitisers.
- Group/camp hygiene (e.g. washing and disinfection of shared crockery and cutlery, construction of appropriate toilet facilities) should be discussed.

3.2.1 Adventure

- Travellers should be advised, and receive written instructions, on the use of medication for self-treatment of travellers' diarrhoea, and know when and how to seek medical assistance. See Box 2-7 in The Pre-Travel Health Consultation Section 2.
- Those travelling as part of a group should report any illness early to the group leader and where possible, a medical opinion sought.

Vector-borne Risks
Venomous Bites
- See Disease Guide Section 5. See Risk Management: 2.3.6 Vector-borne Risks.
- Travellers should be aware of the poisonous snakes, scorpions and spiders that are native to the area.
- It is not appropriate to carry snake or scorpion antivenom. Local specialist advice should be sought.
- Urgent medical attention should be sought following possible envenomation. Travel to a distant specialist centre is usually required to access antivenom. Knowledge of first aid measures is essential. See Resource Guide: 2.3.1a.

Air-borne Risks
- Human-to-human transmission of respiratory infections can occur in groups. Influenza vaccination can be considered.

Histoplasmosis
- Travellers can be exposed to histoplasmosis usually during caving. Appropriate risk reduction strategies should be adopted, including the use of masks. A medical opinion should be sought if symptoms of a febrile or respiratory illness develop 10 days or more after such activities.

Sexual Health and Blood-borne Viral Risks (BBVs)
- Greater risk-taking behaviour, including sexual contact, often occurs when undertaking adventurous travel; this increases potential exposure to sexually transmitted infections (STIs). Protective measures should be emphasised. See Disease Guide Section 5.

Psychological Health
- Travel to challenging environments and/or undertaking adventurous activities can affect an individual's psychological health. Group travel can place a diverse range of people in close, unfamiliar and often confined environments, which some find stressful.
- Awareness of the potential psychological impact and coping strategies should be discussed.

3.2 Special Risk Travel

3 Special Risks

3.2.2 Altitude

Popular high-altitude destinations for UK travellers include the Andes (e.g. Quito, Ecuador; Inca trail, Peru), the Himalayas (e.g. Nepal and Tibet, including Everest Base Camp) and accessible volcanoes such as Mount Kilimanjaro, Tanzania. Travellers should discuss their exact itinerary, including sleeping altitudes, and plans for acclimatisation, with a travel health specialist prior to booking. Those intending to travel to altitude should read the information provided by expeditions, mountain and wilderness societies. See Resource Guide: 3.2.2 Websites.

- Risk management advice should follow that of the general traveller and be tailored as described below.
- Destination-specific risk management advice can be found on the NaTHNaC Country Information Pages[1] www.nathnac.org.
- See Resource Guide: 3.2.2a and 3.2.2b.
- A Health Information Sheet, *Altitude illness*, is available to download from NaTHNaC[1]. See Resource Guide: A26 – Key Resources.

Medical Preparation

- Comprehensive travel insurance is essential for all travellers. A full declaration of medical conditions should be made to the insurers. All equipment and planned activities should be covered.
- Hypoxia (low blood oxygen levels) is one of the main physiological alterations during ascent to high altitude; the body's response is to increase the breathing rate. Over several days, aided by the kidneys, acclimatisation (balancing of the body's response to altitude) usually occurs.
- It is not possible to predict the susceptibility of a traveller to altitude illness; physically fit travellers are not necessarily at lower risk. The best indicator of how altitude will affect a traveller is previous experience at altitude, but even this may be unreliable.
- Risk factors for altitude illness include total altitude gained, rate of ascent, altitude achieved, sleeping altitude and level of exertion. Rapid ascent without a period of acclimatisation puts a traveller at higher risk.
- The most important prevention of altitude illness is adequate acclimatisation and regular rest days. Travellers should be advised to acclimatise at an altitude below 3,000m, and ascend gradually with no more than a 300m to 500m increase in sleeping altitude each day, and a rest day every 3 days.
- Travellers to altitude should be able to recognise the signs and symptoms of acute mountain sickness (AMS), high-altitude cerebral oedema (HACE) and high-altitude pulmonary oedema (HAPE). See Box 3-6.
- If symptoms of altitude illness develop, no further ascent should be made until the traveller has recovered. A rapid descent should be made if severe AMS occurs.

3.2.2 Altitude

- Acetazolamide (Diamox®) has been extensively used as prevention for altitude illness, although it is unlicensed for this purpose. If travellers are to take acetazolamide (Diamox®), trial doses of 125mg twice daily for 2 days should be taken prior to travel. Assuming there are no adverse events it should then be commenced 1 to 2 days prior to ascent to 3,000m and above, and continued for at least 2 days after reaching the highest altitude.
- Acetazolamide (Diamox®) can cause nausea, a mild diuresis, and sensations of oral and finger tingling. More unusual side effects include rashes, flushing and thirst. It is contraindicated in those with an allergy to sulphonamides.
- Acetazolamide (Diamox®) is not an alternative to adequate acclimatisation.
- Travellers with pre-existing medical conditions should receive a medical opinion prior to booking their trip, in order to assess their fitness to travel to altitude. Those planning to exercise/trek at altitude should be physically fit.
- All travellers with pre-existing medical conditions should carefully consider the medical care available to them in case of altitude illness and plan for any emergency.

Treatment of altitude illness

Although mild AMS is unpleasant, it is usually self-limiting, resolving spontaneously over several hours or days if no further ascent is made. Acclimatisation can take between 2 days and 3 weeks depending on several factors including the altitude to be attained. Paracetamol, aspirin or ibuprofen can be used to relieve headache, and antiemetics can be taken for nausea.

Acetazolamide (Diamox®) can be used for treatment but the onset of its effect can be delayed. A person with AMS should never be left unattended in case symptoms worsen. If no improvement occurs, or symptoms worsen, an immediate descent of at least 500m to 1,000m should be made.

The main principle of treatment of severe AMS, HACE or HAPE is immediate descent. Both HACE and HAPE can progress rapidly and death is the likely outcome if a descent is not made as soon as the symptoms are recognised. Oxygen by face mask can help to relieve symptoms. Nifedipine and dexamethasone are useful in the treatment of HAPE, and dexamethasone can relieve symptoms of HACE. These drugs are not routinely recommended for travellers to carry to altitude. They are usually reserved for climbing expeditions to extreme altitudes and administered by persons with extensive experience in the management of high-altitude illness. Portable hyperbaric chambers may also be used by expeditions.

 ## Vaccination

Hepatitis B

- Travellers participating in hazardous sports or activities are at increased risk of accidents and injuries. Invasive medical treatment can expose the traveller to blood-borne viruses. Hepatitis B vaccination should be given.

3.2 Special Risk Travel

3 Special Risks

3.2.2 Altitude

Journey Risks

- Airlines often fly directly to a high-altitude destination allowing limited or no opportunity for gradual acclimatisation. Cities with airports over 2,000m include Bogotá (Colombia), Quito (Ecuador), Cusco (Peru), Mexico City (Mexico), Addis Ababa (Ethiopia), Sana'a (Yemen) and Lhasa (Tibet, China). Travellers should be aware of the altitude at each of their destinations and discuss their itinerary in detail with a health professional, ideally prior to booking.
- Travellers flying directly to high altitude should ensure they are acclimatised to that altitude before ascending any higher.
- Travel to altitude can involve hazardous activities and sports such as climbing and mountaineering. Appropriate training, experience and guiding is essential; safety equipment should be carried or thoroughly checked if sourced overseas.

Food- and Water-borne Risks

- Travel at altitude can cause dehydration and loss of appetite. Travellers should be encouraged to pay attention to their fluid intake and eat small, regular meals.
- Access to safe drinking water is often more difficult in remote areas. Travellers should pay particular attention to water purification advice.
- Travellers should be advised, and receive written instructions, on the use of medication for self-treatment of travellers' diarrhoea, and know when and how to seek medical assistance. See Box 2-7 in The Pre-Travel Health Consultation Section 2.

Skin Health

- Levels of UV radiation are higher at altitude; the risk of sunburn is increased. Sun protection measures should be taken.
- Travel to high altitude can expose the traveller to sub-zero temperatures. Appropriate warm clothing should be worn and skin checked regularly for signs of frostbite.

Psychological Health

- Sleep disturbance and loss of appetite, often experienced during acclimatisation to altitude, can precipitate low mood.
- High-altitude expeditions may involve periods of time living in close proximity to others and in basic accommodation.
- Travellers should be psychologically prepared for their trip.

3.2.2 Altitude

Box 3-6. Signs and symptoms of altitude illness

Altitude illness is a term used to describe a spectrum of illness associated with ascent to altitudes usually higher than 2,500 metres. It can be divided into 3 syndromes:

1. Acute mountain sickness (AMS). This is most common, and usually begins at altitudes of 2,500m to 3,500m (8,200ft to 11,500ft) but can occur at lower altitudes between 1,500m to 2,500m (5,000ft to 8,200ft). Symptoms of AMS typically begin 6 to 12 hours after arrival at altitude, but can begin more than 24 hours after ascent. Initial symptoms include headache, fatigue, loss of appetite, nausea and sleep disturbance. These symptoms usually resolve within 1 to 2 days if further ascent does not occur.

2. High-altitude cerebral oedema (HACE). AMS progresses in less than 10% of cases to the more severe HACE where travellers experience lethargy, confusion and ataxia in addition to the symptoms of AMS. If untreated, HACE will eventually progress to coma and death.

3. High-altitude pulmonary oedema (HAPE) typically occurs in the first 2 to 4 days after arrival at altitudes higher than 2,500m. HAPE is not necessarily preceded by AMS. Initial symptoms of HAPE include shortness of breath with exertion, and a dry cough, progressing to shortness of breath at rest. The cough may become productive with blood-stained sputum. HAPE is frequently accompanied by symptoms of HACE.

3.2.3 Cruises

In 2008, approximately 1.5 million British nationals travelled on cruise ships.

- Health professionals should take a detailed account of both the on-board conditions and the on-shore itinerary, including duration, destinations and planned activities. Suitability of the trip should be discussed, ideally prior to booking.
- Risk management advice should follow that of the general traveller and be tailored as described below.
- Destination-specific risk management advice can be found on the NaTHNaC Country Information Pages[1] www.nathnac.org.
- See Resource Guide: 3.2.3a and 3.2.3b.

Medical Preparation

- Comprehensive travel insurance is essential for all travellers. A full declaration of medical conditions should be made to the insurers. All equipment and planned activities should be covered.
- Medical facilities on board cruise ships vary considerably. Only vessels carrying more than 100 crew members and undertaking an international voyage of 3 days or longer are required by international regulation to provide a physician.
- Travellers are advised to review a ship's procedures for handling medical emergencies, including stabilisation and evacuation of seriously ill passengers, prior to booking. Medical and dental care received on board is usually not free of charge.
- Travellers with pre-existing medical conditions should inform the cruise company/ship's medical team of their medical conditions and carry a written summary of their medical history, and sufficient personal supplies of medication. Obtaining supplies on board should not be assumed; obtaining supplies on shore should be discouraged due to the prevalence in some countries of counterfeit drugs.
- Qualities of medical facilities on shore vary considerably and can be non-existent. Travellers, who require medical intervention, and those undertaking high-risk travel such as remote adventure cruises, should try to obtain information about medical facilities available, and discuss their proposed itinerary with a specialist, prior to booking.

Vaccination

Influenza/pneumococcal disease

- Influenza and pneumococcal vaccination should be given to travellers for whom they are routinely recommended; influenza vaccination can be considered for all travellers.

Yellow fever (YF)

- Vaccination may be required and/or recommended for travel to a country as part of a cruise itinerary.
- Use of waiver letter may be appropriate, if there is no or low risk of exposure, and a high risk of adverse events for vaccination due to age and/or pre-existing medical condition.
- Specialist advice should be sought when necessary.

3.2.3 Cruises

Malaria
- Antimalarials may be necessary if the ship docks or travellers stay on shore, overnight in risk areas. A visit on shore during the daytime, in low-risk areas, does not usually require antimalarials.

Journey Risks
Fitness to Fly
- A long haul flight may be required to join/return from the cruise. Travellers should be fit to fly.

Motion Sickness
- Preventive measures should be advised for motion sickness.

Safety Risks
- Historically, cruise ships have been one of the safest forms of transport due to the application of strict international security regulations.
- FCO advice regarding entry requirements and safety should be reviewed for each destination. See Resource Guide: A12 – Key Resources.
- Falls are a frequent cause of injury on ships. Deck surfaces and stairways may be wet and slippery. Care should be taken whilst on board, particularly in rough seas, and when embarking/disembarking the ship. Because of the risk of falling overboard, passengers should avoid sitting on balcony or deck railings.
- Travellers should familiarise themselves with the ship's emergency evacuation procedures.

Environmental Risks
Heat/Cold
- Travellers may be exposed to extremes of heat and cold on some cruise itineraries. Suitable clothing is advised.

Sun
- Travellers may underestimate the risk from sun exposure whilst on a cruise. Protective measures should be emphasised.

Food- and Water-borne Risks
- Travellers should be advised to moderate their alcohol and food consumption.
- Outbreaks of gastrointestinal infections, such as norovirus, have occurred on cruise ships. Human-to-human transmission can occur more easily in these environments.
- The risk of infection can be reduced by personal hygiene, including hand washing and the use of alcohol-based hand sanitisers. These measures are particularly important during, and on return from, on-shore visits.
- Travellers should report any illness promptly to the ship's crew or medical team. Isolation may be required.

3.2 Special Risk Travel

3 Special Risks

3.2.3 Cruises

Vector-borne Risks

- Cruise itineraries should be carefully reviewed to determine risk of exposure to insect-borne diseases, such as dengue, malaria and YF.

Air-borne Risks

- Outbreaks of respiratory infections, such as influenza and legionellosis, have occurred on cruise ships. Human-to-human transmission can occur more easily in these environments.
- The risk of some respiratory infections can be reduced by personal hygiene, including hand washing and the use of alcohol-based hand sanitisers and keeping a distance from contagious persons
- Due to the risk of legionellosis, special risk travellers, such as the elderly or immunocompromised, should be advised to avoid using whirlpool spas unless it can be established that they have been adequately chlorinated.
- Travellers should report any illnesses early to the ship's medical team/ crew. Isolation may be necessary.

Sexual Health and Blood-borne Viral Risks (BBVs)

- Increased alcohol consumption can result in greater risk-taking behaviour, increasing the risk of exposure to sexually transmitted infections (STIs). Travellers should be advised to moderate their consumption. Protective measures against STIs should be emphasised. See Disease Guide Section 5.

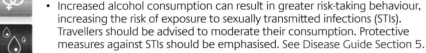

Psychological Health

- Cruises place diverse groups of people in often crowded, unfamiliar and confined environments, which some may find stressful. Awareness of the potential psychological impact and coping strategies should be discussed.
- Cruises may be perceived as safe havens from which to visit different countries and cultures. The potential for culture shock still exists.

3.2.4 Diving

The UK has an estimated 90,000 qualified recreational divers. Many travel to dive with a self-contained underwater breathing apparatus (SCUBA) or with the specific aim to learn to dive.

*   Risk management advice should follow that of the general traveller and be tailored as described below.
*   Destination-specific risk management advice can be found on the NaTHNaC Country Information Pages[1] www.nathnac.org.
*   See Resource Guide: 3.2.4.
*   Travellers may find the Divers Alert Network Dive and Travel Medical Guide useful. See Resource Guide: 3.2.4a.

Medical Preparation

*   Comprehensive travel insurance is essential for all travellers. A full declaration of medical conditions should be made to the insurers. All equipment and planned activities should be covered.
*   Travellers with pre-existing medical conditions should have a specific diving medical assessment prior to booking a trip. They should carry with them a written summary of their medical history, written confirmation of fitness to dive from a health professional, and inform the dive operators on arrival.
*   The Recreational Scuba Training Council (RSTC) Medical Statement is required in order to participate in internationally recognised scuba training programmes; however, it is recommended for all those travelling for the purpose of diving. It lists risk conditions and provides a diver's medical questionnaire and physical examination form to be completed by a physician. See Resource Guide: 3.2.4b.
*   The main contraindications to diving given by the UK Sports Diving Medical Committee are listed in Table 3-6. See Resource Guide: 3.2.4c for full guidelines.
*   Specialist advice should always be sought.

Table 3-6. UK Sports Diving Medical Committee contraindications to diving

Medical condition	Absolute/Relative contraindication to diving	Comments
Cardiovascular/ Cerebrovascular Disease	Angina (unstable). Anticoagulant medication. Arrhythmias. Congestive heart failure. Hyperlipideamia. Hypertension. Intracardiac shunts. Myocardial infarction. Pacemakers. Prosthetic valves. Revascularisation.	Persons with well controlled disease may be allowed to dive; individual medical assessment is required.

(continued)

3.2 Special Risk Travel

3 Special Risks

3.2.4 Diving

Table 3-6. UK Sports Diving Medical Committee contraindications to diving (continued)

Medical condition	Absolute/Relative contraindication to diving	Comments
Diabetes	• Hypoglycaemia within last year. • Diabetes associated retinopathy or neuropathy.	Persons with well controlled diabetes may be allowed to dive; individual medical assessment is required.
Haematology	Sickle cell disease.	Individual medical assessment is recommended before diving for persons with sickle cell trait.
	Bleeding/coagulation disorders.	Individual medical assessment is required.
Neurology	Epilepsy: • Taking antiepileptics. • Seizure within last 5 years. • Nocturnal seizure within last 3 years. Head Injury. Multiple Sclerosis. Other neurological disease	Travellers with epilepsy who have been seizure-free and off medication for 5 years may be allowed to dive. Where seizures were exclusively nocturnal, this time is reduced to 3 years. Individual medical assessment is required.
Obesity	BMI > 30.	Individual medical assessment is required.
Opthalmology	Dependent on condition.	Individual medical assessment is required following eye surgery and recommended for person with glaucoma.
Otolaryngology (Ears, nose and throat)	Tympanic membrane perforation. Infection. Post-surgery.	Individual medical assessment is required.
Post-operative	Dependent on procedure.	Individual medical assessment is required.
Pregnancy	Not recommended throughout pregnancy.	
Psychology	Anxiety traits, depressive illness, psychoses, schizophrenia, history of suicide attempt.	Individual medical assessment is required.
Respiratory	Asthma: • Cold, exercise or emotion induced. • Bronchodilator required within last 24 hours. Infection. Pneumothorax.	Persons with well controlled asthma may be allowed to dive; individual medical assessment is required. Individual medical assessment is required.

3.2.4 Diving

- Travellers should be aware of the full range of injuries and illness associated with underwater pressure changes, including barotrauma, pneumothorax, emphysema, arterial gas embolism, and life-threatening decompression sickness. They should know how to minimise risks, recognise symptoms of illness and know how to access medical care.
- Ear and sinus barotrauma are the most common injuries in divers and are due to failure to equalize pressure changes in the middle ear and sinus spaces on descent. Symptoms of barotrauma include pain, tinnitus, vertigo and reduced hearing. Travellers should be advised to discontinue diving and seek a medical opinion. Infections of the ear, nose and sinuses increase the risk of barotrauma and diving should be avoided until symptoms have fully resolved.
- Decompression sickness can occur in any diver, including those who have followed standard principles of safety and decompression guidelines. Symptoms include joint pain, shortness of breath, cough, behaviour change, loss of coordination or consciousness. High concentration oxygen and fluids should be administered as first aid if possible, and definitive treatment of recompression and oxygen administration in a hyperbaric chamber urgently sought.
- Medical facilities near dive sites, and the availability of hyperbaric chambers, vary considerably worldwide. Travellers should obtain information about hospital facilities in advance, and carry a contact telephone number such as the Divers Alert Network in case of medical emergencies.
- A dental check up is strongly recommended prior to diving; gas under pressure can accumulate in dental cavities.

Malaria

- Mefloquine has not been shown to alter dive performance and may be suitable for those who are known to tolerate the drug. However, mefloquine reduces the seizure threshold, and can be associated with neuropsychiatric adverse events. These can complicate decompression illness. If suitable alternatives are available, it may be prudent to avoid mefloquine if planning to dive.
- Some dive centres do not permit those taking mefloquine to dive.

Journey Risks

Fitness to Fly

- There is an increased risk of decompression sickness when exposed to altitude after a dive. Divers should avoid flying or travelling to an altitude above 2,000m, for a minimum of 24 hours, after surfacing from a dive, in order to reduce the risk of decompression sickness.

3.2 Special Risk Travel

3 Special Risks

3.2.4 Diving

Safety Risks

- Travellers should dive within the safe limits of their training and equipment. Established international and local safety guidelines should be followed.
- Equipment and training should only be received from an accredited source and safety checks performed prior to each dive.
- Dives should always be undertaken with at least one other person; both divers should have knowledge of the dive site and of the calculated dive plan.

Environmental Risks

Water

- Divers are at increased risk of water hazards due the nature of their activity.
- Schistosomiasis may be a risk if diving in fresh water. See Disease Guide Section 5.

Sun

- Divers can be exposed to high intensity sunlight including that reflected on water. Use of protective measures should be emphasised.

Cold

- Divers are at increased risk of hypothermia; appropriate wet/dry suits should be worn.

Food- and Water-borne Risks

- Travellers should remain well hydrated and rested, and avoid alcohol prior to diving.

Vector-borne Risks

Marine Toxins and Venomous Bites

- Travellers should not touch marine creatures and corals. Touching coral is illegal in some countries.
- Some marine species are harmful. Contact with coral can leave small amounts of material in a wound which becomes infected. Wounds should be scrubbed with soap and water, and antiseptic applied. Jellyfish stings should be rinsed with vinegar. Topical antibiotic ointment and/or oral antibiotics can be required for infected wounds. Medical advice should be sought early in the event of severe cuts or infection.

Psychological Health

- Adventurous activities can affect psychological health; travellers may be unaware, or underestimate, the challenging nature of the underwater environment. Awareness of the potential psychological impact and coping strategies should be discussed.

3.2.5 Healthcare Workers

Healthcare workers (HCWs) travel, often at short notice, to work on short- or long-term assignments, in a variety of overseas settings.

- Risk management advice should follow that of the general traveller and be tailored as described below.
- Destination-specific risk management advice can be found on the NaTHNaC Country Information Pages[1] www.nathnac.org.
- See Resource Guide: 3.2.5.

Medical Preparation

- Comprehensive travel insurance is essential for all travellers. A full declaration of medical conditions should be made to the insurers. All equipment and planned activities should be covered.
- HCWs also have a responsibility to declare medical conditions to their employer's medical/occupational health advisers.
- Specialist opinion on the advisability of work related travel should be sought for those with pre-existing medical conditions.
- Employers/organisations have a duty of care to ensure that HCWs have sufficient time, information and opportunity to consider the health risks at their destination.
- Employers/organisations should also guarantee that appropriate preventive strategies are in place.
- The Royal College of Nursing, Working with humanitarian organisations: a guide for nurses, midwives and health care professionals.
- Occupational health clearance must be undertaken by a suitably qualified health professional.
- HCWs should be advised, and receive written instructions, on the use of medication for self-treatment of minor illness, and know when and how to seek independent medical assistance.

Vaccination

- While vaccinations can be indicated for the benefit of individual HCWs, they are also important in preventing transmission of infections to vulnerable patients.

Hepatitis B

- HCWs are at risk of exposure to blood-borne viral diseases such as HIV, hepatitis B and hepatitis C. Hepatitis B vaccination should be given.

Influenza

- Influenza occurs throughout the year in the tropics and seasonally in temperate climates. Influenza vaccine, appropriate for the hemisphere of travel and work, should be considered for HCWs.

Measles/mumps/rubella

- Protection of HCWs is especially important in the context of their ability to transmit measles, mumps or rubella infections to vulnerable groups.

3.2.5 Healthcare Workers

- MMR vaccination should be given according to national recommendations for HCWs. HCWs unable to produce satisfactory evidence of protection (reliable history of appropriate immunisation or positive antibody tests) should receive 2 doses of MMR vaccine at least 1 month apart.

Meningococcal meningitis

- In endemic areas, HCWs may be at increased risk of meningococcal disease due to close contact with local populations. ACW135Y meningococcal vaccination should be considered for those at risk.

Tuberculosis (TB)

- HCWs travelling to areas with a high incidence of TB are at increased of infection. They should know the incidence at their destination and the signs and symptoms of the disease.
- BCG vaccination should be given according to national recommendations for HCWs. The Department of Health recommends that unvaccinated, tuberculin-negative HCWs less than 35 years, who have contact with patients or clinical materials, should receive the BCG vaccine. BCG may be considered for at risk healthcare workers over 35 years of age; there are no data on the protection afforded by BCG vaccine when it is given to adults aged 35 years or over.

Varicella

- Varicella vaccination should be given according to national recommendations for HCWs. HCWs without a reliable history of chickenpox or herpes zoster infection or previous appropriate immunisation should be serologically tested and vaccine offered to those with negative serology.

Safety Risks

- HCWs may work in unstable areas and can be victims of intentional and non-intentional violence. The Foreign and Commonwealth Office provides safety advice that should be observed. See Resource Guide: A12 – Key Resources.
- HCWs must be aware of their employer's emergency procedures, including evacuation plans. Ideally all HCW's should receive safety training prior to departure.

Food- and Water-borne Risks

- Preventive measures, infection control guidelines, and self-treatment options for gastrointestinal illness should be discussed. See Box 2-7 in The Pre-Travel Health Consultation Section 2.

Air-borne Risks

- HCWs are at increased risk of exposure to respiratory diseases due to close contact with infected persons. The importance of applying infection control measures should be emphasised.

3.2.5 Healthcare Workers

Sexual Health and Blood-borne Viral Risks (BBVs)

- HCWs should strictly apply infection control measures overseas in order to reduce their risk.

- HCWs should be advised of their employer's protocols and procedures for protection against and post-exposure management of BBVs.

- All sharps injuries and body fluid exposures should be medically assessed as soon as possible and considered for HIV post-exposure prophylaxis (PEP). First aid measures should be emphasised. See Department of Health, HIV post-exposure prophylaxis: guidance from the UK Chief Medical Officers' Expert Advisory Group on AIDS Resource Guide: 3.2.5a.

- HCWs in areas with a risk of exposure to viral haemorrhagic fevers should follow infection control measures, such as those recommended by the World Health Organization (WHO); see Resource Guide: 3.2.5b.

Psychological Health

- HCWs travelling to low-income areas may find the poverty that they observe adversely affects their psychological well-being. Adequate preparation includes knowledge of the organisation, work and living environment, the skills required, as well as coping strategies. The importance of taking time for rest and relaxation, including full leave entitlement, should be emphasised.

- HCWs workers may witness or be victims of traumatic stress. It is crucial that these individuals are offered confidential opportunities to discuss their experiences with trained professionals.

- It is recommended that employers provide psychological support before, during and after an overseas assignment. HCWs should have knowledge of their employer's procedures for accessing such support.

3.2 Special Risk Travel

3 Special Risks

3.2.6 Last Minute Travel

Travellers who attend for travel advice close to their departure date present a challenge to the healthcare professional. These 'last minute' travellers may be at increased risk of travel-associated illness due to inadequate preparation; this is particularly true for those with pre-existing medical conditions.

- Risk management advice should follow that of the general traveller and be tailored as described below. Risk management advice, and some interventions, even when given at the last minute, can still be beneficial.
- Destination-specific risk management advice can be found on the NaTHNaC Country Information Pages[1] www.nathnac.org.
- See Resource Guide: 3.2.6.

Medical Preparation

- Comprehensive travel insurance is essential for all travellers. A full declaration of medical conditions should be made to the insurers. All equipment and planned activities should be covered.
- Specialist opinion on the advisability of last minute travel should be sought for those with pre-existing medical conditions. Deferment of travel should be suggested when risks are assessed to be high.

Vaccination

- Risks and benefits of last minute vaccination should be considered on an individual basis. Factors to consider include time necessary to develop an immune response (usually 5 to 10 days), the risk of developing an adverse reaction to the vaccine during travel, the length of the trip and the risk of exposure to the disease for which vaccination is being considered.
- Accelerated schedules exist for some vaccinations: See Table 3-7. A vaccine may be contraindicated for use at the last minute due to risks of adverse reactions.
- Partial or sub-optimal immune response can result from incomplete or shortened intervals of administration of doses of a primary vaccination schedule.
- Schedules of recommended vaccines should be started as soon as possible in last minute travellers. These travellers should be advised to complete the series according to the original schedule, even following an extended interval. Courses of parenteral vaccines do not need to be restarted following missed doses.
- Occasionally it is appropriate for further doses of vaccine to be sourced during travel in order to complete the recommended schedule. Carrying vaccine for administration overseas is not usually recommended.
- There is no limit to the number of vaccines that can be given in 1 day, although multiple vaccines given simultaneously can increase the risk of adverse events. See Resource Guide: 3.2.6a.
- The importance of other risk management measures should be emphasised when a sub-optimal response from partial or last minute vaccination is anticipated.
- Booster doses can be given at any time before travel.

3.2 Special Risk Travel

3 Special Risks

3.2.6 Last Minute Travel

Hepatitis A

- Primary or reinforcing doses of hepatitis A vaccine can be given at any time prior to departure and will provide a significant degree of protection.

Japanese encephalitis

- A course of unlicensed Green Cross Corporation® JE vaccine should ideally be completed 10 days prior to departure in order to observe for late-onset adverse reactions. Those travelling within 10 days of the last dose are advised to remain in an area with ready access to medical care. This caution does not apply to the licensed Ixiaro® Japanese encephalitis vaccine.

- Travellers should be informed of the signs and symptoms of adverse reactions associated with Green Cross Corporation® JE vaccines, and know to seek medical care as soon as possible should they occur.

- Under exceptional circumstances, when time constraints preclude giving 3 doses of Green Cross Corporation® JE vaccine over 1 month, a 2 dose schedule at 0, and 7 to 14 days can be administered. A sub-optimal response and shorter duration of protection can result.

Table 3-7. Accelerated vaccine schedules*

Vaccine	Name of vaccine	Accelerated schedule	Comments
Hepatitis A/B	Twinrix®	0, 7, 21 days 4th dose at 12 months	Licensed for adults aged 18 years or above.
Hepatitis B	Engerix B® HB Vax Pro®	0, 1, 2 months 4th dose at 12 months	
	Engerix B®	0,7,21 days 4th dose at 12 months	Licensed for adults aged 18 years or above.
Japanese encephalitis	Green Cross Corporation®	2 doses at days: 0 and 7 to 14 or 3 doses at days: 0, 7, 14	An accelerated course of Green Cross vaccine is recommended for children aged 3 to 17 years, in exceptional circumstances, when time constraints preclude giving the course over a month. The course should be completed 10 days prior to departure, due to risk of delayed reaction.
Rabies	Rabies vaccine BP® Rabipur®	0, 7, 21 days.	
Tick-borne encephalitis	TicoVac®	2nd dose can be given 2 weeks after 1st dose. 3rd dose should be given 5 to 12 months after 2nd dose.	

* Vaccine information should be checked in the 'Green Book' and Summary of Product Characteristics; see Resource Guide: Appendix 1 – Vaccine Compendium.

3.2.6 Last Minute Travel

Vaccination Requirements

- An International Certificate of Vaccination or Prophylaxis becomes valid 10 days after the yellow fever (YF) vaccine has been given. If re-vaccination occurs within 10 years of a previous vaccine, the new certificate is valid immediately. Travellers may be refused entry, quarantined or vaccinated at the port of entry if they do not have valid certification for YF vaccination.

Malaria

- It is better to start antimalarials even with a short interval to departure. When antimalarials are started late, protection may be delayed and unprotected exposure can occur. The need for strict insect bite avoidance measures and prompt reporting of symptoms of possible malaria should be emphasised.

- Chloroquine +/- proguanil (non-prescription medication), and mosquito bite prevention measures, including insect repellent and nets, can often be purchased over-the-counter at the last minute at pharmacies, including those at many UK airports. Chloroquine +/- proguanil should ideally be started 1 week before entering an endemic area. All other antimalarials require a prescription; a travel clinic may be able provide this at short notice if a GP cannot.

- Doxycycline, or atovaquone/proguanil, is useful for last minute travellers as they can be started on the day of travel; ideally they should be started 1 to 2 days before exposure to malaria.

- A three-week trial of mefloquine (i.e. 3 doses) is normally recommended before departure to assess tolerance. Mefloquine should be avoided in last minute travellers, unless the drug has been tolerated previously. Specialist advice should be sought if alternative agents are contraindicated.

- Loading doses of antimalarials are not recommended.

- See Resource Guide: A5 – Key Resources.

3.2.7 Long-Term Travel

The long-term traveller may be defined as those travelling or residing overseas for more than 6 months. This include those residing overseas in order to work or volunteer (expatriates), those going on extended holidays (gap year/backpackers) and those visiting friends and relatives (VFRs). The type and extent of risk to their health can vary considerably.

Long-term travellers may be at increased risk due to cumulative exposure to disease, closer contact with the local environment and population, and reduced vigilance with regard to risk upon adaptation to their new environment. Longer consultation and preparation times are usually required.

*   Health professionals should take a detailed account of their exact destination (and possible onward travel), accommodation/food/water provision, and access to medical care.
*   Risk management advice should follow that of the general traveller and be tailored as described below. Long-term travellers should be strongly encouraged to apply all preventive strategies throughout their length of stay overseas.
*   Destination-specific risk management advice can be found on the NaTHNaC Country Information Pages[1] www.nathnac.org.
*   See Resource Guide: 3.2.7.

Medical Preparation

*   Comprehensive travel insurance is essential for all travellers. A full declaration of medical conditions should be made to the insurers. All equipment and planned activities should be covered.
*   The Department of Health and the Foreign and Commonwealth Office cannot accept responsibility for medical costs incurred by British citizens overseas and are unable to advise on standards of care. British Consular officers will only assist travellers in an emergency. See Resource Guide: A7 and A12 – Key Resources.
*   Travellers should check on their eligibility for an EHIC. See Resource Guide: A9 – Key Resources.
*   Specialist opinion on the advisability of long-term travel should be sought for those with pre-existing medical conditions.
*   Adequate supplies of prescription medication should be carried in order to allow sufficient time to source a reliable local supplier. Difficulties obtaining basic medical supplies can occur; arrangements to send out essential medications may need to be made. Travellers should be aware that counterfeit drugs are a risk in many areas of the world.
*   Travellers who are living long term in one place should make contact with a reputable health professional on arrival in order to discuss local and regional medical facilities and plan for a medical emergency.
*   Medical facilities may be limited and healthcare standards, facilities, advice and nature of treatment overseas will differ from that in the UK. Travel to a distant specialist centre may be required to access reliable care.

3.2 Special Risk Travel

3 Special Risks

---

1   Alternatively see Travax http://www.travax.nhs.uk/ or Fit for Travel http://www.fitfortravel.nhs.uk/

3.2.7 Long-Term Travel

- Travellers should be advised, and receive written instructions, on the use of medication for self-treatment of minor illness, and know when and how to seek medical assistance.
- Comprehensive travel medical kits should be kept in the home, at work and in vehicles. First aid training should be considered.
- Women should ensure they keep up to date with cervical and breast screening according to NHS recommendations.
- A pre-travel departure medical, including a physical and psychological assessment, is appropriate for the long-term traveller, in particular for those travelling for work. Specialist advice should be sought.
- The Institute of Occupational Health and Safety offer advice on 'keeping your staff healthy and safe abroad'. See Resource Guide: 3.2.7b.

Vaccination

- Adequate preparation time is needed for those intending to travel long term in order to complete all routine, recommended and required vaccination schedules.
- Arrangements may need to be made for booster vaccinations to be received overseas in a reliable medical facility.

Hepatitis B

- Hepatitis B vaccination should be considered for long-term travellers.

Rabies

- Long-term travellers are at increased risk of exposure to rabies during travel to endemic areas. Rabies vaccination should be considered.
- Access to post-exposure rabies immunoglobulin and vaccine is often limited and travel to a distant specialist centre may be required.
- Expatriates who keep pets should ensure that they, and their pets, are vaccinated.

Tuberculosis (TB)

- Long-term travellers to areas with a high incidence of TB are at increased of TB. Travellers should be informed of the incidence at their destination and the signs and symptoms of the disease.
- BCG vaccination should be given according to the UK schedule.

Malaria

- Long-term travellers are at risk of malaria throughout their stay, however, the risk of new adverse events from antimalarials decreases over time.
- Despite this, long-term travellers typically become less compliant with malaria prevention measures, including antimalarials. Fear of side effects, complex regimens, and erroneous perception of declining risk, conflicting advice and reduced confidence in efficacy following intercurrent fevers, all play a role. Each of these factors should be discussed in advance.
- VFRs often perceive little risk from malaria and/or believe, incorrectly, that they are immune. They also may be less able to afford long-term antimalarials. See Special Risk Traveller: 3.2.11 Visiting Friends and Relatives (VFRs).

3.2.7 Long-Term Travel

- Expatriates who are based at a single location may be more aware of the risk of malaria in their locality, able to implement mosquito bite avoidance measures in their homes, and able to establish access to reliable medical care. Despite these risk management strategies, up to 30% of expatriates in some areas develop malaria within 2 years. Many of these cases are attributed to poor compliance with antimalarials.

- Backpackers and gap year travellers are often young and inexperienced travellers, less adherent to advice, and less able to afford long-term antimalarials. They usually have less control than expatriates or VFRs over their environment.

- Issues influencing the choice of antimalarials are the same as for short-term use. In addition, considerations specific to the long-term traveller include length of stay, seasonal risk, access to reliable medical facilities for diagnosis and treatment. Licensing criteria may also influence the length of drug administration. Table 3-8 gives the Advisory Committee on Malaria Prevention (ACMP) advice on long-term antimalarial use (may differ from the SPC). See Resource Guide: A5 – Key Resources.

Table 3-8. ACMP advice on long-term antimalarial use in adults (in alphabetical order)*

Antimalarial	Advice on long-term use
Atovaquone/Proguanil	No evidence of harm in long-term use. Can be prescribed with consideration for up to 1 year, and possibly longer.
Chloroquine	Considered safe for long-term use. Ophthalmic examinations every 6 to 12 months should be considered following continuous use for 6 years or longer.
Doxycycline	No evidence of harm in long-term use. Can be prescribed safely for periods of at least up to 2 years.
Mefloquine	No evidence of harm in long-term use, if tolerated short term. Can be prescribed safely for up to 3 years, in the absence of side effects.
Proguanil	Considered safe for long-term use.

*Adapted from ACMP malaria guidelines. See Resource Guide: A5 – Key Resources. Suitable regimens are dependent on the destination. See NaTHNaC Country Information Pages[1] www.nathnac.org. Drug information should be checked in the British National Formulary (BNF); See Resource Guide: A2 – Key Resources.

---

1   Alternatively see Travax http://www.travax.nhs.uk/ or Fit for Travel http://www.fitfortravel.nhs.uk/

3.2.7 Long-Term Travel

- For long-term use, weekly regimens may increase compliance compared to daily regimens.
- Extending 'unlicensed' regimens, switching regimens, seasonal use, or standby self-treatment may be appropriate for selected individuals, but specialist advice should be sought.
- An early medical opinion for symptom assessment, at any time during their stay overseas, should be emphasised.
- Where access to health services are limited, long-term travellers should consider taking with them an emergency self-treatment kit. Advice should be tailored to the individual's circumstances.

Safety Risks

Accommodation

- Obtain secure accommodation and check regularly for hazards relating to water and power supplies as well as building structure.

Personal Safety

- Advice for 'Travelling and living overseas' is offered by the Foreign and Commonwealth Office. See Resource Guide: A13 – Key Resources.
- Register in country with the British Embassy/Consulate and register online at FCO LOCATE. See Resource Guide: A14 – Key Resources.
- Remain alert to their surroundings, take sensible precautions to ensure personal safety and regularly review local advice.

Environmental Risks

- Long-term travellers should not underestimate the time it may take to acclimatise to their new environment.

Food- and Water-borne Risks

- Traveller's adherence to food and water hygiene precautions is known to decrease over time; long-term travellers remain at risk of gastrointestinal illness. The importance of maintaining strict food, water and personal hygiene precautions over the long term should be emphasised.

Sexual Health and Blood-borne Viral Risks (BBVs)

- Long-term travellers may be more likely to engage in risky behaviour, such as unprotected sex. Protective measures should be emphasised.

Skin Health

- Individuals living in or travelling frequently to sunny climates are at increased risk of sun-related skin damage and skin cancer. Protective measures should be emphasised.
- Long-term travellers should inspect regularly for skin changes and consider a medical review on return.

3.2.7 Long-Term Travel

Psychological Health

- Long-term travellers often experience initial excitement on travelling overseas; they then may experience stress when adapting to a new culture, economy, language, and social situation. Security concerns and issues arising from their work/children/family/partner can add to this psychological impact.

- The period of time required for adjustment during long-term travel should not be underestimated. Feelings of anxiety, disorientation and loneliness are common; however, it is typical following a variable period of adjustment to find a gradual acceptance of the new culture. Coping strategies should be discussed.

- Adaptation to life on return from long-term travel can also be challenging and result in 'reverse culture shock'. A lack of confidence, motivation and feelings of disorientation can be experienced. Support from friends and family should be encouraged; referral to a specialist may be appropriate in some cases. See Resource Guide: 3.2.7c.

3.2 Special Risk Travel

3 Special Risks

3.2.8 Medical Tourism

Many people travel to access medical, surgical and dental treatments. A survey of overseas healthcare providers in 2007 reported on 50,500 medical tourists from the UK. Travellers received dental treatment (43%), cosmetic surgery (29%), elective surgery (18%) and infertility treatment (10%). They spent an estimated £161 million. India, Hungary and Turkey were amongst the most common destinations for UK patients. See Resource Guide: 3.2.8a and 3.2.8b.

Services, treatments, costs and standards vary between providers and countries. Travellers should fully understand the potential risks of travelling with a health condition and of receiving treatment overseas. Extensive research, discussion and preparation are essential prior to booking.

- Health professionals should take a detailed itinerary, including recovery period, procedure/s to be undertaken and expected standards of healthcare, in order to make an accurate risk assessment.
- Risk management advice should follow that of the general traveller and be tailored as described below.
- Destination-specific risk management advice can be found on the NaTHNaC Country Information Pages[1] www.nathnac.org.

Medical Preparation

- Comprehensive travel insurance is essential for all travellers. A full declaration of medical conditions should be made to the insurers. All equipment and planned activities should be covered.
- Pre-existing medical conditions, including those for which treatment overseas is being sought, should be stable prior to travel. The impact of travel on existing medical conditions must be considered. Specialist advice should be sought.
- Travellers should be aware that healthcare standards, facilities, advice and nature of treatment overseas differ from those in the UK.
- Travellers should only consider overseas treatment following extensive research, planning and discussion of all aspects of the care to be provided. Issues to consider include:
  - medical staffing (number, qualification, training and experience)
  - pre- and post-treatment care plans
  - success and complication rates
  - capacity for emergency procedures
  - infection control and health and safety standards
  - equipment quality and maintenance
  - administrative services
  - financial implications of receiving treatment overseas.
- Arranging treatment overseas via the internet or in response to an advertisement should not be done. Ideally, a recommendation should be received from a specialist in the UK.

---

1   Alternatively see Travax http://www.travax.nhs.uk/ or Fit for Travel http://www.fitfortravel.nhs.uk/

3.2.8 Medical Tourism

- Under European Union (EU) rules (Regulation 1408/71) UK citizens are entitled to:
  - Public sector healthcare provided in an emergency during a temporary visit to another country within the European Economic Area (EEA), using the European Health Insurance Card (EHIC).
  - Planned public sector healthcare only if prior approval has been received from a UK health authority commissioner, e.g. Primary Care Trust (PCT).
  - See Resource Guide: 3.2.8c.
- Travellers should ensure that they receive a contract with the hospital or clinic providing treatment. It should clearly document the responsibilities for, and costs of, additional treatment/extended stay, in case of complications. Responsibilities for medication and dressings, follow-up treatment if required in-country, medical repatriation and correctional treatment in the UK, should also be clarified.
- Follow-up care in the UK may be difficult to access and may not be available on the NHS.
- The Department of Health and the Foreign and Commonwealth Office, cannot accept responsibility for medical costs incurred by British citizens overseas and are unable to advise on standards of care. British Consular officers will not routinely visit British nationals who have chosen to travel overseas for medical treatment. They may be able to assist travellers in an emergency. See Resource Guide: 3.2.8d.
- Some countries may not have legislation relating to medical malpractice issues and legal redress may not be available if complications occur. Travellers should ensure that the contract they receive with a hospital or clinic details the complaints procedure.
- Counterfeit medications, including fake cosmetic surgery preparations, are common in many areas of the world.
- See the British Association of Aesthetic Plastic Surgeons Safety in Surgery information. See Resource Guide: 3.2.8e.

Vaccination
- Travel vaccinations and medications may need to be adjusted depending on type and timing of the treatment which is planned.

Hepatitis B
- Hepatitis B vaccination should be considered for those travelling in order to receive medical treatment.

Journey Risks

Fitness to Fly
- A health professional should confirm fitness to travel and fly pre- and post-treatment.

3.2 Special Risk Travel

3 Special Risks

3.2.8 Medical Tourism

Deep Vein Thrombosis (DVT)
- Immobility pre- and post-treatment increases the risk of DVT.
- Travellers should seek advice from their health professional prior to travel.
- See Risk Management: 2.3.2 Journey Risks – DVT.

Safety Risks
- Injury or illness acquired during travel may require a change to the planned treatment, and can delay recovery; travellers should consider contingency plans. Risk management strategies to avoid injury and illness should be emphasised.

Air-borne Risks
- There may be an increased risk of exposure to respiratory infections including influenza, pneumococcal pneumonia, tuberculosis, measles/mumps/rubella in healthcare settings. Those travelling in order to receive treatment should be vaccinated according to the UK schedule.

Sexual Health and Blood-borne Viral Risks (BBVs)
- Infection control and blood transfusion standards vary worldwide.
- Travellers should be informed of the incidence of BBVs at their destination and of the risk of exposure to BBVs when receiving invasive treatment overseas.

Skin Health
- Good wound care is essential following surgery in order to avoid infections, especially in hot and humid conditions.

Psychological Health
- Those travelling in order to receive treatment should fully understand, and prepare as much as possible, for the psychological challenges they may face.
- Language and cultural differences may impact on the overall experience and outcome.

3.2.9 Natural Disasters

Natural disasters (e.g. hurricanes, floods, tsunamis and earthquakes) can strike without warning. Individuals may travel to an area affected by a natural disaster to see friends and relatives or to volunteer/work, and often at short notice. See Special Risk Travel: 3.2.6 Last Minute Travel. Those wishing to assist in areas affected by natural disasters should not travel independently but contact appropriate aid/charity agencies for guidance on how best they can help. Travelling to an affected area without adequate preparation may stretch already challenged local emergency services.

- Risk management advice should follow that of the general traveller and be tailored as described below.
- Destination-specific risk management advice can be found on the NaTHNaC Country Information Pages[1] www.nathnac.org.
- See World Health Organization (WHO), Natural disaster profiles, Resource Guide: 3.2.9a.
- A Health Information Sheet, *Natural disasters – advice for travellers to affected areas*, is available to download from NaTHNaC[1]. See Resource Guide: A26 – Key Resources.

Medical Preparation
- Comprehensive travel insurance is essential for all travellers. A full declaration of medical conditions should be made to the insurers. All equipment and planned activities should be covered.
- There may be severe damage to health facilities together with shortages of surgical supplies and medicines. Travellers should carry a personal travel medical kit, including sterile medical equipment.

Vaccination

Cholera, hepatitis A, typhoid
- Damage to sewage systems and contamination of local water supplies can increase the risk of cholera, hepatitis A and typhoid. Vaccination should be considered.

Hepatitis B
- There can be an increased risk of injury, and possible exposure to bodily fluids when caring for injured persons. Personal protective measures should be used. Hepatitis B vaccination should be considered.

Rabies
- Travellers should avoid contact with wild or domestic animal, including bats.
- Access to post-exposure immunoglobulin and vaccine is often limited. Pre-exposure rabies vaccination should be considered.
- Urgent medical attention should be sought if bitten. Travel to a distant specialist centre can be required to access reliable post-exposure care. Insurance, including repatriation coverage, is essential.

Tetanus
- There can be an increased risk of injury. Tetanus vaccination should be up to date according to the UK schedule.

3.2 Special Risk Travel

3 Special Risks

3.2.9 Natural Disasters

Safety Risks

Accommodation

- Accommodation may be basic and facilities lacking.

Personal Safety

- Civil unrest can occur, resulting in increased security risks to people and their property. Travellers should consult the FCO for up-to-date safety and security advice, not travel until advised that it is safe to do so, register their trip with FCO LOCATE and follow local safety instructions carefully. See Resource Guide: A14 – Key Resources.
- Humanitarian workers should remain in contact with their organisation at all times.

Environmental Risks

- The risk of injury after a natural disaster is high. Hazards from downed power lines, structural damage to buildings, roads and basic services each pose a risk.
- Toxic industrial chemicals and hazardous waste may have been released during the devastation.
- Personal protective equipment should be considered.
- The body of a person killed as a result of a disaster does not pose a risk for infection. See Resource Guide: 3.2.9b.

Heat / Cold

- Exposure to extremes of temperature can occur. Travellers should wear appropriate clothing, remain well hydrated and use high factor sunscreen where appropriate.

Food- and Water-borne Risks

- The risk of gastrointestinal illness is increased by unsanitary living conditions, damage to sewage systems, flooding and limited supplies of clean drinking water.
- Personal hygiene may be difficult to maintain; alcohol-based hand sanitisers can be used.
- Reliable sources of bottled water may not be available and water purification may be necessary. Boiling water is not always practical; combining chlorine treatment with filtration of water may be more appropriate.
- Travellers should carry medication for self-treatment of gastrointestinal illness and know when to seek a medical opinion.

Vector-borne Risks

- Flooding and areas of standing water increase the risk for outbreaks of insect-borne diseases. Travellers should take insect bite avoidance measures. Appropriate vaccination and antimalarials should be given.

3.2.9 Natural Disasters

- Natural habitats of animals, snakes, rats and bats can be disturbed and result in closer contact with humans and increased risk of disease transmission.
- Travellers can be at risk of leptospirosis if wading in floodwater. Protective clothing should be worn to reduce direct contact with rodents, sewage or contaminated water. Pre-exposure chemoprophylaxis can be offered if such contact is unavoidable: Doxycycline 200mg weekly, commencing 1 to 2 days prior to exposure, and continued while at risk.
- Travellers should be aware of potential risks and advised to wear protective footwear and clothing.

Air-borne Risks
- Dust inhalation can be a risk for travellers to areas with structural building damage. Personal protective equipment including a mask may be useful.

Skin Health
- Care should be advised if wading in flood waters to reduce the chance of injury. Protective clothing and footwear should be worn, and wounds covered to reduce secondary infections with bacteria such as *Vibrio vulnificus* in areas flooded by salt/sea water.

Psychological Health
- The potential psychological effects of travel in an area affected by natural disaster should not be underestimated. Psychological preparation is essential prior to travel.
- Psychological support, before, during and after travel, should be offered by organisations to those who volunteer/work in disaster settings.

3.2 Special Risk Travel

3 Special Risks

3.2.10 Pilgrimage (Hajj/Umrah)

The Hajj is an annual pilgrimage to Mecca (Makkah) in Saudi Arabia, the birthplace of the prophet Muhammad. Every Muslim, provided they are fit and financially able, is expected to undertake the Hajj at least once in a lifetime.

The Hajj takes place between the 8th and the 12th day of the last month of the Islamic lunar calendar. This calendar is shorter than the Gregorian solar calendar used in the UK, therefore the Hajj date varies from year to year. It is the largest annual mass gathering in the world, attracting over 2 million people. Umrah is an individual act of pilgrimage, which is part of the Hajj, but can also be undertaken at any time of the year.

The government of Saudi Arabia applies strict regulations for travel for the Hajj and Umrah. Pilgrims should familiarise themselves with visa and passport requirements and be aware that these can change from year to year. Pilgrims should only use a travel agent approved by the Saudi Arabia Ministry of Hajj. See Resource Guide: 3.2.10a. Visa applicants must submit proof of their vaccination status at the time of their application: See Vaccination Requirements below. Those intending to travel to Hajj/Umrah from the UK also should check Resource Guide: 3.2.10 Websites.

- Risk management advice should follow that of the general traveller and be tailored as described below.
- Destination-specific risk management advice can be found on the NaTHNaC Country Information Pages[1] www.nathnac.org.
- See Resource Guide: 3.2.10.
- A Health Information Sheet, *Hajj and Umrah – advice for pilgrims*, is available to download from NaTHNaC[1]. See Resource Guide: A26 – Key Resources.

Medical Preparation

- Comprehensive travel insurance is essential for all travellers. A full declaration of medical conditions should be made to the insurers. All equipment and planned activities should be covered. Sharia compliant travel insurance is available.
- Performing the rituals of the Hajj and Umrah is demanding and often involves walking long distances in hot weather. Pilgrims must ensure that they are as physically fit as possible.
- Access to medical facilities may be limited. A travel medical kit should be carried. Pilgrims should be advised, and receive written instructions, on the use of medication for self-treatment of minor illness, and know when and how to seek medical assistance.

Vaccination
Diphtheria/poliomyelitis/tetanus

- Travellers whose last dose of diphtheria, poliomyelitis or tetanus was more than 10 years ago, should receive a booster, using the trivalent tetanus, diphtheria and polio vaccine.

Hepatitis B

- One of the rites of Hajj is male head shaving. Saudi authorities provide licensed barbers with a new blade to use for each pilgrim. Other barbers may not conform to such standards.

1   Alternatively see Travax http://www.travax.nhs.uk/ or Fit for Travel http://www.fitfortravel.nhs.uk/

3.2.10 Pilgrimage (Hajj/Umrah)

- Shaving with a previously used blade carries a risk of hepatitis B and other blood-borne viruses.
- Pilgrims should be advised to use licensed barbers and consider taking a supply of disposable razors.
- Hepatitis B vaccination should be considered for all pilgrims.

Influenza

- Influenza has occurred during the Hajj.
- Pilgrims in higher-risk groups according to UK guidance should receive annual vaccination.
- In 2009 the Ministry of Health of Saudi Arabia required that all pilgrims received a seasonal influenza vaccine.

Meningococcal meningitis

- Meningococcal meningitis has occurred during the Hajj and has spread to other countries in association with returning pilgrims.
- Vaccination is advised for personal protection and is a visa requirement for all pilgrims.

Tuberculosis (TB)

- Pilgrims can be at risk of acquiring TB due to close contact with infectious pilgrims.
- The current UK recommendations for BCG vaccination should be followed.
- Pilgrims should be informed of the signs and symptoms of TB and know when to seek medical advice.

Yellow fever (YF)

- YF is not a risk in Saudi Arabia. However pilgrims may travel on to YF risk areas. There is a certificate requirement for pilgrims arriving from YF endemic countries.

Vaccination Requirements

- The government of Saudi Arabia regularly reviews and revises the vaccination requirements for Hajj and Umrah. It is essential that pilgrims check, and can prove that they have met the requirements for the year of their pilgrimage at the time of their visa application. See Resource Guide: 3.2.10a.
- In recent years, proof of vaccination from all or certain specified groups of travellers has been required for meningococcal meningitis ACW135Y, polio and YF. In 2009 there was also the requirement for seasonal influenza vaccination.
- Certain pilgrims, for example, those travelling from polio endemic countries may also be required to be vaccinated again on arrival in Saudi Arabia.
- Health professionals should ensure that they use up-to-date resources when advising pilgrims. See Resource Guide: 3.2.10.

Malaria

- Malaria is not normally present at any of the Hajj or Umrah sites. However, malaria is a risk in some other areas of Saudi Arabia.

3.2 Special Risk Travel

3 Special Risks

3.2.10 Pilgrimage (Hajj/Umrah)

- Pilgrims may plan to travel before or after Hajj or Umrah to other countries with a malaria risk and should receive appropriate prevention advice.

Safety Risks

Transport Safety

- Trauma and road traffic accidents are a major cause of mortality and morbidity during the Hajj and Umrah, due to the volume of traffic.
- Travellers should ensure that they carefully follow road safety measures.

Accommodation

- Due to the fire risk, cooking in tents is prohibited; designated cooking areas should be used.
- Pilgrims must familiarise themselves with emergency evacuation procedures.

Personal Safety

- Serious injuries have occurred as a result of stampedes during activities such as the stoning rite. Pilgrims should be encouraged to proceed calmly to religious sites at their allocated times and follow local safety advice. Elderly or incapacitated pilgrims may wish to consider appointing a proxy for the performance of the stoning rite.
- Minor injuries are common, particularly to the feet.
- Care should be taken with personal possessions as theft is a risk.
- British pilgrims should carry details of their UK tour operator, Saudi representative and register their trip with FCO LOCATE. See Resource Guide: A14 – Key Resources.
- The FCO send a British Hajj Delegation (BHD) to Saudi Arabia each year to assist UK Muslims undertaking the Hajj. See Resource Guide: 3.2.10b.

Environmental Risks

Heat/Cold

- Extremes of temperature occur throughout the year in Saudi Arabia.
- Pilgrims should ensure that they avoid over-exertion, take frequent rest breaks, seek shade whenever possible and drink plenty of bottled or purified water.

Sun

- Travel to Makkah before the start of Hajj should be considered in order to allow a period of heat acclimatisation.
- It is custom to keep exposed skin to a minimum; high factor sun protection should be used.
- Men are prohibited from directly covering their heads during pilgrimage. Use of an umbrella for shade is permitted and should be encouraged.

Food- and Water-borne Risks

- It is usual for foodstuffs to be prohibited with the exception of canned or sealed foods sufficient for one person for the road journey.

3.2.10 Pilgrimage (Hajj/Umrah)

- Pilgrims should be advised to take food and water hygiene precautions. Toilet and washing facilities may be basic.
- Dehydration can occur as a result of the heat or diarrhoea. Children, the elderly and those with chronic medical conditions are more vulnerable to dehydration.
- Pilgrims should ensure they remain well hydrated and carry fluids for maintaining hydration and medications for self-treatment of gastrointestinal illness. See Box 2-7 in The Pre-Travel Health Consultation Section 2.
- The importance of seeking prompt medical attention for symptoms that do not promptly resolve should be discussed.

Vector-borne Risks

- Pilgrims should be advised to practise insect bite avoidance measures.

Air-borne Risks

- Respiratory diseases are easily transmitted in the crowded conditions of Hajj or Umrah.
- Personal hygiene and respiratory precautions should be emphasised. Pilgrims are advised not to attend pilgrimage if they are unwell.

Sexual Health and Blood-borne Viral Risks (BBVs)

- Sexual contact is prohibited during Hajj/Umrah.

Female Travellers

- Menstruating women are not permitted to perform certain parts of the Hajj/Umrah.
- Prior to travel women may wish to discuss the use of medication to delay menstruation.

Skin Health

- The Hajj and Umrah involve rituals that include long periods of standing, walking and physical activities in hot weather.
- Minor injuries to the feet are common. Desert sand and marble can reach very high temperatures and may burn bare feet. Pilgrims should wear good quality, comfortable, properly fitting, protective footwear. Footwear must be removed during times of prayer. Pilgrims are advised to carry footwear in a bag.
- Sweating promotes skin infections. Advice should be given on maintaining good foot health including the importance of keeping feet clean and dry and treating cuts/abrasions promptly.
- A self-treatment kit for minor injuries and skin infections should be carried.

Psychological Health

- Pilgrims should recognise and anticipate, as far as possible, the mental as well as the physical challenges of pilgrimage; potential sources of support should be identified.

3.2.11 Visiting Friends and Relatives (VFRs)

The term 'VFRs' refers to migrants from low-income countries that reside in high-income countries and return to their country of origin to visit friends and relatives. Second and third generation ethnic travellers can also be termed VFRs.

- Risk management advice should follow that of the general traveller and be tailored as described below.
- Destination-specific risk management advice can be found on the NaTHNaC Country Information Pages[1] www.nathnac.org.
- See Resource Guide: 3.2.11.

 Medical Preparation

- Comprehensive travel insurance is essential for all travellers. A full declaration of medical conditions should be made to the insurers. All equipment and planned activities should be covered.
- VFRs may not present for travel health advice. Health professionals should enquire about travel plans during any consultation with this group.
- VFRs (adults and children) may not have completed routine vaccination according to the UK schedule. The travel health consultation provides an opportunity to update them.
- Child VFRs are often at higher risk for travel-associated morbidity, due to the nature of their journey and because their parents may not have sought appropriate travel health advice.
- Language can be a barrier to an effective consultation. Appropriate use of an interpreter should be made and written advice provided in the traveller's native language.
- See Health Protection Agency (HPA) report: Foreign travel-associated illness – a focus on those visiting friends and relatives. See Resource Guide: 3.2.11a.
- See Resource Guide: 3.2.11b.

 Vaccination

Hepatitis A

- First generation VFRs who have been brought up in endemic areas are often immune to hepatitis A; however this is changing as standards of hygiene improve in some areas of the world. Natural immunity cannot be assumed.
- Travellers with a history of jaundice without documentation of hepatitis A infection can be offered hepatitis A serology. If time is short and serology is not possible, vaccination should be given when appropriate.
- Second and third generation VFRs who were born in the UK will not have developed immunity and should be offered vaccination when appropriate.

Hepatitis B

- Hepatitis B vaccination should be considered, as appropriate for the destination.

3.2.11 Visiting Friends and Relatives (VFRs)

Tuberculosis (TB)

- The majority of cases of TB in the UK occur in non-UK born persons.
- VFRs may be at risk of acquiring TB due to close contact with friends or relatives with TB.
- VFRs should be vaccinated with BCG according to UK recommendations as appropriate to their age and destination.
- Children under the age of 16 years, with a parent or grandparent who was born in a country where the annual incidence of TB is 40 cases/100,000 population or greater, should receive BCG vaccination. Children aged from 6 years to under 16 should be tuberculin tested before receiving BCG.
- Previously unvaccinated travellers under the age of 16 should be offered BCG if living or working with local persons for more than 3 months in a country where the annual incidence of TB is 40/100,000 or greater.
- VFRs should be informed of the signs and symptoms of TB and know when to seek a medical opinion.

Typhoid/paratyphoid

- Rates of imported typhoid and paratyphoid into the UK are highest amongst VFRs, in particular amongst those who had travelled to South Asia.
- Typhoid vaccination should be given, as appropriate for the destination.

Malaria

- Rates of imported malaria are highest amongst VFRs.
- VFRs may mistakenly believe that they are immune to malaria and therefore not take or comply with antimalarial advice, and delay seeking medical assistance if they become ill.
- Advice about malaria prevention, including compliance with antimalarials, should be emphasised. VFRs should know when to seek medical assistance.
- The cost of antimalarials can be a barrier to their use for some travellers.

Food- and Water-borne Risks

- Advice on food and water hygiene must be tailored to the traveller taking into account cultural expectations at meal times.

Sexual Health and Blood-borne Viral Risks (BBVs)

- In 2008, an estimated 66% of newly diagnosed HIV cases in the UK, who were infected heterosexually, were of black African ethnicity. Of these, 74% acquired their infection overseas, the majority in sub-Saharan Africa. VFRs should be informed of the risks of sexually transmitted infections (STIs) and protective measures that can be taken to reduce these risks. See Disease Guide Section 5.

Psychological Health

- VFRs travelling to/from their family's country of origin should be prepared for the psychological challenges they may experience.

3.2 Special Risk Travel

3 Special Risks

The Post-Travel Consultation

Section 4 – contents

4.1 Introduction

This section aims to direct the healthcare professional towards a systematic approach to the initial management of the returned traveller presenting to a primary care setting. Providers also need to understand the public health issues for some imported infections. Readers are referred to Algorithms 4-1 to 4-8.

Around 8% of travellers to low-income regions of the world need medical attention during or after travel. Unwell, returned travellers typically present within the first few months of their return. However, some infections have long incubations periods and travellers may not develop symptoms for several months or occasionally years after their time abroad. In some circumstances, where the consequences of unrecognised disease are a concern, screening for specific infections is appropriate.

In the UK, primary care often provides the first assessment of the ill returned traveller. This can be challenging to those unfamiliar with the country from which the traveller has returned and the health issues associated with that destination. Keys to developing a differential diagnosis include:

- A detailed clinical history, including pre-travel preventive measures.
- Knowledge of geographic risk of disease (destination-specific diagnoses). See NaTHNaC Country Information Pages[1] www.nathnac.org.
- Incubation periods of infections. See Disease Guide Section 5.
- Frequency of specific diagnoses in returned travellers. See Resource Guide: 4.1.1 and 4.1.2.

Early referral to a specialist centre for advice and management is essential for those practioners with little or no experience in managing ill returned travellers. See Resource Guide: C – Source of Specialist Advice.

Doctors in England and Wales have a statutory duty to notify a 'Proper Officer' of the Local Authority of suspected cases of certain notifiable infectious diseases (NOIDS). If a notifiable disease is suspected, the Medical Practitioner should complete an official Formal Notification certificate immediately and return it to their local health authority. See Disease Guide Section 5 and Resource Guide: 5.1.

4 The Post-Travel Consultation

---

1 Alternatively see Travax http://www.travax.nhs.uk/ or Fit for Travel http://www.fitfortravel.nhs.uk/

4.2 The Ill Returned Traveller

The following four syndromes are most commonly seen in ill returned travellers:

- **Febrile illness** – Algorithm 4-1.
- **Diarrhoeal illness** – Algorithm 4-2.
- **Dermatological conditions** – Algorithm 4-3.
- **Respiratory illness** – Algorithm 4-4.

Any traveller presenting with a febrile illness who has travelled to a malarious area must be urgently assessed for malaria. See Algorithm 4-1. Malaria can be rapidly fatal if the diagnosis is delayed; prompt diagnosis on the day the traveller presents with a fever is essential. Since 2005, the number of imported malaria cases in the UK has ranged from 1,370 to 1,758. Those visiting friends and relatives account for more than 70% of cases. Most had not taken antimalarials. Fifty percent of travellers with febrile illness after return do not have a specific cause identified. See Resource Guide: 4.2.1 to 4.2.4.

Gastrointestinal infections are the most common illnesses affecting travellers. Many diarrhoeal illnesses are self-limiting or can be managed through self-treatment, but others will need investigation and physician management. See Algorithm 4-2. See Resource Guide: 4.2.5 and 4.2.6.

Localised skin infection, or generalised rash from a systemic viral illness, is common. Bacterial skin infections often result from difficulties in maintaining skin hygiene following cuts or insect bites. Other skin problems to consider are cutaneous larva migrans, allergic reactions, leishmaniasis and myiasis, and rashes associated with systemic infections, e.g. meningococcaemia, dengue and rickettsial infections. See Algorithm 4-3. See Resource Guide: 4.2.7 and 4.2.8.

Respiratory diseases often present as self-limited upper respiratory tract infections. A chest X-ray should be performed for those with lower respiratory tract infections and empiric antibiotic therapy considered. The clinical history can be helpful when determining the aetiology of lower respiratory tract infections. See Algorithm 4-4. See Resource Guide: 4.2.9.

For returned travellers with potential exposures to HIV, rabies or schistosomiasis. See The Well Returned Traveller (4.3).

4.2 The Ill Returned Traveller

Algorithm 4-1. Febrile illness

Fever in the returned traveller *

Has the traveller been to a malarial area?
See NaTHNaC Country Information Pages¹ www.nathnac.org.
If yes, **urgent** thick and thin films. Confirm result on the same day.
If positive, refer to specialist centre. See Resource Guide: C – Sources of
Specialist Advice.
If negative, consider blood films daily for 2 more days.

Does this person have severe sepsis?
If meningococcal disease suspected, give penicillin or ceftriaxone and refer to
hospital immediately.
If this traveller within 3 weeks of return, consider infections that may require special
infection control measures e.g. viral haemorrhagic fevers, SARS (consider urgent
referral to specialist centre).

Respiratory illness?
See Algorithm 4-4

Diarrhoeal illness?
See Algorithm 4-2

History: Travel history (duration, areas visited), activities (e.g. fresh water exposure, food sources, STI risks), accommodation (nets, screens available), illness and treatment during travel, pre-trip preparation (vaccinations and antimalarials), pre-existing health conditions.
Examination: General, with attention to temperature, level of consciousness, lymphadenopathy, skin rashes, ulcers of eschars, neck stiffness, organomegaly.
Initial Investigations to consider: FBC, U&Es, LFTs, blood cultures, urinalysis and CXR, stool culture and microscopy for ova & parasite, serum for later serology.
Consider: traveller or migrant, incubation period, geographic risk, frequency of syndrome in returned travellers.

Sub-Saharan Africa
consider:

Undifferentiated Fever
Malaria
HIV
Enteric fever
CHIK
VHF

Fever with rash or eschar
HIV
Rickettsial infection
Schistosomisis (acute)
VHF

Fever with jaundice
VHF
YF
Hepatitis, viral

Fever with organomegaly
Amoebic liver abscess
Trypanosomiasis
Visceral leishmaniasis
Hepatitis, viral

South Asia
consider:

Undifferentiated Fever
Malaria
Dengue
HIV
CHIK
Enteric fever
Leptospirosis

Fever with rash
Dengue
HIV

Fever with jaundice
Hepatitis, viral
Leptospirosis

Fever with organomegaly
Leptospirosis
Visceral leishmaniasis
Amoebic liver abscess

South East Asia
consider:

Undifferentiated Fever
Malaria
Dengue
Enteric fever
CHIK
HIV
Leptospirosis

Fever with rash
Dengue
HIV

Fever with jaundice
Hepatitis, viral
Leptospirosis

Fever with organomegaly
Amoebic liver abscess

South and Central America & Caribbean
consider:

Undifferentiated Fever
Malaria
Dengue
HIV
Enteric fever
Leptospirosis

Fever with rash
Dengue
HIV

Fever with jaundice
Hepatitis, viral
Leptospirosis
YF

North Africa, Middle East & Mediterranean
consider:

Undifferentiated Fever
Brucellosis
Enteric fever
HIV

Fever with rash or eschar
HIV
Rickettsial infection

Fever with organomegaly
Brucellosis
Leptospirosis
Visceral leishmaniasis

Fever with jaundice
Hepatitis

Western Pacific
consider:

Undifferentiated Fever
Malaria
Dengue

Fever with jaundice
Hepatitis, viral

* This algorithm is not an exhaustive list of diagnoses, but is a guide for clinician to consider likely possibilities. For a full discussion see Resource Guide: 4.2.1.

¹ Alternatively see Travax http://www.travax.nhs.uk/ or Fit for Travel http://www.fitfortravel.nhs.uk/

4.2 The Ill Returned Traveller

Algorithm 4-2. Diarrhoeal illness

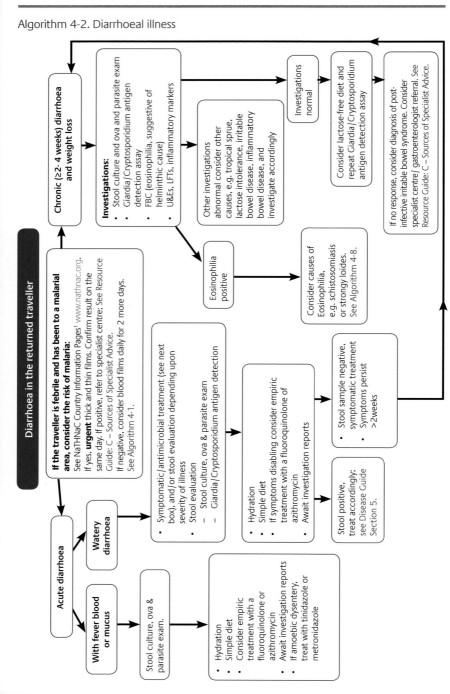

¹ Alternatively see Travax http://www.travax.nhs.uk/ or Fit for Travel http://www.fitfortravel.nhs.uk/

4.2 The Ill Returned Traveller

Algorithm 4-3. Dermatological conditions

Dermatological conditions in the returned traveller						
Bacterial Skin infections	Photosensitivity disorders	Creeping Eruptions	Ulcers	Pruritic conditions	Systemic rash with fever	Urticaria
Infected insect bites	Sunburn	Cutaneous larva migrans	Infected insect bites	Insect bites	**Consider referral to specialist centre:**	Many non-travel/infection related causes, e.g. drug allergy.
Impetigo	Long-term sun exposure: keratoses and skin cancers	Scabies	Cutaneous leishmaniasis	Contact dermatitis	HIV seroconversion illness	
Cellulitis	Drug induced photosensitivity e.g. doxycycline	Strongyloidiasis (larva currens)	Rickettsial tick eschar	Dermatophytosis	Drug reactions	Consider infection related:
Folliculitis		Loiasis	Spider bites	Cutaneous larva migrans	Dengue	Helminth infections, e.g. acute schistosomiasis or strongyloidiasis
		Gnathostomiasis	Cutaneous diphtheria	Scabies	CHIK	
			Cutaneous anthrax	Cercarial dermatitis	Measles	
			Mycobacterium ulcerans	Marine creature contact dermatitis	Rubella	
			Sexually transmitted infections		VHF	
			Genital herpes		Rickettsial infection	
					Syphilis	
					Meningococcaemia	

4.2 The Ill Returned Traveller

Algorithm 4-4. Respiratory illness

Respiratory illness in the returned traveller

- **Has the traveller been to a malarial area?**
  See NaTHNaC Country Information Pages[1] www.nathnac.org.
  If yes, **urgent** thick and thin films. Confirm result on the same day
  If positive, refer to specialist centre. See Resource Guide: C –
  Sources of Specialist Advice.
  If negative, consider blood films daily for 2 more days.
  If the traveller is within 7 days of return consider infections that
  may require special infection control measures e.g. pandemic
  influenza, SARS (consider urgent referral to specialist centre).

- **History:** Detailed travel history, activities, fresh water, bat or farm
  exposure, cruise ship travel.
  Illness during travel and treatment received, details of pre-trip planning
  (vaccinations and antimalarials), determine pre-existing health issues.
  Are symptoms other than respiratory illness and fever present?
- See Algorithm 4-1.
- Consider public health issues and infection control measures.
- **Investigations:** FBC, U&Es, LFTs and CXR.

Lower respiratory tract infections
Typical aetiologies in travellers:

- Viral (e.g. seasonal and pandemic influenza)
- Pneumococcal infection
- Legionnaires disease (hotel, cruise ship)
- Tuberculosis (prolonged travel to country with >40 cases / 100,000 TB, healthcare workers)

Other uncommon to rare aetiologies:

- Influenza (H5N1 "bird flu"), SARS
- Histoplasmosis & coccidioidomycosis (dust and bat exposure)
- Coxiella burnetti (animal farm exposure)
- Paragonimiasis (ingestion of infected raw crabs or crayfish in SE Asia)
- Loeffler's syndrome (ascaris, hookworm, strongyloides), Katayama fever (schistosomiasis)
- Tropical pulmonary eosinophilia; see Resource Guide: 4.3.2 and 4.3.3.
- Filarial infections (wheeze, fever, infiltrates on CXR, eosinophilia; exposure in South and South East Asia)

Upper respiratory tract infections
including sinusitis, pharyngitis, tonsillitis

Aetiologies to consider include:
Viruses, streptococcal pharyngitis

Rare:
Diphtheria (with pharyngeal membrane); travel to areas
such as South East Asia, Indian subcontinent)

Considerations:
Does the patient need hospital admission?
Is there a public health risk? Do they need isolating?
Does the patient need treatment or is the illness likely to be self limiting?

Empirical therapy? Consider amoxicillin, clarithromycin

Does clinical picture suggest alternative diagnosis and management?
See Disease Guide Section 5. Consider referral to a specialist centre. See Resource Guide: C – Sources of Specialist Advice.

4.3 The Well Returned Traveller

Some travellers present to their GP without symptoms, but are concerned that they may have been exposed to one or more infections during travel and request either screening or prophylaxis. This group includes:

- **Asymptomatic post-travel screening** – Algorithm 4-5.
- **Schistosomiasis screening** – Algorithm 4-6.
- **HIV post-exposure prophylaxis** – Algorithm 4-7.

Management of possible rabies exposure for travellers returned to the UK

A possible exposure to rabies from a terrestrial animal or bat should be treated urgently.

- A fresh wound or point of contact should be cleaned and disinfected with soap and copious amounts of water.
- Assess the traveller's past and recent rabies vaccination history (including any doses received since exposure) and type of rabies vaccine given.
- Assess the nature of the exposure, e.g. bite, scratch, saliva, mucous membrane, and whether the skin was broken.
- Assess the patient's immune status to tetanus and consider appropriate antibiotic if bacterial wound infection is a concern.

Consider rabies vaccine and rabies immunoglobulin. Health professionals should contact their relevant health protection agency for advice. See Resource Guide: 5.7.

Post-travel eosinophilia

Post-travel eosinophilia in a well traveller can also be a challenge. Those potentially exposed to schistosomiasis can be screened. See Algorithm 4-6. Other helminth infections including strongyloides should be excluded with a concentrated stool examination and strongyloides serology respectively. Additional investigations depend on the countries visited and referral to special centre should be considered. See Algorithm 4-8. See Resource Guide: 4.3.2 and 4.3.3.

4 The Post-Travel Consultation

4.3 The Well Returned Traveller

Algorithm 4-5. Asymptomatic post-travel screening

Asymptomatic screening of the returned traveller

Assess necessity for screening:
Was the traveller exposed to specific health risks whilst abroad?
Is there a need to alleviate the traveller's concerns?
Has there been an appropriate interval between presentation for screening and the end of the trip to allow detection of latent disease?

Clinical History: Geography, activities, pre-travel immunisations, antimalarials and compliance.
Are there specific disease exposures that may be asymptomatic, based on travel destination and activities?

Health: pre-existing health conditions, illness and treatment during travel, e.g. fever, diarrhoea, rash

Specific enquiries regarding risks:

Food and water general hygiene; ingestion of raw meat or fish, and unpasteurised dairy products

Fresh water contacts e.g. schistosomiasis; see Algorithm 4-6

Soil contact e.g. strongyloides, hookworm

Visits to caves e.g. histoplasmosis and rabies (rare)

Sexual contacts and risks e.g. HIV, syphilis, chlamydia

Blood-borne virus risks (injuries, blood transfusions, tattoos, piercings) e.g. HIV, hepatitis B and C

Healthcare worker e.g. needle stick injury, clinical setting with high rates TB

Game parks and walking safari risk of ticks and tsetse fly bites, e.g. rickettsial infections and trypanosomiasis

Equatorial forests: onchocerciasis, loiasis in Central and West Africa

Accommodation: e.g. mud huts in South America (risk of Trypanosomiasis cruzi infection).

Initial Investigations:
Full blood count
Urea & Electrolytes, liver function tests (C Reactive Protein)
Urinalysis
Stool for ova and parasites
Schistosoma serology (if travel to risk areas in Africa)

Tailor investigations based on clinical history
See relevant disease chapters for appropriate investigations
Consider referral to specialist centre. See Resource Guide: C – Sources of Specialist Advice.

4.3 The Well Returned Traveller

Algorithm 4-6. Schistosomiasis screening

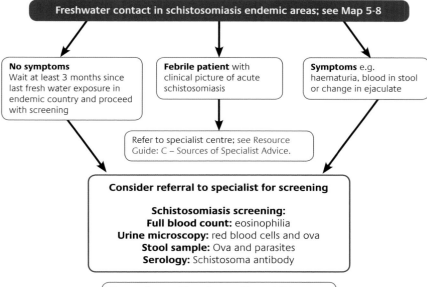

4.3 The Well Returned Traveller

Algorithm 4-7. HIV post-exposure prophylaxis (PEP) in adults

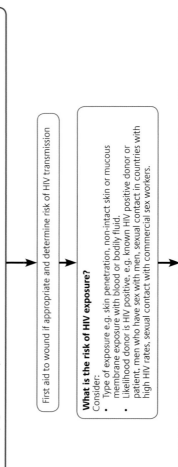

Post-exposure HIV screening

Potential exposure to HIV within 72 hours (generally not recommended after this time; seek specialist advice if >72 hours) e.g.:
- needle stick injury.
- needle shared by injecting drug users.
- receipt of blood or blood products.
- procedures in which contaminated medical instruments may have been used (e.g. tattooing, body piercing).
- unprotected sex (vaginal and anal).

First aid to wound if appropriate and determine risk of HIV transmission

What is the risk of HIV exposure?
Consider:
- Type of exposure e.g. skin penetration, non-intact skin or mucous membrane exposure with blood or bodily fluid.
- Likelihood donor is HIV positive, e.g. known HIV positive donor or patient, men who have sex with men, sexual contact in countries with high HIV rates, sexual contact with commercial sex workers.

If risk of HIV exposure is considered significant and HIV PEP considered appropriate:
- **Take PEP as soon as possible after exposure.**
- **Arrange for donor to be tested for HIV and other blood-borne viruses if possible.**

Refer to current HIV PEP guidance:
- HIV post-exposure prophylaxis: guidance from the UK Chief Medical Officers' Expert Advisory Group on AIDS – see Resource Guide: 3.2.5a
- UK guideline for the use of post-exposure prophylaxis for HIV following sexual exposure – see Resource Guide: 4.3.1

Counsel the individual about HIV testing immediately following an exposure event and again at the 12 week follow up.

4.3 The Well Returned Traveller

Algorithm 4-8. Post-travel eosinophilia

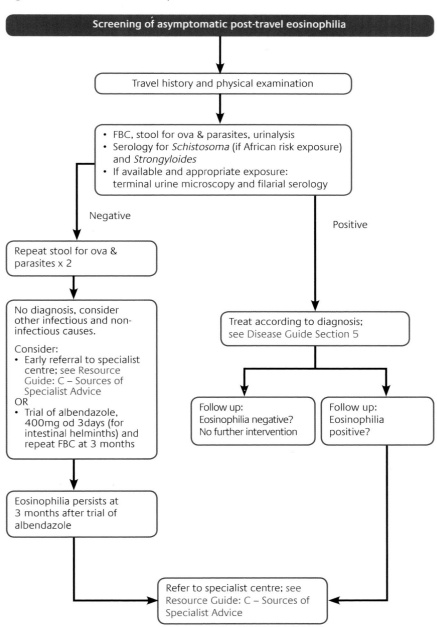

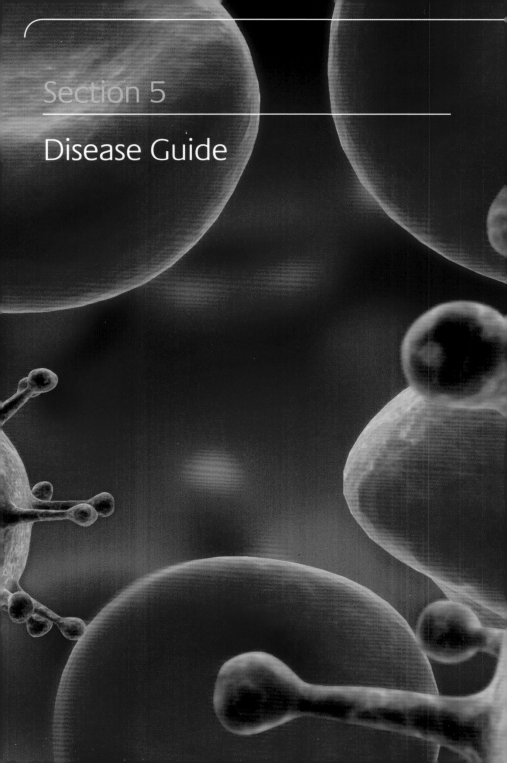

Section 5

Disease Guide

Section 5 – contents

Section 5 – contents

Section 5 – contents

Anthrax

Bacillus anthracis, gram-positive spore-forming bacteria. Bacterial infection of humans and animals.

Risk Assessment

Epidemiology
- Worldwide distribution. Occurs in wild and domestic mammals in Africa, Asia and parts of Europe and the Americas.

Exposure
- Persons acquire anthrax following cutaneous contact with anthrax spores from the hide, hair or wool of animals (usually an occupational risk); through inhalation of spores; or through ingestion of spores in contaminated meat.
- Worldwide, cutaneous anthrax is most common causing >90% of cases.
- Anthrax is rare in travellers.
- Travellers at higher risk include those working with infected animals, carcases, hides or animal products such as wool, bone meal or tallow, some laboratory and construction workers.
- There is concern about deliberate release.

Imported Cases
From 1981 to 2006 there were 18 cases of cutaneous anthrax in England and Wales: 1 was acquired abroad.

Signs and Symptoms
- **Cutaneous anthrax:** 1 to 7 days after exposure a raised, itchy lesion appears and develops into a painless ulcer with a black centre (eschar) and extensive local swelling. Regional lymphadenopathy can occur. Untreated, 20% can progress to bacteraemia and death.
- **Inhalation anthrax:** Non-specific prodrome of fever, cough and headache, followed by rapid onset of fever, dyspnoea, and shock with enlargement of mediastinal lymph nodes, haemorrhage, systemic toxicity. This form is usually fatal if untreated.
- **Intestinal anthrax:** Least common form. Severe abdominal pain, anorexia, fever, malaise, nausea and vomiting with bloody or watery diarrhoea. Bacteraemia develops 2 to 3 days after onset of symptoms. Fatality rate is 20% to 60%.
- Meningitis may complicate any of the syndromes and is usually fatal.

Risk Management
- Avoid contact with infected animals and animal products.
- Anthrax vaccine is reserved for those at occupational risk and in military service.

Anthrax

5 Disease Guide

Anthrax

Diagnosis	Characteristic cutaneous lesion. Microscopy, culture and PCR of a swab or biopsy of affected areas, e.g. cutaneous lesions, bronchial tissue, pleural fluid, blood or cerebrospinal fluid.
Treatment	Intensive support. Antibiotic treatment with ciprofloxacin, doxycycline or penicillin alone or in combination.
Notification	Anthrax is a notifiable infectious disease. See Resource Guide: 5.1.

Anthrax

5 Disease Guide

Anthrax Vaccine

Type of Vaccine	Inactivated vaccine.
Schedule	■ Primary: 3 doses at 3 weekly intervals; 4th dose is given 6 months after the 3rd dose. Booster: Annual if at continued risk.
Recommendations for Travel	Not available for travellers, unless they are at risk because of occupational exposure or military service. See Resource Guide: 5.2.
Contraindications and Precautions	■ Contraindication: A confirmed anaphylactic reaction to previous dose or to any of the constituents of the vaccine. ■ Immunocompromised individuals and those with HIV/AIDS infection can be vaccinated, however, a sub-optimal antibody response can occur. ■ Pregnant and breastfeeding women can be vaccinated if at risk.
Adverse Reactions	■ Common: Pain, swelling or redness at the injection site. ■ Uncommon: Regional lymphadenopathy, non-specific febrile illness, urticaria and other allergic reactions.

Anthrax Vaccine

5 Disease Guide

Amoebiasis

Entamoeba histolytica. E. dispar is morphologically identical, but genetically distinct, and non-pathogenic. Protozoan parasites of humans.

Risk Assessment

Epidemiology
- *E. histolytica* is most commonly found in tropical areas of Latin America, Africa, South Asia and South East Asia. *E. dispar*, worldwide distribution.

Exposure
- Transmitted via the faecal-oral route: Food, human-to-human and water-borne, or during certain sexual practices.
- Travellers are at higher risk in settings of poor sanitation where water may not be adequately purified and there is poor personal hygiene.

Imported Cases

Approximately 100 cases are reported annually in England and Wales. It is presumed that most of these are acquired abroad.

Signs and Symptoms

Intestinal:
- 90% of amoebic infection is asymptomatic; most of this is caused by *E. dispar*.
- Usually gradual onset over 1 to 4 weeks.
- Symptomatic infection ranges from diarrhoea to dysentery. Dysentery (amoebic colitis) characterised by cramping, abdominal pain, tenderness, low-grade fever, bloody stools with mucus, and weight loss.
- Without treatment symptoms can last for weeks to months.

Extra-intestinal, liver abscess:
- Amoebic liver abscess occurs in about 1% of infections.
- Right upper quadrant pain and tenderness, low-grade fever and increased liver enzymes.
- Usually solitary lesion in right lobe of liver occurring in men.

Risk Management

- Practise food and water hygiene precautions.
- Practise personal hygiene with hand washing.

Diagnosis

Intestinal infection: Stool microscopy and antigen detection assays; colonoscopy with biopsy.

Liver abscess: Liver ultrasound or scan, serology.

Treatment

Need to treat invasive parasites with metronidazole or tinidazole and non-invasive, luminal cysts with diloxanide furoate or paromomycin.

Notifications

Infectious bloody diarrhoea is a notifiable infectious disease. See Resource Guide: 5.1.

Avian Influenza

Influenza virus A, highly pathogenic type H5N1; RNA virus of the family *Orthomyxoviridae*. Zoonotic viral infection of birds and humans.

Risk Assessment

Epidemiology

- Avian influenza is primarily a disease of migratory waterfowl (a zoonosis).
- Outbreaks in domestic poultry began in South East Asia in 2003. In 2005, the virus spread beyond its original focus in Asia to affect countries in the Middle East, Europe and Africa.
- Small numbers of human cases have been reported in local persons. As of mid-2009, there were 436 cases worldwide with 262 deaths; the majority of cases have occurred in Indonesia. Cumulative numbers of human cases can be found on the WHO website. See Resource Guide: 5.3.
- Occasionally other mammalian species have been infected.

Exposure

- Humans have been infected following close contact with sick or dead poultry, usually occurring in the domestic setting.
- The virus is not well adapted for humans and only rare human-to-human transmission has occurred.
- To date there have been no travel-associated cases.

Imported Cases

No human cases reported.

Signs and Symptoms

- Incubation period of 3 to 5 days.
- Symptoms: Fever, myalgia, malaise, cough and sore throat. Diarrhoea is common.
- Complications: Pneumonia, encephalopathy and multi-organ failure.
- Case fatality rate of recognised human cases is approximately 60%.

Risk Management

- Avoid visiting live animal markets and poultry farms.
- Avoid contact with surfaces contaminated with animal faeces.
- Do not eat or handle undercooked or raw poultry, egg or duck dishes.
- Do not attempt to bring any live poultry products back to the UK.
- Do not pick up or touch dead or dying birds.
- Exercise good personal hygiene with frequent hand washing.
- Seasonal influenza vaccine is not expected to protect against avian influenza.

Avian Influenza

5 Disease Guide

Avian Influenza

- Oseltamivir prophylaxis or self-treatment is not usually recommended for travellers.
- Travellers should be alert to a respiratory illness for 7 days following return from an area of risk.

Diagnosis	Culture or PCR of nasopharyngeal, throat or nasal swabs; serology.
Treatment	Specialist advice should be obtained. Antiviral therapy with oseltamivir or zanamivir. Supportive care.
Notification	Suspected human cases of avian influenza should be reported to the local Health Protection Unit. An algorithm detailing the initial management and investigation of suspected cases is available on the HPA website. See Resource Guide: 5.3.

Avian Influenza

Babesiosis

Babesia microti and *B. divergens;* most common species causing human infection. Protozoan parasites of humans and animals.

Risk Assessment

Epidemiology Worldwide distribution.

- Most cases occur in North America and are caused by *B. microti*.
  Higher-risk areas in the US are: States along the north-eastern seaboard (New York, Massachusetts, Connecticut and Rhode Island), the upper Midwest (Wisconsin and Minnesota); a few cases are documented in the Pacific Northwest.
- In Europe infection is caused by *B. divergens*. Cases have been reported from England, Scotland, France, Ireland, Spain, Sweden and the former Yugoslavia.
- Prevalence of *Babesia* in malaria-endemic countries is not known.

Exposure
- Babesiosis is transmitted via the bite of an infected *Ixodes* tick.
- Ticks live in vegetation, usually at ground level and can be brushed onto clothing or skin.

Imported Cases Very occasional cases of *B. microti* (less than 1 per year) were acquired from the US.

Signs and Symptoms
- Incubation period is from 1 to 6 weeks.
- About 25% of adults and 50% of children who are infected with *B. microti* are asymptomatic or have mild symptoms.
- Symptomatic disease is characterised by fever, nausea, vomiting, myalgia, jaundice and anaemia. Hepatomegaly, splenomegaly, pulmonary oedema, coagulation problems, respiratory distress and heart and renal failure can occur in severe infection.
- Fulminant and fatal illness occurs in splenectomised individuals and those who are immunocompromised, including those with HIV/AIDS, and those older than 50 years of age.

Risk Management
- Travellers should practise tick bite avoidance measures during outdoor activities.
- Travellers should check themselves for ticks and be knowledgeable about effective tick removal methods.

Diagnosis Blood smear microscopy. Serology for *B. microti*.

Treatment Antimicrobial treatment with clindamycin plus quinine or atovaquone plus azithromycin.

Babesiosis

5 Disease Guide

Brucellosis

Brucellosis, also known as undulant or Mediterranean fever. Bacteria of the genus *Brucella* including *B. melitensi*, *B. abortus* and *B. suis*. Bacterial infection of animals (usually cows, goats, sheep and pigs) and man.

Risk Assessment

Epidemiology	▪ Worldwide distribution. Highest risk regions include the Mediterranean basin, Middle East, South Asia, Africa, South and Central America. The reservoirs of infection are usually cows and goats.
Exposure	▪ Transmission to humans via consumption of unpasteurised dairy products, direct contact with infected animals or animal products, or inhalation of the organism. Human-to-human spread is rare.
	▪ Most travellers are at very low risk.
	▪ Those at higher risk include farmers, veterinarians, butchers and abattoir workers in agricultural areas.
Imported Cases	In England and Wales there were a total of 19 cases in 2004, 8 in 2005, and 11 in 2006. Most cases are presumed to be acquired abroad.
Signs and Symptoms	▪ Incubation period of 1 to 5 weeks.
	▪ There are 3 forms of brucellosis: Acute, relapsing and chronic.
	▪ Acute: Presents weeks after infection as a non-specific 'flu-like' illness of fever, malaise, anorexia, arthralgias and myalgias. The acute form can be self-limiting; however a relapsing illness or chronic disease often develops without treatment.
	▪ Relapsing: Presents months after infection as cyclical fevers associated with features such as large joint arthritis, endocarditis and neurological complications.
	▪ Chronic: Presents years after infection as a chronic fatigue-like syndrome, depression, and arthritis.
	▪ Approximately 2% of those infected develop endocarditis which can be fatal.
Risk Management	▪ Avoid consumption of unpasteurised dairy products.
	▪ Animal handlers should practise personal hygiene and precautions against animal blood and fluids.
Diagnosis	Culture of blood or bone marrow aspirates. Serology.
Treatment	Antibiotic treatment: Doxycycline with rifampicin or an aminoglycoside, for several weeks.
Notification	Brucellosis is a notifiable infectious disease. See Resource Guide: 5.1.

Campylobacter

Campylobacter jejuni, also *C. coli*. Gram-negative bacterial infections of humans and animals.

Risk Assessment

Epidemiology
- *Campylobacter* is distributed worldwide. The organism is prevalent in domesticated poultry and can be found in other animal species including household pets.
- *Campylobacter* is one of the most common bacterial causes of travellers' diarrhoea (TD). It is the most common cause of community acquired diarrhoea in high-income countries.

Exposure
- Transmitted via the faecal-oral route: Food- and water-borne are most common modes. Food items typically at risk are raw or undercooked poultry meat and eggs, unpasteurised dairy products, and other meats.

Imported Cases

There are approximately 50,000 reports of *Campylobacter* infections annually in England, Wales and Northern Ireland. Enhanced surveillance in the early 2000s determined that about 20% of cases were acquired abroad. The countries of acquisition reflect the pattern of UK travel, with most cases coming from Europe. However, highest risk regions are South Asia, North Africa and South East Asia.

Signs and Symptoms

- Incubation period of 2 to 5 days. Infection can be established with 500 or fewer organisms.
- Asymptomatic infections are most common in children and adults in low-income settings.
- Diarrhoea, cramping and fever. Vomiting occurs. Diarrhoea is loose to watery, but also can be bloody with mucus (dysenteric).
- Infection in healthy persons is usually self-limiting over 2 to 10 days.
- Complications are uncommon; they include extra-intestinal spread and bacteraemia.
- Persons with HIV/AIDS can have persistent, severe and extra-intestinal infection.
- Post-infectious Guillain-Barré syndrome (about 1 per 1,000 cases) and reactive arthritis occur.

Risk Management
- Practise food and water hygiene precautions.
- Practise personal hygiene with hand washing particularly after handling potentially contaminated foods.

Diagnosis

Stool culture. Blood can be cultured in bacteraemic cases.

Campylobacter

5 Disease Guide

Campylobacter

Treatment	• Supportive treatment and hydration.
	• Antibiotics should be used to treat very ill persons and those with extra-intestinal spread of infection. Fluoroquinolone resistance is common; azithromycin is an alternative.

Notification	Infectious bloody diarrhoea is a notifiable infectious disease. See Resource Guide: 5.1.

Campylobacter

5 Disease Guide

Cholera

Vibrio cholerae O1, divided into 2 biotypes, Classical and El Tor, and 2 main serotypes, Ogawa and Inaba. *V. cholerae* O139 can also cause cholera. Gram-negative bacterial infections of humans.

Risk Assessment

Epidemiology
- Cholera is predominately a disease of Africa and Asia. WHO reports about 140,000 cases annually with 95% of these from Africa. Surveillance of cholera outbreaks in 2007 indicates 69% were from Africa, 18% from South Asia, 9% from South East Asia and 4% from the Middle East. *V. cholerae* O139 is currently limited to Asia.
- See NaTHNaC Country Information Pages[1] www.nathnac.org.

Exposure
- Transmitted via the faecal-oral route: Food- and water-borne.
- Rare risk for travellers.
- Those at higher risk include humanitarian aid workers and travellers with remote itineraries in areas of cholera outbreaks, who have limited access to safe water and medical care.

Imported Cases
- From 2003 to 2007 an annual average of 15 imported cases of cholera was reported. More than 95% of cases were caused by *V. cholerae* O1, and 77% were acquired in South Asia.

Signs and Symptoms
- Incubation period of 2 to 5 days (can be as short as hours). A high inoculum is required to establish infection, often $\geq 10^5$ organisms.
- Sudden onset of profuse, watery stools with occasional vomiting. Mild diarrhoea and asymptomatic cases are not uncommon.
- Complications occur in 5% to 10% of cases: Dehydration, metabolic acidosis, circulatory collapse.
- 50% of untreated severe cases can die within hours.

Risk Management
- Practise food and water hygiene precautions.
- Practise personal hygiene with hand washing.
- See: Vaccine – Recommendations for Travel.

Diagnosis
Clinical presentation. Stool culture.

Treatment
- Rehydration with oral or intravenous fluids.
- Antibiotics can reduce the volume of diarrhoea and the duration of excretion of *V. cholerae*.
- Case fatality <1% with prompt treatment.

Notification
Cholera is a notifiable infectious disease. See Resource Guide: 5.1.

1   Alternatively see Travax http://www.travax.nhs.uk/ or Fit for Travel http://www.fitfortravel.nhs.uk/

Cholera Vaccine

Type of Vaccine	Inactivated oral vaccine containing bacteria of *Vibrio cholerae* O1 Inaba classical and El Tor biotypes and O1 Ogawa classical biotype with recombinant cholera toxin B. Check 'Green Book' and SPC. See Resource Guide: Appendix 1 – Vaccine Compendium.
Schedule	Adults and children from 6 years: ■ Primary: 2 doses with an interval of at least 1 week between them. If more than 6 weeks has elapsed between doses, the primary schedule should be restarted. ■ Booster at 2 years. If more than 2 years has elapsed, repeat the primary course. Children aged 2 to 6 years: ■ Primary: 3 doses with an interval of at least 1 week between if more than 6 weeks have elapsed between doses, the primary course should be restarted. ■ Booster at 6 months. If more than 6 months has elapsed repeat the primary course.
Recommendations for Travel	The vaccine should be given to travellers visiting areas with cholera of the O1 strain and who are: ■ Aid workers assisting in disaster relief or refugee camps. ■ Travellers with remote itineraries with limited access to medical care in areas with cholera outbreaks.
Contraindications and Precautions	■ Hypersensitivity to active substances or excipients of the vaccine. ■ Current acute gastrointestinal or febrile illness.
Adverse Reactions	Adverse events are uncommon; they include abdominal cramps, diarrhoea and general discomfort.

Cholera Vaccine

5 Disease Guide

Chikungunya (CHIKV)

RNA virus of the genus *Alphavirus*, a member of the *Togaviridae* family. Viral infection of humans and non-human primates.

Risk Assessment

Epidemiology	▪ Tropical and sub-tropical areas of the world. Highest risk regions: West, Central and East Africa, South Asia, South East Asia and the islands in the Indian Ocean, including Réunion, Mayotte, Mauritius and the Seychelles.
Exposure	▪ CHIKV is transmitted via the bite of an infected *Aedes* spp. mosquito. *Aedes* mosquitoes feed predominantly during daylight hours.

Imported Cases

In 2004, 6 suspect or probable cases were reported. In 2005, 19 cases were reported, 11 of which were serving members of the UK armed services in Senegal. In 2006, following an outbreak in South Asia and the islands of the Indian Ocean, 133 cases were reported. The majority of cases were acquired in India and Sri Lanka.

Signs and Symptoms

- The incubation period of CHIKV is 2 to 12 days.
- The number of asymptomatic infections is not known.
- CHIKV usually begins with the sudden onset of severe arthralgias and myalgias accompanied by fever, headache and conjunctivitis. After 2 to 3 days a generalised maculopapular rash can develop.
- Most infections are self-limiting with improvement in 3 to 5 days and full recovery within a few weeks.
- 5 to 10 percent of cases experience persistent joint pain and stiffness, and fatigue lasting weeks or months.

Risk Management

Mosquito bite avoidance measures; *Aedes* mosquitoes feed predominantly during daylight hours, particularly around dusk and dawn.

Diagnosis

Clinical distinction between CHIKV and dengue. PCR or culture of virus. Serology.

Treatment

No specific antiviral treatment. Supportive therapy.

Notification

Notification by diagnostic laboratory. See Resource Guide: 5.1.

Chikungunya

5 Disease Guide

Crimean-Congo Haemorrhagic Fever (CCHF)

RNA virus of the *Nairovirus* genus, family *Bunyaviridae*. Viral infection of humans and animals.

Risk Assessment

Epidemiology
- CCHF occurs in Eastern Europe, particularly in south-western Russia. Also present in the Balkan States, Mediterranean, Middle East, Western China, Central Asia, Africa, and South Asia.

Exposure
- CCHF is transmitted by *Hyalomma* ticks. Numerous animals including rodents, sheep, goats, cattle, hares and some ground-feeding birds are hosts.
- Human infection occurs after a bite, or crushing of an infected tick, or contact with infected animal blood. Rare human-to-human transmission occurs via contact with infected human blood or other bodily fluids.
- Rare risk for most travellers.
- Higher-risk travellers are those in contact with livestock, and healthcare workers in endemic areas.

Imported Cases

One case reported in 1997 in a UK traveller returned from Zimbabwe.

Signs and Symptoms

- Incubation period is 1 to 3 days following a tick bite; 5 to 6 days following exposure to blood or bodily fluids.
- There is frequent asymptomatic infection.
- Sudden onset of fever, headache, myalgia, dizziness, diarrhoea, nausea and vomiting. This can progress over several days to haemorrhagic manifestations: petechiae, extensive bleeding, thrombocytopaenia, hepatitis and shock.
- Case fatality rate is 20% to 35%.

Risk Management

- Travellers should practise tick bite avoidance measures during outdoor activities.
- Travellers should check themselves for ticks and be knowledgeable about effective tick removal methods.
- Those at occupational risk (abattoir workers, veterinarians, farmers) should wear protective clothing to avoid contact with infected blood or other bodily fluids. Healthcare workers should use infection control precautions.
- There is no vaccine commercially available.

Diagnosis

- Clinical syndrome.
- Viral culture of blood, antigen detection, PCR; serology.

Treatment

Supportive treatment and blood and body fluid precautions should be carried out in a high security infectious diseases unit. Antiviral treatment with ribavirin can be tried.

Notification

Viral haemorrhagic fever is a notifiable infectious disease. See Resource Guide: 5.1.

Cryptosporidiosis

Cryptosporidium hominis; also *parvum.* Protozoan parasites of humans and animals.

Risk Assessment		
Epidemiology	■ *Cryptosporidium* is widely distributed in both high- and low-income areas of the world. It is the one of the most common intestinal parasites of man.	
Exposure	■ *Cryptosporidium* is transmitted via the faecal-oral route. Water-borne, human-to-human in settings of poor personal hygiene or during certain sexual practices, and food-borne transmission are the most common modes.	
	■ Travellers are at higher risk in settings of poor sanitation where water may not be adequately purified and there is poor personal hygiene.	

Imported Cases	Approximately 4,000 cases reported annually in England and Wales. The proportion acquired abroad is not known.

Signs and Symptoms	Immunocompetent host: ■ Incubation period of about a week. ■ Prolonged, but usually self-limited watery diarrhoea with cramping, nausea, anorexia and low-grade fever. ■ Diarrhoea may last more than 10 to 14 days, and can be accompanied by weight loss. *Cryptosporidium* contributes to poor nutritional status of children in low-income settings. ■ Prolonged asymptomatic cyst passage is documented in young children. Oocysts may be passed after resolution of symptoms. Immunocompromised host: ■ Most frequently described in AIDS patients and is an AIDS-defining illness. ■ Diarrhoea is usually prolonged (months), voluminous, associated with wasting. ■ Extra-intestinal biliary infection occurs. ■ Generally does not resolve spontaneously unless there is reversal of immunosuppression.

Risk Management	■ Practise food and water hygiene precautions. ■ Practise personal hygiene with hand washing. ■ Avoid untreated water – bring water to a boil or used <1 μm filter. Small volume water halogenation is not reliable.

Diagnosis	Stool for microscopy or antigen detection assays.

Treatment	Immunocompetent host: Hydration, supportive treatment, nitazoxanide. Immunocompromised host: Hydration, supportive treatment, no reliable anti-protozoal therapy. Reversal of HIV/AIDS-induced immunosuppression with Highly Active Anti-Retroviral Therapy.

Notifications	Food poisoning is a notifiable infectious disease. See Resource Guide: 5.1.

Cryptosporidiosis

5 Disease Guide

Cutaneous Larva Migrans

Cutaneous infection by dog or cat hookworms; *Ancyclostoma braziliense*, dogs and cats, and *Ancyclostoma caninum* (dogs). Larval nematode infection of humans.

Risk Assessment

Epidemiology	▪ Widely distributed in tropical and sub-tropical areas, particularly those in South East Asia and the Caribbean.
Exposure	▪ Adult hookworms live in intestines of dogs and cats. Eggs are defecated into the soil or sand, where they mature and hatch, releasing larvae.
	▪ Larvae penetrate the skin of humans when they come into contact with contaminated soil or sand.

Imported Cases	Number of cases in UK travellers is not known, however, it is one of the most common dermatologic conditions seen in returned travellers from endemic areas.

Signs and Symptoms	▪ Incubation period is 10 to 15 days.
	▪ Usually 1 or more erythematous, linear or serpiginous cutaneous lesions, most commonly on the soles of the feet, other parts of the legs, buttocks, trunk or arms. Pruritis is common.
	▪ Other skin features include oedema, vesiculobullous lesions and secondary bacterial infections.

Risk Management	▪ Travellers should wear protective footwear when walking.
	▪ Use a towel to prevent lying directly on beach sand.

Diagnosis	Clinical presentation.

Treatment	Albendazole or ivermectin.

Cyclosporiasis

Cyclospora cayetanensis. Protozoan parasite of humans.

Risk Assessment

Epidemiology
- *Cyclospora* occurs in both high- and low-income areas of the world; prevalence is most common in tropical areas.

Exposure
- *Cyclospora* is transmitted via the faecal-oral route. Food-borne transmission is the most common mode; small water-borne outbreaks are described. Human-to-human transmission is unlikely as parasite needs to mature outside of host before becoming infectious.
- Travellers are at higher risk in settings of poor sanitation.

Imported Cases

Approximately 20 to 60 cases are reported annually in England and Wales. 25% to 50% are presumed to be acquired abroad, but a travel history is often not recorded.

Signs and Symptoms

- Incubation period of about 1 week.
- Asymptomatic infection occurs; most common in children.
- Watery diarrhoea with cramping, nausea, anorexia; weight loss with prolonged illness.
- Without treatment symptoms can persist for weeks.
- Symptoms more severe in AIDS patients.

Risk Management

- Practise food and water hygiene precautions.
- Practise personal hygiene with hand washing.
- Avoid untreated water. Bring water to a boil or use filter of <1 µm pore size. Halogenation is not reliable.

Diagnosis

Stool microscopy.

Treatment

Co-trimoxazole. Long-term suppressive treatment may be necessary in AIDS patients.

Cyclosporiasis

5 Disease Guide

Dengue

RNA viruses of the genus *Flavivirus*, family *Flaviviridae* with 4 distinct serotypes, DEN 1, 2, 3, & 4. Viral infection of humans.

Risk Assessment

Epidemiology	■ Present in more than 100 countries throughout the tropical and sub-tropical areas of the world. Highest risk regions are the Caribbean, South and South East Asia, and Latin America. See Map 5-1.
	■ See NaTHNaC Country Information Pages[1] www.nathnac.org.
Exposure	■ Dengue is transmitted by the bite of an infected *Aedes* spp. mosquito. *Aedes* mosquitoes feed predominantly during daylight hours.

Imported Cases	Approximately 140 cases of dengue fever are reported annually in England, Wales and Northern Ireland. The majority are acquired in Asia and the Americas.

Signs and Symptoms	■ The incubation period of dengue fever is 5 to 8 days.
	■ 15% to 90% of cases are asymptomatic.
	■ Dengue usually starts with a fever lasting 1 to 5 days. Other typical features are headache, myalgia, cough and a blanching, maculopapular rash that begins on the trunk and spreads to the face and extremities. Most infections are self-limiting with improvement and rapid recovery occurring 3 to 4 days after the onset of rash.
	■ Dengue haemorrhagic fever (DHF) is characterised by sudden deterioration between days 2 and 7 with bleeding and hypotension. Mortality rates in the presence of uncontrolled shock have been as high as 40%; however, with treatment, rates should be 1% to 2%.
	■ DHF is more common in children and may occur following re-infection with a different dengue serotype.
	■ DHF is rare in travellers.

Risk Management	Mosquito bite avoidance measures. *Aedes* mosquitoes feed predominantly during daylight hours, particularly around dusk and dawn.

Diagnosis	Clinical distinction between dengue and CHIKV. PCR or viral culture of blood. Serology.

Treatment	No specific antiviral treatment. Supportive therapy.

Notification	Dengue is a notifiable infectious disease. See Resource Guide: 5.1.

---

1   Alternatively see Travax http://www.travax.nhs.uk/ or Fit for Travel http://www.fitfortravel.nhs.uk/

or,

Acknowledgment: Adapted from World Health Organization.

Map 5-1. Dengue Risk Areas, 2009

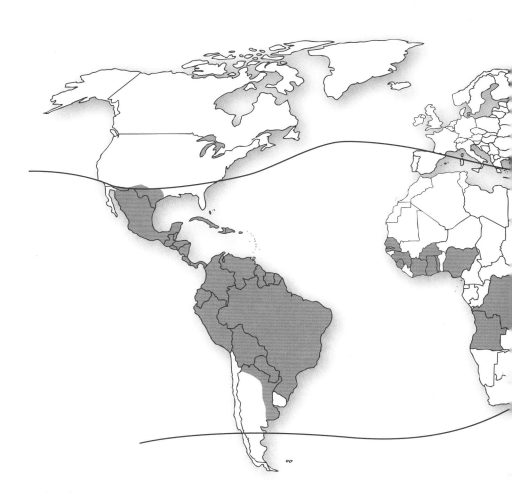

Countries or areas where dengue has been reported

Note: Lines define the boundaries of year-round survival of the dengue mosquito vec
Aedes aegypti, and represents areas where dengue transmission is possible.

Diphtheria

Corynebacterium diphtheriae and *C. ulcerans*. Bacterial infections of man and animals.

Risk Assessment

Epidemiology

- Occurs worldwide. Rarely reported in industrialised countries; sporadic cases that do occur are usually associated with foreign travel or contact with a case who has travelled. Sporadic indigenous diphtheria caused by *C. ulcerans* is known to occur in the UK and other European countries.
- See NaTHNaC Country Information Pages[1] www.nathnac.org.

Exposure

- *C. diphtheriae* is transmitted through the respiratory route, contact with infected objects or exudate from an infected skin lesion.
- *C. ulcerans* is transmitted during close contact with animals that carry it in their nose or throat, or by eating or drinking unpasteurised dairy products.

Imported Cases

- 1986 to 2006, there were 59 isolates of toxigenic *Corynebacterium diphtheriae* in England and Wales; 43 were acquired abroad (25 in South Asia); 8 were classic respiratory diphtheria. There were 2 deaths in the UK from respiratory diphtheria caused by *C. ulcerans*; 1 in 2000 and 1 in 2006.

Signs and Symptoms

- Incubation period is 2 to 7 days.
- **Respiratory form**
  - Tough 'leathery' grey/yellow membrane in the pharyngeal area that can lead to airway obstruction following laryngeal spread.
  - Systemic effects of exotoxin can cause cardiac and neurological symptoms.
  - 5% to 10% of cases are fatal.
- **Cutaneous form**
  - Usually seen in tropical areas.
  - Presents as a chronic non-healing ulcer, often co-infected with *Staphylococci* and *Streptococci*.
  - Systemic symptoms from the cutaneous form are rare.
- Protective immunity following infection may not occur.

Risk Management

- Avoid conditions of overcrowding and poor hygiene.
- Avoid close contact with cattle and other farm animals, and consuming unpasteurised dairy products.
- See: Vaccine – Recommendations for Travel.

Diagnosis

Clinical syndrome. Culture of swabs from throat, nasopharynx or skin. Toxin detection by PCR or immunoassay; serology.

Treatment

Antibiotic treatment with penicillins or macrolides plus administration of diphtheria antitoxin. Antitoxin is available from the Immunisation Department of the Health Protection Agency's Centre of Infection or certain Regional Health Protection Agency and NHS laboratories. See Resource Guide: 5.4.

Notification

Diphtheria is a notifiable infectious disease. See Resource Guide: 5.1.

1 Alternatively see Travax http://www.travax.nhs.uk/ or Fit for Travel http://www.fitfortravel.nhs.uk/

Diphtheria

5 Disease Guide

Diphtheria Vaccine

Type of Vaccine

Inactivated toxoid. Administered as part of combination vaccine (DTaP/IPV/Hib, DTaP/IPV, dTaP/IPV, Td/IPV).
Check 'Green Book' and SPC.
See Resource Guide: Appendix 1 – Vaccine Compendium.

Schedule

Primary course: 3 doses of diphtheria-containing vaccine at monthly intervals
- Infants and children under 10 years:
  - Recommended at 2, 3 and 4 months of age.
  - Higher strength diphtheria dose recommended. This can be given up to 10 years.
- Adults and children aged 10 years and older:
  - Low dose diphtheria-containing vaccine preparation should be used.

Booster doses: 2 doses
- Infants and children under 10 years:
  - 1st booster dose: ideally 3 years after completion of the primary course (but can be minimum of 1 year after primary course when primary vaccination has been delayed).
  - 2nd booster dose: ideally 10 years after 1st booster (but minimum of 5 years where previous dose has been delayed.)
- Adults and children aged 10 years and older who have only received 3 doses of a diphtheria-containing vaccine:
  - 1st booster dose: 1 year following completion of primary course.
  - 2nd booster dose: 5 to 10 years after 1st booster dose.

Recommendations for Travel

- All travellers should ensure they are fully immunised according to the UK schedule.
- A booster dose of a diphtheria-containing vaccine should be given to those who have not received a dose within the previous 10 years.

Contraindications and Precautions

- A history of a confirmed anaphylactic reaction to a previous dose of a diphtheria-containing vaccine or to any of the components of the vaccine.
- A history of neurological complications following a previous dose (defer immunisation until condition stabilised or cause identified).

Adverse Reactions

- Common: Local reactions of pain, redness, swelling at the injection site.
- Rare: In children, fever, convulsions, high-pitched screaming, pallor, cyanosis and limpness (usually following a diphtheria and pertussis containing vaccine).

Diphtheria Vaccine

5 Disease Guide

Filariasis

Eight species of filaria infect humans: *Wuchereria bancrofti*, *Brugia malayi* and *B. timori* causing lymphatic filariasis, *Onchocerca volvulus* causing onchocerciasis (river blindness) See Disease Guide: Onchocerciasis, Loa loa causing loiasis, and *Mansonella perstans*, *M. streptocerca*, and *M. ozzardi*. Nematode infections of humans.

Risk Assessment

Epidemiology

- Lymphatic filariasis: *W. bancrofti* occurs in South and South East Asia, Africa, the Pacific and Americas; *B. malayi* is limited to Asia, and *B. timori* to Indonesia.
- Onchocerciasis: *O. volvulus*, occurs mainly in Africa, with small foci in Latin America and Yemen.
- Loa loa occurs in West and Central Africa.
- *M. perstans* occurs in both Africa and South America, *M. streptocerca* in Africa, and *M. ozzardi* in Central and South America.

Exposure

- Infective larva enter the body via bites from:
  - Mosquitoes: *W. bancrofti*, *B. malayi* and *B. timori*
  - Deer flies *(Chrysops):* Loa loa
  - Black flies *(Simulium):* *O. volvulus* and *M. ozzardi*
  - Midges: *M. perstans*, *M. streptocerca* and *M. ozzardi*
- Most travellers are at very low risk. Expatriates and long-term travellers in endemic areas are at higher risk.

Imported Cases

Filariasis is rare in UK travellers. Between 1998 and 2007, 95 cases of filariasis were reported. The majority of filariasis reported in the UK is loiasis (42), followed by *Mansonella perstans* (25), onchocerciasis (6), *W. bancrofti* (6) and other cases (16) were unspeciated. Travel history is poorly reported; of those with information most cases had been in sub-Saharan Africa and 2 cases with *W. bancrofti* had travelled in Guyana and India.

Signs and Symptoms

- Lymphatic filariasis:
  - Often asymptomatic in persons living in endemic areas, however, asymptomatic individuals can have unrecognised lymphatic and renal pathology.
  - Chronic infection over years can lead to episodes of acute fever and lymphatic inflammation with oedema of the legs, arms, genitals or breast. Over time the changes can become permanent.
  - Chronic lymphoedema in expatriates and long-term travellers is unusual.
  - Tropical pulmonary eosinophilia characterised by fever, wheezing and a persistent cough, can occur in chronically infected persons.

Filariasis

5 Disease Guide

Filariasis

- See Onchocerciasis in Disease Guide.
- Loiasis is often asymptomatic. Intermittent localised oedema (Calabar swellings) of the extremities and subconjunctival migration of an adult worm can occur.
- *Mansonella perstans* is usually asymptomatic, but may be associated with angioedema, pruritus, fever, headaches and arthralgias.
- *Mansonella streptocerca* can cause skin manifestations including pruritus, papular eruptions and pigmentation changes.
- *Mansonella ozzardi* can cause arthralgias, headaches, fever, pulmonary symptoms, adenopathy, hepatomegaly and pruritis.

Risk Management	Travellers should take insect bite avoidance measures.
Diagnosis	• Clinical syndrome. • Identification of microfilariae from appropriate bodily fluid or biopsy. Timing of blood samples is important: *Brugia* and *Wuchereria* after 8pm, Loa loa at midday; *Mansonella* and onchocerciasis, anytime. • Serology.
Treatment	Antifilarial drugs. Seek advice from tropical specialist. Chronic symptoms are not always resolved by drug therapy and may require additional interventions.

Filariasis

5 Disease Guide

Fungal Skin Infections

Fungal skin and mucous membrane infections of humans:

- – Dermatophytes (ringworm or tinea). Three genera: *Trichophyton*, *Microsporum* and *Epidermophyton*. Includes infections of the scalp (tinea capitis), skin (tinea corporis), groin (tinea cruris), feet (tinea pedis) or nails (onychomycosis).
- – Superficial skin and mucosal (thrush, both oral and vaginal) candidiasis. *Candida albicans* is the most common *Candida* species.
- – *Malessezia* spp.: pityriasis versicolor and seborrhoeic dermatitis.

Risk Assessment

Epidemiology
- Dermatophyte infection: Worldwide distribution, more common in tropical areas.
- Candidiasis: Worldwide distribution.
- *Malessezia* spp.: Worldwide distribution of pityriasis versicolor.

Exposure
- Dermatophyte infection: Transmission usually occurs through contact with infected skin scales or hair fragments of humans and occasionally animals.
- Candidiasis: *C. albicans* is a normal commensal of mouth, gastrointestinal tract and vagina. Risk of infection increases with antibiotic use; immunocompromise (including HIV/AIDS), diabetes, and obesity. Hot and humid climates can predispose to infection by leading to warm, moist and macerated skin.
- *Malessezia:* Infections are normal commensals of skin. Risk of infection can increase with warm climates, sun exposure and immunocompromise.

Imported Cases
Fungal skin infections are presumed to be one of the most common skin infections in travellers. The proportion that is acquired abroad is not known.

Signs and Symptoms

- Dermatophyte infection:
  - – Tinea capitis: itching, scaling and alopecia.
  - – Tinea corporis (ringworm): dry scaling, erythematous skin lesions with circular enlargement.
  - – Tinea cruris: pruritic, erythematous plaques with raised margins.
  - – Tinea pedis: scaling, pruritic lesions with maceration and cracking between the toes.
  - – Onychomycosis (Tinea unguium): yellow brown discoloration of the nail bed with hyperkeratosis of the nail.

Fungal Skin Infections

Fungal Skin Infections

- Candidiasis:
  - Cutaneous infections in intertrigenous sites: groin, axilla, under the breasts, and nappy areas. Pruritic, erythematous plaques often with pustular satellite lesions. A whitish scaling is often present.
  - Mucous membrane, oral and vaginal: white plaques often associated with pain.
- *Malassezia* spp.:
  - Pityriasis versicolor: hypo or hyperpigmented macules that can coalesce to form non-pruritic, scaling plaques.
  - Seborrhoeic dermatitis: pruritic, scaling scalp plaques.

Risk Management
- Dermatophyte infection: Skin care, keeping risk areas clean and dry; avoid occlusive footwear.
- Candidiasis: Skin care, avoid unnecessary antibiotic use.
- *Malassezia:* Skin care, avoid excessive sun exposure.

Diagnosis

Clinical syndrome, microscopy and culture of skin scrapings; occasional biopsy.

Treatment
- Dermatophyte infection: Topical antifungals for tinea cruris, coporis and pedis. Oral treatment with an imidazole or other agent for tinea capitis and onychomycosis.
- Candidiasis: Topical nystatin derivatives and/or oral imidazole drug.
- *Malessezia* spp.: Topical azole antifungal cream or shampoo, topical tar-based preparations.

Fungal Skin Infections

5 Disease Guide

Giardiasis

Giardia intestinalis (lamblia). Protozoan parasite of humans and some mammals.

Risk Assessment	
Epidemiology	• Worldwide distribution in both high- and low-income areas. • It is the one of the most common intestinal parasites of humans.
Exposure	• *Giardia* is transmitted via the faecal-oral route. Water-borne, human-to-human in settings of poor personal hygiene or during certain sexual practices, and occasionally food-borne transmission. • Travellers are at higher risk in settings of poor sanitation where water may not be adequately purified and there is poor personal hygiene.
Imported Cases	Approximately 3,000 cases of *Giardia* are reported annually in England, Wales and Northern Ireland. About 14% have a travel history; of these the majority of cases are acquired in Asia and Africa. A travel history is not usually recorded.
Signs and Symptoms	• Incubation period of 1 to 2 weeks. • About 50% will develop symptoms following infection. Asymptomatic infection is most common in children. • Diarrhoea with foul-smelling stools, cramping, nausea, anorexia and malaise. Vomiting and fever are less common. • Prolonged diarrhoea lasting more than 10 days is a helpful distinguishing feature, and is often accompanied by weight loss. Some patients will develop malabsorption; *Giardia* contributes to poor nutritional status of children in low-income settings. • Prolonged asymptomatic cyst passage is documented in young children.
Risk Management	• Practise food and water hygiene precautions. • Practise personal hygiene with hand washing. • Avoid untreated water. Bring water to a boil or use filter of <1 µm pore size. Halogenation is not always reliable.
Diagnosis	Stool microscopy or antigen detection assays.
Treatment	Symptomatic patients should be treated. Treatment is most commonly with tinidazole or metronidazole.
Notifications	Food poisoning is a notifiable infectious disease. See Resource Guide: 5.1.

Giardiasis

5 Disease Guide

Haemophilus Influenzae

Haemophilus influenzae type b (Hib); non-type b *H. influenzae* can cause disease less commonly and are not included in the vaccine. Gram-negative bacteria of the family *Pasteurellaceae*. Bacterial infection of humans.

Risk Assessment

Epidemiology
- Worldwide distribution. Cases of Hib are uncommon in countries that have achieved high vaccine coverage, e.g. Western Europe and North America.

Exposure
- Respiratory transmission from carriers or infected persons.
- Bacteria colonise the nasopharynx of children. Risk of disease is highest between 3 and 11 months of age, and is uncommon over the age of 5.
- Asplenic or hyposplenic individuals can be at increased risk.

Imported Cases

Since the introduction of Hib into vaccination programmes in the UK in 1992, the incidence of invasive Hib disease has decreased by 95% in infants less than 1 year of age. The proportion that is acquired abroad is not known.

Signs and Symptoms
- Incubation period – varies with the type of infection.
- The most common forms of invasive disease caused by Hib are: Meningitis, bacteraemia, and epiglottitis; pneumonia, cellulitis and septic arthritis also occur.
- Manifestations of non-Hib *H. influenzae* include sinusitis, otitis media and bronchitis.
- Approximately 3% to 6% of invasive cases are fatal; up to 20% of surviving patients with meningitis have long-term sequelae such as permanent hearing loss.

Risk Management
- Hand washing and cough hygiene should be practised to minimise respiratory spread: maintaining distance when coughing or sneezing, covering mouth and/or nose with disposable tissues.
- The UK immunisation programme recommends a primary course of vaccination for all children under 10 years of age and unvaccinated asplenic or hyposplenic individuals aged 10 years and over.

Diagnosis

Culture of Hib from a sterile site, such as cerebrospinal fluid, blood, lung puncture, joint or bone. Antigen detection of Hib polysaccharide.

Treatment

Treatment with antibiotics, usually 3rd generation cephalosporins. Supportive treatment.

Notification

Haemophilus influenzae meningitis is a notifiable infectious disease. See Resource Guide: 5.1.

Haemophilus Influenzae Vaccine

Type of Vaccine	Polysaccharide vaccine, conjugated. Usually as part of combination vaccine.
	Check 'Green Book' and SPC.
	See Resource Guide: Appendix 1 – Vaccine Compendium.

Schedule	Primary:
	- Two months to 10 years of age: 3 doses at monthly intervals.
	- Booster: Children aged 1 to 10 years; 12 months after primary course.
	Persons with asplenia of splenic dysfunction:
	- Children under 10 years of age: Complete primary schedule.
	- 10 years and older: 2 doses at an interval of 2 months.

Recommendations for Travel	Children under 10 years of age and asplenic or hyposplenic individuals should be vaccinated.

Contraindications and Precautions	- Contraindicated with history of confirmed anaphylactic reaction to a previous dose of a Hib-containing vaccine or any component of the vaccine.
	- May be given to pregnant women who require protection.
	- May be given to immunocompromised individuals, although the antibody response may be sub-optimal.

Adverse Reactions	- Common: Mild pain swelling and redness at injection site.
	- Rare: Confirmed anaphylactic reaction.

Haemophilus Influenzae Vaccine

5 Disease Guide

Hantavirus

2 syndromes, Haemorrhagic Fever with Renal Symptoms (HFRS) or Hantavirus Pulmonary Syndrome (HPS). In North America *Sin nombre* virus is most common (causing HPS), in Europe *Puumala* virus and in Asia, *Hantaan* virus (causing HFRS). Bunyavirus infections of man and rodents.

Risk Assessment

Epidemiology
- HPS is seen only in the Americas, and has been reported from central and western US, Argentina, Chile, Bolivia, Panama, Uruguay, Paraguay and Brazil.
- HFRS is limited to Europe and Asia, and has been reported from China, Russia, Western Europe and the Balkans.

Exposure
- Transmission is via the respiratory droplet route from infected rodent urine, saliva or faeces.
- Rodents can be persistently infected but are asymptomatic.
- The risk to most travellers is very low. Most reported cases occur in those exposed via peridomestic activities (cleaning rodent-infested buildings) or occupationally (grain farmers, field biologists and industrial workers).

Imported Cases

There are no known cases in travellers from the UK.

Signs and Symptoms

- HFRS:
  - Incubation period typically 2 to 3 weeks (range 1 to 8 weeks).
  - Asymptomatic infections reported.
  - Presents with a fever, lower back pain, bleeding into skin, hypotension, renal failure and varying degrees of bleeding. Recovery may take weeks to months.
  - Case fatality approximately 5% to 15%. Illness with *Puumala* virus may be milder.
- HPS
  - Incubation period typically 1 to 2 weeks (range days to 6 weeks).
  - Presents with a fever, myalgia and gastrointestinal symptoms, followed by abrupt onset of respiratory distress, hypotension and respiratory failure. Recovery may take between 2 to 8 weeks.
  - Case fatality approximately 40% to 50%.
- It is unknown whether long-lasting immunity develops following infection with hantaviruses.

Risk Management
- Avoid rodent infested areas.
- Avoid contact with rodent excreta or contaminated items.
- Food and water precautions and personal hygiene.

Diagnosis

Clinical presentation. Serology, antigen detection in blood or tissues.

Treatment
- HFRS: Intensive supportive care, ribavirin may be useful.
- HPS: Intensive supportive care only.

Notification

Hantavirus infection is a notifiable infectious disease.
See Resource Guide: 5.1.

Hantavirus

5 Disease Guide

Helminth Infection (intestinal)

Divided into roundworms and tapeworms. Roundworms: ascariasis, *Ascaris lumbricoides;* hookworm, *Ancylostoma duodenale* and *Necator americanus;* whipworm, *Trichuris trichiura;* and strongyloidiasis, *Strongyloides stercoralis.* Tapeworms (cestodes), most commonly beef tapeworm, *Taenia saginata* and pork tapeworm, *Taenia solium.* Helminth infections of humans and animals.

Risk Assessment

Epidemiology

- Intestinal helminths are globally distributed, primarily in tropical and sub-tropical areas.
- The intestinal roundworms contribute to extensive morbidity in children; the disease burden from these as measured in Disability Adjusted Life Years (a health gap measure of years lost to premature mortality and / or disability) is secondary only to HIV/AIDS.
- Global estimates of 1.4 billion cases of *Ascaris*, 1 billion of hookworm, 800 million of whipworm, and 200 million of *Strongyloides.*

Exposure

- Transmission is via the faecal-oral route for *Ascaris* and whipworm in conditions of poor sanitation. Penetration of skin by larval forms of hookworm and *Strongyloides* in faecally contaminated soil. Ingestion of raw or undercooked beef or pork for *Taenia* tapeworms.
- The risk to most travellers is low. Helminth infections are usually found in long-term travellers who are exposed to conditions of poor sanitation.

Imported Cases

There are 200 to 300 reports of intestinal helminth infection reported annually in England, Wales and Northern Ireland. *Taenia* spp. and *Ascaris* are most common. A travel history is not usually recorded.

Signs and Symptoms

- Incubation period is variable; from exposure to maturation of adult worms is about 3 months for *Ascaris*, whipworm and the tapeworms, and 1 month for hookworm and *Strongyloides.*
- Asymptomatic infection is common with each of the helminths. There is frequent co-infection with different roundworms.
- All helminth infections can last several years.
- Roundworms:
  - *Ascaris:* Mild abdominal pain.
  - Hookworm: Mild abdominal pain, occasional diarrhoea.
  - Whipworm: Mild abdominal pain and diarrhoea.

Helminth Infection (intestinal)

5 Disease Guide

Helminth Infection (intestinal)

- – *Strongyloides:* Abdominal pain, nausea, diarrhoea and occasional vomiting. Dysentery with high worm burden. Infection may be chronic over years if autoinfection occurs. Occasional cutaneous rash – larva currens.
- Tapeworms:
  - – Mild abdominal discomfort.
- Complications:
  - – *Ascaris:* Pulmonary hypersensitivity during larval migration through lungs; with high worm burden intestinal obstruction (uncommon) and nutritional deficiencies; errant migration of worm to biliary tree with resultant cholangitis.
  - – Hookworm: Anaemia, particularly in childhood and pregnancy.
  - – Whipworm: Rectal prolapse in infants with heavy infections.
  - – *Strongyloides:* Dissemination of larval worms and life-threatening infection in immunocompromised patients with HTLV-1 infection, steroid use or post-transplantation.
  - – Pork tapeworm: Cysticercosis occurs with ingestion of *Taenia solium* (pork tapeworm) eggs or proglottids (tapeworm segments). Tapeworm larvae migrate from the intestine to the tissues, especially affecting the brain (cerebral cysticercosis) causing seizures, focal neurologic deficits and increased intracranial pressure.

Risk Management	<ul><li>Practise food and water hygiene precautions.</li><li>Footwear will protect against hookworm and *Strongyloides*.</li><li>Ensure that beef and pork are thoroughly cooked to prevent tapeworm infection.</li></ul>
Diagnosis	Stool examination for ova and parasites. Head CT or MRI scanning, and serology for cerebral cysticercosis.
Treatment	<ul><li>*Ascaris*, hookworm and whipworm: Albendazole or mebendazole.</li><li>*Strongyloides:* Ivermectin or albendazole.</li><li>Tapeworms: Praziquantel.</li><li>Cysticercosis: Specialist referral recommended.</li></ul>

Hepatitis A

RNA virus of the *Picornaviridae* family. Viral infection of man.

Risk Assessment

Epidemiology	<ul><li>Worldwide distribution. Higher-risk regions are South Asia, sub-Saharan and North Africa, parts of East and South East Asia (not Japan), South and Central America and the Middle East. See Map 5-2.</li><li>See NaTHNaC Country Information Pages[1] www.nathnac.org.</li></ul>
Exposure	<ul><li>Transmitted via contaminated food or water.</li><li>Those at higher risk include travellers visiting friends and relatives (VFRs), long-term travellers, and those exposed to conditions of poor sanitation.</li><li>Travellers to high-income countries are at low risk.</li></ul>

Imported Cases

There has been a steady decrease in the number of hepatitis A cases reported in the UK, with 500 to 1,000 cases reported annually. A travel history is infrequently recorded. Where a travel history was known, South Asia was the most common region of acquisition.

Signs and Symptoms

- Incubation period averages 28 days (range 15 to 50 days).
- Often asymptomatic in children under 6 years. The disease is more severe in adults.
- Prodrome of abrupt onset of malaise, anorexia, nausea and fever followed by jaundice. Recovery is usually within a month.
- Fulminant hepatitis is more likely in those with pre-existing liver disease, and in older individuals.
- 2% case fatality rate in those over 50 years of age.

Risk Management

- Travellers should practise strict food, water and personal hygiene precautions.
- See: Vaccine – Recommendations for Travel.
- In addition to indications for travel, vaccine can be given to those with chronic liver disease, with haemophilia, men who have sex with men, injecting-drug users and those at occupational risk.

Diagnosis

Serology or PCR.

Treatment

Supportive care.

Notifications

Acute infectious hepatitis is a notifiable infectious disease. See Resource Guide: 5.1.

Hepatitis A

5 Disease Guide

---

1 Alternatively see Travax http://www.travax.nhs.uk/ or Fit for Travel http://www.fitfortravel.nhs.uk/

Hepatitis A Vaccine

Type of Vaccine	▪ Inactivated vaccine. ▪ Single antigen vaccine or combined with typhoid or hepatitis B antigens. Check 'Green Book' and SPC. See Resource Guide: Appendix 1 – Vaccine Compendium.

Schedule	▪ Not included in UK schedule.
	▪ Single antigen vaccines: 2 doses 6 to 12 months apart (possible lifetime protection following primary course).
	▪ Combined hepatitis A and typhoid vaccine: Single dose; boost hepatitis A at 6 to 12 months.
	▪ Combined hepatitis A and B vaccine:
	  – Standard schedule: 3 doses; 0, 1 and 6 to 12 months.
	  – Accelerated schedule (aged 18 years and over): 0, 7 and 21 days, 12 months.
	  – 2 dose schedule (children aged 1 to 15 years at low risk during the vaccine course): 0 and 6 to 12 months.

Recommendations for Travel	▪ Vaccination should be given to those at higher risk: VFRs, long-term travellers and those exposed to conditions of poor sanitation. ▪ Because hepatitis A vaccine is well tolerated and affords long-lasting protection, it may be given to all previously unvaccinated travellers.
Contraindications and Precautions	Contraindication: confirmed anaphylactic reaction to previous dose or any component of vaccine including egg. Epaxal® is prepared on hen eggs.
Adverse Reactions	The frequency of adverse events may vary between specific products: ▪ Mild soreness at injection site, fever, malaise, fatigue. ▪ Headache and nausea. ▪ Allergic reactions and convulsions.

Hepatitis A Vaccine

5 Disease Guide

Acknowledgment: Adapted from: HD. Expert Rev Vac 7:535, 2008.

Map 5-2. Hepatitis A Antibody Prevalence

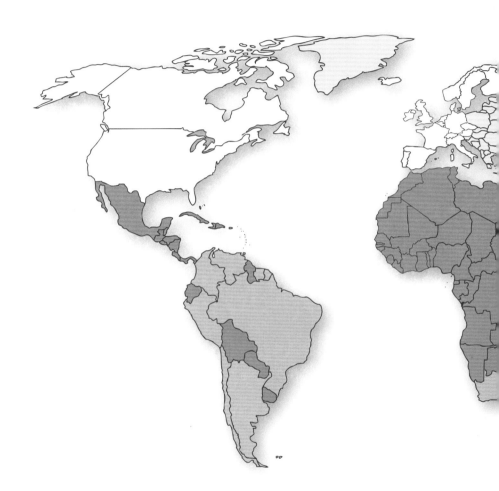

Anti-hepatitis A antibody prevalence

- Low or very low
- Intermediate
- Transitional
- High

Hepatitis B

DNA virus of the *Hepadnavirus* family. Viral infection of man.

Risk Assessment

Epidemiology
- HBV has a global distribution. Approximately 350 million people are estimated to be chronic carriers.
- Prevalence of chronic infection varies worldwide. See Map 5-3.
- See NaTHNaC Country Information Pages[1] www.nathnac.org.

Exposure
- Transmitted via infected blood or body fluids.
- Travellers can be exposed during medical or dental treatment, with direct contact between open skin lesions, or during unprotected sex, contact sports and needle sharing (including injecting-drug use, body piercing, tattoos and acupuncture), and as healthcare workers.
- Children can be infected perinatally, and in settings of high hepatitis B endemicity, child to child.
- Risk is associated with behaviour.

Imported Cases

In England, Wales and Northern Ireland in 2003, heterosexual exposure was reported as a risk factor in 48% of cases of travel-related acute HBV.

Signs and Symptoms
- Incubation period is 40 to 60 days.
- Asymptomatic infection is most common; less than 10% of children and 30% to 50% adults experience symptoms.
- Symptomatic patients experience abdominal pain, anorexia, nausea vomiting and low-grade fever. Jaundice, dark urine and light stools occur.
- Chronic infection develops in 90% of those infected perinatally, 20% to 50% of those infected in early childhood and in approximately 5% of those infected as adults. 20% to 25% of those with chronic infection develop cirrhosis which can progress to hepatocellular carcinoma.
- Case fatality rate in acute infection is approximately 1% in adults.

Risk Management
- Avoid contact with blood or body fluids. If contact is unavoidable, appropriate protective precautions must be taken, including universal precautions if working in medical/dental/high-risk setting.
- A sterile medical kit should be carried.
- See: Vaccine – Recommendations for Travel.
- Vaccine should also be given to those with chronic kidney failure, liver disease or haemophilia, injecting-drug users, men who have sex with men and individuals who change sexual partners frequently.

Diagnosis

Serology and antigen detection in blood.

Treatment

Antiviral drugs are used in chronic infection.
No specific treatment for acute infections, supportive care only.

Notification

Acute infectious hepatitis is a notifiable infectious disease.
See Resource Guide: 5.1.

1   Alternatively see Travax http://www.travax.nhs.uk/ or Fit for Travel http://www.fitfortravel.nhs.uk/

Hepatitis B Vaccine

Type of Vaccine	■ Recombinant hepatitis B surface antigen.
	■ Inactivated single antigen vaccine or combined with hepatitis A antigens.
	Check 'Green Book' and SPC.
	See Resource Guide: Appendix 1 – Vaccine Compendium.
Schedule	■ Number of doses is dependent on the vaccine and age of recipient.
	■ Three dose schedule: 0, 1 and 6 months.
	■ Accelerated schedules:
	– 0, 1 and 2 months, with 4th dose 12 months after 1st.
	– 0, 7 and 21 days, with 4th dose 12 months after 1st (aged 18 years and over).
	■ Renal insufficiency: 0, 1, 2 and 6 months.
	■ Individuals at continuing risk of infection should have a single booster around 5 years after primary immunisation.
Recommendations for Travel	■ Those who may be exposed to blood or blood products through their occupation, e.g. healthcare professionals, aid workers and public service workers such as police and fire fighters.
	■ Travellers who intend to stay for long periods in high prevalence areas.
	■ Those considered being at risk of HBV through their planned activities, e.g. volunteers undertaking manual work, contact sports, casual sex.
	■ Young children who may be in close contact with the local population and therefore at risk of cuts and scratches.
	■ Travellers with pre-existing medical conditions such as renal disease who may be at higher risk of requiring medical procedures abroad.
	■ Pregnant women, who may need medical treatment.
Contraindications and Precautions	■ Confirmed anaphylactic reaction to previous dose or any component of vaccine is a contraindication.
	■ Acute febrile illness – postpone vaccination until fully recovered.
Adverse Reactions	The frequency of adverse events may vary between specific products:
	■ Soreness, erythema and induration at the injection site.
	■ Fatigue, fever, malaise and influenza-like illness.
	■ Guillain-Barré syndrome and demyelinating diseases.

Hepatitis B Vaccine

5 Disease Guide

Acknowledgment: Adapted from Centers for Disease Control and Prevention

Map 5-3. Prevalence of Hepatitis B Virus Chronic Infection, 2006

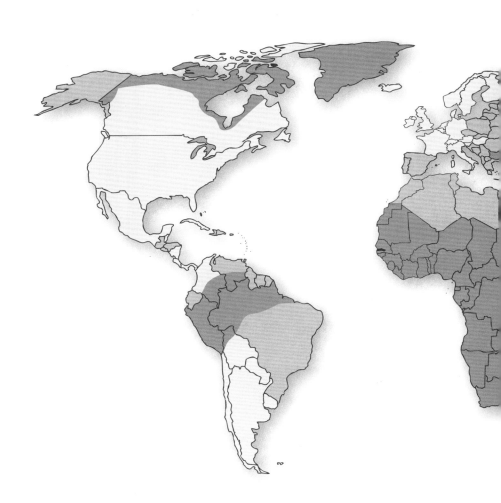

Prevalence of hepatitis B surface antigen

Low <2%
Intermediate 2% - 7%
High ≥8%

Hepatitis C

RNA flavivirus of the genus *Hepacivirus*. Viral infection of man.

Risk Management

Epidemiology
- Worldwide distribution, with a higher prevalence in parts of Africa, Asia, Eastern Europe and South America.
- WHO estimate that approximately 3% of the world's population is infected and 170 million people are chronic carriers.

Exposure
- Transmission via infected blood or body fluids.
- Short-term travel is generally low risk, but risk is associated with behaviour or occupational exposure.
- Healthcare workers and those in occupations with a risk of blood or body fluid exposures (police, prison workers and paramedics) are at higher risk.
- Activities such as unprotected sex, contact sports and needle sharing (including injecting-drug use, body piercing, tattoos and acupuncture) in areas of high endemicity are higher risk.

Imported Cases

7,000 to 9,000 cases of hepatitis C are reported annually in England and Wales. From 1992 to 2004, 295 cases (0.5% of total) were reported as travel-associated; among countries of travel reported cases, Italy, Pakistan and Spain were the most common.

Signs and Symptoms

- Incubation period is 6 to 8 weeks.
- 80% of acute cases are asymptomatic.
- Symptomatic hepatitis: Abdominal pain, loss of appetite, nausea, fatigue, dark urine and jaundice.
- Chronic infection occurs in 75% to 85% of those infected, leading to chronic liver disease in 60% to 70% of individuals. Cirrhosis develops in 5% to 20% of all infected persons and 1% to 5% die from liver failure or hepatocellular carcinoma.

Risk Management

- Avoid contact with blood or body fluids.
- Avoid injecting-drug use, unprotected sex, tattoos, body piercing, acupuncture and beauty treatments with the risk of piercing of skin.
- Healthcare workers and occupational groups, whose work puts them at risk, should follow universal infection control guidelines, and use personal protective equipment.
- A sterile medical kit can be carried where save medical care is not available.
- No vaccine is available.

Diagnosis

Serology and detection of viral RNA.

Treatment

Acute infection – supportive care.
Chronic HCV can be treated with interferon and antiviral drugs.

Notification

Acute infectious hepatitis is a notifiable infectious disease.
See Resource Guide: 5.1.

Hepatitis C

5 Disease Guide

Hepatitis E

RNA virus of the genus *Herpevirus*. Infection in man and some animals (particularly pigs).

Risk Assessment

Epidemiology
- Worldwide distribution; many cases occurring in epidemics particularly in South Asia, Mexico and Africa. Sporadic cases and small outbreaks in high-income countries.

Exposure
- Transmitted via contaminated food and water. Human-to-human transmission is rare. Possible reservoir in animals, particularly pigs.
- Those at higher risk include VFRs, and those visiting areas of poor sanitation.

Imported Cases
In 2006, there were 292 cases reported. Of these, 38% were considered to have been acquired in the UK.

Signs and Symptoms
- Incubation period is 40 days (range 2 to 8 weeks).
- Asymptomatic infection occurs.
- Acute hepatitis: Fever, malaise, nausea, jaundice lasting 1 to 4 weeks.
- Symptomatic illness is more common in young adults and pregnant women in whom fulminant hepatitis can occur.
- No chronic infection.
- Case fatality rate is 1% to 4%, increasing to 20% during third trimester of pregnancy.

Risk Management
- Food and water hygiene precautions particularly for pregnant women.
- No vaccine is available.

Diagnosis
Serology or PCR on blood.

Treatment
Supportive treatment.

Notification
Acute infectious hepatitis is a notifiable infectious disease.
See Resource Guide: 5.1.

HIV/AIDS

Human Immunodeficiency Virus (HIV) and Acquired Immunodeficiency Syndrome (AIDS): RNA virus of the genus *Lentivirus*, retrovirus family. Two major variants of the virus: HIV-1 and HIV-2, and several genotypes or clades of HIV-1. Viral infection of humans.

Risk Management

Epidemiology
- Worldwide distribution. See Map 5-4.
- In 2007: 33 million people living with HIV infection and 2.7 million new infections; 2.0 million deaths due to AIDS.
- 67% of all people living with HIV in 2007 were in sub-Saharan Africa.
- HIV-2 is largely confined to West Africa and countries with close links to West Africa.

Exposure
- Transmission occurs:
  - During exchange of body fluids during unprotected sex (vaginal and anal).
  - Via contaminated needles shared by injecting-drug users.
  - From mother to child perinatally or *in utero*; breastfeeding increases the risk of infection.
  - Via receipt of blood or blood products, contaminated syringes and during procedures in which contaminated medical instruments are used (e.g. tattooing, body piercing).
- There is no evidence that HIV/AIDS is transmitted by insects.

Imported Cases

32,000 persons were newly diagnosed with HIV in the UK between 2004 and 2008. Of those where the country of origin was known, 62% probably acquired their infection abroad: 80% in Africa, 7% in Europe outside the UK, and 13% elsewhere in the world. 80% of those infected through sex between men, acquired the infection in the UK, whereas 80% of those infected heterosexually acquired their infection abroad (mainly in Africa).

Signs and Symptoms

- 6 to 8 weeks after infection a primary or seroconversion illness occurs in about 30%. Symptoms: Fever, malaise, sore throat, myalgia, arthralgia, headache, a maculopapular rash and aseptic meningitis.
- Following a seroconversion illness or asymptomatic primary infection, there is a period of latency that usually last several years.
- A diagnosis of AIDS is made in HIV-infected persons who have an AIDS-defining condition:
  - A specific infectious complication such as: pulmonary tuberculosis, recurrent bacterial pneumonia or *Salmonella* bacteraemia, *Pneumocystis jiroveci pneumonia*, intestinal cryptosporidiosis, central nervous system toxoplasmosis.

HIV/AIDS

5 Disease Guide

HIV/AIDS

– Certain malignancies usually associated with viruses: Kaposi's sarcoma, invasive cervical cancer, Burkitt's lymphoma.
– Chronic HIV-related effects: Wasting and dementia.
– Some countries also use a CD4 lymphocyte count of <200 cells/μL.

Risk Management

- Avoid unprotected vaginal or anal sex. Use condoms that carry the BSI or CE kite-mark.
- Avoid contact with blood or blood products, contaminated syringes and procedures in which contaminated medical instruments are used (e.g. tattooing, body piercing).
- Carry a sterile medical kit.
- Do not inject non-prescribed drugs or share needles, syringe or other medical equipment.
- Post-exposure – seek urgent specialist advice.
- See Algorithm 4-7 in The Post-Travel Consultation Section 4.

Diagnosis

- Clinical presentation.
- Serology in blood, saliva or urine.
- CD4 count.
- Virus or antigen detection in blood, including a viral-load determination.

Treatment

- Seek specialist advice.
- Treatment with Highly Active Anti-Retroviral Therapy (HAART) according to British HIV Association guidelines, should be given to those with:
  – Neurological involvement.
  – Any AIDS defining illness.
  – CD4 cell count persistently <350 cells/μL.
- See Resource Guide: 5.5.
- Treat infectious complications.

Years, 2007

Acknowledgment: Adapted from World Health Organization.

Map 5-4. Prevalence of HIV Infection Among Persons Aged 15 to 49

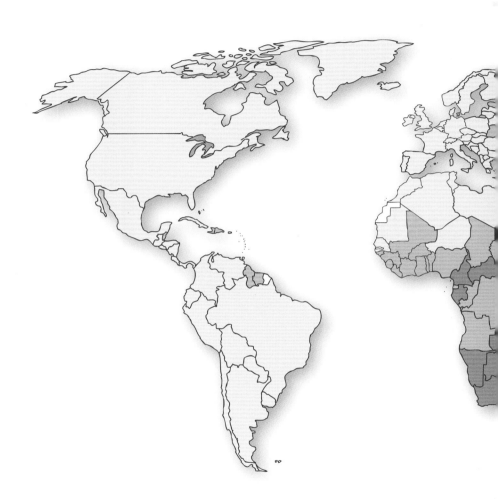

Estimated HIV prevalence

    < 1.0%

    1.0% - 5.0%

    > 5.0%

Histoplasmosis

Histoplasma capsulatum; var. capsulatum and *duboisii*. *Histoplasma* is a dimorphic fungus; it has 2 forms, a mould in the environment and yeast in humans. Fungal infection of humans and bats.

Risk Assessment

Epidemiology
- Worldwide distribution.
- *Histoplasma capsulatum var. capsulatum:* Occurs most commonly in the Ohio and Mississippi River valleys of the United States and in Latin America.
- *Histoplasma capsulatum var. duboisii:* Central and West Africa south of the Sahara and north of the Zambezi River.
- Both grow in soil contaminated with bat and bird droppings.

Exposure
- Infection is acquired by inhaling fungal elements of the mould form.
- Travellers at risk are those who go into bat-infested caves, or work in agriculture or reconstruction of buildings contaminated by bird and bat droppings.
- Low risk for most travellers.
- HIV/AIDS – infected individuals are at greater risk.

Imported Cases

Less than 1% of symptomatic returned travellers attending post-travel screening are diagnosed with histoplasmosis. There are about 8 cases per year referred to the UK Mycology Reference Laboratory; the proportion that is acquired abroad is not known.

Signs and Symptoms
- *H. capsulatum var.capsulatum:*
  - Incubation period is 10 to 14 days (range 3 to 21 days).
  - Approximately 90% infections are asymptomatic, or cause a mild, febrile illness with spontaneous recovery in 10 days to 3 weeks.
  - Acute pulmonary form: Beginning 3 to 17 days after exposure; fever, non-productive cough, chest pain, fatigue, and headache. Arthralgias and erythema nodosum are occasionally present. Patchy pneumonia with mediastinal lymph node enlargement is seen on chest X-ray. Can resolve spontaneously in 4 to 6 weeks.
  - Chronic pulmonary form: Typically in older individuals with pre-existing lung disease. Symptoms of chronic fatigue, fever, sweats, weight loss, dyspnoea, and less commonly, haemoptysis. Upper-lung cavities seen on chest X-ray.
  - Disseminated infection can occur in the immunocompromised, including AIDS patients, and in infants: Fever, malaise, weight loss, hepatosplenomegaly, adrenal insufficiency. Mucous membrane and skin lesions are occasionally seen. If untreated can be fatal.

Histoplasmosis

5 Disease Guide

Histoplasmosis

– Case fatality 40% to 50% for untreated disseminated infection.
- *H. capsulatum var. duboisii:* Skin, subcutaneous and bone infection.

Risk Management	<ul><li>Avoid contact with soil or buildings contaminated with bat and bird droppings.</li><li>High-risk activities include: building, demolition, excavation, farming, gardening, sweeping chimneys, visiting caves (especially bat caves).</li><li>Wear appropriate masks and/or protective equipment.</li><li>No vaccine is available.</li></ul>
Diagnosis	<ul><li>*H. capsulatum var. capsulatum:* Microscopy and culture of affected tissues and body fluids. Antigen detection in urine, serum and bronchiolar lavage; serology.</li><li>*H. capsulatum var. duboisii:* Histology of biopsy.</li></ul>
Treatment	*H. capsulatum var. capsulatum:*<ul><li>Mild acute pulmonary histoplasmosis: Supportive treatment only.</li><li>Severe pulmonary or disseminated infection: Amphotericin-B followed by itraconazole, or itraconazole alone. Seek specialist advice.</li></ul>*H. capsulatum var. duboisii:* Surgical resection and fluconazole.

Histoplasmosis

5 Disease Guide

Influenza

Influenza virus types A, B and C; RNA viruses of the family *Orthomyxoviridae*. Viruses categorised into subtypes based on surface antigens: haemagglutinin (H) and neuraminidase (N), e.g. H3N2. Viruses that have pandemic potential have new antigens to which there is no existing immunity, e.g. pandemic (H1N1) 2009 virus (swine influenza).

Risk Assessment

Epidemiology	■ Worldwide distribution. Temperate climates: seasonal during winter months. Tropical climates: year-round.
	■ Types A and B are responsible for epidemic human disease, with A type accounting for the most severe illness.
	■ Types B and C predominantly affect humans. Type A viruses have been isolated from a wide range of species including birds and pigs.
	■ Pandemic (H1N1) 2009 virus was the agent for the 2009/2010 influenza pandemic.
Exposure	■ Transmission via the respiratory route is most common; hand to mucous membrane spread occurs.
	■ Crowded conditions enhance exposure.
	■ International cruise passengers and Hajj and Umrah pilgrims may be at higher risk due to close proximity with individuals from multiple regions of the world where influenza may be occurring.

Important Cases   The number of cases of seasonal influenza acquired abroad is not known. The importation of pandemic (H1N1) 2009 influenza is detailed in HPA resources. Global pandemics have occurred in 1918, 1957, 1968 and 2009.

Signs and Symptoms

- Incubation period of 2 days (range 1 to 4 days).
- 30% to 50% of infections are asymptomatic.
- Symptoms include fever, dry cough, chills, headache, myalgia, fatigue, sore throat and rhinitis.
- Complications include primary influenza pneumonia, bacterial pneumonia, sinusitis, and exacerbation of underlying medical conditions.
- Febrile seizures can occur in young children, and respiratory failure in severe cases.
- Rarely encephalopathy, myocarditis and Reye syndrome.
- Persons at risk for complications include those who are pregnant, are over the age of 65 years, or have underlying asthma, diabetes, or chronic heart, liver, renal, respiratory or neurological disease and those who are immunocompromised and HIV/AIDS-infected.

Influenza

5 Disease Guide

Influenza

Risk Management	<ul><li>Avoiding contact with known cases, crowded conditions and outbreak areas.</li><li>Hand washing and cough hygiene should be practised to minimise respiratory spread: maintaining distance of at least 2 metres when coughing or sneezing, covering mouth and/or nose with disposable tissues.</li><li>Antiviral drugs can be used to treat influenza-like illness in those considered to be at risk of developing complications, provided treatment is started within 48 hours of symptoms. Not usually recommended for travellers.</li><li>See: Vaccine – Recommendations for Travel.</li></ul>
Diagnosis	<ul><li>Clinical syndrome, but it can be difficult to distinguish from other respiratory infections (influenza-like illness, ILI).</li><li>Specific laboratory tests include viral culture, serology, antigen detection and PCR.</li></ul>
Treatment	Antiviral drugs oseltamivir (Tamiflu®) and zanamivir (Relenza®) can be used for prevention or treatment of influenza in those at increased risk of serious complications. Treatment should ideally be started within 48 hours.
Notification	Human influenza virus caused by a new subtype of influenza virus is a notifiable infectious disease. See Resource Guide: 5.1.

Influenza

5 Disease Guide

Influenza Vaccine

Type of Vaccine	Inactivated vaccine. World Health Organization monitors global virus circulation and makes annual recommendations regarding the strains of type A and B viruses to be included in vaccines. Check 'Green Book' and SPC. See Resource Guide: Appendix 1 – Vaccine Compendium.
Schedule	▪ Annual vaccination. ▪ Adults and children over 13 years: single dose. ▪ Children aged 3 to 12 years: 2 doses, 4 to 6 weeks apart if receiving vaccine for the first time. ▪ Children under 3 years: the dose varies, depending on the manufacturer's instructions.
Recommendations for Travel	In the UK, the vaccine is not recommended specifically for travel. It is offered annually between September and early November to: ▪ All those over 65 years and older. ▪ All those aged 6 months and older with underlying chronic disease such as asthma, diabetes, chronic heart, liver, renal, respiratory or neurological disease and those who are immunocompromised and HIV/AIDS-infected. ▪ In 2009 all travellers to Saudi Arabia for the purposes of Hajj or Umrah were required to be vaccinated and show proof of vaccination.
Contraindications and Precautions	▪ Contraindication: confirmed anaphylactic reaction to previous dose or any component of vaccine including egg. ▪ In immunocompromised individuals, there can be a reduced antibody response. ▪ Pregnant and breastfeeding women with medical conditions that increase the risk of serious complications of influenza should be offered the vaccine.
Adverse Reactions	▪ Common: Mild reaction at injection site, low-grade fever, malaise, fatigue, headache, myalgia and arthralgia, resolving in 1 to 2 days. ▪ Uncommon: confirmed anaphylactic reaction. ▪ Rare: Convulsions, neuralgia, paraesthesiae and transient thrombocytopenia. Guillain-Barré syndrome: a causal relationship has not been established.

Influenza Vaccine

5 Disease Guide

Japanese Encephalitis (JE)

Flavivirus of the family *Flaviviridae*. Viral infection of man, pigs and birds.

Risk Assessment

Epidemiology
- JE occurs in most countries of Asia, in agricultural areas, where rice cultivation and pig farming co-exist. Rural outbreaks are more common, but urban cases can occur. See Map 5-5.
- Rare cases have been reported in the Torres Strait Islands and the tip of Cape York Peninsular on mainland Australia.
- See NaTHNaC Country Information Pages[1] www.nathnac.org.

Exposure
- Transmitted via the bite of an infective *Culex* mosquito.
- Reservoir of infection in birds and other animals (mainly pigs).
- *Culex* mosquitoes are most active during the hours from dusk to dawn.
- Seasonal transmission in temperate areas of Asia and year-round transmission in tropical areas.
- Short-term travellers and those who restrict their visits to urban areas are at very low risk. Those at higher risk include travellers who visit or work in rural agricultural areas such as rice fields and marshland. Long-term travellers and expatriates are also at higher risk.
- Overall estimated risk is 1 case per 5,000 to 1,000,000 visitors.

Imported Cases

There have been 2 reported cases in UK travellers:
- In 1982 a traveller living in Hong Kong died of JE.
- In 1994 a traveller to Thailand acquired JE and recovered fully.

Signs and Symptoms

- Incubation period of 6 to 8 days.
- Asymptomatic infection occurs in the majority of cases.
- Symptoms occur in 1 in 20 to 1 in 1,000 persons infected. They begin with fever, malaise, headache, nausea and aseptic meningitis, and can progress to meningoencephalitis with convulsions (particularly in children) and depressed consciousness.
- Case fatality rate of 20% to 30% in those with encephalitis; neurological sequelae occur in 25% to 30% of survivors.

Risk Management

- Travellers should take insect bite avoidance measures during the hours between dusk and dawn when the *Culex* mosquito is most active.
- See: Vaccine – Recommendations for Travel.

Diagnosis

Clinical presentation, PCR or culture, serology.

Treatment

Supportive treatment, No antiviral drug available.

Notification

Acute encephalitis is a notifiable infectious disease. See Resource Guide: 5.1.

---

1   Alternatively see Travax http://www.travax.nhs.uk/ or Fit for Travel http://www.fitfortravel.nhs.uk/

Japanese Encephalitis Vaccine

Type of Vaccine	Tissue culture derived or mouse brain derived vaccines, inactivated.
	Check 'Green Book' and SPC.
	See Resource Guide: Appendix 1 – Vaccine Compendium.

Schedule

- Tissue culture derived vaccine (Ixiaro®, licensed).
  - For travellers aged 18 years and older.
  - Can be considered for older teenagers, off license.
  - Primary: 2 doses, days 0 and 28.
  - Booster: not currently determined. If at continued risk, seek advice on booster after 3 years.
- Mouse brain derived vaccine (Green Cross®, unlicensed).
  - For travellers aged 1 to 17 years.
  - Three doses, 0, 7 to 14 days and 28 to 30 days.
  - Abbreviated or accelerated: 2 doses, 0, 7 to 14 days or 3 doses at 0, 7 and 14 days.
  - Booster: 1 year following primary course and thereafter 3 yearly.
  - Abbreviated and accelerated schedules can result in lower antibody titres and a shorter duration of protection.

Recommendations for Travel

- Travellers to epidemic or endemic areas whose itineraries take them through areas of rice fields and marshland during the transmission season.
- Risk activities can include fieldwork, camping, or cycling.
- Long stay travellers.

Contraindications and Precautions

Contraindications:

- Confirmed anaphylactic reaction to a previous dose or any component of the vaccine.

Precautions:

- Serious illness or acute active infection.
- Unstable neurological conditions including convulsions within the last year are a precaution for the mouse brain derived vaccine.
- Allergic conditions such as asthma, allergic rhinitis, and drug, food, gelatine or bee sting allergy are a precaution for mouse brain derived vaccine.
- Pregnancy.

Japanese Encephalitis Vaccine

5 Disease Guide

Japanese Encephalitis Vaccine

Adverse Reactions
- Tissue culture derived vaccine:
  - Common: Pain and tenderness at the injection site, headache (20%) and myalgia (13%).
  - Delayed hypersensitivity has not been described with this vaccine.
- Mouse brain derived vaccine:
  - Rare (1%) and include local redness, swelling pain, fever, chills, headache and lassitude.

Japanese Encephalitis Vaccine

5 Disease Guide

Legionnaires' Disease

Legionnaires' Disease: Gram-negative bacteria of the genus *Legionella* with more than 40 species. *Legionella pneumophila* is the most common species. Bacterial infection of humans.

Risk Assessment

Epidemiology
- Worldwide distribution.
- Isolated cases and small outbreaks occur primarily in temperate and sub-tropical areas. Cases from exposure in hotels and cruise ships are not uncommon.

Exposure
- Transmission occurs by the respiratory route.
- Inhalation of respiratory droplets of contaminated water from air conditioning units, hot tubs, showers, spas, water cooling systems and whirlpools.
- The risk for most travellers is low.

Imported Cases

In 2007, there were 441 cases and 53 deaths reported in England and Wales. 165 (44%) cases were associated with overseas travel.

Signs and Symptoms
- Incubation period is 2 to 10 days.
- Symptoms of pneumonia are cough, shortness of breath, and fever with anorexia, headache, malaise and myalgia. Vomiting, diarrhoea, confusion and delirium can also occur.
- Case fatality rate is 10% to 15% and can be higher in the elderly, those with pre-existing lung disease or chronic medical conditions.

Risk Management
- Advise travellers of how *Legionella* is transmitted and avoidance measures.
- Advise of the importance of prompt medical attention in the event of a respiratory illness.
- Those at increased risk of infection and its complications, such as the elderly or those with chronic medical conditions, should avoid high-risk activities such as the use of Jacuzzis and whirlpool spas.
- There is no vaccine available.

Diagnosis

Sputum culture, urinary antigen detection, and serology.

Treatment

Supportive care. Antibiotic treatment with a fluoroquinolone, azithromycin or doxycycline.

Notification

Legionnaires' disease is a notifiable infectious disease.
See Resource Guide: 5.1.

Leishmaniasis

Leishmaniasis (cutaneous (CL), muco-cutaneous (MCL) and visceral leishmaniasis (VL)): protozoan parasites of the genus *Leishmania*, family *Trypanosomatidae*. Species infecting humans include:

– *L. donovani* complex: 3 species; *L. donovani*, *L. infantum* and *L. chagasi*.

– *L. mexicana* complex: 3 main species; *L. mexicana*, *L. amazonensis* and *L. venezuelensis*.

– *L. tropica*, *L. major*, *L. aethiopica*.

– subgenus *Viannia*: 4 main species; *L. (V.) braziliensis*, *L. (V.) guyanensis*, *L. (V.) panamensis*, and *L. (V.) peruviana*

Protozoan infection of humans and animals.

Risk Assessment

Epidemiology	• Found in more than 80 countries in tropical and sub-tropical areas, with an annual global incidence of 1.5 to 2 million cases.
	• CL: 90% of cases in Afghanistan, Algeria, Brazil, Iran, Pakistan, Peru, Saudi Arabia and Syria.
	• VL: 90% of cases in Bangladesh, Brazil, India, Nepal and Sudan.
Exposure	• Transmitted by the bite of female sand flies. Sand flies feed predominantly from dusk to dawn.
	• Mammals, usually rodents, foxes and dogs, are reservoir hosts.
	• Rarely, congenital and blood-borne transmission occurs.

Imported Cases	58 cases (most cases were CL) reported in the UK in 2005 were acquired abroad.
	• CL: Travel to Central America, Afghanistan and South America.
	• VL: Travel to Afghanistan and countries in the Mediterranean basin.

Signs and Symptoms	• Cutaneous leishmaniasis
	– Skin lesions or ulcers that develop weeks or months after an infective sand fly bite. Regional lymphadenopathy can occur.
	– Typically caused by *L. tropica* and *L. major* in the Old World, and members of the *L. mexicana* complex and *Vianna* subgenus in the New World.
	– Ulcers of Old World CL will often self-heal; however, healing can take months. There is a risk of secondary bacterial infection and scarring.
	• Muco-cutaneous leishmaniasis:
	– Occurs when untreated CL (usually caused by *L. brasiliensis*) spreads to mucous membranes of the nose or mouth after a period of months to years. Causes locally destructive lesions.

Leishmaniasis

- Visceral leishmaniasis:
  - Uncommon in travellers and may be sub-clinical. Usually caused by *L. donovani*, *L. infantum* and *L. chagasi*.
  - Symptomatic VL can manifest months or years after infection.
  - Symptoms of VL include anaemia, fever, hepatosplenomegaly, hypogammaglobulinaemia, thrombocytopenia and weight loss. If untreated, visceral leishmaniasis can be fatal.
  - VL and HIV/AIDS co-infection can lead to severe and refractory disease.

Risk Management	• Insect bite avoidance, particularly between dusk and dawn. Sand flies are usually found at ground level and are small enough to go through mosquito nets. Sleeping in hammocks and under insecticide-treated bed nets reduces the risk. • No vaccine or chemoprophylaxis available.
Diagnosis	CL: Skin biopsy with microscopy, culture and PCR. VL: Serology and biopsy.
Treatment	Specialist advice is essential. Drug treatment depends upon the disease manifestation and can include sodium stibogluconate for CL and liposomal amphotericin B for VL.

Leishmaniasis

5 Disease Guide

Leptospirosis

Gram-negative, spirochete bacteria of the genus *Leptospira* with multiple species. Most common species is *L. Interrogans* with many serovars. Bacterial zoonosis affecting man and animals.

Risk Management

Epidemiology
- Worldwide distribution in temperate and tropical areas. Outbreaks can occur following flooding.
- Excreted in the urine by a wide variety of wild and domestic animals, particularly rodents, dogs and livestock.

Exposure
- Transmission occurs through contact with contaminated water or soil, or through direct contact with infected animals.
- Travellers participating in recreational water sports and aid workers in areas where there has been recent flooding can be at risk.

Imported Cases

In 2006, there were 44 laboratory-confirmed reports of human leptospirosis in England and Wales, of which 10 were acquired abroad. Countries visited were France, Malaysia, Borneo, Mexico, the West Indies and Viet Nam.

Signs and Symptoms
- Incubation period is 7 to 12 days (range 2 to 26 days).
- Most infections cause a systemic febrile illness without jaundice; asymptomatic infection occurs.
- Fever, chills, headache, myalgias, conjunctival suffusion, nausea and vomiting, and skin rash. Meningitis can occur.
- Approximately 10% of cases have severe disease known as Weil's disease. This can involve jaundice, renal failure, bleeding and pulmonary distress and myocarditis.
- Case fatality rate is 15% to 40% and higher for those over 60 years of age.
- Partial immunity can develop to the infecting strain.

Risk Management
- Avoid potentially infected animals and limit exposure to fresh water or soil contaminated with animal urine.
- Reduce rodent populations around habitation by clearing rubbish.
- Protective clothing should be worn when in direct contact with contaminated animals, sewage or water.
- Doxycycline (200mg for adults, weekly) can be given to persons with unavoidable occupational or recreational exposure.
- No vaccine is available.

Diagnosis

Clinical syndrome. Serology, microscopy and/or culture of blood, CSF or urine.

Treatment

Supportive treatment. Antibiotic treatment with penicillin or doxycycline.

Notification

Notification by diagnostic laboratory. See Resource Guide: 5.1.

Lyme Disease

Spirochete bacterium of the genus *Borrelia*. *B. burgdorferi* is the most common agent in North America, and *B. afzelii*, *B. garinii*, and *B. burgdorferi* in Europe and Asia. Mice, other rodents and small mammals are the bacterial reservoirs; birds may also be a reservoir. Deer are an important host for adult ticks in the complex transmission cycle of Lyme bacteria. Bacterial zoonosis of humans.

Risk Assessment

Epidemiology
- Temperate forests and fields of Europe, Asia and the north-eastern, mid-Atlantic, north-central and Pacific coastal regions of the US. The highest reported incidence of Lyme borreliosis is found in central Europe, with an estimated 206 cases per 100,000 population in Slovenia and 135 per 100,000 in Austria. In southern Europe, incidence appears to be much lower, at less than 1 per 100,000. In the US, the estimated incidence is 9.1 cases per year.

Exposure
- Transmitted by the bite of an infected *Ixodes* spp. tick.
- Exposure to ticks occurs during outdoor activities in areas of vegetation (gardens, parks, forest fringes, meadows and marshes) during the seasonal transmission period of spring, summer and autumn.
- Ticks reside on ground level vegetation where they can be brushed onto clothing or drop onto passing humans.

Imported Cases
- In 2006, there were a total of 768 cases of Lyme disease in England and Wales: 12% were acquired abroad from the United States, France, Germany, Scandinavia and other northern and central European countries.

Signs and Symptoms
- Incubation period is 7 to 10 days (range 3 to 32 days) after tick exposure.
- Asymptomatic infection occurs.
- Early disease:
  - Classic finding in 80% of persons of enlarging, painless, flat, cutaneous lesion with central clearing termed erythema migrans. May be singular or multiple.
  - Associated symptoms of fever, malaise, myalgias, headache and regional lymphadenopathy.
  - Meningitis, cranial nerve palsies and carditis with heart block can occur within days to weeks following bacterial dissemination.
- Late disease: Months after early disease, intermittent swelling of large joints and chronic arthritis may occur; chronic neurologic symptoms are seen rarely.
- Re-infection can occur.

Lyme Disease

Risk Management	<ul><li>Travellers should practise tick bite avoidance measures during outdoor activities.</li><li>Travellers should check themselves for ticks and be knowledgeable about effective tick removal methods.</li><li>Doxycycline prophylaxis can be offered for a known exposure (*Ixodes* tick bite in an endemic area of North America), if tick attached for 36 to 72 hours.</li><li>No vaccine is available.</li></ul>
Diagnosis	Clinical syndrome with erythema migrans. Serology, occasional PCR of biopsy or joint fluid.
Treatment	Doxycycline, amoxycillin or cefuroxime generally effective for erythema migrans, cranial nerve palsy and arthritis. Parenteral therapy, often with ceftriaxone, for meningitis and late neurological complications.
Notification	Notification by diagnostic laboratory. See Resource Guide: 5.1.

Lyme Disease

nowledgment: Adapted from Centers for Disease Control and Prevention. MMWR. 59(No. RR-1):1, 2010.

Map 5-5. Japanese Encephalitis Risk Areas

Geographical range of Japanese encephalitis

Ack

Malaria

Plasmodium species; *P. falciparum*, *P. ovale*, *P. malariae*, *P. vivax* & *P. knowlesi*.
Protozoan parasites of humans.

Risk Assessment

Epidemiology
- Malaria is endemic in more than 100 countries in tropical and sub-tropical areas of the world, with about 3 billion people exposed. See Map 5-6.
- There is an overlap of malaria species, however, *P. falciparum* is most common in Africa and Hispaniola, and *P.vivax* is most common in South Asia and Latin America. *P. ovale* and *P. malariae* are relatively uncommon.
- Human cases of *P. knowlesi* have recently been reported in peninsular Malaysia and Malaysian Borneo.
- See NaTHNaC Country Information Pages[1] www.nathnac.org.

Exposure
- Malaria is transmitted via the bite of an infected *Anopheles* mosquito. *Anopheles* mosquitoes feed predominately in the hours from dusk until dawn.
- All travellers to malaria endemic areas are at risk.
- Travellers at higher risk of malaria, or from serious complications, include VFRs, pregnant women, infants and young children, the elderly, the immunocompromised, those with homozygous sickle-cell disease, and those with no spleen or severe splenic dysfunction. See Special Risks Section 3.

Imported Cases

In 2008, there were 1,370 cases of malaria acquired abroad, and 6 deaths from malaria. Where the species was known, 79% of cases were of *P. falciparum* and 8% of *P. vivax*. Where a history of prophylaxis was stated, 83% of cases had not taken antimalarials. 77% occurred in VFRs.

Signs and Symptoms
- Incubation period is variable; as short as 8 days in *P. falciparum* infection, and as long as several months in *P. vivax* infection.
- Following a prodrome of fever, headache and myalgias, symptoms of malaria progress to high fever and severe myalgia.
- The fever pattern can become cyclical with hot and cold phases occurring in a 48 hour cycle with *P. vivax*, *P. ovale* and *P. falciparum*, and a 72 hour cycle with *P. malariae*.
- *P. falciparum* infections can progress rapidly to serious complications including coma (cerebral malaria), renal failure, anaemia, shock, pulmonary oedema and death.

Malaria

5 Disease Guide

---

1   Alternatively see Travax http://www.travax.nhs.uk/ or Fit for Travel http://www.fitfortravel.nhs.uk/

Malaria

- Infections with non-falciparum species are less likely to result in severe complications. Morbidity associated with these species is often associated with co-morbidity.

Risk Assessment	See Resource Guide: A5 and A22 – Key Resources.

- **A**wareness of risk: Risk depends on the specific destination, season of travel, length of stay, activities and type of accommodation.
- **B**ite prevention: Travellers should take mosquito bite avoidance measures. *Anopheles* mosquitoes feed predominantly during the hours from dusk to dawn.
- **C**hemoprophylaxis: No malaria prevention tablets are 100% effective. Taking malaria prevention tablets in combination with mosquito bite avoidance measures will give substantial protection against malaria.
  See Tables 5-1 and 5-2. See Special Risks Section 3.
- **D**iagnosis: Travellers who develop a fever of 38°C (100°F) or higher more than 1 week after being in a malaria risk area, or who develop any symptoms suggestive of malaria within a year of return should seek immediate medical care.
- See The Post-Travel Consultation Section 4.

Diagnosis	Thick and thin blood film to detect and speciate malaria parasite. Antigen detection for *P. falciparum* and *P. vivax* and PCR are available.

Treatment	

- *P. falciparum:* Specialist advice is recommended. All patients should be treated in hospital. Drugs depend upon severity of illness. Oral agents: co-artemether or atovaquone / proguanil; parenteral agents: quinine combined with oral doxycycline or clindamycin. Artesunate can be obtained after specialist advice for cases of severe malaria. Official UK guidance should be followed.
- Non-*P. falciparum* species: Chloroquine and primaquine.
- See Resource Guide: 5.6.
- See Table 5-3.

Notification	Malaria is a notifiable infectious disease. See Resource Guide: 5.1.

Malaria

5 Disease Guide

Malaria

Table 5-1. Antimalarials for adults and children*

Drug	Presentation	Adult dosage	Child dosage	Contraindications	Adverse events
Atovaquone/ proguanil	Adult: 250mg atovaquone/100mg proguanil. Paediatric: 62.5mg atovaquone/25mg proguanil.	One tablet daily. Begin 1 to 2 days before travel and continue for 7 days after travel.	< 11kg – not recommended 11 to 20kg – 1 paediatric tablet 21 to 30kg – 2 paediatric tablets 31 to 40kg – 3 paediatric tablets > 40kg – 4 paediatric tablets or 1 adult tablet	Hypersensitivity to atovaquone or proguanil; severe renal failure.	Common – headache, abdominal pain, nausea and vomiting. Rare – rash.
Chloroquine	155mg chloroquine base tablet 50mg/5ml chloroquine syrup	Two tablets weekly. Begin 1 week before travel and continue for 4 weeks after travel.	Under 6kg – ¼ tablet 6 to 9.9kg – ½ tablet 10 to 15.9kg – ¾ tablet 16 to 24.9kg tablet – 1 tablet 25 to 44.9kg – 1 ½ tablets 45kg and over – 2 tablets See Table 5-2 for chloroquine syrup dosage	Epilepsy. May exacerbate psoriasis and myasthenia gravis.	May exacerbate psoriasis. Common – headache, pruritis in those of African descent. Occasionally – blurred vision, partial alopecia. Rare – retinopathy, myopathy, photophobia.
Doxycycline	100mg capsule	One capsule daily. Begin 1 to 2 days before travel and continue for 4 weeks after travel.	<12 years of age – not recommended. >12 years – 1 capsule	Allergy to tetracycline, children <12 years, pregnancy, breastfeeding.	Stains teeth in children < 12 years. Common – gastrointestinal upset, photosensitivity, vaginitis. Rare – allergic reaction, oesophageal ulceration, benign intracranial hypertension.

(continued)

5 Disease Guide

Malaria

Table 5-1. Antimalarials for adults and children* (continued)

Drug	Presentation	Adult dosage	Child dosage	Contraindications	Adverse events
Mefloquine	250mg tablet	One tablet weekly. Begin 2 to 3 weeks before travel and continue for 4 weeks after travel.	< 5kg – not recommended 5 to 15.9kg – ¼ tablet 16 to 24.9kg – ½ tablet 25 to 44.9kg – ¾ tablet > 45kg – 1 tablet	Depression, history of psychosis, epilepsy, cardiac conduction disorders. Caution in pregnancy.	Common – dizziness, nausea, diarrhoea, headache, vivid dreams, insomnia, mood alteration. Rare – seizures, psychosis.
Proguanil	100mg tablet	Two tablets daily. Begin 1 week before travel and continue for 4 weeks after travel.	<6kg – ¼ tablet 6 to 9.9kg – ½ tablet 10 to 15.9kg – ¾ tablet 16 to 24.9kg – 1 tablet 25 to 44.9kg – 1 ½ tablets > 45kg – 2 tablets	Allergy to proguanil. Caution in renal impairment. Folic acid supplements required during pregnancy.	Common – nausea, abdominal pain, headache. Rare – rash.

*Adapted from ACMP malaria guidelines. See Resource Guide: 5.6. Suitable regimens are dependent on the destination; see NaTHNaC Country Information Pages[1] www.nathnac.org. Drug information should be checked in the British National Formulary (BNF); see Resource Guide: A2 – Key Resources.

1 Alternatively see Travax http://www.travax.nhs.uk/ or Fit for Travel http://www.fitfortravel.nhs.uk/

Malaria

Table 5-2. Chloroquine syrup dosage for children*

Weight	Dosage
< 4.5kg	2.5ml
4.5 to 7.9kg	5ml
8 to 10.9kg	7.5ml
11 to 14.9kg	10ml
15 to 16.5kg	12.5ml

Note that these doses are not the same as for chloroquine tablets which have different chloroquine content. Chloroquine syrup contains 50mg chloroquine base per 5ml.

* Drug information should be checked in the British National Formulary (BNF); see Resource Guide: A2 – Key Resources.

Table 5-3. Emergency standby treatment for adults*

Malaria

Standby treatment regimens	Dosage per tablet	Adult dose
Co-artemether	20mg artemether plus 120mg lumefantrine	4 tablets initially followed by further doses of 4 tablets each given at 8, 24, 36, 48 and 60 hours. Total 24 tablets over a period of 60 hours
Atovaquone plus Proguanil	250mg atovaquone plus 100mg proguanil	4 tablets as a single dose on each of 3 consecutive days
Quinine plus Doxycycline	300mg quinine plus 100mg doxycycline	Quinine 2 tablets 3 times a day for 3 days, accompanied by 1 tablet of doxycycline twice daily for 7 days
Chloroquine	155mg chloroquine bases	4 tablets on days 1 and 2, 2 tablets on day 3
Quinine plus Clindamycin	300mg of quinine 75 or150mg (75mg preferred) clindamycin	Quinine 2 tablets 3 times a day for 5 to 7 days, Clindamycin 3 tablets (450mg), 3 times a day for 5 days

* Adapted from ACMP malaria guidelines. See Resource Guide: 5.6. Suitable regimens are dependent on the destination. See NaTHNaC Country Information Pages[1] www.nathnac.org. Drug information should be checked in the British National Formulary (BNF); see Resource Guide: A2 – Key Resources.

5 Disease Guide

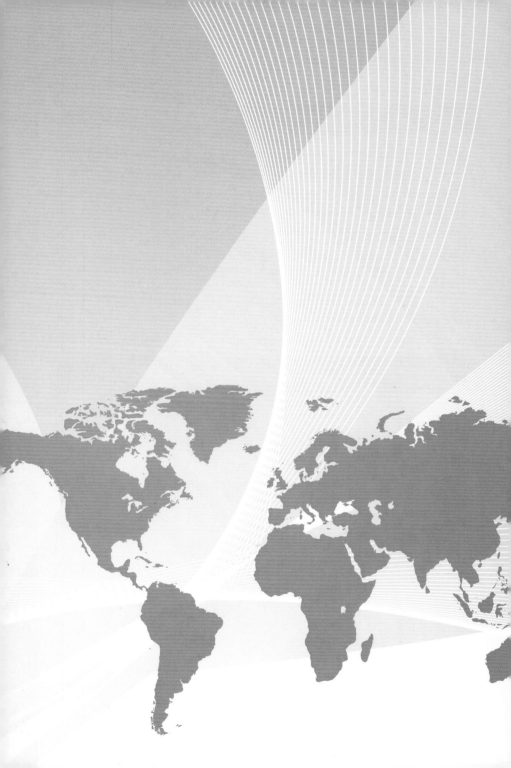

Map 5-6. Malaria Risk Areas, 2009

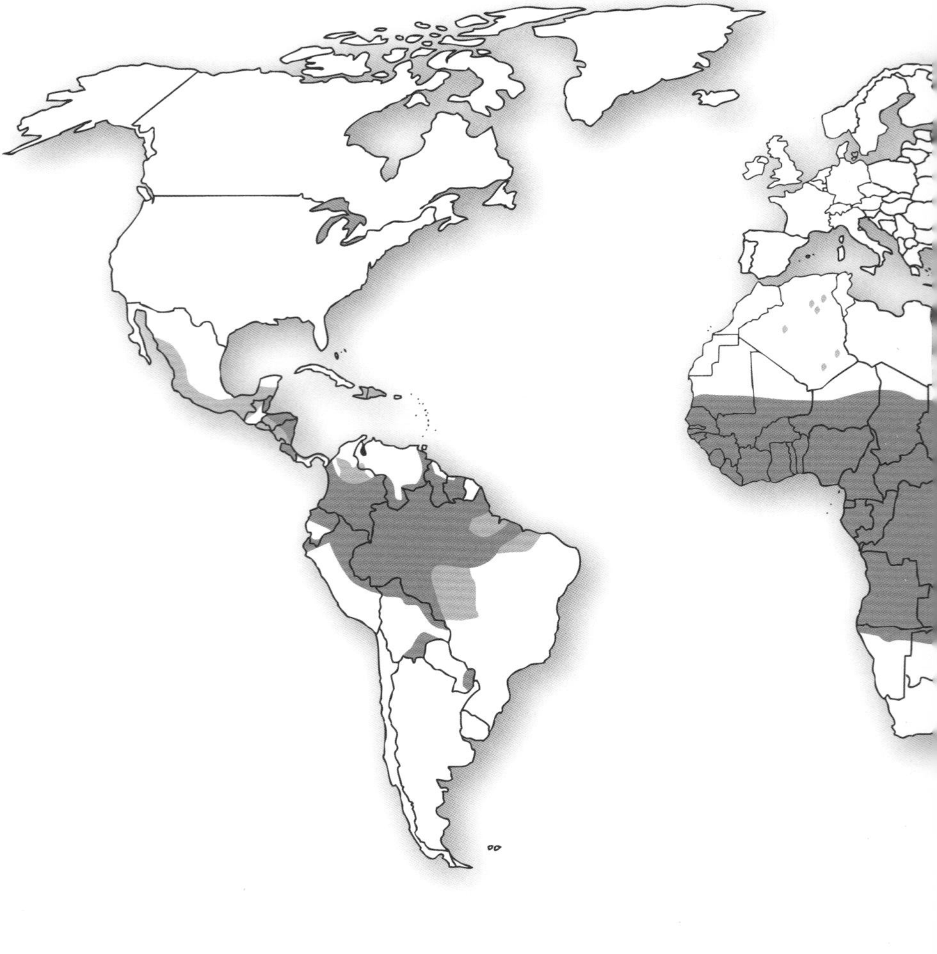

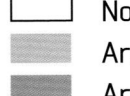

No malaria

Areas with limited risk of malaria transmission

Areas where malaria transmission occurs

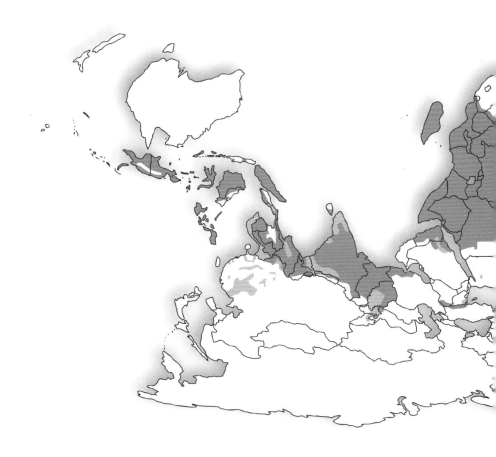

Acknowledgment: Adapted from World Health Organization

Marine Poisoning

Ciguatera, scromboid, tetrodotoxin (pufferfish) and paralytic shellfish poisonings of man.

Risk Assessment

Epidemiology
- Ciguatera, scromboid, and paralytic shellfish poisoning (PSP) have a worldwide distribution.
- Puffer fish poisoning is more common in East Asia.
- Ciguatera is more common in the Caribbean, South Pacific and Indian Oceans.

Exposure
- Ciguatera, puffer fish and PSP occur after ingestion of fish or shellfish that have eaten and concentrated toxins produced by algae or bacteria.
  - Ciguatera: coral reef fish: barracuda, snapper, grouper, sea bass and moray eel.
  - Pufferfish poisoning: caused by tetrodotoxin that is concentrated in the viscera of puffer fish (or fugu), porcupine fish and ocean sunfish.
  - PSP: bivalve shellfish such as mussels, clams, oysters, cockles and scallops.
- Scromboid is the most common condition, and occurs after ingestion of fish that has been inadequately refrigerated, that allows flesh-dwelling bacteria to multiply and produce high levels of histamine.
  - Associated with: bluefin and yellowfin tuna, mackerel, skipjack and bonito.

Imported Cases

The proportion that is acquired abroad is not known.

Signs and Symptoms

- Ciguatera: symptoms occur within 1 to 4 hours.
  - Flushing, headache, nausea, vomiting and urticaria.
  - Sensation of hot and cold temperature reversal, and paresthesiae of the legs, arms, perioral area, tongue.
  - Rarely arrhythmias.
  - Symptoms usually resolve over 1 to 4 weeks with supportive care. Chronic dyesthesias and fatigue can occur.
- Scromboid: symptoms occur within 10 to 60 minutes.
  - Symptoms closely resemble an allergic reaction.
  - Skin flushing, pruritis, throbbing headache, dizziness, nausea, vomiting, abdominal cramps and diarrhoea.
- Puffer fish poisoning: symptoms occur within minutes.
  - Perioral paresthesia, nausea and dizziness within minutes of ingestion.

Marine Poisoning

5 Disease Guide

Marine Poisoning

- Generalised paresthesia can develop together with numbness, ataxia and ascending paralysis, headache, nausea and diarrhoea.
- In severe cases respiratory failure can be fatal in about 7%.
- PSP: symptoms occur within 30 to 60 minutes.
  - Paresthesiae of the face, lips and tongue; headache, nausea, vomiting and diarrhoea can also occur.
  - In severe cases, ataxia and decreased mental status can progress to flaccid paralysis and respiratory failure.

Risk Assessment	<ul><li>Ciguatera: Avoid moray eels, barracuda and reef fish weighing more than 3 kilograms.</li><li>Scromboid: Ensure that fish has been adequately refrigerated before consumption.</li><li>Pufferfish: Always avoid.</li><li>PSP: Travellers should take notice of posted warnings of red tides that signify a risk of PSP.</li><li>Marine shellfish toxins are not inactivated by cooking or freezing.</li></ul>
Diagnosis	Diagnosis is based on clinical presentation.
Treatment	Supportive treatment that can require respiratory support:<ul><li>Scromboid: antihistamines can relieve the symptoms; most cases resolve within 4 hours.</li><li>Pufferfish and paralytic shellfish poisoning: gastric lavage to limit toxin absorption. Specialist advice recommended.</li></ul>

Marine Poisoning

5 Disease Guide

Measles

RNA virus of the genus *Morbillivirus*, *Paramyxoviridae* family. Viral infection of humans.

Risk Assessment

Epidemiology
- Worldwide distribution. A major cause of morbidity in low-income countries with low vaccination coverage.
- Continued cases and outbreaks in high-income countries of Europe.
- In 2007, WHO estimated there were 197,000 measles deaths globally, most in children under the age of 5, with mortality highest in South East Asia.

Exposure
- Respiratory droplet or direct contact with nasopharyngeal secretions from infected individuals.

Imported Cases

990 laboratory confirmed cases in the UK in 2007 of which about 2% are presumed to be acquired abroad (the majority from Asia and Europe).

Signs and Symptoms

- Incubation period 10 to 12 days.
- Fever, malaise, cough, cold symptoms and conjunctivitis.
- Maculopapular rash develops after 2 to 4 days.
- Infectious from 4 days before to 4 days after rash.
- Complications can include otitis media, diarrhoea and pneumonia.
- Rarely: Encephalitis and sub-acute sclerosing pan-encephalitis; death in approximately 1/5,000 cases.

Risk Management

- Travellers should have completed a primary course according to the UK vaccination schedule.
- Persons born in the UK before 1970 are likely to have acquired natural immunity; there is no upper age limit to vaccination and MMR vaccine can be offered if they are not immune and at risk of exposure.

Diagnosis

Clinical syndrome.

Oral fluid for IgM or PCR, nasopharyngeal secretions for viral culture or PCR.

Serology for IgM.

Treatment

Symptomatic treatment. Human Normal Immunoglobulin is used to prevent or reduce the severity of measles infection in the immunocompromised, non-immune persons. It is most effective if given within 72 hours.

Notification

Measles is a notifiable infectious disease. See Resource Guide: 5.1.

Measles

5 Disease Guide

Measles Vaccine

Type of Vaccine	**Measles, Mumps and Rubella (MMR) Vaccine**
	Live vaccine containing attenuated strains of measles, mumps and rubella viruses.
	Check 'Green Book' and SPC.
	See Disease Guide: Appendix 1 – Vaccine Compendium.

Schedule

Children:
- 1st dose at around 13 months.
- 2nd dose pre-school: 3 years and 4 months to 5 years.

Infants of 6 to 13 months:
- If travelling to risk areas should be given MMR.
- Two further doses of vaccine at 13 months and pre-school should be given.

Adults:
- Two doses at least 1 month apart.
- Those born before 1970 are likely to have had natural infection with measles, and if born before 1979, natural infection with mumps and rubella.
- MMR can be offered to travellers at risk of exposure.

Recommendations for Travel

Travellers should have completed a primary course according to the UK vaccination schedule.

Contraindications and Precautions
- Pregnant women.
- Immunocompromised individuals.
- Contraindication: confirmed anaphylactic reaction to previous dose or any component of vaccine including gelatine, neomycin or egg. M-M-RVAXPRO® and Priorix® are produced in chick embryo cells.

Adverse Reactions
- Common: Fever, malaise and occasional rash, approximately 1 week after vaccination; arthritis and arthralgias can occur in adult females approximately 2 to 3 weeks following vaccination.
- Uncommon: Febrile convulsions.
- Rare: Encephalitis and idiopathic thrombocytopenic purpura.

Measles Vaccine

5 Disease Guide

Melioidosis

Burkholderia pseudomallei. Gram-negative bacterial infection of animals and humans.

Risk Assessment

Epidemiology	• Endemic in South East Asia and northern Australia. Most cases have been reported in Thailand. Also occurs in the South Pacific and South Asia.
	• Sporadic cases from countries in Latin America, the Caribbean, Africa and the Middle East.
	• Wide animal reservoir.
	• Organism isolated from soil and water, particularly rice fields, in endemic areas.
Exposure	• Transmitted by:
	– Inoculation of skin abrasions or mucosa with contaminated soil (mud) or water.
	– Inhalation of respiratory droplet-borne bacteria from contaminated water.
	• Human to human and animal to human transmission is rare.
	• Rare risk for travellers.

Imported Cases	1997 to 2007, 23 cases were reported following visits to Thailand, Bangladesh, India, Australia, Malaysia and British Virgin Islands.

Signs and Symptoms	• Incubation period of several days to years. Latent infection is well-described with clinical illness occurring several years after exposure, often following a change to the host such as diabetes or malignancy.
	• Most infections are asymptomatic.
	• Pulmonary infection: cough associated with fever, headache, anorexia, severe chest pain and myalgia, with cavitary pneumonia seen on chest X-ray.
	• Localised infection: skin nodule after inoculation; associated with fever and myalgia; can progress to bacteraemia. Children can develop supportive parotitis, possibly after ingestion of contaminated water.
	• Acute bacteraemia: presents as septicaemia with or without another focus of infection such as skin or lungs. Bacteria can seed and produce abscesses in multiple organs.
	• Relapse is common (13% over 10 years) if treatment is incomplete.
	• Persons with chronic medical conditions (e.g. diabetes, renal failure, corticosteroid use) are at increased risk of infection.
	• Case fatality rate as high as 40% in severe disease.

Melioidosis

5 Disease Guide

Melioidosis

Risk Management	<ul><li>Travellers with skin lesions should avoid contact with soil and standing water in risk areas.</li><li>Footwear should be worn.</li><li>Healthcare professionals should practise blood and bodily fluid precautions.</li><li>No vaccine is available.</li></ul>
Diagnosis	Microscopy and culture of blood, urine, sputum, or skin lesions. Serology.
Treatment	Antibiotic treatment using ceftazidime or imipenem, followed by prolonged course (5 to 6 months) of oral antibiotics (often trimethoprim-sulfamethoxazole with doxycycline; amoxicillin clavulanic acid can be used in children).

Melioidosis

5 Disease Guide

Meningococcal Meningitis

Neisseria meningitidis, with at least 13 serotypes including serotypes A, C, W135, Y. Gram-negative bacterial infection of humans.

Risk Assessment

Epidemiology
- Worldwide distribution. Cases of meningococcal disease occur sporadically and in seasonal outbreaks. See Map 5-7.
- The highest burden of meningococcal disease occurs in the 'African meningitis belt', which extends across the dry, savannah parts of sub-Saharan Africa from Senegal in the west, to Ethiopia in the east.
- Most epidemics occur during the winter-spring period in temperate areas and during the dry season in tropical areas. In the meningitis belt of sub-Saharan Africa, the highest transmission period in West Africa is between November to May/June, with the season variable in east Africa.
- See NaTHNaC Country Information Pages[1] www.nathnac.org.

Exposure
- Transmission occurs via the respiratory route.
- Most travellers are at low risk. Those at higher risk include healthcare workers, VFRs and long-term travellers who have close contact with the local population.
- Vaccination is a requirement for religious pilgrims to Saudi Arabia for the Hajj and Umrah.

Imported Cases

1,152 isolates of *N. meningitidis* were reported in England and Wales in 2006. The proportion that is acquired abroad is not known.

Signs and Symptoms
- Incubation period is 3 to 4 days.
- 5% to 10% of populations living in endemic areas can be asymptomatic carriers.
- Symptoms of meningitis include sudden onset of fever, intense headache, nausea and vomiting. Neck stiffness from meningeal irritation occurs. Delirium and coma can ensue.
- A characteristic petechial or purpuric rash often occurs with septicaemia.
- With early diagnosis and treatment the case fatality rate varies from 5% to 12%.

Meningococcal Meningitis

---

1   Alternatively see Travax http://www.travax.nhs.uk/ or Fit for Travel http://www.fitfortravel.nhs.uk/

Meningococcal Meningitis

Risk Management	<ul><li>Avoid, where possible, overcrowded conditions.</li><li>See: Vaccine – Recommendations for Travel.</li><li>Vaccination is a requirement for religious pilgrims to Saudi Arabia for the Hajj and Umrah.</li><li>Previous vaccination with the meningitis C conjugate vaccine (MenC) does not protect against the other meningococcal serotypes.</li><li>At present there is no available vaccine against serotype B in the UK.</li></ul>
Diagnosis	Clinical syndrome. CSF for microscopy, antigen detection, culture and PCR. Blood for culture and PCR.
Treatment	Antibiotic treatment with a penicillin or advanced generation cephalosporin. Intensive supportive care.
Notification	Meningococcal meningitis and invasive meningococcal disease are notifiable infectious diseases. See Resource Guide: 5.1.

Meningococcal Meningitis

5 Disease Guide

Meningococcal Meningitis Vaccine

Type of Vaccine	Polysaccharide vaccine, quadrivalent, inactivated. A conjugate quadrivalent vaccine is due to be available in the UK in 2010.
	Check 'Green Book' and SPC.
	See Resource Guide: Appendix 1 – Vaccine Compendium.
Schedule	■ Adults and children 2 years and older: Single dose, repeat every 3 years if at risk.
	■ Infants aged 3 months to 2 years: 2 doses at a 3 month interval.
	■ Children under 5 years when first vaccinated should be given a booster if at risk after 2 to 3 years.
	Previous vaccination with MenC does not protect against the other meningococcal serotypes.
Recommendations for Travel	■ Travellers visiting areas at risk of meningococcal disease whose planned activities put them at higher risk including healthcare workers, VFRs and long-term travellers who have close contact with the local population.
	■ All travellers to Saudi Arabia for the purposes of Hajj or Umrah are required to be vaccinated and show proof of vaccination.
Contraindications and Precautions	■ Confirmed anaphylactic reaction to a previous dose or to any constituent of the vaccine.
	■ Conjugate Meningitis C vaccine in the preceding 2 weeks: allow an interval of at least 2 weeks before ACWY vaccine administration.
Adverse Reactions	Refer to the Summary of Product Characteristics of the vaccine for full details:
	■ Mild injection site soreness; fever more common in young children.
	■ Anaphylactic reaction.

Meningococcal Meningitis Vaccine

5 Disease Guide

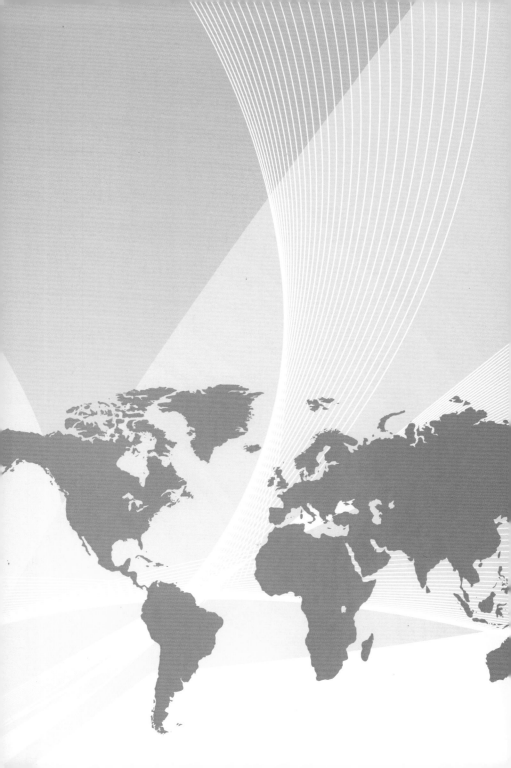

Acknowledgment: Adapted from Centers for Disease Control and Prevention

Map 5-7. Meningococcal Meningitis Belt in Africa

Meningitis belt

Mumps

RNA virus of the genus *Rubulavirus*, *Paramyxoviridae* family. Viral infection of humans.

Risk Assessment

Epidemiology	• Worldwide distribution. In countries where vaccination was introduced and high coverage sustained, the incidence of the disease has dropped and circulation has stopped. In countries where vaccination was not introduced the incidence of mumps remains high, mostly affecting children aged 5 to 9 years.
Exposure	• Respiratory droplet or direct contact with nasopharyngeal secretions from infected individuals.

Imported Cases

There were 1,476 confirmed cases of mumps in the UK in 2007, of which about 3% were linked to travel abroad.

Signs and Symptoms

- Incubation period of 18 days (range 12 to 25 days).
- Frequent asymptomatic or non-specific cases.
- Symptoms of fever, unilateral or bilateral parotitis, sore throat, anorexia and malaise.
- Infectious from 3 days before to 5 days after parotitis.
- Orchitis in 20% to 50% of post-pubertal males.
- Meningitis in approximately 15%.
- Rare: Deafness and encephalitis.

Risk Management

- Travellers should have completed a primary course according to the UK vaccination schedule.
- Persons born in the UK before 1979 may have acquired natural immunity.
- Unimmunised travellers should be vaccinated.

Diagnosis

Clinical syndrome.

Oral fluid for IgM and / or PCR, urine or throat swab for PCR.

Serology for IgM.

Treatment

Symptomatic treatment and treatment of complications.

Notification

Mumps is a notifiable infectious disease.
See Resource Guide: 5.1.

Mumps

5 Disease Guide

Mumps Vaccine

 Type of Vaccine

Measles, Mumps and Rubella (MMR) Vaccine. See Measles Vaccine.

Live vaccine containing attenuated strains of measles, mumps and rubella viruses.

Check 'Green Book' and SPC.

See Resource Guide: Appendix 1 – Vaccine Compendium.

Mumps Vaccine

5 Disease Guide

Myiasis

Infestation of skin by larvae (maggots) of *Diptera* flies; includes *Cordylobia anthropophaga* (tumbu fly) and *Dermatobia hominis* (human bot fly). Wound infestations (wound myiasis) due to other species of flies occur. Larval infections of humans and animals.

Risk Assessment

Epidemiology	• The tumbu fly occurs in sub-Saharan Africa and southern Spain.
	• The bot fly occurs in Central and South America.
Exposure	• Tumbu fly: Female fly lays eggs in clothes left outside to dry. When clothes are worn, the eggs hatch and larvae penetrate skin.
	• Bot fly: Female fly lays eggs on bloodsucking insects (usually a mosquito) or foliage. The eggs are transferred to skin; hatch and the larvae penetrate the skin.
	• Rare in British travellers. Long-term travellers potentially at increased risk.

Imported Cases	Myiasis cases are acquired abroad annually. The exact number is not recorded.

Signs and Symptoms	• Time from skin penetration to emergence of mature larvae: Tumbu fly 8 to 12 days, human bot fly 2 to 6 weeks.
	• Presents as a single or multiple boils that can be painful as the larva grows. There is an air pore for each lesion containing a larva.
	• The person may report movement within the lesion.
	• Myiasis from the tumbu fly tends to be located where clothing covers the body. Lesions with bot fly larvae are usually on exposed areas of the face, scalp, arms and legs.
	• Secondary bacterial infection may occur.

Risk Management	• Insect bite avoidance for the bot fly.
	• Drying clothes indoors and ensuring they are carefully ironed (ironing eliminates eggs laid in clothes) helps reduce risk.

Diagnosis	Clinical presentation.

Treatment	Tumbu fly larvae: Application of petroleum jelly on a cellophane to occlude the air pore. Larvae will exit the lesion and can be manually removed.

Myiasis

5 Disease Guide

Norovirus

Norovirus infection ('viral gastroenteritis'): RNA viruses of the genus *Norovirus*, family *Caliciviridae*. Viral infection of humans.

Risk Assessment

Epidemiology	■ Worldwide distribution in both low- and high-income areas.
	■ Excreted in the faeces and vomit of infected persons.
Exposure	■ Food-borne, human-to-human, and water-borne transmission. Shellfish can concentrate virus. Norovirus can contaminate environmental surfaces that can be a mode of transmission. Possible respiratory droplet transmission.
	■ Outbreaks seen on cruise ships and in healthcare institutions, long-term care facilities and restaurants.

Imported Cases	There are 3,000 to 4,000 cases of norovirus reported in England and Wales annually. The proportion that is acquired abroad is not known.

Signs and Symptoms	■ Incubation period of 12 to 48 hours. Low infectious dose.
	■ Sudden onset of nausea, cramping, vomiting, and watery diarrhoea. Low-grade fever, headache, myalgias and malaise are seen.
	■ Infection is usually self-limiting with recovery after 1 to 3 days.
	■ Children can have more vomiting than adults; infants and the elderly can become dehydrated.

Risk Management	■ Practise food and water hygiene precautions.
	■ Practise personal hygiene with hand washing.
	■ Decontamination of environmental surfaces with dilute bleach.

Diagnosis	Clinical presentation. PCR for virus in stool.

Treatment	Symptomatic treatment with rehydration.

Notification	Food poisoning is a notifiable infectious disease. See Resource Guide: 5.1.

Norovirus

5 Disease Guide

Onchocerciasis (River Blindness)

Onchocerca volvulus. Nematode infection of humans. See Disease Guide: Filariasis.

Risk Assessment	
Epidemiology	▪ Tropical sub-Saharan Africa with small foci in Brazil, Mexico, Guatemala, Venezuela and Yemen.
Exposure	▪ Transmission from the bite of a black fly (*Simulium* species). Black flies breed along fast-flowing rivers and streams.
	▪ Very low risk for most travellers

Imported Cases — Four cases reported between 1998 and 2007, all acquired in West and Central Africa.

Signs and Symptoms

- Following the bite of a black fly, larvae are inoculated into humans and develop over at least 6 months into adult worms.
- Adult worms lie in subcutaneous nodules, mate and produce microfilariae. Adult worms can live up to 15 years.
- Symptoms are related to inflammatory reactions to subcutaneous and ocular migration of microfilarial worms. Subcutaneous nodules containing adult worms are generally asymptomatic.
- Pruritis and itching with rash. Chronic infection can lead to hyperpigmented or hypopigmented papular dermatitis.
- Ocular symptoms range from itching and redness to corneal scarring, night blindness and eventually complete loss of sight.

Risk Management

- Avoid river areas where black flies are prevalent.
- Travellers should use insect bite avoidance measures.

Diagnosis

- Clinical syndrome; travellers usually present with intense itching several months following exposure. Eosinophilia may be present.
- Microscopy for microfilariae in skin snips and adult worms in excised nodules.
- Characteristic eye lesions in chronic infection: corneal opacities and punctate keratitis.
- Mazzotti test: a single dose of diethylcarbamazine can be preformed under specialist supervision.

Treatment — Specialist referral recommended. Ivermectin is drug of choice. Excision of subcutaneous nodules containing adult worms can be considered.

Onchocerciasis (River Blindness)

5 Disease Guide

Pertussis (whooping cough)

Bordetella pertussis and other species of the genus *Bordetella*. Gram-negative bacterial infection of humans.

Risk Assessment	
Epidemiology	▪ Worldwide distribution. ▪ Epidemic peaks occur every 2 to 5 years. In 2006, there were 152,535 cases reported worldwide. ▪ Most cases occur in low-income countries. ▪ Increasing number of cases seen in high-income countries as protection from childhood vaccine wanes.
Exposure	▪ Transmission occurs via the respiratory route. ▪ Persons are most infectious during initial catarrhal stage. If untreated, persons remain contagious for up to 6 weeks after onset of cough. ▪ Most travellers are at low risk.
Imported Cases	1,090 cases reported in England and Wales in 2007. The proportion acquired abroad is not known.
Signs and Symptoms	▪ Incubation period is 7 to 10 days (range 1 to 3 weeks). ▪ Chronic cough may be the only symptom, particularly in adults. Other symptoms include runny nose, conjunctival injection, malaise and low-grade fever. ▪ Severe symptoms include paroxysmal cough followed by characteristic inspiratory 'whoop' and vomiting. ▪ Complications include pneumonia, respiratory distress and cerebral hypoxia. Illness can be protracted, lasting several months.
Risk Management	▪ Avoid contact with nasopharyngeal secretions from infected persons. ▪ Infected individuals should use respiratory precautions. ▪ Prophylactic antibiotics can be considered for susceptible exposed infants, after discussion with local Health Protection Unit.
Diagnosis	Clinical syndrome: prolonged cough with paroxysms, whooping, or post-cough vomiting. Culture and PCR of nasopharyngeal secretions. Serology of limited value in diagnosing acute infection.
Treatment	Antibiotic treatment with a macrolide: treats or decreases severity of infection in the catarrhal stage. Once the cough has developed antibiotics can eliminate *B. pertussis* from the nasopharynx and reduce transmission, but may not be effective in improving symptoms. Supportive care.
Notification	Pertussis is a notifiable infectious disease. See Resource Guide: 5.1.

Pertussis (whooping cough) Vaccine

Type of Vaccine	Acellular pertussis vaccine, inactivated; part of a combined vaccine:
	■ Diphtheria, tetanus, acellular pertussis, inactivated polio, *Haemophilus influenzae* type b (DTaP/IPV/Hib).
	■ Diphtheria, tetanus, acellular pertussis, inactivated polio vaccine (dTaP/IPV or DTaP/IPV).
	Check 'Green Book' and SPC.
	See Resource Guide: Appendix 1 – Vaccine Compendium.
Schedule	Primary course, infants: dose of DTaP/IPV/Hib at 2, 3 and 4 months of age. Reinforcing dose: 3 years following primary course (dTaP/IPV) (or minimum of 1 year following primary course when primary vaccination has been delayed).
	Pertussis vaccination currently not recommended for adults and children 10 years and older in the UK. Adolescent and adult vaccines are available in other countries of Europe and North America.
Recommendations for Travel	■ Travellers should be up to date with routinely recommended vaccinations according to the UK schedule.
Contraindications and Precautions	■ Confirmed anaphylactic reaction to a previous dose or to any constituent of the vaccine including neomycin, streptomycin or polymyxin B.
	■ A history of neurological complications following a previous dose (defer immunisation until condition stabilised or cause identified).
Adverse Reactions	Common: Pain, swelling or redness at the injection site.
	Rare: Fever, convulsions, high-pitched screaming, pallor, cyanosis and limpness (usually following a diphtheria and pertussis containing vaccine).

Pertussis Vaccine (whooping cough)

5 Disease Guide

Plague

Gram-negative bacterial infection caused by *Yersinia pestis* a member of the *Enterobacteriaceae* family. Bacterial zoonosis of man.

Risk Assessment

Epidemiology
- Plague is reported consistently from Africa: Democratic Republic of the Congo, Madagascar and Tanzania; Asia: China, Mongolia and Vietnam; South America: Peru; and south-western United States. More than 80% of cases are reported in Africa.
- Rats are the major reservoir for plague transmission to humans. Other mammals such as prairie dogs and rock squirrels can be hosts in rural areas.

Exposure
- Most cases transmitted by the bite of infected fleas.
- Respiratory droplet spread from human-to-human with pneumonic form.
- Occasional transmission following handling of infected animals.

Imported Cases

No cases have been reported in the UK since 1918.

Signs and Symptoms
- There are 3 forms of plague: bubonic, pneumonic and septicaemic.
- Bubonic:
  - Most common form.
  - Incubation period of 2 to 6 days.
  - Following the bite of an infected flea, bacteria spread from the site to regional lymph nodes causing painful swelling (bubos).
  - Fever, chills, headache and malaise are seen.
- Pneumonic:
  - Incubation period 3 to 5 days.
  - Shortness of breath, blood stained sputum and respiratory failure.
- Septicaemia: both bubonic and pulmonary can progress to septicaemic disease that carries a high mortality.

Risk Management
- Avoid contact with rodents.
- Clear areas around homes of rubbish.
- Practise insect bite avoidance measures to reduce the risk of flea bites.

Diagnosis

Clinical syndrome for bubonic plague. Microscopy and culture of material from lymph node, blood or sputum.

Treatment

Supportive treatment. Antibiotic therapy with an aminoglycoside or a tetracycline.

Notification

Plague is a notifiable infectious disease. See Resource Guide: 5.1.

Plague

Pneumococcal Infection

Streptococcus pneumoniae (pneumococcus). Gram-positive bacterial infection of humans.

Risk Assessment

Epidemiology

- Worldwide distribution. Pneumococcal disease is a major cause of morbidity and mortality in children and adults.
- Pneumococcus is one of the most common causes of otitis media in children, and bacterial pneumonia in all ages. It is the most common cause of bacterial meningitis in adults, and in children where there is high coverage of *Haemophilus influenzae* vaccination.

Exposure

- Transmitted via respiratory droplets or direct contact with respiratory secretions.
- Those at higher risk include travellers in crowded conditions or in close prolonged contact with young children.
- Very young, elderly, immunocompromised, including those with HIV/AIDS, persons without a spleen or with chronic disease, are at higher risk of invasive disease.

Imported Cases

5,000 to 6,000 cases of invasive pneumococcal disease are reported annually in England and Wales. A travel history is not usually recorded.

Signs and Symptoms

- Incubation period of 1 to 3 days.
- Many persons will carry the pneumococcus asymptomatically in their nasopharynx.
- There are several clinical syndromes:
  - Local spread causing sinusitis and otitis media.
  - Pneumonia.
  - Meningitis.
  - Bacteraemia.
- Pneumonia: Fever, cough often with blood-tinged sputum, shortness of breath and pleuritic chest pain.
- Meningitis: Fever, headache, photophobia, neck stiffness and decreased consciousness.
- Bacteraemia: Usually occurs as a consequence of pneumonia or meningitis, but can occur as a primary infection with sepsis, shock and severe illness.
- Case fatality rates dependent on age and underlying disease: pneumonia 5% to 7%, bacteraemia 20% to 60% and meningitis 30% to 80%.

Pneumococcal Infection

5 Disease Guide

Pneumococcal Infection

Risk Management	<ul><li>Hand washing and respiratory precautions when caring for someone with known pneumococcal disease.</li><li>Vaccination is recommended as part of childhood immunisation programme, for those aged 65 years or over, and those in certain clinical risk groups, e.g.<ul><li>– Asplenia or dysfunction of the spleen.</li><li>– Chronic respiratory disease.</li><li>– Chronic heart disease.</li><li>– Chronic renal disease.</li><li>– Chronic liver disease.</li><li>– Immunocompromised.</li><li>– Diabetics.</li><li>– Cochlear implants and those with known CSF leaks.</li></ul></li></ul>
Diagnosis	Clinical presentation. Culture of blood, CSF or sputum. Antigen detection in urine.
Treatment	Antibiotic therapy. Macrolides, penicillin and cephalosporins depending upon resistance patterns of the pneumococcus.
Notification	Pneumococcal meningitis is a notifiable infectious disease. See Resource Guide: 5.1.

Pneumococcal Infection Vaccine

Type of Vaccine(s)	Polysaccharide vaccine representing common pneumococcal types; inactivated. Two vaccines used in the UK: • 23-valent pneumococcal polysaccharide vaccine (PPV). • 7-valent pneumococcal conjugate vaccine (PCV). Check 'Green Book' and SPC. See Resource Guide: Appendix 1 – Vaccine Compendium.
Schedule	Children under 1 year: 2 doses of PCV with an interval of 2 months, booster at 13 months of age. Children 1 year to under 2 years: 1 dose of PCV. Adults 65 years or over: Single dose PPV. Note different schedules for those in clinical risk groups.
Recommendations for Travel	At risk travellers should have received vaccine according to the UK schedule. Not routinely recommended for travel.
Contraindications and Precautions	Confirmed anaphylactic reaction to a previous dose or component of the vaccine.
Adverse Reactions	Common: Mild soreness and redness at injection site.

Poliomyelitis

RNA virus, of the genus *Enterovirus*, *Picornaviridae* family. There are 3 serotypes of the human poliovirus (1, 2 & 3). Viral infection of humans.

Risk Assessment

Epidemiology

- Important gains have been achieved in the global control of polio. The WHO regions of the Americas, Western Pacific and Europe are polio-free.
- In 2008, 4 countries remained polio-endemic: Afghanistan, India, Nigeria and Pakistan.
- Over the last several years, wild polio has been introduced into other countries in Africa, the Middle East, South and South East Asia.
- See NaTHNaC Country Information Pages[1] www.nathnac.org.

Exposure

- Transmission is via the faecal-oral route by exposure to faecally contaminated food or water or by human-to-human contact.
- Travellers are at a very low risk.

Imported Cases

The last case of wild-type polio reported in the UK was in 1993: this was acquired and diagnosed in India.

Signs and Symptoms

- Incubation period ranges from 3 to 21 days.
- The ratio of asymptomatic to paralytic illness is about 200:1.
- Mild, non-specific, self-limited disease accounts for 4% to 8% of infections: upper respiratory tract symptoms, gastrointestinal disturbances and influenza-like illness.
- Aseptic meningitis occurs in 1% to 2% of infections and is characterised by fever, headache and neck stiffness and pain. Lasts from 2 to 10 days with complete recovery.
- Flaccid paralysis occurs in <1% of polio infections. There is a prodrome of fever and myalgias lasting 1 to 10 days followed by paralysis that progresses over 2 to 3 days and stabilises as the temperature returns to normal.
- Paralysis can affect a single or multiple limbs, and also the muscles of respiration.
- 1 in 200 infections result in irreversible paralysis (usually in the legs). Of these cases, 5% to 10% die when respiratory muscles are involved.

Protective immunity following infection may not occur.

---

1   Alternatively see Travax http://www.travax.nhs.uk/ or Fit for Travel http://www.fitfortravel.nhs.uk/

Poliomyelitis

Risk Management	• Travellers should practise strict food, water and personal hygiene precautions.
	• See: Vaccine – Recommendations for Travel.
Diagnosis	Clinical syndrome. Culture or PCR for virus in blood, cerebrospinal fluid, stool or pharynx.
Treatment	Supportive treatment. No antiviral drugs available.
Notification	Poliomyelitis a notifiable infectious disease. See Resource Guide: 5.1.

Poliomyelitis

5 Disease Guide

Poliomyelitis Vaccine

Type of Vaccine	Inactivated virus vaccine, usually combined with other antigens. Check 'Green Book' and SPC. See Resource Guide: Appendix 1 – Vaccine Compendium.

Schedule	Primary:
	• Infants and children under 10 years: 3 doses at monthly intervals, usually 2, 3 and 4 months of age.
	• Adults and children aged 10 years and older: 3 doses at monthly intervals. Adults and children aged 10 years and older require a vaccine containing a low dose of diphtheria.
	Booster:
	• Infants and children under 10 years:
	  – 1st booster: 3 years after completion of the primary course.
	  – 2nd booster: 10 years after the 1st booster.
	• Adults and children aged 10 years and older:
	  – 1st booster: 5 years after the primary course.
	  – 2nd booster: ideally 10 years after 1st booster (but minimum of 5 years where previous dose has been delayed).

Recommendations for Travel	• Travellers should have completed a primary vaccination course according to the UK schedule. • Travellers should practise strict food, water and personal hygiene precautions. • Previous poliomyelitis does not protect against another episode of poliomyelitis. • A booster dose of a polio-containing vaccine should be given to at risk travellers who have not received a dose within the previous 10 years.
Contraindications and Precautions	A history of a confirmed anaphylactic reaction to a previous dose of a polio-containing vaccine or any of the components of the vaccine.
Adverse Reactions	• Common: Local reactions of pain, redness, swelling at the site and mild fever. • Rare: Confirmed anaphylactic reactions.

Q Fever

Coxiella burnetii. Zoonotic, gram-negative bacterial infection of humans and animals.

Risk Assessment

Epidemiology
- Worldwide distribution.
- Wide distribution in animals; also found in ticks.
- *Coxiella burnetii* bacteria produce spores that can survive in the environment for long periods.

Exposure
- Inhalation of respiratory droplet-borne bacteria:
  - After contact with placental products, blood, urine or faeces from an infected animal.
  - From contaminated dust, straw or dried faeces.
- Ingestion of contaminated milk.
- Rare transmission from a tick bite and between humans.
- Travellers to endemic areas who visit farms can be at risk.
- Those who come into contact with ruminants (goats, sheep and cattle) as part of their work are at increased risk of exposure (e.g. farmers, shearers, abattoir workers, butchers).

Imported Cases
Less than 50 cases reported annually. The proportion acquired abroad is not known.

Signs and Symptoms

- Incubation period is 2 to 3 weeks (range 4 days to 6 weeks).
- Asymptomatic infection is common.
- Acute infection: sudden onset of fever (>38°C) headache, malaise, myalgia, and anorexia. Hepatomegaly and elevation of liver enzymes can occur. Infection can be self-limiting.
- Pneumonia: fever, headache, cough and chest pain. Disease is often mild but can progress to respiratory failure.
- Neurologic complications: aseptic meningitis and encephalitis.
- Chronic infection can occur a month or years after initial infection. The most common manifestation is endocarditis, usually affecting abnormal or prosthetic heart valves. Osteomyelitis also occurs.
- Pregnancy can lead to recurrent infection if untreated.
- Case fatality rate approximately 1% to 2% for acute infection, up to 65% in chronic infection.
- Protective immunity may follow infection.

Q Fever

5 Disease Guide

Q Fever

Risk Management	▪ Avoid contact with ruminants particularly during lambing or calving. ▪ If contact unavoidable, practise good hand hygiene and cover open wounds. ▪ If working with infected animals use additional protective equipment such as a face mask and take specialist advice. ▪ Pregnant women and immunocompromised persons should avoid risk environments. ▪ Avoid consumption of unpasteurised dairy products in areas of risk. ▪ Take insect bite avoidance measures. Check body for ticks and remove if found. ▪ No vaccine is available in the UK. Vaccine may be available in parts of the world where the disease is considered an occupational risk.
Diagnosis	Clinical syndrome. Serology; PCR of infected tissues.
Treatment	▪ Acute infection: Antibiotic treatment with doxycycline; macrolides or fluoroquinolones can also be used. ▪ Chronic endocarditis: Combination antibiotic treatment with doxycycline and hydroxychloroquine, or rifampin plus ciprofloxacin for 18 months to 3 years.
Notification	Notification by diagnostic laboratory. See Resource Guide: 5.1.

Q Fever

5 Disease Guide

Rabies

RNA virus of the genus *Lyssavirus*, of the family *Rhabdoviridae*. Viral infection of humans and mammals.

Risk Assessment

Epidemiology
- Rabies is present in many countries worldwide. The burden of clinical rabies in humans is in Asia and Africa.
- See NaTHNaC Country Information Pages[1] www.nathnac.org.

Exposure
- Transmission can occur following contact with the saliva from an infected wild or domestic animal (including bats), most often via a bite, and occasionally via saliva contact with an open wound.
- Most rabies exposures during travel are from a dog bite.
- Risk of exposure is increased by type of activity (e.g. running, cycling), occupation (e.g. veterinarians) and longer duration of stay.
- Children are at increased risk as they are less likely to avoid contact with animals or report a bite or lick.

Imported Cases

In the UK, there have been at least 25 reported deaths from rabies acquired abroad since records began in 1902. The most recent case occurred in 2009. Most cases have been as a result of dog bites.

Signs and Symptoms
- Incubation period of 20 to 90 days (rarely as short as 4 days and as long as several years).
- Initial symptoms can be non-specific: fever, headache, myalgia and fatigue. Paraesthesia can occur at the bite site.
- The virus is neurotropic affecting the central nervous system.
- Rabies in humans is usually 'furious', characterised by laryngeal spasms in response to drinking water, accompanied by a feeling of terror (hydrophobia). A rare form results in progressive paralysis (paralytic rabies) with dysphagia, encephalitis and respiratory failure. Cases progress to coma and death.
- Once symptoms are present, with rare exception, rabies is fatal, usually within 1 to 3 weeks.

Risk Management
- Avoid contact with wild or domestic animals.
- See: Vaccine – Recommendations for Travel.
- Following an animal bite, wounds should be thoroughly washed and an urgent medical assessment sought, even if the wound appears trivial.
- Prompt post-exposure treatment is required, even if pre-exposure vaccine has been received.

---

1   Alternatively see Travax http://www.travax.nhs.uk/ or Fit for Travel http://www.fitfortravel.nhs.uk/

Rabies

Rabies

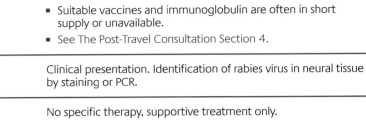

- Suitable vaccines and immunoglobulin are often in short supply or unavailable.
- See The Post-Travel Consultation Section 4.

Diagnosis	Clinical presentation. Identification of rabies virus in neural tissue by staining or PCR.
Treatment	No specific therapy, supportive treatment only.
Notification	Rabies is a notifiable infectious disease. See Resource Guide: 5.1.

Rabies

Rabies Vaccine

Type of Vaccine(s)	Human cell culture (HDCV) or chick embryonated egg (PCEV) vaccines, inactivated. Check 'Green Book' and SPC. See Disease Guide: Appendix 1 – Vaccine Compendium.
Schedule	Pre-exposure: 1 dose on days 0, 7 and 21 or 28. Booster: ■ Travellers at intermittent risk: Single reinforcing dose 2 years after primary course. ■ Regular and continuous risk: Single reinforcing dose, 1 year after primary course. Further doses at 3 to 5 year intervals.
Recommendations for Travel	Pre-exposure vaccination should be given to adults and children who are: ■ Travelling to remote areas where medical care is not readily available. ■ Undertaking higher-risk activities (e.g. cycling, running). ■ Travelling for long periods through rabies-endemic countries. ■ At occupational risk, e.g. vets, animal handlers, and laboratory workers who handle the virus.
Contraindications and Precautions	■ Confirmed anaphylactic reaction to a previous dose of rabies vaccine or any component of the vaccine, including egg. Rabipur® is produced in chick embryo cells.
Adverse Reactions	■ Common: Pain, swelling and redness at injection site; lymphadenopathy, headache, myalgia and arthralgia. ■ Uncommon: Immune complex reaction (urticaria, pruritis and malaise) in persons receiving booster doses of HDCV. ■ Rare: Severe systemic reactions.

Rabies Vaccine

5 Disease Guide

Rickettsial Diseases

Rickettsial diseases: bacteria of the genus *Rickettsia*. Rickettsial infections are of 3 main groups:

- Typhus group: *R. prowazekii* (epidemic typhus), *R. typhi* (murine typhus).
- Spotted fever group (SFG): *R. rickettsii* (Rocky Mountain spotted fever [RMSF]), *R. conorii* (Mediterranean spotted fever also known as Boutonneuse fever) and *R. africae* (African tick bite fever).
- Scrub typhus: *Orientia tsutsugamushi*.

Gram-negative bacterial infections of humans and animals.

Risk Assessment

Epidemiology

Rickettsial infections have a worldwide distribution.

- Typhus group:
  - Murine typhus: worldwide.
  - Epidemic typhus: Africa, South America and Asia, often in impoverished or refugee populations.
- SFG:
  - RMSF: Mid- and south-Atlantic and south-central states of the US; parts of Central and South America.
  - Mediterranean spotted fever: East Africa, Southern Europe, Middle East and Mediterranean basin.
  - African tick bite fever: Occurs in tropical and sub-tropical areas of sub-Saharan Africa and in the eastern Caribbean.
- Scrub typhus: Asia and Western Pacific regions.

Exposure

R. prowazekii: transmitted by the human body louse.

R. typhi: transmitted by rat fleas; can occur via scratching flea faeces into broken skin or conjunctiva.

R. rickettsii, *R. conorii* and *R. africae:* transmitted by different species of ticks.

Orientia tsutsugamushi: transmitted by chigger mite.

Imported Cases

There were 52 rickettsial infections reported in England, Wales and Northern Ireland between 1996 and 2005. 27 were of the spotted fever group. Travel history is not usually reported.

Signs and Symptoms

- Incubation periods:
  - Epidemic and murine typhus, 7 to 14 days
  - SFG, 2 to 14 days.
  - Scrub typhus, 5 to 14 days.

Rickettsial Diseases

- Epidemic typhus *(R. prowazekii)*: Abrupt onset of fever, headache and malaise; trunk and proximal limb rash 2 to 4 days after fever onset. Meningoencephalitis occurs in 50% of cases. Case fatality rate of 20%; less with treatment.
- Murine typhus *(R. typhi)*: Fever, rash, headache and myalgias. Case fatality rate of 1% to 2%.
- RMSF *(R. rickettsiae)*: Abrupt fever onset of fever, myalgias and headache. Nausea, vomiting and abdominal pain can occur. Macular rash develops after 3 to 5 days, particularly on the extremities and can affect the palms and soles of the feet, and become petechial or ecchymotic. Meningoencephalitis and pulmonary complications can occur in severe cases. Case fatality rate of 7% to 10%.
- Mediterranean spotted fever *(R. conorii)* and African tick bite fever *(R. africae)*: An eschar *(tache noire)* is usually present. Regional lymphadenopathy is common with African tick bite fever.
- Scrub typhus: Abrupt onset of fever, headache, myalgia; suffusion of conjunctiva. 50% have an eschar with painful regional lymphadenopathy. Truncal maculopapular rash can occur. Meningoencephalitis occurs in severe cases.

Risk Management	▪ Travellers should practise tick bite avoidance measures during outdoor activities.
	▪ Travellers should check themselves for ticks and be knowledgeable about effective tick removal methods.
	▪ There is no vaccine to prevent rickettsial diseases.
Diagnosis	▪ Clinical presentation.
	▪ Antigen detection, or PCR; serology.
Treatment	Supportive treatment. Antibiotic treatment with tetracyclines.
Notification	Typhus fever is a notifiable infectious disease. See Resource Guide: 5.1.

Rift Valley Fever (RVF)

Rift Valley Fever (RVF): RNA virus of the genus *Phlebovirus*, family *Bunyaviridae*. Zoonotic viral infection of animals and humans.

Risk Assessment

Epidemiology
- RVF occurs in most sub-Saharan African countries, particularly those in East Africa, and Egypt and Madagascar.
- Sporadic cases reported in Saudi Arabia and Yemen.
- RVF virus is maintained in nature through transovarial passage in mosquitoes (usually *Aedes* spp.) and amplified in domestic cattle and sheep.

Exposure
- Transmission via:
  - Bite of an infected mosquito, usually *Aedes* spp.
  - Contact with blood and tissues of infected animals (e.g. sheep, cattle, camels and goats). Respiratory droplet transmission can also occur.
  - Ingestion of unpasteurised milk or undercooked meat from infected animals.
- Rare risk for most travellers.
- Travellers at higher risk are:
  - Those exposed to mosquitoes during epidemics, particularly during rainy seasons.
  - Those with close contact with blood or carcasses of infected animals.

Imported Cases   No reported cases.

Signs and Symptoms
- Incubation period is 2 to 6 days.
- Mild disease: Abrupt onset of fever, headache, muscle and joint pains, photophobia and conjunctivitis, with recovery over several days.
- Severe disease occurs in 1% to 5% of those infected: haemorrhagic, meningoencephalitis, or ocular forms.
  - Haemorrhagic (1%): jaundice, haematemesis, epistaxis, malena and purpura, occurs after 2 to 4 days with high case fatality.
  - Meningoencephalitis (<1%): headache, confusion, convulsions, lethargy and coma, with long-term neurological sequelae.
  - Ocular (up to 10%): retinal lesions develop after 1 to 3 weeks. Permanent visual impairment can occur in 1% to 10% of cases.

Rift Valley Fever

Rift Valley Fever (RVF)

Risk Management	<ul><li>Insect bite avoidance measures.</li><li>Avoid contact with the blood and bodily fluids of infected animals.</li><li>Milk or meat from infected animals should be boiled or cooked before eating.</li><li>No commercially available vaccine.</li></ul>
Diagnosis	Viral culture of blood, antigen detection, PCR; serology.
Treatment	Supportive treatment.
Notification	Acute encephalitis and viral haemorrhagic fever are notifiable infectious diseases. See Resource Guide: 5.1.

Rift Valley Fever

5 Disease Guide

Rotavirus

RNA viruses of the family *Reoviridae*. Multiple strains defined by structural viral proteins, known as 'P' and 'G' proteins. Viral infection of humans.

Risk Assessment

Epidemiology	■ Worldwide distribution. Nearly all children will have been infected by rotavirus by the age of 5 years.
Exposure	■ Faecal-oral transmission: human-to-human contact and contaminated environmental surfaces. Food- and water-borne transmission also occur. Possible respiratory droplet transmission.
	■ Seasonal transmission in temperate climates: winter and spring.

Imported Cases	Approximately 14,000 cases of rotavirus are reported annually in England and Wales. The proportion acquired abroad is not known.

Signs and Symptoms	■ Incubation period of 1 to 3 days.
	■ Sudden onset of fever, vomiting and watery diarrhoea.
	■ Severe, dehydrating illness can occur in infants and young children. Rotavirus causes approximately 50% of hospitalisations for diarrhoeal illness in young children.
	■ Infection is self-limiting with recovery after 3 to 7 days.
	■ Deaths are unusual in high-income countries, but it is estimated that 500,000 childhood deaths occur in low-income countries.

Risk Management	■ Practise food and water hygiene precautions.
	■ Practise personal hygiene with hand washing.
	■ See: Vaccine – Recommendations for Travel.

Diagnosis	Virus or viral antigen detection in stool.

Treatment	Symptomatic treatment with rehydration.

Rotavirus

5 Disease Guide

Rotavirus Infection Vaccine

Type of Vaccine(s)	Two oral, live attenuated vaccines: RotaRix®: monovalent vaccine available in the UK. RotaTeq®: pentavalent vaccine, not available in the UK. Check 'Green Book' and SPC. See Resource Guide: Appendix 1– Vaccine Compendium.
Schedule	▪ RotaRix®: 1st dose at 6 to 16 weeks of age; 4 week interval between doses; complete series by 24 weeks of age. ▪ RotaTeq®: 3 doses given at 2, 4 and 6 months of age; complete series by 32 weeks of age.
Recommendations for Travel	Not specifically indicated for travel but may be given to age-appropriate children who are travelling.
Contraindications and Precautions	▪ Hypersensitivity to the vaccines or any component of the vaccines. ▪ History of intussusception. ▪ Presence of congenital malformation of the gastrointestinal tract. ▪ Immunodeficiency. ▪ Postpone vaccine in infants with acute febrile illness, diarrhoea or vomiting.
Adverse Reactions	RotaRix®: – Common: loss of appetite, irritability, fever, diarrhoea, vomiting and abdominal pain. – Uncommon: constipation, muscle cramps and rash. RotaTeq®: – Common: diarrhoea, vomiting and irritability.

Rotavirus Infection Vaccine

Rubella

RNA virus of the genus *Rubivirus*, *Togavirus* family. Viral infection of humans.

Risk Assessment

Epidemiology

- Worldwide distribution. More common in low-income countries with no vaccination programme or low vaccination coverage, however, cases continue to occur in high-income countries of Europe.
- 251,311 cases were reported worldwide to the WHO in 2007, highest number of reports were from the Russian Federation, China and Poland.

Exposure

- Respiratory droplet or direct contact with nasopharyngeal secretions from infected individuals.
- Maternal-foetal transmission; highest risk in first trimester of pregnancy.

Imported Cases

There were 34 confirmed cases in the UK in 2007, of which about 3% were linked to travel abroad. The majority occurred in migrants to the UK from countries where rubella vaccination is not included in the childhood schedule.

Signs and Symptoms

- Incubation period of 14 days (range 12 to 23 days).
- Sub-clinical infections occur in up to 50% of children.
- Mild fever, rash and lymphadenopathy.
- Infectious from 7 days before to 5 to 7 days after rash onset.
- Complications of arthritis or arthralgias in 70% of adult females.
- Rare: Thrombocytopenia and encephalitis.
- Congenital rubella syndrome: Foetal loss, premature delivery, cataracts, deafness, mental retardation; most common when maternal rubella occurs in first trimester.

Risk Management

- Travellers should have completed a primary course according to the UK vaccination schedule.
- Persons born in the UK before 1979 may have acquired natural immunity.
- Unimmunised travellers should be vaccinated.

Diagnosis

Clinical syndrome.
Oral fluid IgM or PCR, nasopharyngeal secretions for viral culture or PCR.
Serology for IgM.

Treatment

Symptomatic treatment and treatment of complications. Normal human immunoglobulin may be used in the treatment of primary rubella or symptomatic re-infection in pregnant women.

Notification

Rubella is a notifiable infectious disease. See Resource Guide: 5.1.

Rubella Vaccine

Type of Vaccine	Measles, Mumps and Rubella (MMR) Vaccine. See Measles Vaccine.
	Live vaccine containing attenuated strains of measles, mumps and rubella viruses.
	Check 'Green Book' and SPC.
	See Resource Guide: Appendix 1 – Vaccine Compendium.

Salmonellosis

Salmonella enterica. There are more than 2,500 different serovars of *Salmonella*, including Typhoid and Paratyphoid; see Disease Guide: Typhoid / Paratyphoid. Gram-negative bacterial infections of humans and animals.

Salmonellosis *(sidebar)*

Risk Assessment	
Epidemiology	▪ *Salmonella* is distributed worldwide. The organism is prevalent in domesticated poultry and cattle and can be found in many other animal species. ▪ *Salmonella* is one of the most common bacterial causes of travellers' diarrhoea (TD).
Exposure	▪ Transmitted via the faecal-oral route: food-borne is most common mode. Food items typically at risk are raw or undercooked poultry meat and eggs, unpasteurised dairy products, and poorly cooked beef, but any foods can be a risk.
Imported Cases	Approximately 12,000 reports of salmonellosis are reported annually in England, Wales and Northern Ireland. About 20% of cases are acquired abroad; however, travel history reporting is incomplete. The countries of acquisition reflect the pattern of UK travel, with most cases originating from Europe.
Signs and Symptoms	▪ Incubation period of 12 to 72 hours. Need a high inoculum to establish infection, often ≥10^5 organisms. ▪ Diarrhoea, cramping, vomiting and fever (38°C to 39°C). Diarrhoea usually loose to watery, but can be mixed with blood and mucus. ▪ Infection in healthy persons is usually self-limiting over 4 to 7 days. ▪ Complications are more common in very young children, the elderly and immunocompromised individuals, including those with HIV/AIDS. Complications include extra-intestinal spread (bacteraemia) with possible infection of the central nervous system in infants, and other body sites such as bone and blood vessels. ▪ <1% of intestinal infections will result in chronic faecal excretion of *Salmonella*.
Risk Management	▪ Practise food and water hygiene precautions. ▪ Practise personal hygiene with hand washing particularly after handling potentially contaminated foods or animal, e.g. poultry and reptiles.
Diagnosis	Stool culture. Other body fluids (e.g. blood and cerebral spinal fluid) can be cultured in bacteraemic cases.
Treatment	▪ Supportive treatment and hydration. ▪ Antibiotics should be used to treat very ill persons and those with extra-intestinal spread of infection. ▪ AIDS patients may need prolonged treatment.
Notification	Food poisoning is a notifiable infectious disease. See Resource Guide: 5.1.

SARS, Severe Acute Respiratory Syndrome

SARS-associated coronavirus (SARS-CoV) of the family *Coronaviridae*. Viral infection of man and wild animals (e.g. palm civet and raccoon dogs).

Risk Assessment

Epidemiology
- Cases were first identified in Guandong Province, China in late 2002; the virus spread in 2003 to 28 other countries, affecting 8,422 individuals and resulting in 916 deaths. The outbreak was over in July of 2003.
- Wild animals (e.g. palm civets and raccoon dogs) may be a reservoir for transmission of the virus to humans. There is evidence that domestic animals can become infected.
- There are currently no cases of SARS in the world and no risk to travellers.

Exposure
- Transmission occurs via the respiratory route, surface contamination with secretions, and possibly faeces. Respiratory virus excretion is highest during the second week of illness.
- During 2002 to 2003, most cases occurred after close contact with the respiratory secretions of an infected individual, usually in a healthcare or household setting.

Imported Cases
Four probable cases of SARS were reported in the UK during the SARS outbreak in 2003.

Signs and Symptoms
- Incubation period of 4 to 6 days (range 1 to 14 days).
- 2% to 8% of infections were estimated to be asymptomatic.
- Symptoms include high fever, headache, malaise, myalgia, and cough. Diarrhoea affects about 20%.
- Symptoms can progress to dyspnoea and pneumonia with rapid deterioration.
- The overall case fatality rate (CFR) in the 2002 to 2003 epidemic was 11%. The CFR was highest in the elderly and those with pre-existing medical illness.

Risk Management
- These measures apply if cases are occurring:
  - Respiratory hygiene: Cover cough, wash hands.
  - Avoid contact with cases. Healthcare workers should use appropriate protective precautions and follow strict infection control guidelines.
  - Avoid live animal markets and handling uncooked animal products.
  - Prevention of a future epidemic relies on early case detection and implementation of infection control measures to contain local and international spread of the disease.
  - There is no vaccine available.

SARS, Severe Acute Respiratory Syndrome

5 Disease Guide

SARS, Severe Acute Respiratory Syndrome

Diagnosis	Nasopharyngeal swabs and respiratory secretions for culture, antigen detection and PCR. Faecal samples for PCR. Serology.
Treatment	No specific antiviral treatment. Isolation and intensive supportive care.
Notification	SARS is a notifiable infectious disease. See Resource Guide: 5.1.

SARS, Severe Acute Respiratory Syndrome

5 Disease Guide

Schistosomiasis

Parasitic trematode (flatworm or fluke) of several species of *Schistosoma*. Most common are *S. mansoni*, *S. haematobium* and *S. japonicum*. *S. intercalatum* and *S. mekongi* are less common. Parasites of humans.

Risk Assessment

Epidemiology
- Approximately 200 millions cases of schistosomiasis worldwide, primarily in Africa and South America. See Map 5-8.
- *S. mansoni:* Africa and South America (primarily Brazil; *S. haematobium:* Africa; *S. japonium:* Central China and the Philippines; *S. intercalatum:* Central Africa; *S. mekongi:* Laos and Cambodia around Mekong River.
- See NaTHNaC Country Information Pages[1] www.nathnac.org.

Exposure
- Eggs are excreted in human faeces or urine *(S. haematobium)* and hatch in freshwater. The larvae (miracidia) infect freshwater snails where there is multiplication of the parasite and another larval form (cercariae) emerges.
- Cercariae penetrate human skin exposed to fresh water in streams, rivers or lakes during activities such as wading, swimming, working, washing or bathing.

Imported Cases
From 2003 to 2007, 340 cases were reported in England and Wales. 71% of identified species were due to *S. haematobium*. Of those with a travel history most cases were acquired in sub-Saharan Africa.

Signs and Symptoms

- Schistosomiasis has 3 stages of infection: a cercarial dermatitis, acute and chronic schistosomiasis.
- Cercarial dermatitis also known as 'swimmer's itch':
  - Coincides with cercarial penetration of skin, erythema, papular lesions and itching.
- Acute schistosomiasis, also known as 'Katayama fever':
  - Symptoms coincide with maturation of schistosome worms and production of eggs. Occurs weeks to months after exposure with fever, malaise, urticaria and eosinophilia.
  - Cough, diarrhoea, weight loss, haematuria, headache, joint/ muscle pain and liver/spleen enlargement can also be seen.
  - Central nervous system involvement occurs rarely, producing seizures or transverse myelitis, when eggs enter the brain or spinal cord.
  - *S. mansoni, S. japonicum, S. intercalatum* and *S. mekongi* primarily produce intestinal disease, and *S. haematobium* bladder and urinary tract disease.

Schistosomiasis

5 Disease Guide

1 Alternatively see Travax http://www.travax.nhs.uk/ or Fit for Travel http://www.fitfortravel.nhs.uk/

Schistosomiasis

- Chronic infection:
  - *S. mansoni* and *S. japonicum*, liver fibrosis, portal hypertension with ascites and oesophageal varices.
  - *S. haematobium*, bladder scarring, renal obstruction, chronic urinary infection (often with *Salmonella*) and possibly, bladder cancer.

Risk Management	- Avoid swimming, wading, washing or bathing in freshwater rivers, streams and lakes in endemic countries. - Swimming in well maintained, chlorinated swimming pools or sea water is not a risk activity. - No vaccine or drug prophylaxis available. - Use of insect repellents prior to exposure or towel drying afterwards does not prevent infection.
Diagnosis	Microscopy of stool or rectal biopsy *(S. mansoni, S. japonicum, S. intercalatum and S. mekongi)* or microscopy of urine and semen *(S. haematobium)*. Serology. See Algorithm 4-6 in The Post-Travel Consultation.
Treatment	Specialist referral recommended. Antiparasitic treatment with praziquantel.

Schistosomiasis

5 Disease Guide

Acknowledgment: Adapted from Centers for Disease Control and Prevention

Map 5-8. Geographical Distribution of Schistosomiasis

Schistosomiasis Endemic Areas

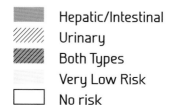

Hepatic/Intestinal
Urinary
Both Types
Very Low Risk
No risk

Sexually Transmitted Infections (STIs)

Sexually Transmitted Infections (STIs) are a group of viral, bacterial and parasitic infections affecting humans. They include:

- Chancroid *(Haemophilus ducreyi).*
- Chlamydia *(Chlamydia trachomatis).*
- Genital herpes (*Herpes simplex* 1 and 2).
- Gonorrhoea *(Neisseria gonorrhoeae).*
- Granuloma inguinale (Donovanosis; *Klebsiella granulomatis*).
- Hepatitis A (hepatitis A virus); see Disease Guide.
- Hepatitis B (hepatitis B virus, HBV); see Disease Guide.
- Hepatitis C (hepatitis C virus); see Disease Guide.
- Human Immunodeficiency Virus (HIV); see Disease Guide.
- Human papillomavirus (HPV) (genital warts and cervical cancer).
- Lymphogranuloma venerum (LGV)(*Chlamydia trachomatis* L1, L2, L3).
- Scabies *(Sarcoptes scabiei).*
- Syphilis *(Treponema pallidum).*
- Trichomoniasis *(Trichomonas vaginalis).*

Risk Assessment

Epidemiology
- Worldwide distribution.
- In adults aged 15 to 49 years, an estimated 340 million new infections of curable STIs (e.g. chlamydia, gonnorrhoea, syphilis and trichomonas) occur annually. The highest number is in South and South East Asia followed by sub-Saharan Africa, Latin America and the Caribbean.
- Genital herpes (*Herpes simplex* type 2) is the leading cause of genital ulcers.
- Certain STIs have specific geographical distributions:
    - Chancroid: Africa, South East Asia, and Papua New Guinea.
    - Granuloma inguinale: Papua New Guinea, India, Vietnam, Japan, southern Africa, Brazil and among the Aboriginal people of Australia.
    - LGV: Africa, India, parts of South East Asia, parts of South America and the Caribbean. Sporadic cases in Australia, North America and Europe.

Exposure
- Transmission of STIs predominantly occurs during exchange of body fluids during unprotected sex (oral, vaginal or anal), or during intimate skin-to-skin contact.
- Blood-borne viruses (i.e. HIV, Hepatitis B and C) can be transmitted via blood or blood products, contaminated syringes, during medical instrumentation (e.g. tattooing, body piercing), dental procedures, or by sharing needles during injecting-drug use.

Sexually Transmitted Infections

5 Disease Guide

Sexually Transmitted Infections (STIs)

- STIs can be transmitted from mother to child either *in utero* (syphilis), during delivery (chlamydia, genital herpes, gonorrhoea, HIV) or breastfeeding (HIV).

Imported Cases

- In 2007, UK Genitourinary clinics reported about 400,000 new STIs. The proportion acquired abroad is not known.
- In 2005 in England and Wales, 965 cases of gonorrhoea were reported. Travel information was available for 104 cases and 12% had sexual contact abroad in the 3 months before diagnosis; Western Europe and the Caribbean were the most reported regions of travel.
- In 2002 to 2005, 6,176 cases of syphilis were reported; 10% were acquired abroad.

Signs and Symptoms

There are 3 main syndromes associated with STIs; some syndromes overlap and persons can have more than 1 infection:

- Genital ulcers:
  - Genital herpes and syphilis most common; also chancroid, LGV, and granuloma inguinale.
- Urethritis and cervicitis:
  - Chlamydia and gonorrhoea.
- Vaginitis:
  - Trichomoniasis, bacterial vaginosis (BV), candidiasis.

Specific STIs:

- Chancroid: Incubation period of 3 to 7 days. Painful genital ulcer causing destruction with tender, suppurative inguinal lymphadenopathy.
- Chlamydia: Incubation period of 6 to 19 days. Asymptomatic infections are common. Typical syndrome is urethritis in men; pharyngitis can occur after oral sex and proctitis after anal sex. Epididymitis, prostatitis and Reiter's syndrome are complications. Females can be asymptomatic or have increased vaginal discharge, and pelvic inflammatory disease (PID). Risk of ectopic pregnancy, fallopian tube scarring, or infertility.
- Genital herpes:
  - Primary infection: Multiple painful genital vesicles or ulcers, inguinal lymphadenopathy, and occasional systemic, 'flu-like' symptoms. Complications of aseptic meningitis and urinary retention can occur.
  - Recurrence of lesions is common without suppressive treatment.
- Gonorrhoea: Incubation period 2 to 7 days.
  - Asymptomatic in up to 50% of women and 10% of men.

Sexually Transmitted Infections (STIs)

- Men: Purulent penile discharge that can lead to epididymitis and urethral stricture.
- Women: Asymptomatic in up to 50% of infections. Can develop vaginal discharge, dysuria and post-coital bleeding. Risk of ectopic pregnancy, fallopian tube scarring, or infertility.
- Complications in both men and women: Disseminated gonococcal infections with pustular cutaneous lesions and gonococcal arthritis; uncommonly meningitis and endocarditis.

- Granuloma inguinale: Incubation period 3 to 40 days. Painless genital ulcer extending into skin folds in anogenital areas. Complications include secondary infection and elephantiasis.
- Human papillomavirus:
  - Genital warts: >90% caused by HPV serotypes 6 and 11. Incubation period 2 weeks to 8 months. Warts are flat, papular or pedunculated lesions usually on the external genital mucosa. The virus can also infect the cervix, vagina, anus and mouth.
  - Cervical HPV infection: Certain serotypes of HPV (serotypes 16 and 18 account for 65%) are associated with cervical cancer. HPV can also lead to anal cancer.
- LGV: Incubation period 3 to 30 days. A papule or ulcer at the site of inoculation associated with tender inguinal or femoral lymphadenopathy. Rectal LGV can lead to a proctocolitis with pain and rectal discharge. Complications of colorectal fistula and stricture.
- Scabies: Intensely itchy, nodular lesions, commonly between the fingers and toes, abdomen, axillae and groin.
- Syphilis: Untreated, syphilis has primary, secondary and tertiary phases.
  - Primary: Painless ulcer (chancre) occurs 10 to 70 days after exposure and heals without treatment.
  - Secondary: 3 to 6 weeks after 1° infection, diffuse maculo-papular rash that also involves the palms and soles, generalised lymphadenopathy, and occasional meningitis.
  - Tertiary: Untreated, 1° or 2° disease can become latent for a prolonged period (months to years). It can recur (3° syphilis) leading to cardiac or neurologic (cognitive, motor, auditory or ocular) disorders.
- Trichomoniasis: Females develop vaginal itch and frothy vaginal discharge. Men often asymptomatic, but urethral discharge and urinary discomfort occur.

Risk Management
- Travellers should not have unprotected oral, vaginal or anal intercourse. British standard condoms should be used in preference to those available abroad.

Sexually Transmitted Infections

5 Disease Guide

Sexually Transmitted Infections (STIs)

- Travellers should avoid contact with blood or blood products, needles and syringes, and procedures in which contaminated medical instruments may be used (e.g. tattooing, body piercing).
- Consider carrying a sterile medical kit.
- Travellers should not inject non-prescribed drugs or share needles or other medical equipment.

Diagnosis	<ul><li>Genital ulcers:<ul><li>– Clinical syndrome; serological testing for syphilis, culture or antigen testing for herpes, special culture for chancroid; culture, PCR for LGV; microscopy/biopsy for granuloma inguinale.</li></ul></li><li>Urethritis and cervicitis:<ul><li>– Swab for microscopy, PCR and culture.</li></ul></li><li>Vaginal discharge:<ul><li>– Microscopy, pH testing (trichomonas and BV usually pH >4.5), PCR, nucleic acid probes, and culture.</li></ul></li><li>HPV:<ul><li>– Genital warts: Clinical syndrome.</li><li>– Cervical infection: cytology with nucleic acid testing.</li></ul></li><li>Scabies: Clinical presentation, lesion scrapping and microscopy.</li></ul>Consider HIV testing for all those with STDs.
Treatment	<ul><li>Chancroid: Azithromycin, ceftriaxone or ciprofloxacin.</li><li>Chlamydia: Azithromycin or doxycycline.</li><li>Genital herpes: Systemic antivirals (e.g. acyclovir, famiciclovir and valacyclovir).</li><li>Gonorrhoea: Ceftriaxone or cefixime.</li><li>Granuloma inguinale: Azithromycin, co-trimoxazole doxycycline, or ciprofloxacin.</li><li>HPV:<ul><li>– Genital warts: Topical drugs, cryotherapy, laser ablation, intralesional interferon.</li><li>– Cervical infection: Specialist referral.</li><li>– HPV vaccine is included in child and adolescent immunisation programme.</li></ul></li><li>LGV: Doxycycline or erythromycin.</li><li>Scabies: Topical permethrin or oral ivermectin.</li><li>Syphilis: Benzyl penicillin.</li><li>Trichomoniasis: Metronidazole or tinidazole.</li></ul>
Notification	Acute infectious hepatitis (e.g. hepatitis A, B and C) is a notifiable infectious disease. See Resource Guide: 5.1.

Shigellosis

Shigella spp.; *S. sonnei* (the most common species), *S. flexneri*, *S. dysenteriae* (usually seen in low-income countries), and *S. boydii*. Gram-negative bacterial infections of humans.

Risk Assessment

Epidemiology	■ *Shigella* is distributed worldwide.
	■ The organism is only a pathogen of man (and non-human primates), and in low-income countries is seen in settings of poor faecal-oral hygiene. In high-income countries it occurs in households, residential care facilities, amongst men who have sex with men, and in water-borne outbreaks.
Exposure	■ Transmitted via the faecal-oral route: food, human-to-human and water-borne, or during certain sexual practices.

Imported Cases	Approximately 1,500 cases of Shigellosis are reported annually in England, Wales and Northern Ireland. 15% to 20% of cases are acquired abroad; however, travel history reporting is incomplete. Where a travel history is recorded, South Asia and North Africa are the most commonly reported regions of acquisition.

Signs and Symptoms	■ Incubation period of 1 to 3 days. Infection can be established with as few as 100 organisms.
	■ Diarrhoea, fever and cramping. Dysentery frequently occurs: severe cramping (tenesmus), bloody stools and mucus. Dysentery more common with *S. dysenteriae* and *S. flexneri* compared with *S. sonnei*.
	■ Mild and asymptomatic infections occur.
	■ Infection lasts 5 to 7 days.
	■ Complications most common in children under the age of 2 years and include high fever and seizures, and proctitis.
	■ Post-infectious Reiter's syndrome seen in 2% of cases of *S. flexneri*.
	■ *S. dysenteriae* that produces 'shiga toxin' is associated with haemolytic uraemic syndrome: haemolytic anaemia, renal failure and thrombocytopaenia.

Shigellosis

5 Disease Guide

Shigellosis

Risk Management	■ Practise food and water hygiene precautions. ■ Practise personal hygiene with hand washing.
Diagnosis	Stool culture. Blood can be cultured in bacteraemic cases.
Treatment	■ Supportive treatment and hydration. ■ Treatment with antibiotics shortens the duration of clinical symptoms, prevents complications and eliminates the organism from the intestine. ■ Avoid antimotility agents.
Notifications	Infectious bloody diarrhoea is a notifiable infectious disease. See Resource Guide: 5.1.

Shigellosis

5 Disease Guide

Smallpox

Variola virus. RNA virus of the genus *Orthopoxvirus*. Viral infection of humans.

Risk Assessment

Epidemiology
- World Health Organisation declared the global eradication of smallpox in 1980. The last reported case of indigenous smallpox was reported in Somalia in 1977.
- There has been concern about its re-introduction as an agent of bioterrorism.

Exposure
- Transmission is via respiratory droplets or following direct contact with infected bodily fluids.
- There is currently no risk to travellers.

Imported Cases
- No cases reported in UK. The last reported case of indigenous smallpox was reported in Somalia in 1977.

Signs and Symptoms
- Incubation period is 7 to 17 days.
- Febrile prodrome that can have headache, chills, vomiting and prostration, occurring 1 to 4 days before the characteristic rash.
- The rash begins on the face and extremities and spreads to the trunk. Rash characterised by round, hard vesicles that progress to pustules and then scabs over 1 to 2 weeks, leaving scars as they heal. Can affect the oral mucosa and palms.
- Case fatality rate about 30%.

Risk Management
- There is currently no risk to travellers.
- Vaccine is available for some laboratory staff and specific workers at risk in response to re-introduction of smallpox. Contact Health Protection Agency. See Resource Guide: 5.8.

Diagnosis
- Suspected cases should be notified to appropriate national agencies immediately.
- PCR or vesicle swab microscopy.

Treatment
Supportive treatment. Antiviral treatment is experimental. Vaccine can prevent or lessen the severity disease if given within 2 to 3 days of the initial exposure.

Notification
Smallpox is a notifiable infectious disease. See Resource Guide: 5.1.

Smallpox

5 Disease Guide

Tetanus

Clostridium tetani; anaerobic, spore forming bacillus. Bacterial infection of humans and animals.

Risk Assessment

Epidemiology
- Worldwide distribution in both temperate and tropical countries. *C. tetani* spores are present in animal faeces, and therefore ubiquitous in the environment.
- Neonatal tetanus remains an important problem in low-income countries.
- See NaTHNaC Country Information Pages[1] www.nathnac.org.

Exposure
- Spores present in soil and manure and occasionally in contaminated injecting-drug paraphernalia, can be introduced through cuts, wounds, punctures and injection sites. Wounds may often be trivial.
- Most travellers from high-income countries are at a very low risk due to high vaccination coverage.

Imported Cases

Since 1991 an average of 8 cases has been reported annually in England and Wales. Most cases have occurred in persons over the age of 65 who were unvaccinated or incompletely vaccinated; in recent years cases have occurred in injecting-drug users. The proportion acquired abroad is not known.

Signs and Symptoms

- The incubation period averages 7 days (range 3 to 21 days).
- Generalised tetanus: most common syndrome caused by systemic circulation of the toxin of *C. tetani*, tetanospasm.
- Spasms of the facial muscles causing lock jaw (trismus) with characteristic facial expression (risus sardonicus) followed by spastic paralysis of the muscles of the back, thorax and the extremities. Spasms may occur for 2 weeks.
- Complications include respiratory failure, convulsions, bone fractures, and autonomic dysfunction with hypertension and cardiac arrhythmias.
- Case fatality rate up to 50%, but with intensive support and treatment, mortality reduced to about 10%.
- Tetanus immunity does not occur after infection.

Risk Management

- Clean all wounds and seek medical attention.
- See: Vaccine – Recommendations for Travel.

Diagnosis

Clinical syndrome. Analysis for toxin in blood. Culture of wound.

Treatment

Prompt administration of human tetanus immunoglobulin.
Antibiotic treatment to prevent further toxin production.
Intensive support.
Vaccinate following recovery.

Notification

Tetanus is a notifiable infectious disease. See Resource Guide: 5.1.

1   Alternatively see Travax http://www.travax.nhs.uk/ or Fit for Travel http://www.fitfortravel.nhs.uk/

Tetanus Vaccine

Type of Vaccine	Tetanus toxoid, inactivated, usually part of a combined vaccine. Check 'Green Book' and SPC. See Resource Guide: Appendix 1 – Vaccine Compendium.

Schedule	**Primary course:**
	■ Infants and children under 10 years: 2, 3 and 4 months of age; can be given at any stage from 2 months to 10 years.
	■ Adults and children over 10 years: 3 doses of a tetanus-containing vaccine (usually combined with polio and low-dose diphtheria) with a monthly interval between each dose.
	Booster doses:
	■ Infants and children under 10 years: 3 years after completion of the primary course; subsequently after 10 years, if at risk.
	■ Adults and children over 10 years:
	  – 1st booster: at least 5 years after completion of the primary course.
	  – 2nd booster: 10 years after the 1st (but minimum of 5 years where previous dose has been delayed).

Recommendations for Travel	■ All travellers should ensure they are fully immunised according to the UK schedule. ■ Travellers who will not have ready access to medical care, and whose last dose of a tetanus-containing vaccine was more than 10 years ago, should have a booster dose; even if they have received 5 doses previously.
Contraindications and Precautions	■ Confirmed anaphylactic reaction to a previous dose of a tetanus containing vaccine or any component of the vaccine. ■ A neurological complication following an earlier immunisation against diphtheria or tetanus is a precaution. ■ Immunisation should be postponed in those who have an acute febrile illness.
Adverse Reactions	■ Common: Pain, redness and swelling at the injection site. ■ Rare: Anaphylactic reaction; convulsions, high-pitched screaming, pallor, cyanosis and limpness are rare following tetanus and pertussis-containing vaccines.

Tetanus Vaccine

5 Disease Guide

Tick-borne Encephalitis (TBE)

RNA virus of the genus *Flavivirus*, family *Flaviviridae*. There are 3 virus subtypes of TBE: Western (Central European encephalitis), Far Eastern (Russian spring/summer encephalitis) and Siberian subtypes. Viral infection of humans and animals.

Risk Assessment

Epidemiology
- Western subtype occurs primarily in the forested areas of Central and Eastern Europe.
- Far Eastern subtype occurs in the former USSR, east of the Ural Mountains, and in parts of China.
- Siberian subtype occurs in eastern Russia.
- See Map 5-9.
- See NaTHNaC Country Information Pages[1] www.nathnac.org.

Exposure
- Transmitted by:
  - The bite of an infected *Ixodes* spp. tick.
  - Consumption of unpasteurised dairy products from infected animals.
- Exposure to ticks occurs during outdoor activities in areas of vegetation (forest fringes, meadows and marshes, gardens and parks) below 1,400m.
- Transmission season is from April to November; the Eastern subtype is more common in the spring and the Western subtypes in autumn.
- Ticks reside on ground-level vegetation where they can be brushed onto clothing or drop onto passing humans.

Imported Cases

No reported cases.

Signs and Symptoms

- Incubation period is 7 to 14 days (range 4 to 28 days) after tick exposure.
- The ratio of asymptomatic to symptomatic infection is about 250 to 1.
- Two thirds of symptomatic patients have a self-limited febrile illness lasting from 1 to 8 days: fever, fatigue, headache, myalgia and nausea.
- After an asymptomatic period of 1 to 20 days, about one third of patients proceed to a second phase of illness with a sudden rise in temperature and central nervous system involvement with headache and meningitis.
- Progression to encephalitis is more common in persons older than 40 years.

Tick-borne Encephalitis

5 Disease Guide

Tick-borne Encephalitis (TBE)

- Case fatality rate (CFR): Far Eastern subtype 5% to 20%, European subtype 1% to 2%. There is little information about the CFR for the Siberian subtype. Persons who recover are frequently left with neurologic deficits.
- Protective immunity is likely to follow infection.

Risk Management	<ul><li>Travellers should practise tick bite avoidance measures during outdoor activities.</li><li>Travellers should check themselves for ticks and be knowledgeable about effective tick removal methods.</li><li>Avoid consumption of unpasteurised dairy products.</li><li>See: Vaccine – Recommendations for Travel.</li></ul>
Diagnosis	Clinical syndrome. Antibody detection in blood or CSF; PCR detection of virus.
Treatment	Supportive treatment. No antiviral drugs available.
Notification	Acute encephalitis is a notifiable disease. See Resource Guide: 5.1.

Tick-borne Encephalitis Vaccine

Type of Vaccine	Inactivated virus vaccine Check 'Green Book' and SPC. See Resource Guide: Appendix 1 – Vaccine Compendium
Schedule	Primary course: • Three dose schedule: 0, 1 to 3 months, and 5 to 12 months after the second dose. • Accelerated schedule: 0 and 2 weeks, and 5 to 12 months after the second dose. Booster doses: • < 60 years: at 3 years and then after 3 to 5 years. • > 60 years: 3 yearly.
Recommendations for Travel	• Persons living in TBE-endemic areas. • Those at occupational risk in endemic areas, e.g. farmers, forestry workers, soldiers. • Travellers to rural, endemic areas below 1,400m, during late spring and summer, e.g. campers, hikers.

Contraindications and Precautions	• Contraindication: confirmed anaphylactic reaction to previous dose or any component of vaccine including egg. TicoVac® and TicoVac® Junior are produced in chick embryo fibroblast cells.
	• Precautions:
	  – Acute febrile illness; postpone vaccination until recovered.
	  – Known or suspected autoimmune disease.
	  – Known pre-existing cerebral disorders.
	  – Pregnant or breastfeeding women.

Adverse Reactions	• Common: Soreness, erythema, induration and pain at the injection site. Mild fatigue, malaise, headache and myalgia. • Rare: Meningitis and neuritis.

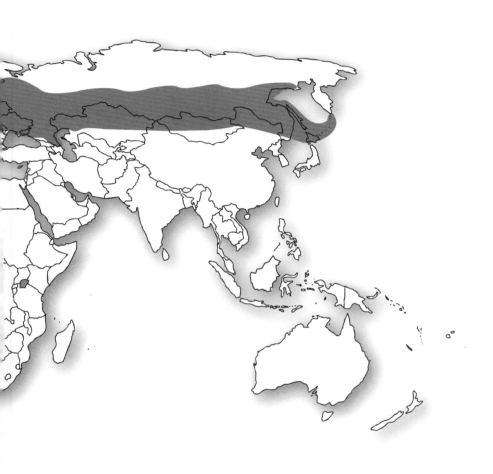

Acknowledgment: Adapted from Lindquist L, Vapalahti O. Lancet Infect Dis. 271:1861, 2008.

Map 5-9. Tick-borne Encephalitis Risk Areas

Countries or areas at risk for tick-borne encephalitis

Travellers' Diarrhoea (TD)

Common syndrome caused by 1 or more enteric bacteria, virus, parasite, and/or bacterial toxin.

Risk Assessment

Epidemiology

- TD is the most common illness in travellers, affecting between 20% and 60% of those going to low-income areas of the world.
- Most common aetiologies are bacteria (30% to 60%): Enterotoxigenic *Escherichia coli*, enteroaggregative *E. coli*, *Salmonella*, *Shigella* and *Campylobacter*. Enteric viruses (5% to 20%): Norovirus and rotavirus; protozoan parasites (≤5%): *Giardia* and *Cryptosporidium*; and acute food poisoning from toxins of *Staphylococcus aureus*, *Bacillus cereus* or *Clostridium perfringens* (≤5%).

Exposure

- Transmitted via the faecal-oral route by contaminated food and water.
- All travellers are at risk, but exposure to conditions of poor sanitation, improperly cooked and stored foods, and ground-grown leafy vegetables and fruits that cannot be peeled by the traveller are risk items.

Imported Cases

Most cases occur overseas, but imported disease is common. See individual infections for more information.

Signs and Symptoms

- Incubation period of hours to a few days.
- Watery diarrhoea (usually 3 or more stools per 24 hours), cramping, nausea and low-grade fever. Vomiting and blood in the stool are less common.
- About 25% of travellers will alter their plans because of TD.
- Illness often worse in young children.
- TD may spontaneously resolve over 3 to 6 days, but many persons will self-treat.

Risk Management

- Practise food and water hygiene precautions.
- Practise personal hygiene with hand washing.
- Antibiotic prophylaxis not usually recommended.
- Risk avoidance not always successful and self-treatment common.
- The oral cholera vaccine (Dukoral®) provides modest protection against *E. coli* that produce LT toxin. It will protect 7% or less of travellers and should not generally be used for this purpose.

Travellers' Diarrhoea

5 Disease Guide

Travellers' Diarrhoea (TD)

Diagnosis	TD is a clinical syndrome. Aetiology determined by obtaining a stool for: Bacterial culture, ova and parasites, or virus detection.
Treatment	■ Maintain hydration; oral rehydration solution can be given to young children, the elderly and those with chronic medical problems.
	■ Loperamide can be used to control symptoms when there is no blood in the stool and a temperature < 38°C. It should not be used in children < 2 years.
	■ A short course of an antibiotic (single dose to 3 days), usually a quinolone or azithromycin, will resolve symptoms.
Notification	■ Food poisoning is a notifiable disease. See Resource Guide: 5.1.

Travellers' Diarrhoea

5 Disease Guide

Trypanosomiasis
(Sleeping Sickness and Chagas Disease)

Protozoan parasites of the genus *Trypanosoma*. Two clinical syndromes: African trypanosomiasis or sleeping sickness (caused by 2 sub-species of *T. brucei*, *rhodesiense* and *gambiense*), and American trypanosomiasis or Chagas disease (caused by *T. cruzi*). Protozoan infections of humans and animals.

Risk Assessment

Epidemiology	■ Sleeping sickness: *T. brucei rhodesiense* occurs mainly in east Africa (Uganda to Mozambique), and *T. brucei gambiense* occurs mainly in West and Central Africa (predominantly from Cote d'Ivoire to DR Congo and Angola).
	■ Humans are the main reservoir for *T. brucei gambiense* and wild and domestic animals such as antelope and cattle are the main reservoirs for *T. brucei rhodesiense*.
	■ Chagas disease: *T. cruzi* occurs in Latin America; it is a disease of man and wild and domestic mammals.
Exposure	■ Sleeping sickness: Transmitted by tsetse flies of the genus *Glossina;* tsetse flies inhabit savannahs, including game reserves.
	■ *Chagas disease: transmitted following contact with the faeces of an infected reduviid bug (triatome bugs). Reduviid bugs inhabit cracks in the walls and roofs of buildings constructed with mud or thatch.
	■ Transmission of both species can also occur via blood transfusion, organ transplantation, contaminated needles or the congenital route. Chagas disease has been occasionally transmitted via ingestion of contaminated juices.

Imported Cases	Between 1990 and 2007 14 cases of African trypanosomiasis were reported in England, Wales and Northern Ireland; most of these were of east African type. There have been no cases of Chagas disease reported since 1983.

Signs and Symptoms	■ Sleeping sickness:
	– East African disease: Usually more acute and rapidly progressive compared with West African disease. A chancre (skin ulcer) often occurs at the site of the tsetse fly bite, and is accompanied by regional lymphadenopathy. High fever with progression to multi-organ involvement (including the CNS, and occasionally the heart) over days to weeks. Untreated illness is often fatal.
	– West African disease: More chronic course. Inoculation site chancre is unusual. Cervical lymphadenopathy common (Winterbottom's sign). Invasion of CNS over months leads to coma and death.

Trypanosomiasis

5 Disease Guide

Trypanosomiasis (Sleeping Sickness and Chagas Disease)

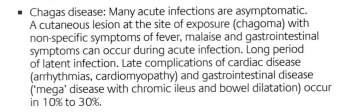

- Chagas disease: Many acute infections are asymptomatic. A cutaneous lesion at the site of exposure (chagoma) with non-specific symptoms of fever, malaise and gastrointestinal symptoms can occur during acute infection. Long period of latent infection. Late complications of cardiac disease (arrhythmias, cardiomyopathy) and gastrointestinal disease ('mega' disease with chromic ileus and bowel dilatation) occur in 10% to 30%.

| Risk Management | - Insect bite avoidance measures: |

- Insect bite avoidance measures:
    - Tsetse flies can bite through loose-weave fabrics and are unaffected by many insect repellents. Travellers are advised to wear insecticide treated, neutral coloured, close-weave clothing.
    - To prevent being bitten by a reduviid bug, travellers residing in buildings constructed with mud or thatch should sleep under a mosquito net and treat bedding with an insecticide solution.

Diagnosis

- Sleeping sickness: Microscopy of blood, CSF (for CNS invasion), lymph nodes, or bone marrow. Serology is of limited value.
- Chagas disease; acute infection: microscopy of blood; late infection: serology.

Treatment

Specialist referral.

Sleeping sickness:

- West African: Early, pentamidine or suramin; late, eflornithine with/without nifurtimox or melarsoprol.
- East African: Early, suramin; late, melarsoprol.

Chagas disease:

- Acute: Nifurtimox or benznidazole.
- Late: Symptomatic support, antiparasitic treatment controversial.

Trypanosomiasis

5 Disease Guide

Tuberculosis (TB)

Mycobacterium tuberculosis (MTB) of the genus *Mycobacterium*; *M. africanum* causes disease in sub-Saharan Africa; *M. bovis* found in cattle, and *M. caprae* found in goats, can also cause tuberculosis in man. Mycobacterial infection of humans.

Risk Assessment

Epidemiology

- Worldwide distribution. Approximately one third of the world's population is infected with MTB; there are 9 million new cases and nearly 2 million deaths annually.
- See Map 5-10.
- The regions with most new cases are sub-Saharan Africa, South Asia and the Russian Federation.
- The 5 countries with the highest burden of infection are: India, China, Indonesia, South Africa and Nigeria.
- The prevalence of HIV/AIDS infection in sub-Saharan Africa and multi-drug resistance particularly in Eastern Europe and the Russian Federation, contribute to the ongoing problem of global TB.
- See NaTHNaC Country Information Pages[1] www.nathnac.org.

Exposure

- Transmission occurs via the respiratory route.
- Uncommonly, TB (usually *M. bovis*) can be transmitted through ingestion of infected milk products.
- Most travellers are at very low risk.
- Travellers at higher risk include healthcare workers, VFRs (particularly children under 5 to 6 years), long-term travellers, and those who have close contact with an infected individual.
- Immunocompromised or HIV/AIDS-infected individuals and persons with diabetes or renal failure are also at higher risk.

Imported Cases

8,417 cases were reported in the UK in 2007. 72% of the cases where a country of birth was known were in foreign-born persons, usually from South Asia or sub-Saharan Africa. The proportion of all reported cases that have been acquired abroad is not known.

Signs and Symptoms

- Most exposures to MTB result in a subclinical or asymptomatic infection: latent tuberculosis.
- Latent tuberculosis infection can lie dormant for years, with a 10% to 15% lifetime risk of reactivation.
- Children under the age of 5 years and AIDS patients are more likely to experience primary tuberculosis following exposure.
- Reactivation TB is usually pulmonary: productive cough, breathlessness and chest pain, weight loss, malaise and night sweats. There can be cavity formation, often in the upper lobes of the lungs.

Tuberculosis

5 Disease Guide

Tuberculosis (TB)

- Extrapulmonary tuberculosis occurs less commonly and can affect the lymph nodes, bones (e.g. vertebral TB, called Pott's disease), kidneys and central nervous system. It can also disseminate throughout the body.

Risk Management	<ul><li>Avoid close contact with individuals known to have infectious pulmonary tuberculosis.</li><li>Healthcare workers should take appropriate respiratory precautions.</li><li>Children in defined risk categories less than 16 years of age should be vaccinated with BCG according to current UK guidance.</li><li>See: Vaccine – Recommendations for Travel.</li><li>Pre- and post-travel assessment of tuberculosis infection can be performed using either tuberculin skin testing (TST) or an interferon gamma release assay (IGRA). These tests should be done 2 to 3 months after return.</li></ul>
Diagnosis	<ul><li>Clinical presentation.</li><li>Culture and acid-fast staining of sputum and/or biopsy specimens.</li><li>Assessment of tuberculosis infection can be done using either by using either TST or an IGRA.</li><li>TST can be difficult to interpret in those who have been vaccinated with BCG. Interpretation of IGRA is not affected by previous BCG vaccination.</li></ul>
Treatment	<ul><li>Specialist referral.</li><li>Antimycobacterial treatment for 6 or more months depending upon the TB syndrome.</li><li>Initial therapy usually with isoniazid (INH), rifampicin (RIF), ethambutol and pyrazinamide for 2 months followed by INH and RIF for 4 months.</li><li>Therapy should be observed; drug resistance needs to be considered.</li></ul>
Notification	Tuberculosis is a notifiable infectious disease. See Resource Guide: 5.1.

Tuberculosis

5 Disease Guide

Tuberculosis Vaccine

Type of Vaccine	BCG Vaccine: Statens Serum Institut (SSI)®, live attenuated vaccine. Check 'Green Book' and SPC. See Disease Guide: Appendix 1 – Vaccine Compendium.
Schedule	Single intradermal dose. A booster is not recommended. Mantoux TST is required prior to vaccination for: ■ All individuals aged 6 years and older. ■ Infants and children under 6 years of age with a history of residence or prolonged stay (more than 3 months) in a country with an annual TB incidence of ≥40/100,000. ■ Those who have had close contact with a person with known TB. ■ Those who have a family history of TB within the last 5 years. BCG can be given up to 3 months following a negative TST.
Recommendations for Travel	Vaccine is recommended for: ■ Previously unvaccinated persons, under 16 years of age, who are going to live for more than 3 months in a country where the annual incidence of TB is ≥ 40/100,000. ■ Healthcare workers under 35 years of age travelling to a country where the annual incidence of TB is ≥ 40/100,000, irrespective of duration of stay. ■ Healthcare workers over 35 years of age who are at particular risk of TB can consider vaccination following careful risk assessment.
Contraindications and Precautions	Vaccine should not be given to those who have/are: ■ Previously had a BCG vaccine. ■ A past history of tuberculosis. ■ An induration of 6mm or more following TST. ■ A confirmed anaphylactic reaction to a component of the vaccine. ■ Neonates in a household where an active tuberculosis case is suspected or confirmed. ■ Immunocompromised. ■ Acutely unwell. ■ Pregnant.

Tuberculosis Vaccine

5 Disease Guide

Tuberculosis Vaccine

Adverse Reactions A successfully administered BCG vaccine is associated with induration at the vaccine site followed by development of a lesion that may ulcerate before it heals, leaving a small, round, flat scar.

Undesirable adverse events include:

- Uncommon: Headache, fever, enlargement of regional lymph node, ulceration with discharge at the site of vaccination.
- Rare (<1 / 1,000): Disseminated BCG with osteomyelitis, confirmed anaphylactic reaction, abscess formation.

Tuberculosis Vaccine

5 Disease Guide

000

Acknowledgment: Data from World Health Organization

Map 5-10. Countries with Tuberculosis Incidence of ≥40 Cases/100, Population per Year, 2007

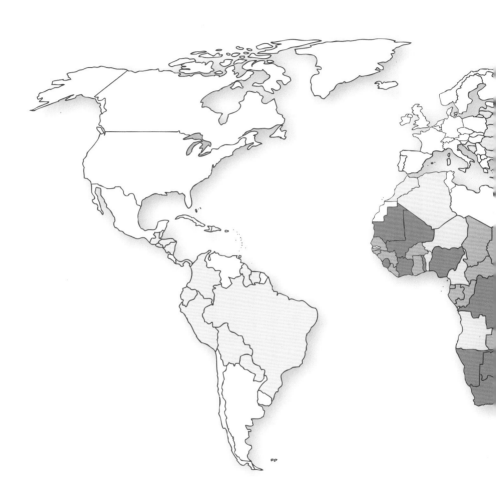

Incidence of tuberculosis, cases/100,000

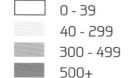

0 - 39
40 - 299
300 - 499
500+

Tungiasis (Jigger or Chigoe flea)

Infestation of skin by the sand flea *Tunga penetrans*. Parasitic infection of humans and animals.

Risk Assessment

Epidemiology
- The flea occurs in Central and South America, the Caribbean, Africa and South Asia.

Exposure
- Flea lives in sandy soil. Pigs are the natural host.

Imported Cases

The number of cases reported in the UK is not known.

Signs and Symptoms

- Gravid female flea burrows into skin.
- A black papule develops into a nodule at the site of penetration. Flea eggs are expelled from the nodule.
- Usually occurs on the feet and ankles, particularly in the periungal area.
- Secondary bacterial infections can occur.
- The flea dies 3 to 4 weeks after penetration.

Risk Management

- Wear protective footwear.
- Do not lie directly on infested sand or soil.

Diagnosis

- Clinical presentation.
- Identification of flea.

Treatment

- Excision and curettage of flea with sterile needle.
- Antibiotic treatment of secondary infection if present.

Typhoid / Paratyphoid (Enteric Fever)

Salmonella enterica serotype Typhi (typhoid fever) and S. Paratyphi A, B or C (paratyphoid fever). Gram-negative bacterial infections of humans.

Risk Assessment

Epidemiology

- Worldwide distribution, however, the highest risk regions are in South Asia; Latin America and Africa are a lesser risk. *S.* Typhi is the most common organism.
- See NaTHNaC Country Information Pages[1] www.nathnac.org.

Exposure

- Transmitted via the faecal-oral route: food-, water-borne and human-to-human.
- Travellers at higher risk include VFRs, young children, long-term travellers, and those exposed to conditions of poor sanitation.

Imported Cases

About 250 cases each of *S.* Typhi and *S.* Paratyphi occur annually in England, Wales and Northern Ireland. Approximately 90% are acquired abroad, mainly from South Asia in VFRs.

Signs and Symptoms

Typhoid:

- Incubation period of 7 to 14 days. Need high inoculum to establish infection, usually $\geq 10^5$ organisms.
- Fever (>39ºC), chills, headache, malaise, weakness, and anorexia, with abdominal pain; diarrhoea may occur early in the course. Moderate hepatosplenomegaly occurs in about 50% of cases. Faint, pink macular rash (rose spots) can be seen occasionally.
- Complications can occur in up to 10% to 15% of cases: intestinal perforation, bacteraemia, meningitis (usually in young children).
- Chronic carrier state (*S.* Typhi excretion in stool for more than a year) occurs in <3% of infected persons.
- Previous typhoid illness does not confer reliable immunity.

Paratyphoid:

- Symptoms similar to those with *S.* Typhi, but can be less severe and of shorter duration.

Risk Management

- Practise food and water hygiene precautions.
- Practise personal hygiene with hand washing.
- See: Vaccine – Recommendations for Travel.
- Current vaccines against *S.* Typhi are only 50% to 80% protective and do not protect against *S.* Paratyphi.

Diagnosis

Culture of stool, blood or bone marrow.

Treatment

- Antibiotic treatment, using a fluoroquinolone or cephalosporin; azithromycin when resistance considered.
- Case fatality <1% with prompt treatment.

Notification

Typhoid and paratyphoid fever are notifiable infectious diseases. See Resource Guide: 5.1

---

1 Alternatively see Travax http://www.travax.nhs.uk/ or Fit for Travel http://www.fitfortravel.nhs.uk/

Typhoid Vaccine

Type of Vaccine(s)	Inactivated and live oral vaccines against *S*. Typhi: • Vi polysaccharide, inactivated single antigen vaccines or combined with hepatitis A antigen. • Ty21a, oral, live attenuated Vaccines do not protect against *S*. Paratyphi. Check 'Green Book' and SPC. See Resource Guide: Appendix 1 – Vaccine Compendium.
Schedule	• Vi polysaccharide: single dose. Reinforcing dose at 3 yearly intervals if at risk. • Live oral vaccine: 3 capsules, day 1, 3 and 5. Boost at 1 year.
Recommendations for Travel	Vaccine should be given to travellers whose planned activities put them at higher risk. Those at higher risk include: • VFRs. • Young children. • Long-term travellers. • Travellers exposed to conditions of poor sanitation.
Contraindications and Precautions	• Hypersensitivity to the vaccines or any component of the vaccines; the combined hepatitis A/typhoid vaccines contain traces of neomycin. • Acute febrile illness. • Vivotif®: acute gastrointestinal illness, congenital or acquired immune deficiency.
Adverse Reactions	Vi polysaccharide vaccines: • Common: Pain, redness and swelling at injection site. • Uncommon: Headache, nausea, diarrhoea and abdominal pain. Live oral vaccine: • Common: Gastrointestinal symptoms, fever, influenza- like symptoms and headache. • Uncommon: Skin reactions and confirmed anaphylactic reaction.

Typhoid Vaccine

5 Disease Guide

Varicella (Chickenpox)

Varicella zoster virus, DNA virus of the *Herpesvirus* family. Viral infection of man.

Risk Assessment

Epidemiology	▪ Worldwide distribution
Exposure	▪ Transmitted by the respiratory route or with direct personal contact with varicella vesicles.
	▪ Most travellers are not at risk due to previously acquired immunity.
	▪ Those at higher risk include non-immune healthcare workers and travellers who will have close contact with the local population.

Imported Cases   The number of cases acquired abroad is not known.

Signs and Symptoms

- Incubation period is between 14 to 16 days (range 10 to 21 days).
- Infected individual are infectious 1 to 2 days before the rash appears and until vesicles are dry.
- Illness begins with 1 to 2 days of fever and malaise. Vesicles appear first on the head and spread to the trunk and extremities, affecting the entire body. New vesicles continue to appear over several days.
- Complications include pneumonia, secondary bacterial skin infections and viral meningitis and encephalitis. These are more common in adults, immunocompromised persons and pregnant women.
- Congenital varicella infection can occur when women acquire varicella in the first 20 weeks of pregnancy.
- Case fatality rate of 1 / 100,000 in children and 25 / 100,000 in adults.
- Herpes zoster (shingles) affects a single dermatome, is caused by reactivation of the varicella virus, and is more common in the elderly. Post-herpetic neuralgia can be debilitating.
- Varicella usually results in life-long immunity.

Risk Management
- Avoid contact with infected persons.
- Infected persons should be excluded from public places until vesicles are dry.
- See: Vaccine – Recommendations for Travel.

Varicella (Chickenpox)

Diagnosis	Clinical syndrome. Culture, PCR or fluorescent antibody detection of virus vesicles. Serology for past infection.
Treatment	Early administration of antiviral drugs can shorten the severity of illness. Varicella zoster immunoglobulin (VZIG) is given to those at increased risk of severe varicella infection and who do not have existing antibodies to Varicella Zoster virus.

Varicella (Chickenpox)

5 Disease Guide

Varicella (Chickenpox) Vaccine

Type of Vaccine	Live attenuated virus Check 'Green Book' and SPC. See Resource Guide: Appendix 1 – Vaccine Compendium.
Schedule	▪ Children from 1 year to less than 13 years: single dose. ▪ Children over 13 years and adults: 2 doses, 4 to 8 weeks apart.
Recommendations for Travel	▪ Not routinely recommended for travel. ▪ Recommended for non-immune persons who are at risk of serious illness, healthcare workers or household contacts of immunocompromised individuals.
Contraindications and Precautions	▪ Confirmed anaphylactic reaction to a previous dose or vaccine component including neomycin or gelatin. ▪ Pregnancy should be avoided for 3 months post vaccination. ▪ Immunocompromised individuals.
Adverse Reactions	▪ Common: Mild infection site soreness. ▪ Uncommon: Fever and varicella rash (approximately 5 lesions).

Varicella (Chickenpox) Vaccine

5 Disease Guide

Venomous Bites

Venomous bites and stings from snakes, scorpions, spiders and aquatic species.

Risk Assessment

Epidemiology
- Snake bites: Worldwide distribution with highest burden in South Asia, South East Asia, and sub-Saharan Africa.
- Scorpion stings and spiders bites: Worldwide distribution.
- Aquatic species: Worldwide in tropical and temperate coastal waters and reef systems.

Exposure
- Bites or stings from snakes, scorpions and spiders.
- Bites and stings from aquatic species such as eels, fire coral, jellyfish, octopus, sea urchins, stonefish and stingrays.

Imported Cases

The number of exposures occurring abroad is not known.

Signs and Symptoms

- Snake bites: Injury depends on snake species:
  - Viper envenomations (e.g. Russell's viper) typically cause local injury: Pain, swelling, tissue damage and coagulopathy.
  - Elapid envenomations (e.g. cobras and kraits) cause local injury and neurotoxicity that can result in respiratory failure.
- Scorpion stings: Local pain and injury; occasional systemic symptoms and neurotoxicity that can result in death, e.g. American *Centruroides* species.
- Spider bites: Can cause necrosis at the site of the bite, e.g. recluse spider *(Loxosceles)* bites can cause local necrosis and can be associated with systemic effects such as renal or liver failure, and haemolysis. Neurotoxic envenoming can occur, e.g. black widow spiders *(Lactrodectus)* and Australian funnel web *(Atrax)* causing pain locally, muscular spasms and sometimes death.
- Aquatic species bites or stings: Species-specific symptoms ranging from extreme pain at site of exposure to respiratory paralysis and death.

Risk Management

- Seek local advice about potential hazards.
- Avoid contact with spiders, snakes, scorpions or aquatic animals.
- Snake bites: Wear boots and long trousers and use a torch and walking stick when outdoors at night. Avoid sleeping directly on the ground. Rubbish should be stored away from houses / campsites; grass / foliage should be cut short.
- Scorpion stings and spider bites: Avoid bed nets and bed clothes touching the floor; shake shoes and clothing before wearing.

Venomous Bites

5 Disease Guide

Venomous Bites

- Aquatic species bites or stings: Wear plastic shoes in and around water.
- Do not touch coral.

Diagnosis	Clinical presentation.

Treatment	<ul><li>Supportive treatment; tetanus boosting and antibiotics may be necessary.</li><li>Snake bites: keep the patient and affected area still. Pressure immobilisation with bandages can be applied by a skilled medical specialist. Use of tourniquets, incisions and suction is **not** recommended and can be harmful. Prompt medical attention to obtain antivenom if possible. Neurotoxic envenomations: consider anticholinesterases to improve paralytic symptoms.</li><li>Scorpion stings and spider bites: Wound care and supportive treatment. For neurotoxic bites and stings, pressure immobilisation with bandages and antivenom if available.</li><li>Aquatic species bites and stings:<ul><li>Marine fish, e.g. urchin, stonefish, remove spines and spine fragments and immerse in hot water (120° F / 50ºC) taking care not to burn the patient.</li><li>Soft coral and certain jellyfish carefully remove nematocysts and consider topical alcohol or vinegar to deactivate the nematocysts of some species.</li></ul></li></ul>

Venomous Bites

5 Disease Guide

Viral Haemorrhagic Fevers (VHFs)

Clinical syndromes of severe illness caused by Lassa virus (*Arenaviridae* family), Ebola and Marburg viruses (*Filoviridae* family) and other viruses (e.g. yellow fever, dengue, hantavirus: See individual descriptions). Viral infections of humans and animals.

Risk Assessment

Epidemiology

- Lassa is endemic in West Africa; Ebola and Marburg are endemic in East and Central Africa. A few cases of Ebola have occurred in West Africa; a strain that is non-pathogenic in humans (Ebola Reston) occurs in the Philippines.
- Lassa: Rodents are the reservoir.
- Ebola: unknown reservoir in Africa; non-human primates can become ill with Ebola virus. Ebola Reston has a reservoir in pigs.
- Marburg: Possible reservoir in cave or mine-dwelling fruit bats.

Exposure

- Lassa: Broken skin or mucous membrane contact with urine and/or faeces of rats.
- Ebola: Initial exposure possibly to an infected animal, then transmission between humans through bodily fluids, including the preparation of bodies for burial.
- Marburg: Initial exposure possibly through bats in mines or caves, then transmission between humans through bodily fluids, including the preparation of bodies for burial.
- Travellers are at a very low risk.
- Healthcare workers are at increased risk through direct contact with bodily fluids.

Imported Cases

In the UK, 12 reported cases of Lassa have been reported since 1971, including 2 cases in 2009. All cases were acquired in West Africa. There have been no known imported cases of Ebola or Marburg reported in the UK.

Signs and Symptoms

- Lassa: Incubation period of 7 to 10 days (range 3 to 21) with early symptoms of fever, headache and malaise. Illness can progress to pharyngitis, cough and abdominal pain following by bleeding and multi-organ failure with death in about 15% of hospitalised patients. Pregnancy carries a higher risk of a fatal outcome for both mother and foetus. Sensorineural deafness occurs in up to 25% of those who recover.
- Ebola and Marburg: Incubation period of 4 to 10 days (range 3 to 19). Sudden onset of fever, headache, myalgias, arthralgias and weakness, followed by diarrhoea, vomiting, confusion, bleeding and organ failure with death in 50% to 90% of cases.

Viral Haemorrhagic Fevers

5 Disease Guide

Viral Haemorrhagic Fevers (VHFs)

Risk Management	■ Strict infection control guidelines in healthcare, laboratory and postmortem settings to prevent transmission of each of the viruses. See Resource Guide: 5.9.
	■ Lassa: Avoid contact with rodents. Reduce rodent populations by clearing rubbish around dwellings, and preventing access into buildings.
	■ Ebola and Marburg: Avoid contact with infected patients. Avoid caving in Central and East Africa where Marburg virus may be a risk.
	■ No vaccines are available.
Diagnosis	■ Clinical syndrome following travel to risk areas.
	■ Serology for antibody; detection of virus by PCR and culture of blood, urine and post-mortem tissue.
Treatment	■ Treatment and isolation must be carried out in a high security infectious diseases unit.
	■ Intensive supportive treatment.
	■ Lassa: Treatment with ribavirin.
Notification	Viral haemorrhagic fever is a notifiable infectious disease. See Resource Guide: 5.1.

Viral Haemorrhagic Fevers

5 Disease Guide

West Nile Virus (WNV)

Virus of the *Flaviviridae* family, of the genus *Flavivirus*. Zoonotic viral infection of birds, animals and humans.

Risk Assessment

Epidemiology
- First isolated in West Nile district, Uganda in 1937. Indigenous to Africa, Asia, Australia, the Middle East and North America.
- Outbreaks and sporadic cases occur in Europe.
- First cases occurred in the US in 1999 which spread over the next several years throughout the US and into Canada. Cases have been reported in Central America, Mexico and the West Indies.
- In the last several years 2,500 to 4,500 cases reported in the US.
- Main host of WNV is birds; man incidentally infected.

Exposure
- Transmitted via the bite of a mosquito, usually *Culex* spp., that feed predominately during the hours between dusk and dawn.
- Transmission can occur via blood transfusion, and rarely *in utero* and during breastfeeding.
- Rarely reported in travellers.

Imported Cases

Since surveillance began in 2002, 2 cases have been reported in the UK, each in 2007 and 2008; both cases were acquired in Canada.

Signs and Symptoms
- Incubation period is 1 to 14 days.
- 80% of cases are asymptomatic or mild.
- Symptomatic persons usually experience a mild, self-limited illness with fever, headache, myalgia and occasionally a maculopapular rash.
- Approximately 1 in every 150 cases progresses to neuroinvasive disease, meningitis or encephalitis that carries a case fatality rate of 4% to 14% (15% to 29% in the elderly). Persistent neurologic disability can occur in persons who survive.
- Immunity is considered to follow infection although duration is unknown.

Risk Management
- Mosquito bite avoidance measures.
- There is no vaccine available.

Diagnosis
- Culture or PCR for virus in blood, CSF or tissue sample. Serology on blood or CSF.

Treatment
- No specific antiviral treatment. Supportive treatment.

Notification
- Acute encephalitis is a notifiable infectious disease. See Resource Guide: 5.1.

West Nile Virus

5 Disease Guide

Yellow Fever (YF)

RNA virus of the genus *Flavivirus*, a member of the *Flaviviridae* family. Viral infection of humans and monkeys.

Yellow Fever

Risk Assessment

Epidemiology	▪ Risk of yellow fever transmission in tropical areas of Africa and South America, eastern Panama and Trinidad in the Caribbean.
	▪ See Map 5-11. **New WHO-approved yellow fever vaccination maps are expected to be published in 2010.**
	▪ See NaTHNaC Country Information Pages[1] www.nathnac.org.
	▪ In South America there can be 2 YF transmission cycles:
	  – A sylvatic (jungle) cycle maintained by monkeys and tree-hole breeding mosquitoes (usually *Haemagogous* spp.).
	  – An urban cycle between humans and *Aedes aegypti* mosquitoes.
	▪ In Africa 3 cycles can occur:
	  – A sylvatic, rainforest cycle between monkeys and *Aedes* spp. mosquitoes.
	  – A savannah cycle that can be maintained by both humans and monkeys and *Aedes* spp. mosquitoes.
	  – An urban cycle between man and *Aedes aegypti* mosquitoes.

Exposure	▪ Yellow fever is transmitted via the bite of an infected *Aedes* spp. mosquito. (In the sylvatic cycle of yellow fever in South America, *Haemagogous* spp. mosquitoes can transmit infections). *Aedes* spp. mosquitoes feed predominantly during daylight hours.
Imported Cases	No cases reported.
Signs and Symptoms	▪ Incubation period of 3 to 6 days. ▪ Infection is asymptomatic in approximately 50% to 85% of infections. ▪ Symptomatic infection can present as an acute illness with fever, malaise, headache, lower back pain, and nausea and vomiting. ▪ After a short period of improvement, the illness can progress in 15% to 25% to more severe disease with jaundice, haemorrhagic complications, and renal and liver failure. ▪ 20% to 50% case fatality rate.
Risk Management	▪ Mosquito bite avoidance measures. *Aedes* mosquitoes bite predominantly during daylight hours. ▪ See: Vaccine – Recommendations for Travel.
Diagnosis	Clinical syndrome. Culture of virus or PCR detection in blood or tissue. Serology.
Treatment	No specific antiviral treatment. Supportive therapy.
Notification	Yellow Fever is a notifiable infectious disease. See Resource Guide: 5.1.

5 Disease Guide

Yellow Fever Vaccine

Type of Vaccine	Live attenuated vaccine. Check 'Green Book' and SPC. See Resource Guide: Appendix 1 – Vaccine Compendium.
Schedule	Primary course: Single dose. Re-vaccination is recommended every 10 years for those at risk. An International Certificate of Vaccination or Prophylaxis (ICVP) is valid from the 10th day after primary vaccination and immediately after re-immunisation if re-immunisation occurs within the 10-year period.

Recommendations for Travel

- Travellers should take mosquito bite avoidance measures. *Aedes* spp. mosquitoes feed predominantly during daylight hours.
- Vaccination should be given to those aged 9 months and older, travelling to areas with a risk of yellow fever transmission.
- Vaccination can also be required by certain countries as a condition of entry under International Health Regulations.

Contraindications and Precautions

Contraindications:

- Aged 5 months and younger.
- Confirmed anaphylactic reaction to previous YF vaccine or to any component of vaccine.
- Confirmed anaphylactic reaction to egg. Stamaril® is produced in chick embryos.
- Thymus disorder.
- Immunocompromised status due to congenital condition, disease process or treatment.

Precautions:

- People aged 60 years and older.
- Pregnancy.
- Breastfeeding.
- Children aged from 6 months up to 9 months of age.
- Human Immunodeficiency Virus positive with CD4 counts >200 cells/mm^3.

Adverse Reactions

- Common: soreness at injection site, low-grade fever, headache, myalgia, occurs in 10% to 30% of recipients.

Yellow Fever Vaccine

5 Disease Guide

Yellow Fever Vaccine

- Rare:
  - Confirmed anaphylactic reaction: 1 case per 56,000 to 250,000 doses.
  - Vaccine Associated Neurologic Disease (VAND), approximately 3 to 5 cases per 1,000,000 doses.
  - Vaccine Associated Viscerotropic Disease (VAVD), approximately 5 cases per 1,000,000 doses.
  - Increased risk of VAND and VAVD in people aged over 60 years, approximately 25 cases per 1,000,000 (1:40,000).
- Adverse reactions should be reported.
  See Resource Guide: 5.10.

Acknowledgment: Adapted from World Health Organization

Map 5-11. Yellow Fever Risk Areas, 2010

Yellow fever risk areas

Section 6

Resource Guide

Section 6 – contents

A – Key Resources

A1   Atlas, e.g. The Times Comprehensive Atlas of the World. 12th ed. Times Books. London, 2008.
http://www.timesatlas.com/FindThatPlace/Pages/Search.aspx

A1   British National Formulary (BNF).
http://www.bnf.org

A2   British Travel Health Association (BTHA).
http://www.btha.org/

A3   Centers for Disease Control and Prevention (CDC). Health Information for International Travel 2010. US Department of Health and Human Services. Atlanta, 2009.
http://wwwnc.cdc.gov/travel/default.aspx

A4   Chiodini P, Hill D, Lalloo D, et al. Guidelines for malaria prevention in travellers from the United Kingdom 2007. Health Protection Agency (HPA) Advisory Committee on Malaria Prevention (ACMP) for UK Travellers. London, 2007.
http://www.hpa.org.uk/webw/HPAweb&HPAwebStandard/HPAweb_C/1203496943315?p=1249920576136

A5   Civil Aviation Authority (CAA). Assessing fitness to fly. Guidelines for medical professionals from the Aviation Health Unit. UK Civil Aviation Authority. 2009.
http://www.caa.co.uk/docs/923/FitnessToFlyPDF_FitnesstoFlyPDF%20Feb%2009.pdf

A6   Department of Health (DH), England.
http://www.dh.gov.uk/en/index.htm

A7   Electronic Medicine Compendium (EMC). Summaries of Product Characteristics (SPC).
http://www.medicines.org.uk/

A8   European Health Insurance Card (EHIC).
http://www.ehic.org.uk/InternetRes/home.do

A9   Faculty of Travel Medicine. Royal College of Physicians and Surgeons of Glasgow.
http://www.rcpsg.ac.uk/Travel%20Medicine/Pages/mem_spweltravmed.aspx

A10 Fit for Travel.
http://www.fitfortravel.nhs.uk/

A11 Foreign and Commonwealth Office (FCO).
http://www.fco.gov.uk/en/

A12 Foreign and Commonwealth Office (FCO). Travelling and living overseas.
http://www.fco.gov.uk/en/travelling-and-living-overseas/

A13 Foreign and Commonwealth Office (FCO). LOCATE.
http://www.fco.gov.uk/en/travelling-and-living-overseas/Locate/

A14 Foreign and Commonwealth Office (FCO). Know Before You Go.
http://www.fco.gov.uk/en/travelling-and-living-overseas/about-kbyg-campaign/

6 Resource Guide

A – Key Resources

A15   Health Protection Agency (HPA), England.
       http://www.hpa.org.uk/

A16   Health Protection Agency (HPA). Travel Health Reports.
       http://www.hpa.org.uk/HPA/Publications/InfectiousDiseases/
       TravelHealth/

A17   Health Protection Scotland (HPS).
       http://www.hps.scot.nhs.uk/travel/index.aspx

A18   Hospital for Tropical Diseases (HTD).
       http://www.thehtd.org/Default.aspx

A19   Liverpool School of Tropical Medicine (LSTM).
       http://www.liv.ac.uk/lstm/

A20   London School of Hygiene and Tropical Medicine (LSHTM).
       http://www.lshtm.ac.uk/

A21   Malaria Reference Laboratory (MRL).
       http://www.hpa.org.uk/HPA/ProductsServices/InfectiousDiseases/
       LaboratoriesAndReferenceFacilities/1200660023262/

A22   MedicAlert® Foundation.
       http://www.medicalert.org.uk/

A23   Medicines and Healthcare products Regulatory Agency (MHRA).
       http://mhra.gov.uk

A24   National Travel Health Network and Centre (NaTHNaC).
       http://www.nathnac.org

A25   National Travel Health Network and Centre (NaTHNaC). Health Information
       Sheets for travellers.
       http://www.nathnac.org/travel/factsheets/index.htm

A26   NHS Choices.
       http://www.nhs.uk/Pages/HomePage.aspx

A27   NHS Wales.
       http://www.wales.nhs.uk/

A28   NHS Scotland.
       http://www.show.scot.nhs.uk/index.aspx

A29   Northern Ireland Department of Health, Social Services and Public Safety.
       http://www.dhsspsni.gov.uk/

A30   Royal College of Nursing (RCN). Competencies: an integrated career and
       competency framework for nurses in travel health medicine. RCN. London, 2007.
       http://www.rcn.org.uk/publications/pdf/travel_health_medicine.pdf

A31   Salisbury D, Ramsay M & Noakes K. Immunisation against infectious
       disease. 'The Green Book'. Department of Health. TSO. London, 2006.
       Includes access to updated chapters.
       http://www.dh.gov.uk/en/Policyandguidance/Healthandsocialcaretopics/
       Greenbook/DH_4097254

A – Key Resources

A32 Travax.
http://www.travax.nhs.uk/

A33 Vaccine Administration Task Force. UK guidance on best practice in vaccine administration. 'The Purple Book'. Shire Hall Communications. London, 2001.
http://www.rcn.org.uk/__data/assets/pdf_file/0010/78562/001981.pdf

A34 World Health Organization (WHO). International Health Regulations (IHR) 2005. Geneva, 2005.
http://www.who.int/ihr/en/

A35 World Health Organization (WHO). International travel and health. Geneva, 2010.
http://www.who.int/ith/en/index.html

A36 Yellow Card Scheme. Medicines and Healthcare products Regulatory Agency (MHRA).
http://yellowcard.mhra.gov.uk/

B – Resources for Travellers

The following resources provide general information and advice for travellers. However, travellers are advised to discuss any specific needs with a health professional in advance of planned travel.

Destination-specific health advice

- National Travel Health Network and Centre (NaTHNaC).
  http://www.nathnac.org/travel/index.htm
- Fit for Travel.
  http://www.fitfortravel.nhs.uk/home.aspx
- The Hospital for Tropical Diseases.
  http://www.thehtd.org/
  - Pre-recorded travel advice line: 020 7950 7799.

General travel health information (including downloadable Health Information Sheets)

- National Travel Health Network and Centre (NaTHNaC).
  http://www.nathnac.org/travel/factsheets/index.htm
- Fit for Travel.
  http://www.fitfortravel.nhs.uk/advice/advice-for-travellers.aspx

Safety and security advice

- The Foreign and Commonwealth Office (FCO):
  - Travel advice by country.
    http://www.fco.gov.uk/en/travel-and-living-abroad/
  - Know Before You Go campaign.
    http://www.fco.gov.uk/en/travel-and-living-abroad/about-kbyg-campaign/
  - FCO LOCATE enables British nationals to document their travel plans so that embassy and crisis staff can provide assistance in an emergency.
    http://www.fco.gov.uk/en/travel-and-living-abroad/staying-safe/Locate/

Access to healthcare overseas

- The Department of Health (DH), England:
  - Going abroad.
    http://www.direct.gov.uk/en/TravelAndTransport/TravellingAbroad/index.htm?cids=Google_PPC&cre=TravelandTransport
  - Access to healthcare abroad.
    http://www.nhs.uk/nhsengland/Healthcareabroad/pages/Healthcareabroad.aspx
- The International Association for Medical Assistance to Travellers (IAMAT) is a not-for-profit organisation that provides travel health advice and coordinates an international network of qualified medical practitioners to assist travellers in need of emergency medical care. Requires subscription and login.
  http://www.iamat.org/about_our_work.cfm
- International Society of Travel Medicine (ISTM) promotes healthy travel worldwide and has a global travel clinic locator.
  http://www.istm.org/

B – Resources for Travellers

Travel health books

- Marie Stopes International. Back pocket travel guide to sexual health. http://www.mariestopes.org/documents/travelguide.pdf
- The Essential Guide to Travel Health (2009). Wilson-Howarth J. Cadogan Guides London
- The Rough Guide to Travel Health. Jones N. London: Rough Guides; 2004.
- The Travellers' Good Health Guide. Lankester T. London: Sheldon Press; 2006.
- Travel Health Berlitz Pocket Guide. Lankester T. Berlitz Publishing; 2008.
- Travellers' Health: How to Stay Healthy Abroad. 4th ed. Dawood R. Oxford University Press; 2002.
- Your Child Abroad: A travel health guide. Wilson-Howarth J, Ellis M. Bradt Travel Guides; 2004.

C – Sources of Specialist Advice

Telephone and facsimile (FAX) advice lines

- National Travel Health Network and Centre (NaTHNaC):
  - 0845 602 6712 (telephone only)
  - Hours: weekdays 9 am – 12 noon; 2 pm – 4:30 pm
  - http://www.nathnac.org
- Travax (free access for Scottish NHS users, subscription only for others):
  - 0141 300 1130 (telephone only)
  - Hours: weekdays 2 – 4pm
  - http://www.travax.co.uk
- Malaria Reference Laboratory (MRL):
  - Non-urgent advice on malaria chemoprophylaxis. Download PDF risk assessment form, complete and FAX; reply within three working days.
  - http://www.hpa.org.uk/HPA/ProductsServices/InfectiousDiseases/LaboratoriesAndReferenceFacilities/1200660023262/
  - 020 7637 0248 (FAX only)

Health protection agencies

- Health Protection Agency (HPA), England.
  http://www.hpa.org.uk/HPA/
  - Details of local Health Protection Units:
    http://www.hpa.org.uk/web/HPAweb&Page&HPAwebAutoListName/Page/1158945066055
- Health Protection Scotland (HPS).
  http://www.hps.scot.nhs.uk
- Northern Ireland Department of Health, Social Services and Public Safety.
  http://www.dhsspsni.gov.uk/
- NHS Wales.
  http://www.wales.nhs.uk/

Yellow fever and rabies serology

- Yellow fever antibody testing (under special circumstances only): The Doctors Laboratory, 60 Whitfield Street, London. Tel: 020 7307 7373. http://www.tdlpathology.com/
- Rabies antibody testing (under special circumstances only): Rabies High Security Unit, Vet Lab, Weybridge, Addlestone, Surrey. Tel: 01932357645.

Post-travel advice

Health professionals should contact their nearest Infectious Disease Unit or:

- Hospital for Tropical Diseases (HTD), London:
  - 24hr telephone advice for doctors available on 0845 155 5000 (UCLH switchboard) and ask for the on-call tropical medicine registrar.
  - Post-travel advice for doctors considering referral:
    http://www.thehtd.org/Fordoctors.aspx

C – Sources of Specialist Advice

- Liverpool School of Tropical Medicine (LSTM):
  - Post-travel telephone advice for health professionals available on: 0151 705 3100 (ask for duty doctor)
  - Details of the diagnostic laboratory service: http://www.liv.ac.uk/lstm/travel_health_services/diagnos_lab.htm
- Health Protection Agency (HPA), England. http://www.hpa.org.uk/HPA/
- Guidelines relating to post-exposure prophylaxis for rabies: http://www.hpa.org.uk/HPA/Topics/InfectiousDiseases/InfectionsAZ/1191942176103/. See Resource Guide: 5.7.
- Health Protection Scotland (HPS). http://www.hps.scot.nhs.uk
  - Guidelines relating to post-exposure prophylaxis for rabies: See Resource Guide: 5.7.

1 Introduction to UK Travel Health

1.1 Provision of Travel Health Services in the UK

1.1.1 UK Travel Medicine Courses (in alphabetical order):

Health Protection Scotland (HPS):

- The Foundation Course in Travel Medicine.
- The Diploma in Travel Medicine.
  http://www.travelcourses.hps.scot.nhs.uk/home.aspx

Liverpool School of Tropical Medicine (LSTM):

- Travel and Expedition Medicine course.
  http://www.liv.ac.uk/lstm/learning_teaching/short_creds/ShortTravMed.htm

London School of Hygiene and Tropical Medicine (LSHTM):

- Travel Medicine attended course.
  http://www.lshtm.ac.uk/prospectus/short/stm.html
- Travel Medicine online course.
  http://www.lshtm.ac.uk/prospectus/cpd/travel_med.html

University College London (UCL):

- MSc Travel Health and Medicine.
  http://www.ucl.ac.uk/slms/courses/postgraduate/show.php?progid=215

Vaccine manufacturers often run one day travel health courses; they may be aimed at marketing a vaccine or other product.

1.2 The UK Travel and Tourism Industry

1.2.1 United Nations World Tourism Organization (UNWTO) Yearbook of Tourism Statistics, 2009.
http://www.unwto.org/statistics/publications/publications.htm

1.2.2 Civil Aviation Authority (CAA) Air Travel Organiser's License.
http://www.caa.co.uk/default.aspx?catid=27

1.2.3 Foreign and Commonwealth Office (FCO). British Behaviour Abroad Report.
http://www.fco.gov.uk/en/news/latest-news/?view=News&id=20759995

1.2.4 European Union (EU) Package Travel Directive.
http://www.opsi.gov.uk/si/si1992/uksi_19923288_en_1.htm

1.2.5 Federation of Tour Operators (FTO). Legal Requirements - Implications of the EC Package Travel Directive 1993 and financial protection for holidaymakers.
http://www.fto.co.uk/operators-factfile/legal-requirements/

1.2.6 Association of British Travel Agents (ABTA). Code of Conduct.
http://www.abta.com/about/industry_standards

2 The Pre-Travel Consultation

2.3 Risk Management

2.3.1 Medical Preparation

2.3.1a   St John Ambulance. First Aid Advice.
http://www.sja.org.uk/sja/first-aid-advice.aspx

2.3.1b   St John Ambulance, St Andrew's Ambulance and the British Red Cross. First aid manual; step by step guide for everyone. 9th ed. Penguin. London, 2009.
http://www.stjohnsupplies.co.uk/products/default.asp?productID=P95118

2.3.1c   HM Revenue and Customs (HMRC). Taking medicines with you when you go abroad. HMRC, 1998.
http://customs.hmrc.gov.uk/channelsPortalWebApp/channelsPortalWebApp.portal?_nfpb=true&_pageLabel=pageTravel_InfoGuides&propertyType=document&id=HMCE_CL_001589

2.3.1d   International Association for Medical Assistance to Travellers (IAMAT).
http://www.iamat.org

2.3.1e   Joint Commission International (JCI).
http://www.jointcommissioninternational.org/

2.3.1f   The International Society of Travel Medicine (ISTM).
http://www.istm.org/WebForms/SearchClinics/

2.3.1g   Foreign and Commonwealth Office (FCO). Find an Embassy.
http://www.fco.gov.uk/en/travel-and-living-abroad/find-an-embassy/

2.3.1h   International commercial databases (Note: recommendations may differ to those in the UK).
■ Travax Encompass (requires subscription and login).
http://www.travax.com/scripts/login/login.asp?sUrl=%2Fscripts%2Fmain%2Findex%2Easp
■ International SOS (requires subscription and login).
http://www.internationalsos.com/en/

2.3.2 Journey Risks

2.3.2a   British Medical Association. The impact of flying on passenger health: a guide for healthcare professionals. 2004.
http://www.bma.org.uk/images/Impactofflying_tcm41-20362.pdf

2.3.2b   World Health Organization Research into Global Hazards of Health (WRIGHT) project. Geneva, 2007.
http://www.who.int/cardiovascular_diseases/wright_project/phase1_report/en/index.html

2.2.3 Safety Risks

2.3.3a   World Health Organization Global status report on road safety; time for action. Geneva, 2009.
http://whqlibdoc.who.int/publications/2009/9789241563840_eng.pdf

2 The Pre-Travel Consultation

2.3.3b   Department of Transport: Aviation safety.
          http://www.dft.gov.uk/pgr/aviation/safety/

2.3.3c   European Commission Transport: List of airlines banned within the EU.
          http://ec.europa.eu/transport/air-ban/list_en.htm

2.3.3d   Royal Society for the Prevention of Accidents. Water sports safety
          abroad. 2007.
          http://www.rospa.com/leisuresafety/information/water_sports_
          safety_abroad.htm

2.3.4 Environmental Risks

2.3.4a   The Met Office World Weather Forecast.
          http://www.metoffice.gov.uk/weather/world/world_forecast.html

2.3.4b   Health Effects from Ultraviolet Radiation: Report of an Advisory Group
          on Non-Ionising Radiation. National Radiological Protection Board.
          Health Protection Agency (HPA). Documents of the NRPB 2002; 13(1).
          http://www.hpa.org.uk/webw/HPAweb&HPAwebStandard/HPAweb_
          C/1254510590307?p=1219908766891

2.3.4c   Sunsense: Protecting Yourself from Ultraviolet Radiation. Health
          Protection Agency (HPA). 2009.
          http://www.hpa.org.uk/webw/HPAweb&HPAwebStandard/HPAweb_
          C/1215501685726?p=1158934607683

2.3.4d   Epstein Y, Moran D. Extremes of temperature and hydration. In:
          Keystone J, Kozarsky P, Freedman D, eds. Travel Medicine, 2nd ed.
          Elsevier. Philadelphia. 2008:413-22.

2.3.4e   The Health and Safety Executive. A short guide to the Personal
          Protective Equipment at Work Regulations. 1992.
          http://www.hse.gov.uk/pubns/indg174.pdf

2.3.4f   World Health Organization (WHO). Air quality guidelines for
          particulate matter, ozone, nitrogen dioxide and sulphur dioxide.
          Global update 2005.
          http://www.euro.who.int/document/e90038.pdf

2.3.4g   Centers for Disease Control and Prevention (CDC). Harmful Algal
          Blooms.
          http://www.cdc.gov/hab/cyanobacteria/facts.htm

2.3.5 Food- and Water-borne Risks

2.3.5a   Hill D, Ryan E. Management of travellers' diarrhoea. Brit Med J
          337:863-7, 2008.

2.3.5b   DuPont HL, Ericsson CD, Farthing MJ, et al. Expert review of the
          evidence base for self-therapy of travelers' diarrhea. J Travel Med
          16:161-71, 2009.

2.3.5c   DuPont HL, Ericsson CD, Farthing MJ, et al. Expert review of the
          evidence base for prevention of travelers' diarrhea. J Travel Med
          16:149-60, 2009.

2 The Pre-Travel Consultation

2.3.5d   Backer HD. Water disinfection for international travelers. In: Keystone J, Kozarsky P, Freedman D, eds. Travel Medicine, 2nd ed. Elsevier. Philadelphia, 2008:47-58.

2.3.5e   World Health Organization. Preventing Travellers' Diarrhoea: How to Make Drinking Water Safe. WHO/SDE/WSH/05.07. Geneva, 2005.
http://www.who.int/water_sanitation_health/hygiene/envsan/sdwtravel.pdf

2.3.6 Vector-borne Risks (including animals)

2.3.6a   Committee to Advise on Tropical Medicine and Travel (CATMAT). Statement on personal protection measures to prevent arthropod bites. Update 2005.
http://www.phac-aspc.gc.ca/publicat/ccdr-rmtc/05vol31/asc-dcc-13/index-eng.php

2.3.7 Air-borne Risks

2.3.7a   World Health Organization. Tuberculosis and Air Travel – Guidelines for Prevention and Control. 3rd edition. Geneva, 2008.
http://www.who.int/tb/publications/2008/WHO_HTM_TB_2008.399_eng.pdf

2.3.8 Sexual Health and Blood-borne Viral Risks

2.3.8a   World Health Organization (WHO) Joint United Nations Programme on HIV/AIDS.
http://www.unaids.org/en/default.asp

2.3.8b   World Health Organization (WHO): Global Prevalence and Incidence of Selected Curable Sexually Transmitted Infections. Overview and Estimates. Geneva, 2001.
http://www.who.int/hiv/pub/sti/pub7/en/index.html

2.3.8c   Marie Stopes International. Back pocket travel guide to sexual health around the world. London, 2004.
http://www.mariestopes.org.uk/documents/travelguide.pdf

2.3.8d   Family Planning Association: Sexual Health Information Service/Find a Clinic.
http://www.fpa.org.uk/Information

2.3.8e   Blood Care Foundation.
http://www.bloodcare.org.uk/html/home.htm

2.3.8f   Foreign and Commonwealth Office (FCO). Rape and sexual assault abroad.
http://www.fco.gov.uk/en/travelling-and-living-overseas/things-go-wrong/rape

2.3.9 Skin Health

2.3.9a   The British Skin Foundation. Skin Information.
http://www.britishskinfoundation.org.uk/162

6 Resource Guide

2 The Pre-Travel Consultation

2.3.9b   Williams H, Ravenscroft J, Lawton S et al. Atopic eczema: sun, holidays and fun. Queen's Medical Centre Nottingham University Hospital NHS Trust. Nottingham, April 2005.
http://www.nottinghameczema.org.uk/nsgccedata/derm_advice_4.pdf

2.3.10 Psychological Health

2.3.10a   Sugden R. Fear of flying – Aviophobia. In: Keystone J, Kozarsky P, Freedman D, eds. Travel Medicine, 2nd ed. Elsevier. Philadelphia, 2008:361-65.

2.3.10b   Lovell-Hawker D. Cultural adaptation. In: Keystone J, Kozarsky P, Freedman D, eds. Travel Medicine, 2nd ed. Elsevier. Philadelphia, 2008:379-85.

2.3.10c   Beny A, Paz A, Potasman I. Psychiatric problems in returning travelers: features and associations. J Trav Med 8:243-46, 2001.

2.4 Principles of Vaccination

2.4.1   World Health Organization (WHO). Countries.
http://www.who.int/countries/en/.

2.4.2   The Red Book - Statement of Fees and Allowances. The Stationery Office (TSO).
http://www.redbook.i12.com/Index.htm

2.4.3   General Medical Council (GMC), 0-18 years: guidance for all doctors. 2007.
http://www.gmc-uk.org/guidance/ethical_guidance/children_guidance_index.asp

2.4.4   Care Quality Commission (CQC).
http://www.cqc.org.uk/.

2.4.5   Scottish Commission for the Regulation of Care.
http://www.carecommission.com.

2.4.6   Health Protection Agency (HPA). National Minimum Standards for Immunisation Training. June 2005.
http://www.hpa.org.uk/webw/HPAweb&HPAwebStandard/HPAweb_C/1204100464376?p=1249920573012

3 Special Risks

3.1 Special Risk Traveller

3.1.1 Cardiovascular and Cerebrovascular Disease

3.1.1a British Heart Foundation. Holiday and travel top tips.
http://www.bhf.org.uk/keeping_your_heart_healthy/top_tips_for_
keeping_healthy/travel_tips.aspx

3.1.1b British Committee for Standards in Haematology. Guidelines on oral
anticoagulation (warfarin). Br J Haematol 132:277-85, 2005.
http://www.bcshguidelines.com/pdf/oac_guidelines_190705.pdf

3.1.1c Frequently Asked Questions on Malaria Prevention. Compiled by the
HPA Malaria Reference Laboratory and the National Travel Health
Network and Centre (NaTHNaC). 14 March 2008.
http://www.nathnac.org/pro/misc/faq_malaria.htm#warfarin

3.1.2 Children

3.1.2a World Health Organization (WHO) Vaccine Preventable Diseases
Monitoring System Global summary. 2009.
http://www.who.int/vaccines/globalsummary/immunization/
countryprofileselect.cfm

3.1.2b British National Formulary for Children (BNFC). Pharmaceutical Press.
2009.
http://www.pharmpress.com

3.1.2c Centers for Disease Control and Prevention (CDC) educational tool for
children about rabies.
http://www.cdc.gov/rabiesandkids/

3.1.2d Pollard A, et al. Children at high altitude: an international consensus
statement by an ad hoc committee of the International Society for
Mountain Medicine, 12 March 2001.
http://www.ismmed.org/ISMM_Children_at_Altitude.htm

3.1.2e Third Culture Kids.
http://www.tckworld.com/

3.1.2f Wilson-Howarth J, Ellis J. Your child abroad; a travel health guide. Bradt
Travel Guides. Buckinghamshire, 2004.
http://www.bradt-travelguides.com/details.asp?prodid=126

3.1.3 Diabetes

3.1.3a Diabetes UK: Travelling with diabetes.
http://www.diabetes.org.uk/Guide-to-diabetes/Living_with_diabetes/
Everyday_life/Travelling_with_diabetes/

3.1.3b Chandron M, Edelman SV. Have insulin, will fly: diabetes management
during air travel and time zone adjustment strategies. Clin Diabetes
21:82-5, 2003.
http://clinical.diabetesjournals.org/content/21/2/82.full

3.1.4 Disability

3.1.4a Association of British Travel Agents (ABTA). Accessible Travel - Checklist
for disabled and less mobile passengers. 29 April 2008.
http://www.abta.com/consumer-services/accessible_travel

3 Special Risks

3.1.4b   Disabled Persons Transport Advisory Committee - Door to Door: a travel guide for disabled people.
http://dptac.independent.gov.uk/door-to-door/index.htm

3.1.4c   Pet Travel Scheme.
http://www.defra.gov.uk/wildlife-pets/pets/travel/pets/index.htm

3.1.4d   Foreign and Commonwealth Office (FCO). Disabled Travellers.
http://www.fco.gov.uk/en/travelling-and-living-overseas/ta-relevant-to-you/disabled-travellers

3.1.4e   Home Office Crime Reduction. Keep Safe. A guide to personal safety for people with learning disabilities. 2006.
http://www.crimereduction.homeoffice.gov.uk/keepsafe.htm

3.1.4f   Blue Badge Scheme.
http://www.direct.gov.uk/en/DisabledPeople/MotoringAndTransport/DG_4001061

3.1.5 Gastrointestinal Conditions

Patient Associations

- Cancer Backup – Travel. Advice on travelling if you have a stoma. 2008.http://www.macmillan.org.uk/Cancerinformation/Livingwithandaftercancer/Practicalissues/Travel/Ifyouhaveastoma.aspx
- Coeliac UK.
http://www.coeliac.org.uk/
- Colostomy Association.
http://www.colostomyassociation.org.uk/
- National Association for Colitis and Crohn's Disease.
http://www.nacc.org.uk/content/home.asp

3.1.6 Haematological Conditions

Coagulation Disorders

3.1.6a   Baglin T, Cousins D, Keeling D, et al. Safety indicators for inpatient and outpatient oral anticoagulant care. Recommendations from the British Committee for Standards in Haematology and National Patient Safety Agency. Brit Haematol 136:26-9, 2006.
http://www.bcshguidelines.com/pdf/NPSA_040107.pdf

3.1.6b   British Committee for Standards in Haematology Guidelines.
http://www.bcshguidelines.com/

Porphyria

3.1.6c   British Porphyria Association.
http://www.porphyria.org.uk/

3.1.6d   Welsh Medicines Information Centre, University Hospital of Wales, Cardiff.
http://www.wmic.wales.nhs.uk/

3 Special Risks

Hyposplenia/Asplenia

3.1.6e Davies JM, Barnes R, Milligan D. Update of guidelines for the prevention and treatment of infection in patients with an absent or dysfunctional spleen. Clin Med 2:440-3, 2002.
http://www.christie.nhs.uk/pro/cs/pmp/docs/Splenectomy Guidelines.pdf

3.1.6f Department of Health (DH). Splenectomy: information for patients. The Stationery Office, London. 2006.
http://www.dh.gov.uk/en/Publicationsand statistics/Publications/PublicationsPolicyandGuidance/DH_4113581

Patient Associations

- British Porphyria Association.
  http://www.porphyria.org.uk/
- The Haemophilia Society.
  http://www.haemophilia.org.uk/
- The Sickle Cell Society.
  http://www.sicklecellsociety.org/
- UK Thalassaemia Society.
  http://www.ukts.org/

3.1.7 Hepatic Conditions (Liver)

3.1.7a European Medicines Agency. Guideline on the evaluation of the pharmacokinetics of medicinal products in patients with impaired hepatic function. CPMP/EWP/2339/02. February 2005.
http://www.emea.europa.eu/pdfs/human/ewp/233902en.pdf

Patient Associations

- The British Liver Trust.
  http://www.britishlivertrust.org.uk/home.aspx
- Children's Liver Disease Foundation.
  http://www.childliverdisease.org/
- The Hepatitis C Trust.
  http://www.hepctrust.org.uk/Living+with+Hepatitis+C/travel/

3.1.8 HIV/AIDS

3.1.8a The global database on HIV related travel restrictions.
http://www.hivtravel.org/

3.1.8b Hoffmann C, Rockstroh JK Kamps BS. Travelling with HIV. HIV Medicine. 15th ed. Flying Publisher. Paris, 2007.
http://www.hivmedicine.com/hivmedicine2007.pdf

3.1.8c British HIV Association (BHIVA) guidelines for immunization of HIV-infected adults, 2008 HIV Med 9:795-848, 2008.
http://www.bhiva.org/Immunization2008.aspx

3.1.8d Cavassini ML, D'Acremont V, Furrer H, et al. Pharmacotherapy, vaccines and malaria advice for HIV-infected travellers. Expert Opin Pharmacother 6:891-913, 2005.

3 Special Risks

3.1.8e   University of Liverpool HIV drug interactions.
http://www.hiv-druginteractions.org/

Patient Associations

- Terrence Higgins Trust.
http://www.tht.org.uk/
- National AIDS Trust (NAT).
http://www.nat.org.uk/Living-with-HIV/Useful-information/
International-travel.aspx

3.1.9 Immunocompromised Travellers (excluding HIV/AIDS)

3.1.9a   Steroid Treatment Card. British National Formulary (BNF).
http://bnf.org/bnf/.

3.1.9b   Vaccinations in the immunocompromised person – guidelines for the
patient taking immunosuppressants, steroids and the new biologic
therapies. British Society for Rheumatology. January 2002.
http://www.rheumatology.org.uk/includes/documents/cm_
docs/2009/v/vaccinations_in_the_immunocompromised_person.pdf

3.1.9c   Immunisation of the immunocompromised child. The Royal College of
Paediatrics and Child Health. 2002.
http://www.rcpch.ac.uk/doc.aspx?id_Resource=1768

3.1.9d   Ljungman P, Engelhard D, de la Camara R, et al. Vaccination of stem
cell transplant recipients: recommendations of the Infectious Diseases
Working Party of the European Bone Marrow Transplant (EBMT). Bone
Mar Trans 35:737-46, 2005.
http://www.ebmt.org/5workingparties/idwp/wparties-id5.html

3.1.10 Neurological Conditions

3.1.10a   Rutschmann OT, McCrory DC, Matchar DB. Immunization and MS: a
summary of published evidence and recommendations. Neurology
59:183-43, 2002.
http://www.neurology.org/cgi/content/full/59/12/1837

3.1.10b   Giovanetti F. Travel medicine interventions and neurological disease.
Travel Med Infect Dis 5:7-17, 2007.

3.1.10c   Fischer PR, Walker E. Myasthenia and malarial medicines.
J Travel Med 9:267–8, 2002.

Patient Associations

- The MS Society.
http://www.mssociety.org
- Epilepsy Action.
http://www.epilepsy.org.uk
- Epilepsy Research UK.
http://www.epilepsyresearch.org.uk/

3 Special Risks

3.1.11 Older Travellers

3.1.11a   Leder K, Weller P, Wilson M. Travel vaccines and elderly persons;
a review of vaccines available in the United States. Clin Infect Dis
33:1553–66, 2001.
http://www.journals.uchicago.edu/doi/full/10.1086/322968
?cookieSet=1

3.1.11b   Khromava AY, Eidex RB, Weld LH, et al. Yellow fever vaccine: an
updated assessment of advanced age as a risk factor for serious
adverse events. Vaccine 23:3256-63, 2005.

3.1.11c   Lindsey NP, Schroeder BA, Miller ER, et al. Adverse event reports
following yellow fever vaccination. Vaccine 26:6077-82, 2005.

3.1.11d   Domingo C, Niedrig M. Expert Opinion: safety of 17D derived yellow
fever vaccines. Expert Opin Drug Saf 8:211-21, 2009.

3.1.11e   Hackett PH, Rennie D, Levine HD. The incidence, importance and
prophylaxis of acute mountain sickness. Lancet 11 27;2(7996):1149–
55, 1976.

Patient Associations

- Age Concern. Leisure and Travel information.
http://www.ageconcern.org.uk/

- Help the Aged. Financial services – insurance.
http://www.helptheaged.org.uk/en-gb/OnlineShop/Insurance/

3.1.12 Pre-conception, Pregnancy and Breastfeeding

3.1.12a   Chen L, Zeind C, Mackell S, et al. Breast feeding travelers: precautions
and recommendations. J Trav Med 17:32-47, 2010.

3.1.12b   Greer IA. Air Travel and Pregnancy. Royal College of Obstetricians and
Gynaecologists. 2nd edition, 2008.
http://www.rcog.org.uk/files/rcog-corp/uploadedfiles/SAC1Air
TravelPregnancy2008.pdf

Websites

- The Pregnant Traveller.
http://www.pregnanttraveler.com/

3.1.13 Psychological Conditions

3.1.13a   World Health Organization (WHO). Psychological Health. Wkly
Epidemiol Rec 18:151-60, 2009.
http://www.who.int/wer/2009/wer8418.pdf

3.1.14 Renal Conditions

3.1.14a   Global dialysis.
http://www.globaldialysis.com/

3.1.14b   Thain Z. Travelling and vaccines. In Ashley C, Morlidge C. Introduction
to Renal Therapeutics. Pharmaceutical Press, London, 2008.

3 Special Risks

Patient Associations

- UK National Kidney Federation.
  http://www.kidney.org.uk/

3.1.15 Respiratory Conditions

3.1.15a   British Lung Foundation. Going on holiday with a lung condition.
http://www.lunguk.org/holidays-travel.asp

3.1.15b   British Thoracic Society Standards of Care Committee. Managing
passengers with respiratory disease planning air travel: British Thoracic
Society recommendations. Thorax. 2004.
http://brit-thoracic.org.uk/Portals/0/Clinical%20Information/Air%20
Travel/Guidelines/FlightSummary04.pdf

3.1.15c   World Health Organization (WHO). Tuberculosis and Air Travel – Guidelines
for Prevention and Control. 3rd ed. Geneva, 2008.
http://www.who.int/tb/publications/2008/WHO_HTM_TB_2008.399_
eng.pdf

3.1.15d   Luks AM, Swenson ER. Travel to high altitude with pre-existing lung
disease. Eur Respir J 29:770-92, 2007.
http://www.erj.ersjournals.com/cgi/content/full/29/4/770

3.1.16 Rheumatological Conditions

3.1.16a   British Society for Rheumatology. Vaccinations in the
immunocompromised person: guidelines for the patient taking
immunosuppressants, steroids and the new biologic therapies. 28
January 2002.
http://www.rheumatology.org.uk/includes/documents/cm_docs/
2009/v/vaccinations_in_the_immunocompromised_person.pdf

3.1.16b   Ledingham J, Deighton C. Vaccination. Update on the British Society
for Rheumatology guidelines for prescribing TNF blockers in adults with
rheumatoid arthritis.
http://rheumatology.oxfordjournals.org/cgi/content/full/44/2/157

3.1.16c   O'Neill SG, Isenberg DA. Immunizing patients with systemic lupus
erythematosus: a review of effectiveness and safety. Lupus 15:778-83,
2006.
http://www.lupus-journal.com

3.1.17 Women

3.1.17a   Jean D, Leal C, Kriemler S, et al. Medical recommendations for women
going to altitude. A Medical Commission UIAA consensus paper. High
Alt Med Biol 6:22-31, 2005.

3.1.17b   Foreign and Commonwealth Office (FCO). Travelling and Living
Overseas – Women Travellers.
http://www.fco.gov.uk/en/travelling-and-living-overseas/ta-relevant-
to-you/women-travellers

3 Special Risks

3.2 Special Risk Travel

3.2.1 Adventure

3.2.1a   Johnson C, Anderson S, Dallimore J et al. Oxford Handbook of Expedition and Wilderness Medicine. Oxford University Press. Oxford, 2008.

3.2.1b   Auerbach PS. Wilderness Medicine, 5th ed. Mosby. Philadelphia, 2007.

3.2.1c   Winser S (Ed.). The Royal Geographical Society Expedition Handbook. The Profile Books. London, 2004.

> Websites
> - UIAA – International Mountaineering and Climbing Federation.
>   http://www.theuiaa.org/
> - The British Mountaineering Council.
>   http://www.thebmc.co.uk/
> - Wilderness Medical Society.
>   http://www.wms.org/

3.2.2 Altitude

3.2.2a   UIAA – International Mountaineering and Climbing Federation. Travel at High Altitude.
http://www.theuiaa.org/upload_area/files/1/Travel_at_high_altitude_2009.pdf

3.2.2b   Committee to Advise on Tropical Medicine and Travel. Statement on high-altitude illnesses. CCDR 33:ACS5, 2007.
http://www.phac-aspc.gc.ca/publicat/ccdr-rmtc/07vol33/acs-05/index_e.html

> Websites
> - UIAA – International Mountaineering and Climbing Federation.
>   http://www.theuiaa.org/
> - The British Mountaineering Council.
>   http://www.thebmc.co.uk/
> - Wilderness Medical Society.
>   http://www.wms.org/

3.2.3 Cruises

3.2.3a   World Health Organization. Travel by sea: health considerations. Wkly Epidemiol Rec 82:305-8, 2007.
http://www.who.int/wer/2007/wer8234.pdf

3.2.3b   Committee to Advise on Tropical Medicine and Travel (CATMAT). Statement on cruise ship travel. CCDR 31:ACS8, 2005.
http://www.phac-aspc.gc.ca/publicat/ccdr-rmtc/05vol31/acs-dcc-8-9/8-eng.php

3.2.4 Diving

3.2.4a   Divers Alert Network Dive and Travel Medical Guide.
http://www.diversalertnetwork.org

3.2.4b   Recreational Scuba Training Council Medical Statement.
http://www.wrstc.com/downloads.php

6 Resource Guide

3 Special Risks

3.2.4c   UK Sport Diving Medical Committee standards.
http://www.uksdmc.co.uk/standards/Standards.htm

3.2.5 Healthcare Workers

3.2.5a   Department of Health. HIV post-exposure prophylaxis: guidance from the UK Chief Medical Officers' Expert Advisory Group on AIDS. 19 September 2008.
http://www.dh.gov.uk/en/Publicationsandstatistics/Publications/PublicationsPolicyAndGuidance/DH_088185

3.2.5b   World Health Organization (WHO). Infection control for viral haemorrhagic fevers in the African health care setting. 2008.
http://who.int/csr/resources/publications/ebola/WHO_EMC_ESR_98_2_EN/en/

3.2.5c   Royal College of Nursing. Working with humanitarian organisations: a guide for nurses, midwives and healthcare professionals. 2007.
http://www.rcn.org.uk/__data/assets/pdf_file/0007/78757/003156.pdf

3.2.6 Last Minute Travel

3.2.6a   Borner N, Muhlberger N, Jelinek T. Tolerability of multiple vaccinations in travel medicine. J Travel Med 10:112-6, 2003.

3.2.7 Long-Term Travel

3.2.7a   Chen LH, Wilson ME, Davis X et al. Illness in long-term travelers visiting GeoSentinel Clinics. Emerg Infect Dis 15:1773-82, 2009.
http://www.cdc.gov/eid/content/15/11/1773.htm#cit

3.2.7b   Institute of Occupational Health and Safety. Safety in the global village – Keeping your staff healthy and safe abroad. 2008.
http://www.iosh.co.uk/information_and_resources/guidance_and_tools.aspx

3.2.7c   World Health Organization (WHO). Psychological Health. Wkly Epidemiol Rec 84:151-60, 2009.
http://www.who.int/wer/2009/wer8418.pdf

3.2.8 Medical Tourism

3.2.8a   Treatment Abroad. Medical Tourism Survey. 2007.
http://www.treatmentabroad.net/about/medical-tourism-survey/?locale=en

3.2.8b   Treatment Abroad. Guide to Medical Tourism.
http://www.treatmentabroad.net/guide

3.2.8c   NHS Choices: Healthcare abroad. 2010.
http://www.nhs.uk/Healthcareabroad/Pages/Healthcareabroad.aspx

3.2.8d   Foreign and Commonwealth Office (FCO). Travelling abroad for medical treatment. 2007.
http://www.fco.gov.uk/en/travel-and-living-abroad/your-trip/medical-treatment

3 Special Risks

3.2.8e   British Association of Aesthetic Plastic Surgeons. Safety in Surgery.
          http://www.baaps.org.uk/

3.2.9 Natural Disasters

3.2.9a   World Health Organization (WHO). Natural disaster profiles.
          http://www.who.int/hac/techguidance/ems/natprofiles/en/index.
          html

3.2.9b   Morgan O. Infectious disease risks from dead bodies following natural
          disasters. Rev Panam Salud Publica 15:307–12, 2004.
          http://publications.paho.org/pdf/dead_bodies.pdf

3.2.10 Pilgrimage (Hajj/Umrah)

3.2.10a   Kingdom of Saudi Arabia Ministry of Hajj Information.
          http://www.hajinformation.com/

3.2.10b   Foreign and Commonwealth Office (FCO). Hajj pilgrims.
          http://www.fco.gov.uk/en/travelling-and-living-overseas/ta-relevant-
          to-you/hajj-pilgrims#

          Websites
          ■ Association of British Hujjaj (Pilgrims).
             http://www.abhuk.com/index.htm
          ■ Muslim Council of Britain.
             http://www.mcb.org.uk/

3.2.11 Visiting Friends and Relatives (VFRs)

3.2.11a   Health Protection Agency (HPA). Foreign travel-associated illness –
          a focus on those visiting friends and relatives. London, 2008.
          http://www.hpa.org.uk/webw/HPAweb&HPAwebStandard/HPAweb_C
          /1231419801008?p=1158945066450

3.2.11b   Leder K, Tong S, Weld L, et al. Illness in travelers visiting friends and
          relatives: a review of the GeoSentinel Surveillance Network. Clin Infect
          Dis 43:1185-93, 2006.
          http://www.journals.uchicago.edu/doi/abs/10.1086/507893

4 The Post-Travel Consultation

4.1 Introduction

4.1.1   Health Protection Agency (HPA). Foreign travel-associated illness in England, Wales, and Northern Ireland: 2007 report. London, 2007.
http://www.hpa.org.uk/web/HPAweb&HPAwebStandard/HPAweb_C/1204186178825

4.1.2   Freedman DO, Weld LH, Kozarsky PE, et al. Spectrum of disease and relation to place of exposure among ill returned travelers. N Engl J Med 354:119-31, 2006.
http://content.nejm.org/cgi/content/full/354/2/119

4.2 The Ill Returned Traveller

Febrile illness

4.2.1   Johnson V, Stockley JM, Dockrell D, et al. Fever in returned travellers presenting in the United Kingdom: recommendations for investigation and initial management. J Infect 59:1-18, 2009.

4.2.2   British Infection Society and Health Protection Agency. Malaria Guidelines BIS algorithm. 2007.
http://www.britishinfectionsociety.org/drupal/sites/default/files/MalariaAlgorithm07.pdf

4.2.3   Lalloo DG, Shingadia D, Pasvol G, et al. (on behalf of the HPA Advisory Committee on Malaria Prevention in UK Travellers). UK malaria treatment guidelines. J Infect 54:111-21, 2007.
http://www.hpa.org.uk/webw/HPAweb&HPAwebStandard/HPAweb_C/1195733815652?p=1191942128258

4.2.4   Wilson ME, Weld LH, Boggild A, et al 2007. Fever in returned travelers: results from the GeoSentinel Surveillance Network. Clin Infect Dis 44:1560-68, 2007.
http://www.journals.uchicago.edu/doi/full/10.1086/518173?cookieSet=1

Diarrhoeal illness

4.2.5   Swaminathan A, Torresi J, Schlagenhauf P, et al. A global study of pathogens and host risk factors associated with infectious gastrointestinal disease in returned international travelers. Infect 59:19-27, 2009.

4.2.6   Greenwood Z, Black J, Weld L, et al. Gastrointestinal Infection among international travelers globally. J Travel Med 15:221-28, 2008.

Dermatological conditions

4.2.7   Caumes E, Carrière J, Guermonprez G. et al. Dermatoses associated with travel to tropical countries: a prospective study of the diagnosis and management of 269 patients presenting to a tropical disease unit. Clin Infect Dis 20:542-8, 1995.

4.2.8   Hochedez P, Caumes E. Common skin infections in travellers. J Travel Med 15:223-33, 2008.

4 The Post-Travel Consultation

Respiratory illness

4.2.9   Leder K, Sundararajan V, Weld L, et al. Respiratory tract infections in travelers: a review of the GeoSentinel Surveillance Network. Clin Infect Dis 36:399-406, 2003.
http://www.journals.uchicago.edu/doi/full/10.1086/346155

4.3 The Well Returned Traveller

HIV post-exposure prophylaxis

4.3.1   Fisher M, Benn P, Evans B, Pozniak A, et al. Clinical Effectiveness Group (British Association for Sexual Health and HIV). UK guideline for the use of post-exposure prophylaxis for HIV following sexual exposure. Int J STD AIDS 2006 Feb;17(2):81-92.

Post-travel eosinophilia

4.3.2   Checkley AM, Chiodini PL, Dockrell DH, et al. Eosinophilia in returning travellers and migrants from the tropics: UK recommendations for investigation and initial management. J Infect 60:1-20, 2010.

4.3.3   Meltzer E, Percik R, Shatzkes J, et al. Eosinophilia among returning travelers: a practical approach. Am J Trop Med Hyg 78:702-9, 2008.
http://www.ajtmh.org/cgi/content/full/78/5/702

5 Disease Guide

5.1 Notifiable Infectious Diseases (NOIDS)

All suspected cases of notifiable disease in England must be reported immediately to the Health Protection Agency (HPA) via an offical Formal Notification certificate. See Notifications of Infectious Diseases (NOIDS).
http://www.hpa.org.uk/HPA/Topics/InfectiousDiseases/InfectionsAZ/
1191942172952/

Alternatively, contact:

NOIDS Section
Centre for Infections
Health Protection Agency
61 Colindale Avenue
London NW9 5EQ
Telephone: 020 8200 4400.
Fax: 020 8200 7868
Email: noids@hpa.org.uk

Any suspected case of a notifiable disease or health risk state in Scotland must be reported to health boards who in turn must send a return, in writing (in practice electronic transmission via Scottish Infectious Disease Surveillance System (SIDSS2), to Health Protection Scotland (HPS).
See http://www.scotland.gov.uk/Resource/Doc/924/0090868.doc

5.2 Anthrax

All suspected anthrax cases must be reported to HPA via NOIDS (see above). The HPA's Novel and Dangerous Pathogens (NADP) laboratory, based at the Centre for Emergency Preparedness and Response, Porton Down, provides specialist diagnostic services for dangerous diseases, including anthrax.
http://www.hpa.org.uk/HPA/ProductsServices/ResearchAndTesting/
NovelAndDangerousPathogens/

HPA Guidelines include algorithms for clinical evaluation and management of potential anthrax cases.
http://www.hpa.org.uk/HPA/Topics/InfectiousDiseases/InfectionsAZ/
1191942145757/

5.3 Avian Influenza

The World Health Organization (WHO) is coordinating and monitoring worldwide response to human avian influenza. Further information, including technical guidelines, is available at:
http://www.who.int/csr/disease/avian_influenza/en/index.html

HPA have produced specific Avian Influenza Guidance, including management algorithms.
http://www.hpa.org.uk/web/HPAweb&HPAwebStandard/HPAweb_C/
1195733851442

5.4 Diphtheria

All suspected or confirmed cases must be reported to HPA via NOIDS; diphtheria is a notifiable disease. Horse serum-derived diphtheria antitoxin is available from the Immunisation Department of the HPA's Centre for Infections or Regional HPA and NHS laboratories. It is given only in confirmed or suspected diphtheria, carries

5 Disease Guide

the risk of anaphylaxis, and should be given in a hospital setting. See Chapter 8 of the HPA's Immunoglobulin Handbook.
http://www.hpa.org.uk/web/HPAwebFile/HPAweb_C/1194947358556

Immunisation Department
Centre for Infections
Health Protection Agency
61 Colindale Avenue
London NW9 5EQ
Telephone: 020 8200 6868

Further information about diphtheria can be found on the Diphtheria Surveillance Network website.
http://www.dipnet.org/general.public.php

5.5 HIV

British HIV Association guidelines for the treatment of HIV-1 infected adults with antiretroviral therapy 2008.
http://www.bhiva.org/TreatmentofHIV1_2008.aspx

5.6 Malaria

HPA ACMP Guidelines for malaria prevention in travellers from the United Kingdom 2007.
http://www.hpa.org.uk/webw/HPAweb&HPAwebStandard/HPAweb_C/1203496943315?p=1249920576136

Lalloo DG, Shingadia D, Pasvol G, et al. (on behalf of the HPA Advisory Committee on Malaria Prevention in UK Travellers). UK malaria treatment guidelines. J Infection 54:111-21, 2007.
http://www.hpa.org.uk/webw/HPAweb&HPAwebStandard/HPAweb_C/1195733815652?p=1191942128258

5.7 Rabies

Health professionals in England, Wales and Northern Ireland should refer to HPA Centre for Infections Clinical Rabies Service information for regularly updated management of rabies post-exposure treatment.
http://www.hpa.org.uk/servlet/ContentServer?c=HPAweb_C&cid=1224745729371&pagename=HPAwebFile

Advice regarding rabies post-exposure prophylaxis is available from:

HPA Virus Reference Division, Colindale. Tel: 0208 200 4400. If unavailable contact:

- Duty doctor at the HPA Centre for Infections. Tel: 0208 200 6868.
- Liverpool School of Tropical Medicine duty doctor. Tel: 0151 705 3100
- London School of Hygiene and Tropical Medicine on-call tropical medicine registrar. Tel: 0845 155 5000

Health professionals in Scotland should refer to the HPS website (www.hps.scot.nhs.uk) or telephone 0141 300 1100 for current rabies guidance, including provision of vaccine and rabies specific immunoglobulin, and treatment algorithms.

5 Disease Guide

Rabies vaccine and immunoglobulin is available on the NHS via local Health Protection Agency Units.

Assessment of rabies risk by country:

Note: Country risk assessment may differ between sources.

- NaTHNaC Country Information Pages www.nathnac.org.
- HPA Centre for Infections Clinical Rabies Service (see above).
- For Scotland, refer to Travax (health professionals)
  http://www.travax.nhs.uk/
  or Fit for Travel (public)
  http://www.fitfortravel.nhs.uk/.

5.8 Smallpox

HPA Smallpox Vaccination: Q&As for Health Care Workers. 2008.
http://www.hpa.org.uk/webw/HPAweb&HPAwebStandard/HPAweb_C/1204100459087?p=1204100455754

CDC Emergency preparedness and response. Smallpox.
http://www.bt.cdc.gov/agent/smallpox/

5.9 Viral Haemorrhagic Fevers (VHFs)

WHO Interim infection control recommendations for care of patients with suspected or confirmed filovirus (Ebola, Marburg) haemorrhagic fever. March 2008.
http://www.who.int/csr/bioriskreduction/filovirus_infection_control/en/index.html

HPA: Management and Control of VHF.
http://www.hpa.org.uk/HPA/Topics/InfectiousDiseases/InfectionsAZ/1191942148931/

5.10 Yellow Fever (YF)

Medicines and Healthcare products Regulatory Agency (MHRA). Reporting suspected adverse drug reactions.
http://www.mhra.gov.uk/Safetyinformation/Reportingsafetyproblems/Medicines/Reportingsuspectedadversedrugreactions/CON001906

Sanofi Pasteur MSD. Adverse Events Reporting.
http://www.spmsd.co.uk/doc.asp?catid=427&docid=806

NaTHNaC Yellow Fever Vacccination Centres (YFVCs): Reporting suspected Yellow Fever Vaccine-Associated Neurologic Disease (YEL-AND) or suspected Yellow Fever Vaccine-Associated Viscerotropic Disease (YEL-AVD).
http://www.nathnac.org/nathnac_protected/reportingaes.htm

Appendix 1 – Vaccine Compendium

Table 6-1 is an index of travel vaccines available in the UK at time of going to press. The information in the table below should be checked to ensure that it is up to date.

- Salisbury D, Ramsay M & Noakes K. Immunisation against infectious disease. 'The Green Book'. Department of Health. TSO. London, 2006. Includes access to updated chapters.
  http://www.dh.gov.uk/en/Policyandguidance/Healthandsocialcaretopics/Greenbook/DH_4097254

- Summary of Product Characteristics
  http://emc.medicines.org.uk/

Table 6-1. Vaccines available in the UK (April 2010) (in alphabetical order)

Disease	Vaccine name	Manufacturer/Distributor
Cholera	Dukoral®	Crucell/Masta
Diphtheria	Infanrix-IPV® Infanrix-IPV+Hib® Revaxis®	GlaxoSmithKline UK GlaxoSmithKline UK Sanofi Pasteur MSD
Haemophilus influenza type b (Hib)	Infanrix-IPV+Hib® Menitorix® Pediacel®	GlaxoSmithKline UK GlaxoSmithKline UK Sanofi Pasteur MSD
Hepatitis A	Avaxim® Epaxal® Havrix Junior Monodose® Havrix Monodose® Vaqta Paediatric®	Sanofi Pasteur MSD Masta GlaxoSmithKline UK GlaxoSmithKline UK Sanofi Pasteur MSD
Hepatitis A/B combined	Ambirix® Twinrix Adult® Twinrix Paediatric®	GlaxoSmithKline UK GlaxoSmithKline UK GlaxoSmithKline UK
Hepatitis A/typhoid combined	Hepatyrix® ViATIM®	GlaxoSmithKline UK Sanofi Pasteur MSD
Hepatitis B	Engerix B® 10mcg/ml Engerix B® 20mcg/ml HBVaxPRO® 5mcg HBVaxPRO® 10mcg	GlaxoSmithKline UK GlaxoSmithKline UK Sanofi Pasteur MSD Sanofi Pasteur MSD
Influenza (pandemic H1N1)	Celvapan® Pandemrix®	Baxter Healthcare GlaxoSmithKline UK
Influenza (seasonal)	Agrippal® Begrivac® Enzira® Fluarix® Fluvirin® Imuvac® Inactivated Influenza Vaccine BP® Influenza Vaccine Ph. Eur. ® Influvac® Optaflu Vaccine® Viroflu®	Novartis Vaccines Novartis Vaccines Wyeth Pharmaceuticals (Pfizer) GlaxoSmithKline UK Novartis Vaccines Solvay Healthcare Ltd Sanofi Pasteur MSD Wyeth Pharmaceuticals (Pfizer) Solvay Healthcare Ltd Novartis Vaccines Sanofi Pasteur MSD

(continued)

Appendix 1 – Vaccine Compendium

Table 6-1. Vaccines available in the UK (continued)

Disease	Vaccine name	Manufacturer/Distributor
Japanese encephalitis	Green Cross® Ixiario®	Green Cross Corporation/Masta Intercell AG/Novartis Vaccines
Measles Mumps Rubella	M-M-RVAXPRO® Priorix®	Sanofi Pasteur MSD GlaxoSmithKline UK
Meningococcal meningitis	ACWY Vax®	GlaxoSmithKline UK
Pertussis	Infanrix-IPV® Infanrix-IPV+Hib® Pediacel® Repevax®	GlaxoSmithKline UK GlaxoSmithKline UK Sanofi Pasteur MSD Sanofi Pasteur MSD
Pneumococcal	Prevenar® Pneumovax® II Synflorix®	Wyeth Pharmaceuticals (Pfizer) Sanofi Pasteur MSD GlaxoSmithKline UK
Polio	Infanrix-IPV® Infanrix-IPV+Hib® Revaxis®	GlaxoSmithKline UK GlaxoSmithKline UK Sanofi Pasteur MSD
Rabies	Rabies Vaccine BP® Rabipur®	Sanofi Pasteur MSD Novartis Vaccines/Masta
Rotavirus	Rotarix®	GlaxoSmithKline UK
Tetanus	Infanrix-IPV® Infanrix-IPV+Hib® Revaxis®	GlaxoSmithKline UK GlaxoSmithKline UK Sanofi Pasteur MSD
Tick-borne encephalitis	TicoVac® TicoVac Junior®	Baxter/Masta Baxter/Masta
Tuberculosis	Tuberculin PPD RT 23 SSI®, 2 T.U/0.1ml BCG Vaccine SSI®	Statens Serum Institut Statens Serum Institut
Typhoid	Typherix® Typhim Vi® Vivotif®	GlaxoSmithKline UK Sanofi Pasteur MSD Istituto Sieroterapico Berna s.r.l./Masta
Varicella	Varilrix® Varivax®	GlaxoSmithKline UK Sanofi Pasteur MSD
Yellow fever	Stamaril®	Sanofi Pasteur MSD

Appendix 2 – List of Abbreviations (in alphabetical order)

ABTA	Association of British Travel Agents
ACMP	Advisory Committee on Malaria Prevention in UK travellers
BBV	Blood-borne Virus
BHIVA	British HIV Association
BIS	British Infection Society
BMC	British Mountaineering Council
BNF	British National Formulary
BTHA	British Travel Health Association
CAA	Civil Aviation Authority
CDC	US Centers for Disease Control and Prevention
CQC	Care Quality Commission
DAN	Divers Alert Network
DEET	N, N-diethylmetatoluamide
DH	Department of Health (England)
EHIC	European Health Insurance Card
EU	European Union
FCO	Foreign and Commonwealth Office
FTO	Federation of Tour Operators
GP	General Practitioner
HPA	Health Protection Agency
HPS	Health Protection Scotland
HTD	Hospital for Tropical Diseases
IAMAT	International Association for Medical Assistance to Travellers
ISMM	International Society for Mountain Medicine
ISTM	International Society of Travel Medicine
INR	International Normalized Ratio
LSHTM	London School of Hygiene and Tropical Medicine
LSTM	Liverpool School of Tropical Medicine
MHRA	Medicines and Healthcare products Regulatory Agency
MRL	Malaria Reference Laboratory
NaTHNaC	National Travel Health Network and Centre
NOIDS	Notifiable Infectious Diseases
PCR	Polymerase Chain Reaction
PGD	Patient Group Direction
POM	Prescription Only Medicine
PSD	Patient Specific Direction
RCN	Royal College of Nursing
RDT	Rapid Diagnostic Test
SPC	Summary of Product Characteristics
UK	United Kingdom
VFR	Visiting Friends and Relatives
WER	Weekly Epidemiological Record
WHO	World Health Organization
YFVC	Yellow Fever Vaccination Centre

Index

Index

Index

Index

Index

Index

Index

Index

Index

Index

Index

Index

Index